After Exegesis

Carol A. Newsom

After Exegesis
Feminist Biblical Theology
Essays in Honor of Carol A. Newsom

Patricia K. Tull and Jacqueline E. Lapsley
Editors

BAYLOR UNIVERSITY PRESS

Unless otherwise stated, Scripture quotations are from the New Revised Standard
Version Bible, copyright 1989, Division of Christian Education of the National
Council of the Churches of Christ in the United States of America. Used by
permission. All rights reserved.

Cover design: Will Brown
Cover art: Detail from plate 674, fragment 3 of 4Q400 – 4QShirShabb[a] (Songs of
the Sabbath Sacrifice[a])

Library of Congress Cataloging-in-Publication Data

After exegesis : feminist biblical theology : essays in honor of Carol A. Newsom /
[edited by] Patricia K. Tull and Jacqueline E. Lapsley.
312 pages cm
Includes bibliographical references and index.
ISBN 978-1-4813-0380-4 (hardback : alk. paper)
1. Bible. Old Testament—Feminist criticism. 2. Feminist theology. I. Newsom,
Carol A. (Carol Ann), 1950- honouree. II. Tull, Patricia K., editor.
BS1181.8.A38 2015
230'.041082—dc23
2015002500

Printed in the United States of America on acid-free paper with a minimum of 30
percent post-consumer waste recycled content.

CONTENTS

CHAPTER 1

INTRODUCTION
Wisdom Rebuilds Her House

Jacqueline E. Lapsley and Patricia K. Tull

When Carol Newsom and Sharon Ringe first considered creating the edited book now known as the *Women's Bible Commentary*, they wondered whether they could find enough women scholars to author short commentaries on each of the Bible's sixty-six books. By the time they were writing the introduction to their third edition twenty years later, the problem had been transformed into an embarrassment of riches, with far more potential contributors than chapters to write. By 2012, not only among white North American women feminists, but among womanist, mujerista, Asian, African, European, male feminist, queer, differently abled, and other liberation-oriented scholars, the abundance of perspectives and possibilities had blossomed into an interpretive Eden.

Feminist biblical interpreters, and female interpreters who identify with liberation theologies but for diverse reasons do not call themselves feminists, vary widely in preferred exegetical methods, social locations, training, and faith and faith stances. Yet there are some characteristics that can be named as widespread.

First, most feminists reject the idea that interpreting Scripture as women is an exegetical "method" alongside of, and on the same plane as, historical criticism or rhetorical criticism. Rather, individuals who hold feminist or

1

liberationist sensibilities can and do employ an eclectic range of exegetical tools, tools both traditional and recently developed.

Second, unlike traditional scholars who have presumed that their views held universal relevance, and therefore that their own particular social settings had little impact on their studies, feminist biblical scholars recognize that social location shapes interpretation. It formulates who the interpreter is and what questions and concerns that interpreter will bring to particular texts. In fact, a feminist writer's social location is often named explicitly. Unlike scholars who systematically avoid personal pronouns, we seldom disguise our own agency.

Third, feminists tend not to predetermine what the assumed "center" of biblical theology must be, nor do we view our chosen starting points as givens. Accordingly, we seldom oblige ourselves either to ignore or to smooth over the diverse theological positions of biblical writers themselves—a practice that underinterprets or ignores texts that threaten a central idea's prominent place. Instead, feminist interpreters acknowledge and even celebrate fundamental diversities among biblical passages and writers.

Fourth, although some of us adhere to faith more than others, few feminist biblical interpreters set out only to defend or to debunk the Scriptures. Instead we engage in a complex, often dialogical process of acquainting ourselves with the "other" whose authorship underlies the text, seeking in sympathy to understand before responding. As we construct our reading of an ancient text, our work may be compared to home remodeling: having examined the materials available, we highlight what has been hidden from view, reclaim everything we can, repurpose or recycle what we must, and carefully refuse what we can no longer consider appropriate to the project of life-affirming inquiry—recognizing full well that other readers in other places or times may beg to differ.

Fifth, such complex layering of thought is built into feminism itself, which resists organizing the world into the wholesale, weighted dichotomies that earlier philosophers and theologians often employed. Such dualisms have valued, for instance, mind over body, male over female, reason over emotion, control over creativity, one over many. Within polarities such as these, all too often, "the female body becomes a metaphor for the corporeal pole of this dualism, representing nature, emotionality, irrationality and sensuality . . . all that needed to be tamed and controlled by the (dis)embodied, objective, male scientist."[1] Feminists often draw attention to sources of knowledge or ways of knowing that are disparaged or ignored in such dualities, such as experiences known not through reason first but through emotion and bodily, lived events.

The project of constructing feminist theology in conversation with an ancient book written mostly if not wholly by men in a male-dominated culture may seem, at least at first glance, doomed to failure. But significantly, the Bible in general and the Old Testament in particular, when examined closely, are more amenable than one might think to feminist thought. First, Scripture itself is eclectic in its own messages and genres. Second, few passages of Scripture claim universality. Rather, its writings are positioned within specific times, places, and circumstances, and are often surrounded by other texts that bring into serious question the universality of particular claims. Third, the Bible points to no thematic center. Even God—who is almost but not quite ubiquitous in Scripture—is not imagined in any set way. In fact, reducing God to one image is considered idolatry. Fourth, while there are some biblical figures who are celebrated without reserve or rejected without mercy, and some actions that are categorically proscribed or everywhere commended, Scripture itself maintains a certain ambivalence about the character of most everyone and everything under the sun, even that of God. Its production, in fact, entailed a continuous process of reevaluation, renovation, recycling, rejection, and reintegration of earlier views. And fifth, Scripture itself is unsystematic and unphilosophical. Its writers and its figures live in gendered bodies, in time, in pain, in longing, in experience, in confusion, in hope. In fact, much of the Bible's long-standing readability derives from the recognizable day-to-day experience of ancient people whose bodies and minds resemble our own. Thus, as this volume's contributors will demonstrate, Scripture itself offers many examples of personal, temporal, specific, and experiential ways of knowing.[2]

Given all this, one would think that, nearly forty years since both feminist theology and feminist biblical interpretation first emerged, plenty of feminist biblical theologies would have been produced. But in reality, while biblical *readings, interpretations,* and even *hermeneutics* by female biblical scholars from around the world have burgeoned, and while constructive theologies by female theologians from a wide variety of social settings have likewise flourished, very little has emerged in feminist biblical theology as such.

Back in 1989, before several of the contributors to this volume had yet entered graduate studies (or, in some cases, high school), Phyllis Trible reviewed the masculine history of biblical theology, asking, "Can feminism and biblical theology meet?"[3] Her own response was a qualified yes—but not yet. Nevertheless, she suggested some "overtures," projecting what a feminist biblical theology might look like should it be written. She viewed the project as constructive and hermeneutical, not simply descriptive; as belonging to diverse communities, neither essentially nor necessarily Christian; as varied in its interpretive methods, organizations, and expositions; and as springing from exegesis—in particular, highlighting neglected texts and reinterpreting familiar ones, especially those dealing with women. She called for grounding theology in creation, particularly regarding the theological meaning of gender; for opposing the absolutizing of any particular image of God; for welcoming meanings that have not been anticipated by writers and readers before; and for wrestling with models of authority.

All that she pointed out was already being practiced by Trible herself and by other feminist biblical interpreters before 1989 and has continued since. But by the mid-2000s, when both Leo Perdue and James Mead drew on her overtures in their own discussions of biblical theology, feminist work that was specifically called biblical theology had seen almost no significant development.[4] Even today, as biblical theology has enjoyed resurgence, very few women have ventured into book-length biblical theologies, much less explicitly feminist biblical theology.[5]

There may be several reasons for this. Biblical theology itself has been somewhat less certain since its failed mid-twentieth-century attempts to discover a central theme around which to organize. In contrast to the magisterial multivolume works of Gerhard von Rad, Walther Eichrodt, and others in biblical theology's heyday, contemporary biblical theologies usually pursue less ambitious programs for unifying their works. Biblical theology has also suffered from some confusion about its goals, confusion dating back to its origin: Should biblical theology be descriptive or constructive? If it is descriptive of the thought of ancient Israelite writers, feminists have clearly been working in this area for quite some time, often without calling it biblical theology. But some of the most important work in biblical theology has been constructive, not purely descriptive.

Although Carol Newsom does not call herself a biblical theologian, her contributions to rethinking the problems and possibilities of biblical theology are vast and fundamental. They come to clear theoretical expression in her 1996 article "Bakhtin, the Bible, and Dialogic Truth"[6] and are exemplified in her work on the book of Job.[7]

Newsom opens her 1996 article by recounting a scene familiar to many seminary professors. In a job interview, a candidate for a position in Old Testament reaches an impasse with a theologian on the committee over the nature of the Bible. The theologian inquires about the Hebrew Scriptures' theological center or primary theme. The biblical scholar resists repeatedly, insisting on the Bible's variety and particularity, leading to the theologian's exasperated response: "I'm just trying to find something that theology can work with."

Newsom quotes a series of prominent biblical theologians from the past who have given theology something it could work with, but at the expense of distorting the Bible's own nature. The problem, she says, is that the monologic sense of truth that has dominated Western thought does not suit the Bible or its theological quest. Drawing from Mikhail Bakhtin's "Discourse in the Novel" and *Problems of Dostoevsky's Poetics*, Newsom offers instead a description of dialogical, or polyphonic, truth capable of negotiating the compositional and ideological complexity of biblical texts.[8] Dialogic truth "exists at the point of intersection of several unmerged voices"[9]—as a conversation among different consciousnesses embodied as persons. It is not systematic, but rather it is manifest in "event"—in the dynamic interaction of perspectives that do not merge with one another, and remain open, "unfinalizable."

Bakhtin gave Dostoevsky credit for creating such dialogic events in his novels. Within the Bible, Newsom acknowledges, only the book of Job shows evidence of similar orchestration. However, the biblical redactors' practice of leaving the voices of source materials unmerged, much as it may frustrate a seeker of monologic truth, invites investigation into the (usually implicit, but occasionally explicit) dialogues among texts and their authors. By way of example, she notes side-by-side creation accounts, interpolated flood narratives, and repeated and varied treatments of such themes as identity, land, and outsiders in the patriarchal narratives. "Would it be possible," Newsom asks, "for biblical theology to 'play Dostoevsky' to the various ideas and worldviews of the biblical text? There are many implicit quarrels in the Bible which need only a little prodding to make them explicit."[10] A biblical theologian's role, then, Newsom said, "would not be to inhabit the voice, as the novelist does, but rather to pick out the assumptions, experiences, entailments, embedded metaphors, and so on, which shape each perspective and to attempt to trace the dotted line to a point at which it intersects the

claims of the other"—to "self-consciously go beyond what the texts themselves explicitly say to draw out the implications of their ideas."[11]

It is instructive to compare Trible's and Newsom's suggestions with the
expressed aims of the most prominent recent writer of biblical theology,
Walter Brueggemann. He defines Old Testament theology as the "coherent, wholistic [sic] presentation of the faith claims of the canonical text, in
a way that satisfies the investigations of historical-critical scholarship and
the confessional-interpretive needs of ongoing ecclesial communities."[12]
Several aspects of this definition are worth comment. First, as has already
been observed, and as Newsom has made explicit, feminist biblical theology
resists the idea that a holistic or comprehensive treatment is necessary to
qualify for the title "biblical theology." Feminist biblical theology may well
take up the larger categories of systematic theology ("sin," "grace," "redemption," etc.), but it is likely to do so in ways that differ from those of the
dominant tradition. Readings of individual texts, explicit engagement with
present-day social and political realities, reflection on themes occurring in a
minority of texts, and so on—these, without apology, are often the purview
of feminist biblical interpretation. To be sure, while Brueggemann offers
the above description as the "aim and task" of Old Testament theology, he
acknowledges that there are many "legitimate" means of inquiry and that
particularity in perspective is necessary. Yet many biblical theologians suggest, implicitly or explicitly, that comprehensive approaches are preferable.
Feminist thought, by contrast, prefers to eschew totalizing schemas since
they have tended to reflect androcentric bias—and this includes the way
feminists do biblical theology. Second, while feminist biblical theology certainly attends to historical-critical scholarship and may well present the
"faith claims of the canonical text," both of these are tools in a larger project of constructively engaging the biblical text in theological conversation
on current realities and contexts. Third, in agreement with Brueggemann's
definition, as well as the concerns of Trible and Newsom, most but not all
feminist biblical scholars do their work with and for confessional communities that seek to understand how the biblical texts may inform life lived
before God.

Few feminist biblical interpreters understand their work as participating in the construction of theology per se. Nevertheless, the field of biblical
theology is here to stay, and since biblical theology shapes the church and
other confessional communities in powerful ways, to leave this field to men
is to neglect our influence with the people who care the most about the

Bible. Feminist biblical theology can have a positive role in facilitating the church's participation in loving the people and the world God has made. In addition, while feminist constructive theologians outside the field of biblical studies are understandably more reluctant to begin with an ancient text that is, if not consistently or irretrievably patriarchal, at least sometimes discouraging to read and interpret, it is important to them to know what feminist biblical scholars perceive regarding Scripture and the central theological themes that our forebears derived from it—creation, sin, suffering, grace, and others.

Constructing a list of themes that ought to be covered in a feminist biblical theology proved challenging for us. Not all themes traditional to systematic theology are amenable either to what the Old Testament offers or to what interests women, and some topics that are extremely interesting both to the biblical writers and to contemporary women (such as inclusion and exclusion, moral agency, violence, and leadership) suffer neglect at the hands of traditional biblical theologians. Ultimately we chose to balance the book between what might be possible to treat in depth and what kind of breadth seemed called for, between what we hoped for ideally and what emerged among real people in their real-life settings, between aspirations and time limitations. Because the trails are not yet blazed, much less trampled, we view our efforts as preliminary and suggestive forays into the field, explorations to see what might be discovered. Yet we believe that the essays in this volume address important issues that can help shape discourse on what the church might be.

Wishing to make the volume more cohesive than is often possible in edited works, we set out with certain parameters and methods in mind for engendering conversation both within each essay and among them. This is what we did:

First, since this volume is intended to honor the life, work, mentorship, trailblazing, and collegiality of our friend Dr. Carol Newsom and to gesture toward her significant work in the *Women's Bible Commentary*, we made the difficult decision to limit the volume to women—recognizing full well the fine male scholars, many of them feminists, who have also been her colleagues and students. Every contributor to this volume has at least one debt to pay to Carol, either as friend, as colleague, or as protégée (the majority of us were her students at Emory)—and all as learners from her own finely reasoned work. Most of us were contributors to the third edition of *WBC*, though only two of us contributed to the second edition and only one, Jo Ann Hackett, appeared in the first edition.

Echoing Carol's suggestion that biblical texts need only a little prodding to begin to quarrel, we offered each scholar a theme to explore, asking that they do so by means of two or more specific scriptural passages of their choosing, researched in some depth and placed in dialogue with one another. Some contributors chose two passages that they balanced in dialogue. Others chose one central passage, brought into question or expanded in significance by its resonance or discrepancy with two to five others. Some chose passages from the same book of Scripture, and others chose from across the canon.

We first asked each contributor to write a brief abstract explaining what they expected to do. After we collected these abstracts and distributed them to all participants, almost all of us met face-to-face over coffee and pastries early one morning at the November 2012 annual meeting of the Society of Biblical Literature in Chicago, graciously hosted by Carey Newman in the Baylor University Press hotel suite. These abstracts and this meeting allowed us to discuss the book we envisioned; to draw lines of connection among the essays we were writing; to air our confusions, insecurities, and questions; and by our embodied presence to support one another in a shared project that we found both daunting and exciting.

During 2013 all contributors wrote first drafts of their chapters, which were then shared by e-mail. Although we would have liked to discuss individual contributions in depth when we met for a second time at the November 2013 annual meeting in Baltimore (again, thanks to Carey Newman and Baylor University Press), we were forced to confine ourselves to general discussion of the common themes, shared frustrations, divergent methods, and "aha" moments that had emerged during the drafting process. The sense of gratitude for common experience, frankly shared, was palpable in the room.

Before, between, and after these two meetings, we (Jacq and Trisha) continued to confer with each contributor and with each other, questioning, shaping, prodding, sometimes virtually wrenching finished products from hands unwilling to give any less than their best, even in the midst of lives filled with the daily realities of child rearing, elder care, job interviews and moves, illnesses, tragedies, travel, classes, and grades. The two of us had met several times to shape the project before it began, and as the chapters were being written we continued to meet in person and by phone to plan, confer, and edit. Early on, we consulted Carol's supportive (and proud) spouse, Rex Matthews, who also snuck peaks at Carol's CV and social calendar for us.

Our roster of contributors is limited primarily, but not completely, to Christian European-Americans (some of whom live abroad), in part because this population is somewhat self-selected by association with Carol. Rather than attempting tokenism, which was rightly rejected by the editors of the WBC, we accepted our cultural limitations (great though they may be, in a group of fifteen) or parochialism (as the WBC editors said, in the sense of "based in the neighborhood") in the hope that, just as constructive theology and biblical exegesis are expanding among women worldwide, female biblical scholars worldwide will also develop biblical theologies based in their own neighborhoods.

In the first essay, Patricia Tull joins with ecofeminist scholarship to discuss the variety of scriptural presentations of creation and the natural world, beginning with the Bible's first two chapters, augmented with other depictions of creation particularly in Isa 40, Ps 104, and Job 38–39. In light of the varieties of roles the Hebrew Bible portrays for humans in relation to the rest of creation, Tull suggests that the time has come to reevaluate who and what in creation matters most.

Eunny Lee shows how the book of Ruth characterizes divine providence. She reflects on the ways that God—who is silent in the book and is evoked only by the characters and narrator—nonetheless acts through the agency of people who are traditionally most excluded from the main action—namely, women and foreigners.

Carleen Mandolfo, pondering the presence and absence of God, puts Joban texts in conversation with Psalms and finds that Job offers a rich resource for rethinking our core claims about the character and actions—and inactions—of God.

In her exploration of salvation and redemption in Isa 51:9–52:12 and Ps 62, Katie Heffelfinger reaffirms the traditional doctrine of salvation while ringing changes on what salvation means and how it manifests in the human world, emphasizing in particular the experiences of "real bodies, lived lives." Salvation is not unilateral; rather, it "dawns at the mysterious meeting point of divine deliverance and human response."

Jacqueline Lapsley, treating the theme of praise, discusses Ps 146, which she sets in relationship to Pss 104 and 148. Human beings praise God from their context within the rest of creation. Her feminist reading of these psalms decenters humanity and resituates us as one part of the whole world that God would see flourish.

Anne Stewart considers a feminist biblical approach to justice. After surveying understandings of, and images for, justice among the Psalms and prophets, and in the Bible's wisdom literature, she focuses on the self-description of Woman Wisdom in Prov 8:22-31. She draws insight for understanding justice today not only from Woman Wisdom but also from Scripture's wide diversity of claims about justice.

Cameron Howard examines the theme of authority by looking at the two women in the Hebrew Bible who are portrayed as authors, Esther and Jezebel. For all their differences, the depiction of these women as writers suggests something important about writing: that it is not writers, but *readers*, who wield ultimate power.

A pair of essays follows that both deal with the sticky problem of community boundaries and the effects of these boundaries on those standing outside. First, Suzanne Boorer reads two passages in Numbers (chapters 12 and 20) that pertain to the leadership roles and fortunes of Moses and his two siblings, Aaron and Miriam. She explores the shifting status of these three characters as insiders and outsiders within the book, and the implications of these stories for a feminist theological reading of Numbers.

Julie Galambush explores the coexistence in the Torah of the evidently incompatible commands to kill the Canaanites and to protect resident aliens. She presents a history of origins for both Israel and its pentateuchal commands that recasts this apparent ethical disparity, and she reflects on the problems these stories have raised for subsequent interpretation.

Sarah Melcher examines the actions of two women—Rahab in Josh 2 and Esther in the book by her name—who exercise moral agency on behalf of family members in their dealings with more powerful adversaries. In light of the biblical texts, Melcher explores theories of moral agency in order to expand our understanding of what motivates moral action.

Employing trauma studies to assist in her reading of Ps 102 and other psalms, Amy Cottrill explores the problem of suffering. The lament psalms especially offer ways of talking about suffering and trauma that take seriously our bodily existence and provide a "fleshly authority" with significant potential for feminist theology.

Jo Ann Hackett treats the theme of violence against women by putting a modern problem in conversation with a biblical text. The contemporary problem of "missing women," including the loss of infant girls through sex-selected infanticide and abortion, is juxtaposed with the problem of "missing women" in Judg 19–21. The chaos depicted in the biblical text throws the predicament of so many modern societies into high relief.

Ingrid Lilly engages in a contextual feminist theology of reconciliation by examining several passages in Zechariah in which postconflict rebuilding is central. Lilly finds a comparison to South Africa's reconciliation process illuminating, since it reveals the gendered nature of reconciliation. With such a lens, Zechariah yields profound and surprising insights for a feminist biblical theology of reconciliation.

The final two essays deal with aspirations for both the present and the future. Christine Roy Yoder examines how the wisdom tradition views "the good life." In its presentation of multiple images for what constitutes flourishing, Prov 1–9 affirms that there is no single answer to this question. The wise understand that sometimes truths exist in tension with one another and that context is crucial when discerning truth.

Finally, Amy Merrill Willis considers the theme of hope in Isa 65:17-25 and Dan 12:1-3 through a feminist lens. In these texts hope requires emotional and moral work on the part of readers in order to engage in an "act of counterimagination." Hope is active; it entails "small and large practices of wisdom, compassion, and justice."

Even as authors were asked to write on specific topics, a number of themes emerged across several essays. Agency was perhaps the most prevalent theme. Reflection on the nature of human agency, especially under difficult conditions, appeared in many of the essays, highlighting the ways women and other traditionally excluded groups exercise their agency, authority, and power (Lee, Howard, Boorer, Galambush, Melcher). A similar recurrent theme is divine agency (Lee, Mandolfo, Merrill Willis). Notably, the biblical texts are shown to offer portraits of divine agency that stand in considerable tension with the dominant portraits presented by biblical theology, suggesting potentially rich resources for feminist theology.

Two essays (Tull and Lapsley) suggest that the context for feminist biblical theology must be understood more broadly than it traditionally is—that is, that all theology must consider the whole of creation, with humanity situated within our interdependent relationships with the living world. While these two highlight creation theology particularly, the theme of creation also plays into the essays by Lee, Mandolfo, Heffelfinger, Stewart, Cottrill, Yoder, and Merrill Willis.

The embodied nature of human being is explored by Heffelfinger, Lapsley, and Cottrill, among others. Taking bodily experience seriously is a hallmark of feminist thought. These authors reveal how central it is to many biblical traditions as well as how it enriches theological discourse. Not surprisingly, given feminist theology's concern for the brokenness of the world, that is, for the suffering of people and the groaning of creation, several authors put suffering and trauma at the center of their reflections (Mandolfo, Cottrill, Hackett). Each in her own manner finds the biblical text to offer a powerful entrée into reflection on the ways in which people suffer from oppression, often systemic, at the hands of the powerful. And finally, truth as a multivocal, not a univocal, reality comes to the fore explicitly in several essays (Tull, Stewart, Lilly, Yoder) and is affirmed implicitly in many more.

Finding the words to convey our appreciation of and respect for Carol Newsom leaves us somewhat tongue-tied (which, perhaps not coincidentally, is how many of us felt when we were students sitting in her office face-to-face with the most nimble and sophisticated thinker we had ever encountered). Besides the many contributors who knew her as teacher, there are others who know her as former classmate, colleague, mentor, and respected senior scholar. In all cases she has exemplified everything we hold dear as a scholar, as a teacher, as a colleague, as a human being. She is keen witted, creative, and inquisitive, reading more deeply outside the field of Hebrew Bible for insight and models than anyone we know. She demands sharp-minded rigor in her own work and models it for her students. She speaks with authority and confidence, yet with respectful, self-forgetting humility, demonstrating delight in the process of inquiry itself and not in the honor or recognition that may come of it. Unfailingly generous with her time and insight, Carol takes seriously the charge to nurture other scholars. Her graciousness in both formal and intimate settings has encouraged many of us to view our own actions through the lens of hospitality. In short, Carol has no peer.

One contributor remembers waiting for Carol outside her office to discuss a dissertation chapter and overhearing Carol talking with a divinity school advisee. The advisee was in some distress, and Carol's response was so deeply pastoral, so caring, that it shifted the hearer's way of thinking about her own vocation. Carol had always represented the best in *scholarship*, but here Carol was equally, if not more, interested in the care of the person in front of her. Her embodiment of the highest virtues of the vocation of scholar-teacher inspires love and admiration among her students, colleagues, and friends.

We are most grateful to Rex Matthews for his help in deciding the shape of the book; to Carey Newman and the staff of Baylor University Press for their enthusiastic support throughout; to our contributors, each of whom we found to be founts of wisdom, knowledge, insight, and grace, and who have so generously contributed to this book; to each other for the happy partnership; and of course most of all to our mentor and friend Dr. Carol Newsom, who taught us all to take ourselves seriously (though not too seriously) and to reach inside for the gifts we each possess.

Chapter 2

JOBS AND BENEFITS IN GENESIS 1 AND 2
A Feminist Biblical Theology of Creation

Patricia K. Tull

One day last summer, my spouse Don conducted a funeral for a church member. Loren had been the sixty-year companion and longtime caregiver for his wife Carol, who is both wheelchair bound and blind. The sanctuary filled with stories expressing gratitude for his life, tears over his large family's loss, and majestic music: "Be Still My Soul"; "I Know That My Redeemer Liveth." At the graveside, Carol received the folded flag, and a young bugler lingered over each lonely arpeggio of Taps.

That night Don said, "I saw the saddest thing today." I thought he would say something about Loren's funeral. But he continued, "There is a mourning dove lying dead in front of our neighbor's house. Its mate was hovering all around it, calling out, trying to protect its body. It wouldn't leave its side. A mourning dove, mourning. And there was nothing I could do." We have rituals confirming the dignity of fallen and bereaved humans. But when a citizen of the natural world dies, what can we give? We have elaborate celebrations of human worth but very little that contributes meaningfully to other life.

Some might call my husband's compassion anthropomorphic or even sentimental. Yet anyone who pays attention knows that animals convey joy, grief, fear, anger, and welcome in much the way we do—and not only to their own kin. Ethologist Marc Bekoff says continuity between the feelings, awareness, communication, and behaviors of humans and other animals simply makes

15

sense, given our evolutionary connections and genetic similarities.[1] Christian theology, including biblical theology, is beginning to depart from our centuries-old fixation on human ascendancy and to attend more to Scripture's representations of the living world beyond ourselves.[2] In this essay I will first examine the twin ideas of "dominion" and *imago Dei* that traditional understandings of creation have derived from Gen 1:26-28. Then I will reexamine Gen 1 overall, as well as other creation accounts, beginning with Gen 2, in order to describe a biblical theology of the human place in creation that accords with Scripture and promotes a healthier approach to contemporary ecological issues.

A Truncated Theology of Creation

For many centuries, theologians, philosophers, and biblical scholars have fixed inordinate attention on only three of the thirty-four verses of Gen 1:1–2:3, which is only one of the Bible's many descriptions of the created world. In fact, if two words could summarize Western Christian understanding of a biblical relationship between humans and all the rest of creation, they would be "have dominion." Theologians' focus on the divine plan announced in Gen 1:26 for humankind to "have dominion over the fish of the sea, and over the birds of the air, and over the cattle, and over all the wild animals of the earth, and over every creeping thing that creeps upon the earth" has made this one of the Old Testament's better known verses, virtually guaranteed to enter most contemporary environmental conversations, whether as defense of human actions or—increasingly—as opportunity to deflect blame to the past for what humans are doing now to the earth and its inhabitants. Within the same verse stands the counterpart of "dominion," through whose obscure, evocative wording centuries of Christians have pondered our own significance: "Let us make humankind in our image, according to our likeness" (v. 26). Theological attention to the *imago Dei*, the "image of God," has inspired generations of speculation over what this apparently unique connection with God means for human being.[3]

Like any construction project, theological anthropology proceeds incrementally. The notion of *imago Dei* evidently reflects a democratizing step in an ancient Near Eastern milieu in which kings alone were thought to bear God's image.[4] Further on in Genesis, this wording interdicts murder, "for in God's own image God made humankind" (9:6). Historically, the concept of *imago Dei* has supported the dignity of many outsiders to power.[5] The outworkings of such an insight continue to unfold. Early feminist biblical theology, tracing the implications of "male and female he created them," suggested gender as the substance of *imago Dei*.[6] Contemporary theologies around the world credit the concept of *imago Dei* with articulating humanity's fragile dignity.[7]

But in 1967, historian Lynn White laid the growing ecological crisis at the door of biblically based Western Christian ideas about "dominion," ideas that, he said, shaped medieval Europe and the industrial era and made Christianity "the most anthropocentric religion the world has seen,"[8] so that "no item in the physical creation had any purpose save to serve man's purposes" and "although man's body is made of clay, he is not simply part of nature: he is made in God's image."[9] Despite White's protest and its many echoes in subsequent ecological literature, theologians have continued pondering these verses, scrutinizing them for substantive or functional significance.[10] Detailed debate continues over how these terms should be understood today, and whether the concept can be expanded to include nonhuman creation, with whom we possess genetic ties;[11] over what responsibilities of stewardship are entailed in this verse; over just what meaningful theological and ethical distinctions can be made between humans and other sentient beings; over what it means to be uniquely made in God's image.

But as Sallie McFague pointed out, "A theology that is not commensurate with reality as culturally understood is not credible."[12] To be socially relevant and even prophetic, theology must, among other things, begin with sound biblical exegesis and knowledge of the winding interpretive paths that brought us here. It should be conversant with science, particularly the empirical evidence showing that the rest of the natural world got along very well before our arrival and could continue to get along well without us, if not better,[13] and that the genetic chain leading to *Homo sapiens* has no definitive break-point distinguishing us qualitatively from other animals. Especially since the time of Francis Bacon, readers have erred in picking out of the several creation accounts in the Bible, and out of the first creation account in Gen 1, a narrow focus on humans that seldom wanders from these three verses.[14] As Nicola Hoggard Creegan has put it, "*Imago Dei* has allowed humans to make all manner of assumptions about how special and different we are."[15]

Much has come to light about the ancient worldview underlying the dual notions of "image of God" and "dominion," which stem from the identity of ancient kings as "divine image-bearers, appointed representatives of God on earth," who placed statues, or images, of themselves throughout their empires to remind subjects of their presence.[16] Biblical scholars have long noted that the edifices that have been built on the foundation of these concepts have been far too grandiose. According to Peter Enns, Gen 1:26 does not describe what makes us humans rather than animals. It says merely that "humans represent God in the world, nothing less but certainly nothing more."[17] The Bible has much more to say than these three verses about the place of humans in creation, much that stands at odds with notions of human godlikeness and dominion. The first wave of feminist ecotheology came and went in the 1980s and 1990s before the wider church was ready to hear its wisdom. As churches increasingly seek to address the ecological crisis, we would be well advised to reread much of this literature, and to read Scripture more fully and more carefully.

Reading in Context

"No cherry-picking" is a fundamental principle in biblical interpretation. To isolate verses—ignoring their context, both immediate and broad—is counterproductive.[18] A sound theology of creation is rooted in the larger passage from which these verses come, which is in turn rooted in the larger garden of Scripture.

There are two scriptural contexts to consider here. First, when these three verses are read in the context of the other thirty-one in this passage, much that has been ignored is illuminated. Second, and even more strikingly, other biblical accounts of creation portray humans as far less powerful, far less central, than Gen 1 does. Though humans' mirroring of God is repeated in further Priestly texts (Gen 5:1; 9:6), and what the NRSV translates as "dominion" reappears using a different Hebrew term in Ps 8:6, the relationship moderns have made so much of is actually a minority view among Scripture's writers. In what follows, I will examine Gen 1 and 2 to show how these texts portray humanity as less central than they have traditionally been interpreted as claiming. Then I will turn to other creation texts that even more explicitly place humanity within creation's larger context.

Genesis 1

Creationism and its softer cousin "intelligent design" grab headlines in school curriculum battles. But a broad swath of mainline Christians and an increasing number of evangelicals find that scientific cosmology and Darwin's evolutionary theory, as it has itself evolved, fit their worldviews well. Just as Christians today believe that the earth revolves around the sun (despite Gen 15:12 and other biblical references to the sun's rising and setting) and that rain comes from rain clouds rather than windows in heaven's dome (despite Gen 7:11 and other references to heavenly architecture), many feel no need to reconcile the theologically majestic story of creation in seven days with the scientifically compelling story of the universe's development since the big bang. Distinguishing between literary and scientific writing allows many to view the account of God's calling creation into being piece by piece, day by day—formless void, firmament, sea monsters, and all—as a poet's way of crediting God for the universe's complex order.

Yet, while untroubled by "seven days" and other verbal antiquities, many Christians would like to reconcile humanity's presumed centrality with a healthier environmental ethic.[19] Having been taught that Gen 1:26-28 defines humans' place in creation, many Christians yearn to hear something more consistent with what they know. Placing these three verses in their proper context calls forth the following observations that counter notions of humanity as God's sole or first concern:

- According to Gen 1:1-25, most of creation precedes humans. This order resembles that of scientific accounts, which situate hominids on the cosmic timeline "within three hours of the stroke of midnight on New Year's Eve, and *Homo sapiens* a mere twenty seconds before the hour."[20]
- In this account God speaks creation into being as if it possessed intelligence. The light, earth, sky, vegetation, and animals respond immediately and directly to God's voice. In the five and a half days before we enter the picture, God calls creation "good" six different times, displaying pleasure with the prehuman world.
- The tenfold repetition in Gen 1:11-25 of the term *min* ("kind," "species," as in "of every kind")—referring to plants, fruit trees, sea creatures, birds, land animals both (from the human viewpoint) wild and domesticated, and "creepers"—indicates divine fascination not with a single species but with a wide variety of swarming, teeming life on earth, what Gen 2:1 calls "their multitude" or "their vast array" (*tseva'am*).
- Humans are by no means the first to be blessed and commanded to multiply. That honor goes to sea creatures and birds (1:22). Nor are we the last to be blessed—the Sabbath holds that distinction (2:3). Unlike light on the first day and Sabbath on the seventh, we humans are not honored with an entire day to ourselves but—underscoring continuity—enter on the sixth day after other land animals.

+ Even the command to "have dominion" (NRSV) or to "rule" (NIV) implies neither greed nor exploitation. If, as these verses claim, humans reflect God's image, human rule is not self-seeking but generative. Further, the list of dominion's subjects is far from exhaustive. Animals are named, but if we accept the NRSV's and NIV's correction of verse 26 on the basis of the Syriac and in accord with surrounding verses, the world's plants and nonliving elements are not included.[21] The creation story does not authorize destruction of mountains, rivers, or coastlines.

+ All animals, including humans, are offered the same food supply, intended for all together (vv. 29-30). In fact, according to this account, Plan A was universal vegetarianism. These verses do not support indirect killing through destruction of habitats and food systems, much less direct killing for food, fur, or fun.

+ It is not until all is complete that anything is described as "very good." This divine approval applies not to humans alone but to everything, the sum total (v. 31).

With so many qualifiers to human importance embedded even within an account that enthrones us, we might wonder why readers have for so long fixated on human centrality. All these observations about God's direct relationship to the whole living world weigh in especially now, when biodiversity is at risk, seas are fished out, and the intricate web of creation is coming unraveled. Many Christians, troubled by the disconnect between contemporary ecological realities and what they have assumed about human dominion, are ready to hear something different. Fortunately, there is much more to hear in Scripture.

Genesis 2

Two different accounts of creation in the Bible's first two chapters suggest deliberate breadth of vision even within tiny ancient Israel. In Gen 2's account, even though the human's appearance precedes that of other species, this earthling is not called ruler but servant to the ground. Translations have obscured this role.[22] The NRSV, for instance, reads Gen 2:15 in this way: "The LORD God took the man and put him in the garden of Eden *to till it and keep it*" (cf. Tanakh; NIV ["to work it and take care of it"]; CEB ["to farm it and to take care of it"]; NJB ["to cultivate and take care of it"]). The final verb *leshamrah* ("to keep, watch, guard") is translated accurately enough. But the preceding one, *le'avdah*, when thinned down to "till," "work," "farm," or "cultivate," loses its semantic resonance. Intransitive, this verb can mean "to work." But when transitive, as here, its meaning does not become, as in English, "to work it"—that is, "to make it work." Rather it means "to serve" the Garden of Eden, to "work for" it.[23] Genesis 2 pictures the human's role not as ruler but as groundskeeper or tenant farmer.[24]

Sharp distinctions between humans and animals are difficult to draw from Gen 2.[25] Both humans and animals are called *nephesh hayah*, "living creatures." This phrase applies to aquatic life (Gen 1:20, 21), land animals (1:24; 2:19; 9:10), birds (9:10), and in fact "all flesh" (9:15, 16)—and in 2:7 it also applies to humans. Translators have obscured this: almost all recent Bibles read "living being" for the man in Gen 2:7 and "living creatures" for animals everywhere else. But the ancient writer did not make this distinction.[26]

In addition, whereas in Gen 1 each group of living creatures arises from its own habitat, in Gen 2 we all come from the same place. In this agriculturally infused story, humans are formed from the ground just as all other life is:

> Then the LORD God shaped the man from dust from the ground. (2:7, author's trans.)
> Then the LORD God caused to grow from the ground every tree. (2:9, author's trans.)
> Then the LORD God shaped from the ground every animal of the field and every bird of the air . . . every living creature. (2:19, author's trans.)

In fact, God's making and bringing potential animal helpers to the man is not mere trial and error. The word "helper" implies that his problem is not loneliness but aid in the farm work God has given him.[27] "Helper" here does not mean "assistant"—in fact, the same word often describes God as divine helper, as in Ps 33:20. In ancient agrarian economies, animals indeed lived and worked alongside humans, as they do today in many places. The woman is part of the agrarian project, yet she is also human like the man, "bone of my bones and flesh of my flesh" (Gen 2:23).

Nor does the human's naming of the animals necessarily imply superiority. As a book of origins, Genesis depicts the human penchant for naming not only animals and offspring but memorable places (11:9; 19:22; 21:31; 22:14; 28:19; 32:2, 31; 33:17; 50:11), markers (31:45-49), wells (26:18-22, 33), trees (35:8), altars (33:20; 35:7), and even God (16:13)—presumably without asserting rule over the divine. Discussing evolution's propensity to develop traits in species on an as-needed basis, Marc Bekoff points out that, so far as we know, some animals possess a sense of "me-ness" or selfhood and even recognize one another, without assigning names: "Knowing *who* you are is not necessarily better than knowing you are not another individual."[28] Naming is something we humans do because it suits our social patterns and needs. This is a distinction we make between individuals, though we cannot, like dogs, recognize the distinctive odors of every individual we meet.

In short, to place humans first, last, best, and ruling over all is to read against both of the creation stories with which Scripture begins. Ancient writers told stories far more complex, of human embeddedness in a larger sphere, of divine delight in the animals, of human work to care for the ground, of the company of animal companions.

Other Creation Descriptions

Genesis 2 is by no means alone in drawing the human role differently from that in Gen 1:26-28. Psalm 104 places humans in a timeshare with the lions, who roam the same haunts at night that humans do in the day (vv. 21-23). Although the psalm displays interest in and knowledge about the natural world—from meteorology to astronomy to physical geography to natural habitats of many species—it nowhere implies that humans are any more than one of the many fascinating creatures that reflect, in their dependence, life, and death, their creator's glory.

Descriptions of creation in Isa 40:12-31 and in the divine speeches in Job 38–39 emphasize not human centrality or control but our transience, our weakness, even our noncomprehension of the created world: "The nations are like a drop from a bucket," the exilic prophet proclaims (Isa 40:15). Human rulers are as ephemeral as winter wheat: "Scarcely are they planted, scarcely sown, scarcely is their shoot rooted in the earth when God breathes on them and they dry up, and the tempest carries them off like stubble" (v. 24, author's trans.).

For his part, Job, who was not present when God laid the earth's foundations, cannot claim to know anything about its processes:

What is the way to the place where the light is distributed,
    or where the east wind is scattered upon the earth?
Who has cut a channel for the torrents of rain,
    and a way for the thunderbolt,
to bring rain on a land where no one lives,
    on the desert, which is empty of human life,

to satisfy the waste and desolate land,
    and to make the ground put forth grass? (Job 38:24-27)

Job cannot explain the life cycles of mountain goats and deer (39:1-4), or tame wild animals (vv. 5-12), or comprehend God's affection for creatures that seem foolish (vv. 13-18). Even a domesticated horse is too powerful for human command (vv. 19-25).

And though the translation is ironically and aptly obscure, perhaps the author of Eccl 3:11 hits the nail on the head when describing a human reach that far exceeds its grasp: God "has made everything suitable for its time; moreover he has put a sense of past and future into their minds, yet they cannot find out what God has done from the beginning to the end." Ecclesiastes repeatedly invites humans to let go of anxious ambition and to be content.

Many other scriptural writers likewise imagine humans inhabiting a world far more powerful than we, which we can neither understand nor control. It is populated by wild animals and wild vegetation (Isa 34:11-15). It is characterized by wild forces—earthquakes (Ps 68:8), storms (Ps 57:1), floods (Ps 69:2), drought (Jer 14:1-6). The Psalms portray the natural world in poetry resplendent with awe. Isaiah constantly compares humans to field grass, to trees, to vines and other vegetation. The book of Proverbs instructs humans to learn from ants, spiders, lions, and eagles. Sometimes majestically and sometimes terrifyingly, biblical poetry and narrative announce that we are anything but in control, making the command to take charge seem like one ancient writer's pipe dream or, better, an encouragement to human self-esteem in an overwhelming social and natural world. The Scriptures as a whole voice reverence and care for, not self-centered rule over, the larger-than-human world.

In fact, there is some irony in the statement in Jas 3:7-9 that "every species of beast and bird, of reptile and sea creature, can be tamed and has been tamed by the human species, but no one can tame the tongue—a restless evil, full of deadly poison. With it we bless the Lord and Father, and with it we curse those who are made in the likeness of God." James's claim that humans can tame all other species is clearly hyperbolic, but his main points, that we cannot tame our own words and that we use these words to wreak havoc, are as true in the case of our anthropocentrism as in any other. With questionable scriptural justification, Christians have for centuries placed humans at the center of the cosmos, and we have been more than willing to carry this role to its logical conclusion in ecological crisis. In the face of the many examples of creation's complexity as described in Genesis, Psalms, Isaiah, Job, and elsewhere, theologies that raise "dominion" and *imago Dei* as twin banners over against the rest of the world fall short. They are true neither to scriptural roots nor to human experience.

As Christians we can and must adopt a broader understanding of our relationship to all we say God has made, and carry this understanding through to actions, since what we embody in life practices expresses what we believe in our depths. Just as the church's message has spread the dominion idea through Western culture, now it is time to lean forward toward a more resilient view of our living neighborhood on earth.

What If?

What would happen if biblical readers backed away once and for all from placing Gen 1:26-28 at the center of creation theology, where even those who dispute its meaning still bow to its centrality?[29] What if we could take a different starting point, even a different one within Gen 1? Just for the sake of argument, what if we took most seriously not just the late afternoon of our own creation but the third day, on which all the earth's lush vegetation sprouts and grows; and the fifth day, on which both sea and sky are filled with creatures; and the morning of the sixth day, when all the other land animals are made? Surely distinctions between creature and creator are greater than those among genetically intertwined beings. What if we declared a moratorium on talking further about humans outside the context of all else? As Ivone Gebara has pointed out, "Every being is different from all the others . . . every being is absolutely unique and irreplaceable."[30] What if we, at seven billion and still growing, declared ourselves an evolutionarily secure species—one now endangered more than anything by our own success? What if we chose a different mantra than *imago Dei* and dominion? Recognizing the alarming rate of anthropogenic species extinctions occurring now, what if we chose, for instance, "every living creature of every kind" and spent the foreseeable future—the next two thousand years, say—pondering the significance of the other 8.7 million species with which we share the earth? Broadening our frame to encompass the scope of creation would not diminish human particularity any more than interfaith acknowledgment diminishes Christian particularity, or accepting gay marriage diminishes heterosexual unions, or learning from world cultures diminishes European heritage, or welcoming the gifts of women diminishes manhood. On the contrary, in a larger sphere, all are enhanced. Gebara proposes a vision that is "not a mechanical interdependence but a living one: a sacred interdependence that is vibrant and visceral."[31] As Catholic priest and cosmologist Thomas Berry says,

> The ecological age fosters the deep awareness of the sacred presence within every reality of the Universe. There is an awe and a reverence due to the stars in the heavens, the sun, and all heavenly bodies; to the seas and the continents; to all living forms of trees and flowers; to the myriad expressions of life in the sea; to the animals of the forests and the birds of the air.[32]

Biologist E. O. Wilson is among those warning of the urgency of our present rate of species extinction. Without swift action, achievable and affordable, to avert this trend, by the end of this century the earth's species decline will rival that in the five earlier great extinctions, including the one that killed the dinosaurs sixty-five million years ago.[33] It took the earth ten million years to recover from each of the previous extinctions. As Wilson says, "A new ten-million-year slump is unacceptable. Humanity must make a decision, and make it right now: conserve Earth's natural heritage, or let future generations adjust to a biologically impoverished world."[34] Once dead, these species cannot be replaced within any time scale meaningful to humans. John Cobb puts the problem of extinctions in a distinctly theological context when he says, "The extinction of species is now opposed not only because something of value to human beings may be lost, but also because each species is of value to its own members, and each species is of value to God."[35]

Every Living Creature of Every Kind

What would it mean to honor the intrinsic worth of living creatures in a way that is commensurate with Christian teachings and practice on the value of human life? It can mean a great many things, certainly some that no one has yet explored. I will suggest four themes consistent with a feminist biblical theology.

(1) *Life, including human life, is founded on, and lived among, the elements grandly spoken into being in Gen 1: sunlight, waters, earth, and air.* Though not thought of as living themselves, these are the media through which life originally sprang and continues to emerge. Little distinction is made biblically between these and the living world. According to Gen 1, the light, the atmospheric expanse, the seas, and the dry land organize themselves at God's word *yehi*, "let there be." According to Ps 90, God gave birth to the mountains and the earth itself. In Job 38 the stars sing and

the sea bursts from the womb. In Ps 104 and elsewhere, waters flee and springs gush at God's bidding. In Ps 19 the heavens declare glory and the sun runs its course like a racer. In Isa 44, 49, and 55, the heavens above, the depths below, and the steadfast mountains burst out singing. These are just a few of the animations Scripture records of the habitat of the living creatures. In biblical idiom, the elements themselves live and breathe in response to their creator. Surely these are too sacred to defile.

(2) *Like the human body, like the body of Christ as Paul describes it, all creation is interconnected.* "If one member suffers, all suffer together with it; if one member is honored, all rejoice together with it" (1 Cor 12:26). No part can say to another, "I have no need of you" (v. 21). Sallie McFague speaks of the world itself as God's body, saying:

> While that notion may seem a bit shocking, it is a very old one with roots in Stoicism; it tantalized many early Christian theologians, including Tertullian and Irenaeus: it surfaces in a sacramental understanding of creation—the world charged with the glory of God, as poet Gerard Manley Hopkins puts it.[36]

McFague points out the following: (1) Such a metaphor is not distant but close to us, easily conceptualized by seeing life all around us. (2) Such a metaphor overcomes the dualistic split between spirit and body, making it easier to see salvation as social, political, and economic. (3) As in Jesus' incarnation, God's bodily presence in the world is vulnerable to harm, as nature is, by human choices. She concludes, "Were this metaphor to enter our consciousness as thoroughly as the royal, triumphalist one has, we would live differently. We could no longer see God as worldless or the world as godless."[37]

(3) *All life, including human life, is absolutely dependent and interdependent. Providential, unearned grace is mediated not just through other people but throughout creation.* Psalm 104 describes the utter dependence of all creation on God's continuous care:

> O LORD, how manifold are your works!
>> In wisdom you have made them all;
>> the earth is full of your creatures.
>
> . . . .
>
> These all look to you
>> to give them their food in due season;
> when you give to them, they gather it up;
>> when you open your hand, they are filled with good
>> things.
> When you hide your face, they are dismayed;
>> when you take away their breath, they die
>> and return to their dust.

> When you send forth your spirit [or your breath], they are
> created;
> and you renew the face of the ground. (Ps 104:24, 27-30)

This care comes not simply spiritually, ethereally, or through other humans but through sun and rain, breath and harvest, even through the well-being of these relationships. In his book *I and Thou*, Martin Buber contrasts seeing a tree as an "it" that is observed, classified, studied, and counted, with seeing the tree as a "you," a living being with whom one is bound up in relationship.[38] He likewise describes relationships with individual animals whose "eyes have the power to speak a great language," in whose glances "the world of *Thou* has shown out from the depths."[39] Vicki Hearne draws on the speeches of God in Job to suggest that what humans owe animals even more than love is respect.[40] Stephen Webb develops a theology of grace through the sympathetic love between humans and animals. He describes grace as "the inclusive and expansive power of God's love to create and sustain relationships of real mutuality and reciprocity."[41] Such grace, he says, is present in our relationships with animals as well as other humans. Since animals give to us, it is right for humans "to attend to their giving and return their gifts appropriately."[42] Such grace makes available to us a different economy for living, an economy of abundance rather than scarcity, a "wealth that is actualized only as we give it away, and in giving we see something that we could not see before."[43]

(4) *The basic command, given to other creatures and to ourselves, to "be fruitful and multiply" can be fulfilled only in an earth whose conditions foster life.* The Bible is filled with concern for future generations and their well-being. We are fortunate heirs to this concern, voiced thousands of years ago by writers who could not imagine us yet somehow foresaw us. To spend down the resources needed by our own offspring and those of other species who were commanded to be fruitful is to dishonor the gift passed to us. No theology capable of learning from the past encourages waste out of a disparagement of earthly life or reliance on either God or science to provide a substitute. Theologies of eminent "rapture" from earth, and philosophies that justify destructive exploitation of the earth's resources in hope that science and technology will fix the damage, equally radiate disrespect for God's handiwork and unconcern for future generations.

Refocusing attention on creation's breadth as envisioned in God's concern for "every living creature of every kind" will do nothing to diminish human life on earth. On the contrary, it will open theological imagination to the abundant, vulnerable world that surrounds us, and in turn to both our own abundance (of grace received, of capacity to give back) and our own vulnerability. If there is security in knowing our neighbors on the block, there is more security to be found for human life in rich knowledge of, and respectful appreciation for, the nonhuman neighborhood that surrounds us. In this way we can continue, in accord with biblical theology, to reacquaint ourselves with the realm with which we are blessed to be interdependent.

Recently, two neighboring religious orders—the Sisters of Loretto in Bardstown and the Trappist monks at Gethsemani, where Thomas Merton once lived—protected their collective three thousand acres in the rolling hills of central Kentucky by refusing access for a proposed natural-gas liquid pipeline. As Dominican Sister of Peace Claire McGowen explained, this pipeline "would risk much of what makes Central Kentucky dear to us: the beauty of our landscape, the abundance of good water, the health of our air, the peaceful quietness of our rural areas, and the general sense of security from unexpected disasters." More churches and religious bodies are waking up to the sense expressed by Sister Maria Visse of Loretto about their land: "It's a gift. It's not a commodity."[44]

Anglican Martin Palmer has noted that religious groups "own about 8 percent of the habitable land surface of the planet."[45] These institutions, including churches, can become—and in fact are becoming—powerful collective forces modeling humility toward the larger created world and on-the-ground conservation practices. In the quest for a more resilient relationship with other creatures, we have allies in ancient scriptural writers. The Bible, closely read, can stir readers to attend to the vast array of creation, what it gives to us, and what it needs from us.

For Further Reading

Bekoff, Marc. "Considering Animals—Not 'Higher' Primates: Consciousness and Self in Animals; Some Reflections." *Zygon* 38 (2003): 229–45.

Gebara, Ivone. *Longing for Running Water: Ecofeminism and Liberation; Biblical Reflections on Ministry.* Minneapolis: Augsburg Fortress, 1999.

Hiebert, Theodore. *The Yahwist's Landscape: Nature and Religion in Early Israel.* New York: Oxford University Press, 1996.

Hoggard Creegan, Nicola. "Being an Animal and Being Made in the Image of God." *Colloquium* 39 (2007): 185–203.

McFague, Sallie. *The Body of God: An Ecological Theology.* Minneapolis: Fortress, 1993.

————. "An Earthly Theological Agenda." Pages 84–98 in *Ecofeminism and the Sacred*. Edited by Carol J. Adams. New York: Continuum, 1993.

Tull, Patricia K. *Inhabiting Eden: Christians, the Bible, and the Ecological Crisis*. Louisville, Ky.: Westminster John Knox, 2013.

————. "Persistent Vegetative States: People as Plants and Plants as People in Isaiah." Pages 17–34 in *The Desert Will Bloom: Poetic Visions of Isaiah*. Edited by J. Everson and P. Kim. Atlanta: Society of Biblical Literature, 2009.

CHAPTER 3

WOMEN'S DOINGS IN RUTH
A Feminist Biblical Theology of Providence

Eunny P. Lee[*]

It may seem odd to speak of divine providence in a book that features a God who largely remains "in the shadows."[1] The book of Ruth says little directly about God; only twice does the narrative report divine activity (1:6; 4:13) and, in the first of those instances, only obliquely. There are no mighty acts of God; there is no glorious deliverance from above. Neither does God speak. Ruth, like Abraham the paragon of faith, boldly leaves her native place to go to an unknown land (2:11; cf. Gen 12:1), but without the divine call and grand promises that accompanied the man.[2] Naomi's bitter lament against YHWH after the loss of her family (1:13, 20-21) recalls Job's heroic protest (see especially Job 27:2), but no voice responds from the whirlwind.[3] Instead, God in the book of Ruth remains silent and works unobtrusively behind the scenes, while seemingly ordinary people and ordinary events take center stage.

Yet, if one is interested in a theology of providence that invites the participation of those commonly excluded from the main action, Ruth is an eminently appropriate text. God is very much at work in this book. But the

[*] I have long admired Carol Newsom for her scholarship, among the most creative and provocative in the field of biblical scholarship. She has taught me and inspired me mostly from afar. Mostly, I say, because a series of personal interactions at an early stage in my career provided encouragement that I still hold dear. It is an honor to be counted among her grateful students and colleagues in this volume.

narrative depicts that activity in a way that valorizes human agency—and the agency of women in particular—in the fulfillment of God's good purposes. Indeed, the narrator's tendency to remain relatively silent about God gives a greater narratological role to the women. Thus, while divine initiative plays a vital part in the movement of the narrative, it does not overshadow or restrict human initiative; quite the contrary, it creates and yields space for a commensurate initiative on the part of human agents.

Ruth tells the story of a Bethlehem family facing extinction due to famine, displacement, childlessness, and the death of its men (1:1-5). In the first place, it is a women's tale. Naomi and her daughter-in-law, vulnerable widows whose own lives are now at risk, must find a way to survive their losses.[4] But their plight also has far greater ramifications. The continuity of the family line and, it turns out, nothing less than the future of the Davidic dynasty (4:17, 18-22) are at stake. The God who safeguarded Israel's endangered ancestresses in the past must intervene again to care for Naomi and Ruth and ensure their family's survival.[5] But that deliverance happens only through the full cooperation and ingenuity of the women themselves as well as of their Bethlehem kinsman. Divine presence does not control events with a heavy hand but manifests itself through a gracious partnership with God-centered people who are willing to do what is right. God's "mighty acts" thus give way to the everyday courageous acts of women and men who commit themselves to sustaining life and enacting God's blessing in their world.

This essay will begin with a brief overview of the theology of providence that undergirds the book of Ruth, with its accent on a God who gives and gives way to human agents. I will then offer a closer look at the book's climactic moment (4:11-13), in which the Bethlehem community celebrates the shared agency at work in the preservation of an endangered family. What is especially striking about this text is its public acclaim of women as the primary "builders" of the house of Israel. The final section will consider the implications for this house when women, including a foreign woman, are acknowledged as its builders. The inclusion of a Moabite within the house of Israel disrupts and opens its boundaries, forcing interpreters ancient and modern to wrestle ever anew with the meaning of "home."

The God Who Gives

Many commentators have observed that the narrator of Ruth explicitly mentions divine activity only twice. Yet these theological assertions occur at key moments. First, in 1:6, Naomi hears that "the LORD had considered his people and given them food." The gift of food reverses the problem of the barren land that had precipitated Naomi's crisis. The mere report of God's attentive care is enough to rouse her to action, to begin her homeward journey. Hence, divine initiative sets the narrative in motion, reminding readers at the outset that the fate of the land and its inhabitants ultimately lies in God's hands.

God the giver then makes a second appearance at the end of the book, this time to address the problem of the barren womb.[6] The God who provided seed for harvest now provides human seed: "So Boaz took Ruth and she became his wife. When they came together, the LORD made her conceive, and she bore a son" (4:13b). To one degree or another, all of Israel's matriarchs required divine intervention to conceive (Sarah [Gen 21:1-2]; Rebekah [25:21]; Leah [29:31; 30:17]; Rachel [30:22-23]). Each time, there is a theological affirmation that fertility is not just a product of human sexuality or parental planning but a gift of God. In Ruth 4:13, however, the Hebrew text employs unique language that especially highlights YHWH's involvement in the mystery of procreation. It reads literally, "the LORD *gave* her conception." For the ancient rabbis, the odd verbiage demanded an explanation, and they imagined that Ruth "had no ovary, so the Holy One . . . formed an ovary for her."[7] Of course, it is just as possible that Ruth's deceased husband had been the cause of their infertility and that God "gave conception" by giving Ruth a husband able to father a child. However one speculates on the matter, the peculiar language of the biblical text underscores the crucial role of providence in childbearing.

In both of these instances of divine initiative, God acts decisively to resolve a major human predicament. The gift of food provides immediate sustenance and gets the story going. The gift of a child brings it full circle, completing Naomi's redemption (4:14-15) and securing the family's continuity. The God who gives thus frames the narrative and forms the book's broad theological horizon. The affirmation that God creates and sustains life is foundational.

While the narrator refrains from elaborating further on divine activity, God's name proliferates on the lips of characters who pray for and bless one another, even in routine greetings. Indeed, this short story offers a dense collection of the Old Testament's various forms of prayer. And these prayers both reflect and shape the theological perspectives of those who pray and, by extension, the theological orientation of the book.[8] The steady stream of prayers thus reinforces the notion of a God who gives. They appeal to God to provide security (1:8-9), refuge (2:12), reward (2:12), progeny (4:11-12), and redemption within the family's protective circle (2:20; 4:14-15).

At the same time, the way these prayers function in the narrative upholds the importance of human agency alongside the divine. Indeed, as the story progresses, the prayers are fulfilled by the very people who utter them. The purposeful repetition of key words reinforces this connection. Naomi invokes YHWH as the one to grant her daughters-in-law "security" in the house of a husband (1:9); she later takes it upon herself to find that "security" for Ruth (3:1). Boaz prays that Ruth would find refuge under God's "wings" (plural of Heb. *kanaph*, 2:12), but Ruth calls upon him to make good on that prayer by spreading his "wing" or "cloak" (*kanaph*, 3:9) over her in marriage. This literary strategy conveys the book's theology of double agency. The fundamental theological claim is that God acts on behalf of those in need. But just as important are human actions that make God's gifts an experienced reality.

The interplay is also evident in the very rhetoric of blessing. When Naomi hears of Ruth's "accidental" encounter with Boaz (2:3-4), she declares, "Blessed be he by the LORD, whose kindness [*hesed*] has not forsaken the living or the dead!" (2:20). In the ambiguous Hebrew syntax, "kindness" may be attributed to either YHWH or Boaz (cf. Gen 24:24; 2 Sam 2:5). Indeed, Naomi's eyes are opened to God's kindness precisely because of Boaz's kindness. Similarly, in 4:14-15, the women of the town celebrate Obed's birth, saying, "Blessed be the LORD, who has not left you this day without next-of-kin; and may his name be renowned in Israel! He shall be to you a restorer of life." Whose name is in view: YHWH's or the newborn's? Who will restore Naomi's life? The ambiguity reinforces the notion that the child's significance cannot be separated from the God who provides.[9]

As an important counterpoint, Naomi's initial complaint concerning YHWH's harsh treatment (1:13, 20-21) points to the dark side of providence. When God removes all the things that gave her meaning and security, Naomi protests as bitterly as Job. Her charge that God caused her calamities amounts to a widow's cry for redress. Couched as biblical lament, this speech too plays a critical part in the reversal of her plight. Thus, in the story's deft construction, God acts through both human speech and human behavior.[10]

A Community's Blessing (4:11-12)

Divine and human agency are similarly interwoven in the communal invocation that caps Boaz's negotiations at the city gate, in which Boaz reunites
Naomi with her family estate and pledges to marry Ruth. The women are
finally reintegrated into the family's protective circle, and the witnesses
commemorate the redemptive moment:

> May YHWH grant[11] that the woman coming into your house
> be like Rachel and Leah, who together built the house of Israel.
> Thus may you flourish in Ephrathah!
> Thus may you proclaim a name in Bethlehem!
> May your house be like the house of Perez whom Tamar bore to Judah
> from the seed which YHWH will grant you from this young woman.
> (4:11-12 author's trans.)

One scholar likens this text to a mise en abîme, a miniature representation
of a larger work, which summarizes, reflects, and intensifies the narrative
of which it is a part.[12] The invocation points both back to Israel's founding
mothers and forward to the founding of David's dynasty. It thus represents
an important moment not only for the book of Ruth but also for the community's larger story.[13] The preservation of Naomi's family is bound up with
the metanarrative concerning Israel's destiny.

The expansive purview of the blessing is reinforced by its central motif,
"house." The Hebrew *bayit* may refer to a physical structure or habitation
(Boaz's house; Bethlehem, "house of bread") but also the family that occupies it (Boaz's household). It takes on a broader meaning when it refers to
the descendants of a particular tribe or clan ("house of Israel"; "house of
Perez"), or even the Israelite people as a whole ("house of Israel"). When
the house in question belongs to a king, it can signify a palace or a dynasty,
a usage that is distantly but clearly in view here via the Davidic genealogy
that concludes the book.

The blessing is effusive and celebratory, with a nicely balanced structure. Syntactically, two parallel jussives ("May YHWH grant" and "May
your house be") surround two parallel imperatives ("Thus may you flourish" and "Thus may you proclaim") that express the desired outcome for
Boaz.[14] The first imperative *'aseh hayil* can mean "do valiantly/triumph"
(Num 24:18; 1 Sam 14:48; Ps 60:12), "achieve wealth" (Deut 8:17-18), or
"do great things/exercise power/act worthily" (Prov 31:29). The ambiguity
stems from the noun *hayil*, which may refer to various forms of strength,

including physical and military prowess, socioeconomic influence, intellectual power, and strength of character. Some interpreters argue that in this context the word means "procreative power" or "virility," yielding something like "may you produce children" (NRSV).[15] Such a translation is appealing, since it recognizes (in)fertility to be just as much a male issue as a female one. But this rendering is unnecessarily restrictive, especially since the word *ḥayil* elsewhere refers to Boaz's substantial wealth and good standing in Bethlehem (2:1) and to Ruth's worthy character (3:11). Those nuances are also in view here, and a rendering like "may you flourish" (cf. JPS, "prosper") better captures the multivalence.

The meaning of the second imperative *qere' shem* (literally, "proclaim a name") is also uncertain. The precise idiom occurs only here, and it remains unclear whose name is in view, Boaz's own good name (thus JPS, "perpetuate your name") or the naming of his progeny (thus NRSV, "bestow a name"; cf. 4:14, 17). However it is read, the heart of the blessing focuses on the flourishing of Boaz's household into the future (cf. 4:14, 17-22).[16]

But the man's interests cannot be divorced from the woman's. Indeed, the dominant note sounded by the blessing is a celebration of God's work in and through women. As noted above, the imperatives directed toward Boaz are best understood as the consequence of the opening clause, "May YHWH grant that the woman coming into your house be like Rachel and Leah." Similarly, the blessing concludes with the declaration that Boaz's thriving household will be actualized through "the seed which YHWH will grant you from this young woman." The structure of this blessing thus echoes the larger theological framework of the book. A twofold reference to YHWH's "giving" surrounds and grounds the blessing. It holds it together and is foundational for the burgeoning family envisioned here. At the same time, the blessing recognizes that God's gift is actualized through female agency. YHWH's "giving" is parallel to women's "building" and "bearing," indicating a shared agency at work in the founding of this house.

The House That Women Built

Women are of course needed to produce children, and their instrumental value is a commonplace in patriarchal discourse. In this instance, however, Israel's matriarchs are credited with building the house of Israel. The language is remarkable, given that the subject of the verb is typically male. Important houses are built by men of royal or priestly background (2 Sam 5:9; 1 Kgs 5-9 passim; Neh 3:1). Even ordinary homes have male builders

(e.g., Deut 25:9). Ultimately, however, building houses is God's prerogative. As the psalmist declares, "Unless the LORD builds the house, those
who build it labor in vain" (Ps 127:1). The accent on divine prerogative is
even more prominent in 2 Sam 7, where YHWH disallows David's lofty
plans to build a house for God (v. 5) and pledges instead to establish a
house for David (vv. 11, 16, 27). This text too plays on the multiple meanings of "house." David's offspring will eventually build a temple (bayit) for
YHWH, but even that will signify YHWH's faithfulness in establishing
David's royal line (bayit).[17] Indeed, 2 Sam 7 is a comprehensive recital of
God's beneficent activity on behalf of David, in which God claims all the
action (twenty-three verbs) and puts the king in his proper place.

In Ruth 4:11-12, however, divine action embraces and promotes women
who would build. Rachel, Leah, and Tamar all ensured their families' continuity, sometimes despite their husbands. The Genesis narratives, however,
tend to highlight the painful and unflattering dimensions of their stories.
In the case of Rachel and Leah, their bitter rivalry drives the narrative.[18]
Feminist interpreters point instead to a hidden cooperation beneath the
surface of the text (see Gen 30:14-15).[19] The claim in Ruth 4:11 that the two
sisters *together* built the house of Israel pays tribute to their collaboration.
Indeed, according to Ilana Pardes, the portrayal of the bonding between
Ruth and Naomi throughout the book offers an "idyllic revision" of the
Genesis rivalry.[20]

By attending to the female *togetherness* noted in Ruth 4:11, feminist critics have thus recovered a suppressed element in the biblical narrative—the
female solidarity that enabled Israel's growth. But just as important is the
extraordinary claim that these women "*built* the house of Israel." In Genesis,
Israel's foremothers appear as subjects of the verb *banah* when, unable to
bear offspring of their own, they attempt "to be built up" through surro-
gates (Sarah in Gen 16:2; Rachel in Gen 30:3).[21] The passive verb highlights
the helplessness of reproductively challenged women. But in Ruth 4:11, the
matriarchs are transformed from passive to active subjects who exercise creative power of their own. The text recasts their struggle positively. Their
initiative and their agency receive appropriate recognition in this alternative
account of Israel's origins. Ruth's revisionism thus highlights collaboration
not just among women but also between women and God. The matriarchs
are acknowledged as the master builders of the house of Israel, empowered
by God the chief architect. Women work in concert with one another, and
in concert with God, to build up Israel.

This emphasis on women's agency is altogether in keeping with a book that acknowledges the importance of the "mother's house" (1:8). The maternal attribution is quite unusual (occurs elsewhere only in Gen 24:28; Song 3:4; 8:2).[22] Examining this phrase in light of ancient Israel's social context, Carol Meyers finds that it surfaces in texts that feature female characters, their experience, their voice, and their agency. These occurrences signal the possibility that Israelite women played "a role equal to if not greater than their husbands" in the domestic setting of the household and even beyond.[23] The references to "mother's house" and women "builders" in Ruth thus prompt readers to rehabilitate the dignity of female autonomy, indelibly inscribed even within the male-centered discourse of ancient Israel.

The significance of women builders may be further elucidated when we consider that the language of building belongs in the semantic field of creation theology. The verb *banah* has to do with bringing things—strong and durable things—into existence through generative power. Its initial occurrence in Gen 2:22 concerns God's work in creating (literally, "building") Eve. Moreover, "building" implies skill and know-how, as evidenced by its frequent collocation with various words for "wisdom," most notably *hokhmah* ("wisdom" or "expertise"), *tevunah* ("understanding," "intelligence," or "competence"), and *da'at* ("knowledge"). This same group of words occurs in the description of the building of God's "houses" (the tabernacle [Exod 31:1-3; 35:30-31; 36:1]; the temple [1 Kgs 7:14; cf. 5:9-26]) as well as the creation of the world, God's cosmic house (Prov 3:19-20; cf. Isa 40:14; Jer 10:12; 51:15; Pss 104:24; 136:5; Job 12:13-14).[24] One may thus argue that the proficient construction of any house presupposes harmony with God's creative work. It is sacred labor, requiring God-given wisdom both practical and ethical.

This wisdom association illumines yet another dimension of female building activity. When women build houses, their agency is not limited to their reproductive abilities. The capacity to bear children is of course a crucial element. But just as important is the ongoing work of nurturing and raising the young to maturity, tending to the family's physical needs, and directing the moral formation of children. In fact, in the symbolic world of Proverbs, a feminine brand of wisdom is a key ingredient for building a good house. Proverbs 14:1 states, "The wise woman builds her house." Even in its brevity, the aphorism names both the wisdom (its multiple dimensions) and the house as *hers*.[25] The poem that rounds out the book of Proverbs then expands on the nature and scope of "her house" (31:15, 21, 27).

It sings the praises of the "woman of strength" ('eshet-hayil, NRSV "capable wife" [v. 10]; cf. Prov 12:4), the very embodiment of wisdom, who works with unflagging energy, skill, and resourcefulness to build up and supply her household, assuming duties typically associated with warrior, king, prophet, and priest.[26] Her base of operations is her home, but she moves beyond it to care for the larger community (vv. 20, 24). Indeed, her power and dignity mirror God's own (vv. 17, 25; cf. Ps 93:1; Job 40:10). The hymn to this woman thus catalogues her achievements from A to Z, in the form of an acrostic. And it ends with a call to "[g]ive her her due from the fruit of her hands, and let her works praise her in the gates" (v. 31, author's trans.), for the woman's agency and the fruit it bears deserve public acclaim.

Outside of Proverbs, the only woman to be characterized as a "woman of strength" is Ruth, who exercises her agency in tacit partnership with God to enter the house of Israel and build it up. It is fitting that she too is recognized for her courageous initiative (3:11) and that the witnesses at the gate pray for the prosperity of her house (4:11).

Open House

Divine providence in Ruth features a God who gives and shares agency. The deity acts behind the scenes, enabling women to emerge as builders of the house of Israel. In Ruth 4:11-12, the house that Rachel and Leah built together opens to welcome a foreigner within its fold and to give her a share in the work of building up Israel. The openness of this house reflects God's own willingness to yield power and space to human agents. Indeed, it is by YHWH's "grant" (Hebrew natan [4:11]) that Ruth enters this house and joins the ranks of Israel's matriarchs.

But the formation of this "open house" is no easy matter. Homes are exclusive by nature, establishing boundaries between those who belong within and those who do not. The term bayit may in fact designate what is "inside," as opposed to what is "outside" (see Gen 6:14; 2 Sam 5:9; 1 Kgs 6:15-16; 7:25). The Moabite must therefore break through Bethlehem's ethnic and socioeconomic barriers. She must exercise her own initiative with dogged determination to claim her God-given place.

Indeed, Ruth's arduous journey into Israel can be tracked by examining the narrative occurrences of the verb "to come." She first returns to Bethlehem with a Judean mother-in-law who vehemently resists her "coming" (1:19). When the women appear together in Bethlehem, they are utterly empty-handed, so Ruth must "come" to Boaz's field (2:3, 7) and glean for food like a pauper. Boaz receives her and provides bountiful sustenance for the day; but beyond that, he piously commits her to YHWH's care, under whose wings she has "come" for refuge (2:12). He neglects to claim her or Naomi as family until Ruth "comes" to him again (3:7, 14), stealthily and scandalously, to call him to account as their kinsman-redeemer (3:9). In 4:11, Ruth finally "comes" into Boaz's house; she has arrived. She comes to this house not only as a beneficiary of the protection and security it offers but as one who will continue the generative work of Israel's matriarchs. The witnesses who commemorate her "homecoming" thus offer a moral testimony about the inclusive nature of this house (4:10b, 11a).

Ruth's incorporation into Boaz's household is remarkable, given her Moabite "baggage." Biblical narratives reveal general animosity toward Moab and unease about Moabite women in particular (Gen 19:30-38; Num 22; 25:1-5; Judg 3; Jer 48; Ezra 9–10; Neh 13). Because of this ancient hostility, Deut 23:3-6 forbids Moabites from entering Israel's religious assembly, and this prohibition later becomes the rationale for excommunicating foreign wives in Ezra and Nehemiah.

In the book of Ruth, the anxiety is registered more subtly through recurring emphasis on the Moabite's ethnicity (1:22; 2:2, 6, 21; 4:5, 10) and insistent interrogation of her identity (2:5; 3:9, 16; cf. 1:19).[27] But those who question Ruth are forced to reevaluate their constructions of identity and difference and to reconsider the truth of their own roots. The nineteenth-century rabbinic exegete Malbim suggested that the reference to Israel's matriarchs in Ruth 4:11-12 serves as a subtle reminder of the Israelites' own questionable pedigrees: although Jacob goes to Paddan-Aram to avoid marrying a Canaanite (Gen 28:1-2), Rachel and Leah are nevertheless daughters of the idolatrous Laban.[28] The sanction against marrying "a woman as a rival to her sister" (Lev 18:18) suggests, in the context of the Genesis stories, that all Israelites are the offspring of a prohibited marriage. Likewise, the union of Judah and his daughter-in-law Tamar, another woman deemed potentially dangerous to Israelite men (Gen 38:11), is also an illicit yet necessary one.[29] It would seem that from its inception, the house of Israel was built through transgressive yet "right" relations (cf. Gen 38:26).

The question of Ruth's place in the house of Israel becomes all the more pressing because of her link to David. Indeed, in early Jewish interpretation, David's dubious ancestry posed a scandal that had to be addressed exegetically and theologically. That the rabbis were exercised over his Moabite connection is evident in their repetitive citation of an amendment to the

Deuteronomic injunction: "a Moabite is prohibited, but not a Moabitess" (cf. Deut 23:3-6). The classic source for this gendered reading, a Talmudic tractate concerning permitted and forbidden marriages, reveals the urgency of the issue. There, Doeg the detractor challenges David's legitimacy on the basis of the original Deuteronomic law and is swiftly silenced:

> Immediately Amasa girded on his sword like an Ishmaelite and exclaimed: "Whoever will not obey the following rule will be stabbed with the sword. This rule emanated from the Prophet Samuel's Beth Din: . . . a Moabite [if unfit] but not a Moabitess."
>
> (Babylonian Talmud, *Yebamoth* 76b, 77a)

The vehemence with which David's rightful place is defended registers a profound anxiety about Israel's very identity.[30] The Moabite within Boaz' house—and David's house by extension— represents a destabilizing force that necessitates an ongoing openness to the other. As Julia Kristeva writes, "If David is *also* Ruth, if the sovereign is *also* a Moabite, peace of mind will never be his lot, but a constant quest for welcoming and going beyond the other in himself."[31]

Such implications were not lost on the rabbis, it seems. In *Ruth Rabbah*, they revisit the question of David's legitimacy. When Doeg rises to discredit the king, David's advocate appeals yet again to the new law: "a Moabite is prohibited, but not a Moabitess." This time Doeg counters by arguing that if Moabite women are now welcome, the law may then be broadened even further to include Edomite women, Egyptian women, and so on (cf. Deut 23:7-8). The implications exposed by Doeg's logic cause David's defense to falter for a moment.[32] As one interpreter asserts, "Ruth shakes the foundations." Her inclusion in Israel means that "a most significant precedent obtains for *anyone* desiring to enter the assembly of Israel."[33] And not only the assembly of Israel. For those who read Ruth as a part of the Christian Scriptures, David's genealogy is picked up in the Gospel of Matthew, where Ruth is named—together with Tamar, Rahab, and "the wife of Uriah"—as belonging to the line of Jesus the Christ. Ruth's presence in Israel thus challenges narrow exclusivism whenever and wherever it is found.

Homes mark boundaries between insiders and outsiders. Whenever border crossings occur, as in Ruth, home is no longer fixed and stable; boundaries become permeable.[34] But the "open house" in Ruth has theological moorings as well. The openness reflects the book's theological orientation, in which God yields space and shares agency with human partners. Whenever women work together to build homes that include the "other," they model God's own willingness to include human agents in the workings of providence.[35]

Concluding Thoughts

I have argued that Ruth offers a theology of providence working through multiple agents. This theology affirms both God's sovereignty and the dignity of human (specifically female) autonomy. Theologians have long struggled with the tension between these two notions.[36] When divine sovereignty is pressed to its extreme, it denies human freedom. Similarly, unrelenting focus on human agency leaves no room for providence. But the Old Testament does not engage in theoretical discussions to reconcile these seemingly opposing principles. It simply upholds both, presenting multiple ways of construing the interaction. We are left to ponder and describe "thickly" where and how they coexist, intersect, and differentiate.

For much of the twentieth century, the dominant paradigm of Old Testament theology focused on God's dramatic acts of salvation in Israel's history. According to one biblical theologian, the rise of this interventionist mode of theological discourse coincided with an unfortunate neglect of creation theology. This trend reinforced a dualism serving masculine logic and denigrating the more "feminine-maternal" themes of creation, life, and blessing.[37] Unsurprisingly, then, the turn to creation theology in recent decades has dovetailed with the rise in feminist approaches to biblical scholarship. As Phyllis Trible notes, "Creation theology undercuts patriarchy."[38] It helps us to retrieve what female and male are meant to be, equal partners who together reflect the image of God (Gen 1:27).

Ruth is not often associated with creation theology. Yet the motif of "building houses" belongs in its purview, especially in the broader understanding of creation that has been the focus of renewed scholarly interest.[39] The book's central concern is preserving life—the lives of two women, their family, their land, and eventually their nation. It recognizes humanity's deep dependence on God, who gives and sustains life at every level. At the same time, Ruth attends closely to the ongoing creative efforts of women. Indeed, this is where the narrative invests most of its energy. God delivers the "house" at risk not by miraculous demonstrations of power but through human acts of boldness and kindness in the rhythmic flow of everyday life.

Ruth's fundamental theological claim centers on the God who gives to and shares power with human partners.[40] In Ruth, the shared agency yields a salutary outcome because the people involved align themselves with

God and God's covenantal faithfulness. When people thus embody God's intention for creation, even the mundane acts depicted in Ruth—building families, caring for the needy, welcoming the other, being accountable for one's prayers—gain redemptive significance. Remarkably, these acts are just as critical for securing Israel's national destiny as God's mighty acts. Divine initiative undergirds this dynamic. But providence is experienced in the glory of the ordinary, through the agency of women who faithfully and courageously model God's ways. The result is the creation of a home that flourishes (reflecting God's own creative powers) and is open to the other (mirroring divine willingness to share power and space).

For Further Reading

Kwok Pui-lan. "Finding Ruth a Home: Gender, Sexuality, and the Politics of Otherness." Pages 100–121 in *Postcolonial Imagination and Feminist Theology*. Louisville, Ky.: Westminster John Knox, 2005.

LaCocque, André. *Ruth: A Continental Commentary*. Translated by K. C. Hanson. Minneapolis: Fortress, 2004.

Lapsley, Jacqueline E. "The Word Whispered: Bringing It All Together in Ruth." Pages 89–109 in *Whispering the Word: Hearing Women's Stories in the Old Testament*. Louisville, Ky.: Westminster John Knox, 2005.

Pardes, Ilana. "The Book of Ruth: Idyllic Revisionism." Pages 98–117 in *Countertraditions in the Bible: A Feminist Approach*. Cambridge, Mass.: Harvard University Press, 1992.

Sakenfeld, Katharine Doob. *Ruth*. Interpretation: A Bible Commentary for Teaching and Preaching. Louisville, Ky.: Westminster John Knox, 1999.

Tull, Patricia K. *Esther and Ruth*. Interpretation Bible Studies. Louisville, Ky.: Westminster John Knox, 2003.

CHAPTER 4

JOB AND THE HIDDEN FACE OF GOD
A Feminist Biblical Theology of Divine Judgment

*Carleen Mandolfo**

God's absence and judgment are inextricably linked in many texts of the Hebrew Bible. The overriding impression a reader gets is that God's absence portends ill for individual or corporate Israel. The Jewish tradition has long commented on this phenomenon, naming it *hester panim* ("hiding of the face"), debating whether it is an element of God's nature or rather an activity of the divine, whether God hides "his"[1] face arbitrarily or whether human action forces God to hide his face. But the relationship between God's absence and God's judgment is more nuanced than a simple reading would suggest. In some texts it is God's presence that is directly related to, even responsible for, personal or corporate calamity. Whether or not God's judgment is a reflection of his absence or his presence, biblical notions of justice line up for the most part with the Deuteronomistic belief in a "doctrine of retribution"—that is, God punishes those who disobey his *torah* and rewards those who are faithful.

Of particular interest to feminist theology is the whole premise of a god who rewards and punishes. That is, a god who is present or absent for the primary purpose of rewarding and punishing is a reflection of the patriarchal

* While I can never hope to achieve the kind of singular insight and rigorous scholarship Carol unfailingly contributes to our discipline, I attempted in this essay to reflect in a small way her admirable commitment to interdisciplinary dialogue. I am deeply grateful for her direct mentorship as well as her continuous modeling of unrivaled scholarship.

values of most biblical writers. In this scenario, the idea of God's presence encompasses a traditional binary and reflects hegemonic reasoning in which humankind is judged according to its adherence to YHWH's *torah*. Those who are obedient are understood to deserve God's redemptive intervention; those who are disobedient are deserving of God's wrath and subsequent acts of judgment. This hierarchical and unidirectional arrangement is a hallmark of the patriarchal values of these texts, an arrangement that is challenged by feminist post-Holocaust thinker Melissa Raphael, who argues for a more relational understanding of God than is dominant in the Bible, based on the philosophy of Emmanuel Levinas and on her own work in archives retrieving women's recollections of living and dying in the death camps of Europe during World War II. While not a biblical scholar, Raphael's observations will serve as a touchstone for the theological and hermeneutical reflections that follow.

This essay will first reconsider how God's absence and presence might be construed through a feminist lens. Then, a survey of texts will follow in which the hiding of God's face is depicted. While in some prophetic texts God's hiding his face is the result of the sinfulness of the people, in the Psalms God's absence is construed not as the result of sin but as an inexplicable phenomenon. In several texts in Deuteronomy where hiding the face appears in a way that is reminiscent of the prophetic texts, hiding the face represents divine judgment. With these texts as background, I will examine several passages in the book of Job, and specifically I will consider Job's presentation of the hiding of God's face. Job's distinctive presentation of this image offers a potentially powerful resource for a feminist reconstrual of divine (in)activity.

Rethinking God's Absence and Presence

Raphael's main objection to the (almost exclusively male) post-Holocaust thinkers that preceded her is that they often argue that God, through his absence, had somehow failed Israel in the Holocaust,[2] or that the Holocaust provided an opportunity for God to demonstrate his masculine prowess in (re)securing the land of Israel for his people.[3]

> Despite the holocaustal abjection of God and his people, God must be shown to have world and cosmos at his masculine command and in the name of the men to whom he has promised land and power. Theologies of protest have equally assumed God's sovereign power and will: but in God's failure to exercise them he is found guilty by his subjects.[4]

Whether God "failed" or ultimately came through for his people in the end amounts to the same patriarchal conception of the deity. No matter how one looks at it, the theological vision is a martial one—YHWH, the warrior king.

Raphael argues instead for a theology of presence that is reciprocal and nurturing. Drawing on Jewish notions of the Shekinah (God's feminine presence in the world), as well as Levinasian ethics,[5] Raphael contends that God was indeed in the death camps—his "presence" could be found in the women who were simply present (*hinneni*)[6] with the suffering of the other, who looked into (rather than past) the face of the other.

> In women's care for the other—emblematized in the wiping of filth from a face—God's face was revealed as present and visible to the eye of spiritual perception in the facing image.[7]

Unlike a patriarchal god, this god could not rescue the interned from death, but it could buoy up their humanity in the face of every effort to extinguish it. In short, the theological issue for Raphael is divine-human reciprocity rather than an emphasis on "God the father," whose primary purpose is to redeem and/or punish.

The notion of a saving or punishing god finds its foundational expression in biblical images. While the metaphors used of God in the Bible are diverse, the presentations of a rescuing and judging deity are foundational for Judeo-Christian traditions insofar as they are featured throughout so many biblical texts. The book of Exodus of course presents the prototypical portrayal of Israel's God as a god who "muscles" his people out of their bondage in Egypt (at the expense of many "innocent" as well as "guilty" Egyptians). The Exodus narrative has rightly played a crucial role in the liberational vision of oppressed peoples across millennia and across continents, but it has also been critiqued for glorifying the violent overthrow of those who contested Israel's right to enter a land already occupied on their way out of Egypt.[8] Likewise, while prophetic texts are often venerated for God's concern with the poor and oppressed, they are texts likewise filled with metaphoric violence against women as well as hegemonic demands of strict adherence to the laws against worshipping other deities, a demand that, it can be argued, serves primarily to uphold YHWH's "honor" and dominion, rather than serving some inherently just moral code.

The post-Holocaust thinkers Raphael is addressing are beholden to this conception of a rescuing and judging deity, but Raphael wants to move away

from a mostly biblical and thus largely patriarchal understanding of God to
a vision that is more relational, less hierarchical, and less martial.

> It may be asked what purpose was served by the maternal, grieving pres-
> ence of Shekinah if it could not offer actual deliverance from evil *then*,
> nor in a time to come. But within the logic of the model of God I am
> proposing it is not meaningful to ask why God did not protect us at the
> time because it is not the nature or function of God to be reduced to that
> of a fortification against particular suffering. God is not a supernatural
> arsenal.[9]

The martial depiction of God is especially true in parts of the Pentateuch
(e.g., Exodus) and prophets, but it is not difficult to discern elsewhere in the
Bible, as well. The nurturing and reciprocal presence of God that Raphael
posits as a replacement for the patriarchal God to which post-Holocaust
thinkers are beholden is scarce indeed.[10]

There are texts, however—such as the Psalms and Job—that make
some room for human subjectivity and give us a foundation upon which to
build a more promising (if not easy) notion of divine presence and divine-
human reciprocity than we witness in the "God is a mighty warrior" texts.
This essay will examine selections from Job that are amenable to Raphael's
feminist theological vision. Job might seem an odd choice, given the harsh
answer God delivers to Job at the end of the book, but the overall rhetorical
thrust of Job's speech, as well as God's response, honors human agency in
a way that many biblical texts fail to do. The selected texts from Deuteronomy, the prophets, and Psalms that I will examine first will serve as a
contrast to Job and will help to refine my observations.

"Hiding the Face"

Because the issue of God's presence/absence/judgment in the Bible is
immense—even if primarily focused on Job—I will use as a point of reference the phrase *hester + panim* ("hiding" + "face") as it applies to the divine
in order to assess to what degree the combination of that phrase along
with God's acts of judgment emphasizes binary, hierarchical, and patriarchal concerns over more relational, holistic concerns. In other words, some
of the questions I will be asking are, How is the hiding of the divine face
understood? What does God's hiding reveal about the nature of the divine-
human relationship? The phrase *hester + panim* (in some form) in reference
to God occurs only twenty-nine times: in the Pentateuch (4×), the prophets (11×), Psalms (12×), and Job (2×).[11] It is perhaps not surprising that

the phrase occurs primarily in the prophets and Psalms: while the prophets provide some of the most scathing depictions of God's anger, the Psalms offer human responses to perceptions of God's anger. Whereas the voice of Israel is nearly nonexistent in the prophetic texts to which I will refer, the primary voice in the Psalms, by contrast, is that of the people, of Israel.

"Hiding the Face" in Deuteronomy

Three of the four instances of *hester + panim* in the Pentateuch occur in Deuteronomy, and all support the observations made above about God's presence and its connection to God's disciplinary nature.

> The LORD said to Moses, "Soon you will lie down with your ances-tors. Then this people will begin to prostitute themselves to the foreign gods in their midst, the gods of the land into which they are going; they will forsake me, breaking my covenant that I have made with them. My anger will be kindled against them in that day. I will forsake them and *hide my face* from them; they will become easy prey, and many terrible troubles will come upon them. In that day they will say, 'Have not these troubles come upon us because our God is not in our midst?' On that day *I will surely hide my face* on account of all the evil they have done by turning to other gods." (Deut 31:16-18)

The divine image portrayed here is that of a "suzerain" against whom his "vassals" have rebelled. God constructs a justification of their future suffering that leaves no room for a counterclaim, a justification that will be employed with horrifying effect in many preexilic prophetic texts.

Levinas speaks of precisely this kind of justification as immoral: "For an ethical sensibility—confirming itself, in the inhumanity of our time, against this inhumanity—*the justification of the neighbor's pain* is certainly the source of all immorality."[12] It is hard to imagine a more trenchant critique of the Deuteronomic and prophetic doctrine of retribution, whereby human suffering is justified on the backs of the very ones suffering. The following chapter of Deuteronomy offers much of the same:

> They sacrificed to demons, not God,
>   to deities they had never known,
> to new ones recently arrived,
>   whom your ancestors had not feared.
> You were unmindful of the Rock that bore you;
>   you forgot the God who gave you birth.
> The LORD saw it, and was jealous;

> he spurned his sons and daughters.
> He said: *I will hide my face* from them,
>   I will see what their end will be;
> for they are a perverse generation,
>   children in whom there is no faithfulness. (32:17-20)

In both Deuteronomic texts, God "hides his face" because the people have broken the covenant by worshipping other deities. In Deut 32:19, God "saw" (*r'h*), with a gaze that is unidirectional, one that scrutinizes and passes judgment. What God "sees" in most English translations is his people worshipping "demons" (*shedim*), a word with roots that probably go back to an Akkadian term *sedu*, which means something more like a "protective spirit,"[13] though the Akkadian carries a double meaning that includes "demon" as well.[14] These beings are apparently lesser, personal deities meant to protect the humans with whom they are associated. Although it cannot be denied that these "protective spirits" are indeed not YHWH, rethinking the term "demons" already decenters YHWH's absolutist claims in which the people are rendered "perverse" (v. 20). On their surfaces, these texts betray not a hint of the people's point of view. Their subjectivity is simply erased in order to justify the punitive inclinations of their deity.

Also drawing on Levinasian ethics, Judith Butler explains how violence follows from such justificatory representations of the other:

> The face over there . . . the one whose meaning is portrayed as *captured by evil* is precisely the one that is not human, not in the Levinasian sense. The "I" who sees that face is not identified with it: the face represents that for which no identification is possible, an accomplishment of dehumanization and a condition for violence.[15]

A number of prophetic texts unfortunately resonate with Butler. And they foreshadow the troubling "predictions" made in Deuteronomy by the way they articulate divine judgment.

"Hiding the Face" in Prophetic Texts

The phrase *hester* + *panim* occurs eleven times in the prophetic books. Six of these occurrences are in Isaiah,[16] but only four refer to God's hiding of his face.[17] The phrase also appears in Ezek 39:23, 24, 29; Mic 3:4; and Jer 33:5. In Isa 8:17, the prophet laments expectantly, "I will wait for the LORD, *who is hiding his face* from the house of Jacob, and I will hope in him." This comes in the context of God telling the prophet that YHWH himself will bring the Assyrians upon them like a mighty overflowing river because the people have not trusted in YHWH. Here God's hiding is directly linked to judgment against a rebellious people, as predicted in Deuteronomy.[18] Ezekiel makes particularly explicit the direct connection between God's hiding and his judgment against his people: "And the nations shall know that the house of Israel went into captivity for their iniquity, because they dealt treacherously with me. So I *hid my face* from them and gave them into the hand of their adversaries, and they all fell by the sword" (Ezek 39:23). We hear the same in Jeremiah: "The Chaldeans are coming in to fight and to fill them with the dead bodies of those whom I shall strike down in my anger and my wrath, for I have *hidden my face* from this city because of all their wickedness" (Jer 33:5). In each case YHWH's hiding and subsequent wrath is justified by the misdeeds of the people—"their iniquity" (*'avonam*) or "their wickedness" (*ra'atam*). YHWH feels betrayed, and his response is uncompromising; the texts betray no acknowledgment of the complexity of human behavior. The labels ascribed to the people of Israel in the prophetic texts of doom have served as all the warrant needed to turn many readers' faces away from suffering expressed there.

In a similar vein in Micah, the people are constructed as perversions of humanity:

> [Y]ou who hate the good and love the evil,
> who tear the skin off my people,
>   and the flesh off their bones;
> who eat the flesh of my people,
>   flay their skin off them,
> break their bones in pieces,
>   and chop them up like meat in a kettle,
>   like flesh in a caldron.
> Then they will cry to the LORD,
>   but he will not answer them;
> *he will hide his face* from them at that time,
>   because they have acted wickedly. (3:2-4)

Here, God accuses a portion of Israel of monstrosities against their fellow citizens. And again we have the connection between God's hiding and the people's "wickedness." Many readers understandably accept YHWH's characterization of certain Israelites and thus take no issue with his response to their "wickedness."

But my thesis is not so much about guilt or innocence, though this issue has been the subject of plenty of scholarly ink. I am taking my cue from

Raphael and merely noting the portrayal of YHWH as a warrior king who relates to his people from a position of power, either as a rescuer or as a destroyer. Of further note in this verse is mention of the people's appeal to YHWH. The ability to appeal would seem to be an intrinsic component of the covenantal agreement; and YHWH's dismissal of their attempts at communication seems a principal indicator of the patriarchal and objectifying propensities of the prophetic judgment texts. The lament psalms are our primary evidence that the covenant between YHWH and Israel in fact included a reciprocal element that served as a discursive counterpoint to the one-sided prophetic accusations.

"Hiding the Face" in Psalms

It is particularly in the lament psalms that we are provided a glimpse into the human point of view that is neglected in the prophetic texts. The near total absence of guilt and sin from the suppliants' perspective is notable. Throughout much of the Hebrew Bible, we are treated to God's demands of his people as well as his disappointment over their failures; but in these psalms we get a glimpse into the liturgical life of Israel, the context in which the people voiced their disappointment over God's apparent failure to fulfill his side of the covenant. This expectation is made clear in the several references to God's negative presence—that is, the hiding of his face (hester + panim). Of the twenty-nine biblical occurrences of this phrase, twelve occur in the Psalter (Pss 10, 13, 22, 27, 30, 44, 51, 69, 88, 102, 104, 143), more than in any other book. Unsurprisingly, most of the occurrences in the Psalter are in lament psalms, individual lament psalms in particular. Eight of those are explicitly *complaint* psalms, often containing an interrogative directed at God's apparent lack of positive attention—for example, "How long, O Lord?" (13:1).

Generally speaking, the psalmists seem to have an expectation of YHWH's protection against misfortune. They do not blame themselves—neither do they seem to see their ill fortune as a matter of judgment, or at least not just judgment. They perceive God's "hiding" as an injustice or an oversight. In stark contrast to the prophetic texts we considered, these psalms do not connect absence to judgment, and thus YHWH's "face" (i.e., "presence") is understood as an unequivocal good:[19]

> Do not *hide your face* from your servant,
>   for I am in distress—make haste to answer me.

> Draw near to me, redeem me,
>> set me free because of my enemies. (Ps 69:17-18)

Psalm 44, the single clearly communal lament, beseeches God to make his presence known to Israel in a time of need. According to the psalmist, the people have kept their side of the bargain, so their expectation (based, we can assume, on some form of the promises in Deut 28) that God be present with them is not misplaced:

> All this has come upon us,
>> yet we have not forgotten you,
>> or been false to your covenant.
> Our heart has not turned back,
>> nor have our steps departed from your way. . . .
> . . . .
> Why do you *hide your face?*
>> Why do you forget our affliction and oppression?
> For we sink down to the dust;
>> our bodies cling to the ground.
> Rise up, come to our help.
>> Redeem us for the sake of your *hesed* ["loving faithfulness," author's trans.]. (44:17-18, 24-26)

The interrogative in verse 24 demonstrates the suppliants' surprise and disappointment at the turn of events, whereby God was once beneficially present to their ancestors, as asserted in verse 3:

> [F]or not by their own sword did they win the land,
>> nor did their own arm give them victory;
> but your right hand, and your arm,
>> and the light of your countenance [lit., "face"],
>> for you delighted in them. (Ps 44:3)

With few exceptions, the meaning of "presence"/"face" in the Psalms is that God's presence advantages his people, both individually and corporately.

It might seem like a lot of unnecessary work to have arrived at a conclusion that most would take for granted. But laying it out allows us to see clearly how the connection between absence and judgment in the Psalms differs so markedly from their connection in prophetic texts. Two striking differences are evident. First, Israel's voice is primary in the Psalms, and it is a voice that flatly contradicts the prophetic claims about the alleged aberrant behavior of the people (of course, this voice and the target of the prophetic judgments may well reference distinct groups). Their personhood, their "face," cannot be denied, even if one were to contest their specific claims. Second, although they are complaining about their god, that very complaint is evidence of a more reciprocal divine-human relationship that is not discernible in the prophetic texts.

We have noted the general differences between prophetic and psalmic notions of divine hiding/judgment. What is less explicitly obvious is an observation made possible by Raphael's understanding of the martial characterization of God found in many biblical texts (and extending all the way to the post-Holocaust thinkers). Although the subjectivity and agency of YHWH's people is a hallmark of these psalms, the theological assumptions are strikingly similar to those in the prophets: God is expected to defend or rescue his people. Even if he is failing to do so, the expectation remains. The converse can be assumed: if the suppliants had indeed sinned, then they would deserve the judgment putatively marked by God's absence.

"Hiding the Face" in Job

We are finally in a position to see the ways in which God's presence, absence, and judgment in Job are genuinely unique in the biblical corpus, and furthermore how these references accord more fully, though counterintuitively, with Raphael's call for a less martial, patriarchal, and even hierarchical theology. In Job, the human voice, as in the Psalms, is paramount, but Job's complaint cannot be read so easily as a celebration of presence, as it might be in the Psalms. *Hester* + *panim* occurs a mere two times in Job (13:24 and 34:29). But only the former passage is voiced by Job and thus has a bearing on our comparison with the suppliants of the lament psalms.

Job articulates his complaint that God hides his face as follows:

How many are my iniquities and my sins?
    Make me know my transgression and my sin.
Why do you *hide your face*,
    and count me as your enemy?
Will you frighten a windblown leaf
    and pursue dry chaff? (13:23-25)

The assessment of the relative benefit of God's presence in the book of Job results in a mixed verdict. Job's speech here sounds quite like what we find in the lament psalms, only he makes his complaint with more vitriol. The section begins with interrogatives meant to challenge God's actions vis-à-vis the suppliant, and Job is dismayed at God's absence. In verse 23 he demands that God explain to him his wrongdoing. In this way, he simply makes more explicit the claim of innocence that is a hallmark of the lament psalms. For Job, the consequences of God's hiding his face are much more dire and pro-tracted than they are in the lament psalms. In fact, God's hiding does not seem particularly passive at all, as it often does in the psalms, where the suppliants are suffering because God is not actively caring for them. In Job, God's absence has a dynamic—even lethal—quality to it: "Why do you hide your face, and count me as an enemy? Will you frighten a windblown leaf and pursue dry chaff?" (Job 13:24-25). In short, God's absence mani-fests as a presence of sorts.

Job may complain once about God's absence or hiding, but there are three other occasions in the book in which God's presence—in the form of divine "watchfulness"—appears to be even more problematic than his absence. In 10:14, Job says, "If I sin, you *watch me*, and do not acquit me of my iniquity." In 13:27 Job exclaims: "For you put my feet in the stocks and *watch* all my ways, hampering my progress."[20] And in 14:16, he says, "For then you would not number my steps, you would not *keep watch* over my sin." The sense in these verses is that God is overly vigilant/"present" when it comes to human faults.

Furthermore, there is an interesting phrase that occurs twice in Job, inversely related to the notion of "watching." It has to do with God's pres-ence (found only once in the Psalms, in Ps 119, but in a very different con-text). The phrase translates to "look away" and features a rare Hebrew root (*sh'h*). In chapters 7 and 14 of Job, we are treated to some of the angriest statements in the Bible. Subversively referencing Ps 8, Job begs God:

> What are human beings . . . that you set your mind on them?
> . . . .
> Will you not *look away* from me for a while,
>   let me alone until I swallow my spittle?[21] (7:17-19)

Here, God's presence/gaze is such an oppressive force that Job wishes God would turn his face elsewhere, even just long enough for Job to swallow!

In chapter 14 he translates this personal experience into the sad fate of every person:

> *Look away* from him, and let him be at ease,
>   until he, like a laborer, finishes out his day. (14:6, author's trans.)

Unlike the suppliants in the lament psalms, Job is not redeemed but bur-dened by God's presence. But God's response to Job at the end of the book suggests that Job's understanding of his experience has more to do with his

preconceived theological expectations of God than of the God presented in
chapters 38–41. The divine speech at the end of Job takes us in a very different direction than either the prophetic or the psalmic texts. God suggests
that theological understanding that is limited by human ethical expectations may be off the mark. Job may not be suffering as a result of God's
absence or presence.

God's response suggests that both the prophetic and psalmic attempts
to know God fall short in their own way, being developed as they are from
a limited human point of view. Job's God is not a deity who rewards and
punishes based on his assessment of human behavior. God is, rather, the
creator of the universe:

> Can you bind the chains of the Pleiades,
> > or loose the cords of Orion?
> Can you lead forth the Mazzaroth in their season,
> > or can you guide the Bear with its children?
> Do you know the ordinances of the heavens?
> > Can you establish their rule on the earth? (Job 38:31-33)

Humans indeed suffer, but, according to the book of Job, the prophets and
the psalmists misunderstand God's role in that suffering. In other words,
the book of Job suggests that humans have assigned God an ethical role as
arbiter of reward and punishment based on a doctrine of retribution, but
God's answer to Job is at least in part meant to dispel any such theological
arrogance. God may be none of the things Job and his friends expect him
to be. Rather, in his response to Job, God's nurturing Shekinah is on full
display.

In Job 38–41, God rehearses all the ways in which his presence is manifest, including and especially to nonhuman creation:

> Who has cut a channel for the torrents of rain,
> > and a way for the thunderbolt,
> to bring rain on a land where no one lives,
> > on the desert, which is empty of human life,
> to satisfy the waste and desolate land,
> > and to make the ground put forth grass? (Job 38:25-27)

> Who has let the wild ass go free?
> > Who has loosed the bonds of the swift ass,
> to which I have given the steppe for its home,
> > the salt land for its dwelling place?

It scorns the tumult of the city;
    it does not hear the shouts of the driver.
It ranges the mountains as its pasture,
    and it searches after every green thing. (Job 39:5-8)

God's answer makes clear that he is profoundly "present" in creation but that his presence has little to do with reward and punishment. The exchange between God and Job, as uncomfortable as it might make some readers, may be the best example of reciprocal relating. Both Job and God speak a truth that expresses their authentic selves. Job does not let himself be boxed in by the customary theological understanding (i.e., the doctrine of retribution) represented by his friends' discourse. God's answer may have seemed overwhelming, but the divine awesomeness on display represents a truth about God's essence that humans may need to accept if they are not to limit God in a manner similar to the theological characterizations in the prophets and Psalms.

Conclusion

For the prophets, God's presence is marked by the objectifying gaze of the one standing in the subject position. In these texts, God scrutinizes and objectifies humankind primarily for purposes having to do with the maintenance of his honor. There is virtually no attempt in prophetic texts of doom to view the events in question from the point of view of suffering, struggling, colonized Israel. The Psalms, on the other hand, offer the reader a theological reciprocity approaching that imagined by Raphael. In the Psalms, God's face may be hidden (or God has hidden it), but God's hiding is neither a cause of human suffering, nor is human disobedience the cause of divine hiding. Furthermore, human voices speak their own truth and experience, a discourse notably absent in the prophetic texts under consideration. The book of Job, however, may offer us the most nuanced and fruitful understanding of divine-human reciprocity. There the rhetorical arena belongs to Job in a way that is not true even of the suppliants in the psalms of lament. The psalmic discourse is constrained somewhat by its setting in the official cult of Israel, while the genre of speculative wisdom literature allows Job to balk freely at the unfairness of his situation. Job's theology is much more sophisticated than the psalmists' but also less naïve. It speaks with integrity to the experience of much of humanity: our expectations of fairness belong to the realm of the ethical but perhaps have little bearing on the Absolute.

A God who saves might be an attractive theological construct, but a God who saves must, conversely, be a God who does not save and who even punishes. Raphael's emphasis on a God who neither saves nor punishes sidesteps this conundrum. If Raphael's God had been the divine figure of the book of Job, Job's friends would never have challenged Job's account of his suffering. They would have merely sat with him, tended to his sores, and dried his tears. They could not have saved him, but they could have given him back some semblance of the humanity that was stripped from him by his circumstances. Their adherence to a theology of retribution only ensured the further contraction of Job's personhood.

Melissa Raphael struggles with the idea that God's presence is supposed to serve a protective role in the material (and often martial) sense. For her, the human expectation that God is our rescuer is misguided by patriarchal assumptions about salvation. Post-Holocaust thinkers proclaim that God was absent during the Holocaust—some blame God, some blame Jewish disobedience, but all have an understanding of the covenant in which God is supposed to "rescue" his people.[22] Raphael blames this kind of thinking for the despair that overtook many Jewish thinkers after the Holocaust, prompting some to go so far as to proclaim the death of God.[23] This ultimate challenge to faith could have been avoided had they not started with the presumption of a patriarchal image of God in the first place. The combination of absence plus judgment that we see in the prophets is inarguably the most challenging to Raphael's desire that we move away from an inflexible theology of reward and punishment. The idea that suffering is always the fault of those who suffer can be maintained only by those who have enjoyed unchecked power and privilege.

In none of these texts, however, do we encounter in full the "Mother-God" that Raphael posits through the tradition of the Shekinah. But within the received canonical tradition, the lament psalms and the book of Job offer us the closest example of a theology that respects both the subjectivity of humankind and the alterity of the divine. Job goes beyond the Psalms in this regard, not presenting a one-sided relationship in which humans plead and God saves. Job protests with integrity, and God honors his personhood by providing a thoughtful and thorough, if terrifying, response meant to reorient Job's expectations. It is not exactly the comforting or nurturing presence Raphael found among the women interned in the death camps, but it is a reciprocal presence that acknowledges the "face" of the other.

For Further Reading

Balentine, Samuel. *The Hidden God: The Hiding of the Face of God in the Old Testament*. New York: Oxford University Press, 1983.

Braiterman, Zachary. *(God) after Auschwitz*. Princeton, N.J.: Princeton University Press, 1998.

Brueggemann, Walter. "A Fissure Always Uncontained." Pages 62–75 in *Strange Fire: Reading the Bible after the Holocaust*. Edited by Tod Linafelt. New York: New York University Press, 2000.

Burnett, Joel. *Where Is God? Divine Absence in the Hebrew Bible*. Minneapolis: Fortress, 2010.

Butler, Judith. *Precarious Life: The Powers of Mourning and Violence*. New York: Verso Books, 2004.

Harris, Beau, and Carleen Mandolfo. "The Silent God in Lamentations." *Interpretation* 67 (2013): 133–43.

Kepnes, Steven. *The Text as Thou: Martin Buber's Dialogical Hermeneutics and Narrative Theology*. Bloomington: Indiana University Press, 1992.

Levinas, Emmanuel. *Totality and Infinity: An Essay on Exteriority*. Duquesne, Pa.: Duquesne University Press, 1969.

Mandolfo, Carleen. "Finding Their Voices: Sanctioned Subversion in Psalms of Lament." *Horizons in Biblical Theology* 24 (2002): 27–52.

Newsom, Carol A. *The Book of Job: A Contest of Moral Imaginations*. Oxford: Oxford University Press, 2009.

Raphael, Melissa. "The Female Face of God in Auschwitz." Pages 648–62 in *Wrestling with God: Jewish Theological Responses during and after the Holocaust*. Edited by S. Katz, S. Biderman, and G. Greenberg. Oxford: Oxford University Press, 2007.

Schwartz, Regina. *The Curse of Cain: The Violent Legacy of Monotheism*. Chicago: University of Chicago Press, 1998.

CHAPTER 5

EMBODIMENT IN ISAIAH 51–52
AND PSALM 62
A Feminist Biblical Theology of Salvation

*Katie M. Heffelfinger**

The claim that we live in a broken world—that in a variety of ways people experience a need for deliverance—lies at the heart of salvation theology. As Glenn Morrison so eloquently says, "The heart—broken, scarred and called by God—journeys along an endless crooked road."[1] While popular culture has often thought of salvation as a soul's eternal heavenly bliss, the Bible describes salvation as embodied and as transforming the toils and trials of life as we know it. Scholars insist that the Hebrew Bible depicts salvation in "this-worldly" or "earthly, landed" terms.[2] But biblical salvation's being grounded does not mean it is narrow in scope. Instead, the Bible envisions God overturning life's limits. Salvation is an embodied, this-worldly theme, but it echoes with cosmic repercussions.[3]

The two texts this essay examines share this sense that the world is broken. Each expects salvation to come from the LORD. Yet the two poems present distinctive glimpses of what it is like to expect salvation. In Isa 51:9–52:12, a human voice, using cosmic battle images, pleads with the LORD to intervene. The divine voice rebukes the human voice and insists that its fears

* It is an honor and a privilege to offer this essay to the Festschrift for Carol Newsom, an inspiring teacher and mentor. Her influence on me extended far beyond what she taught me about the Hebrew Bible, which was considerable. She also modeled how to be a generous teacher and a collegial and careful scholar.

are misplaced. In a very different way, Ps 62 commends waiting for God in "stillness" (v. 1).[4] It expresses trust in the LORD through images of stability and refuge. These two poetic responses to the broken world offer different ways of engaging salvation and demonstrate fruitful reflection on living in that broken world.

Salvation, Liberation, and Feminist Theology

Not surprisingly, the biblical theme of salvation resonates with feminist writings, for "feminist theology is predicated upon the assumption that something is dramatically wrong with contemporary existence."[5] Both the biblical vision of divine intervention as salvation and the feminist project share a trajectory toward flourishing. They each look to see the created order transformed on both micro and macro levels. Are the two visions of flourishing compatible, and can they inform and enrich each other? There are certainly feminist scholars who claim that the biblical world is so deeply patriarchal that women should not trust its vision of flourishing.[6] I recognize the patriarchal nature of the world that produced the Hebrew Bible. However, acknowledging this patriarchy does not require wholesale rejection of the Hebrew Bible's themes.[7] Indeed, when we recognize the ways interpretations of biblical texts have been used through history to diminish women's experiences, we see how these interpretations stand at odds with the ultimately liberative emphases of the biblical text itself. Elsa Tamez helpfully names these liberative emphases as "the Gospel's spirit of justice and freedom."[8]

Salvation is a theme well suited for focusing on this spirit of justice and freedom. The biblical vision of salvation is profoundly liberative. Biblical texts use both exodus and re-creation images to show what they mean by salvation, denouncing oppression and injustice as contrary to God's desires. In the poems this essay considers, salvation appears as deliverance from oppression (Isa 51:13; 52:4) and from injustice (Ps 62:10). The Bible depicts human flourishing as coming about because the LORD overturns the current conditions of human existence. This does not mean that the Bible's vision of human flourishing avoids reflecting the patriarchy of the world it comes from or that we should read biblical salvation texts uncritically. Yet we must remember that our own perspectives are biased as well. These texts, whose concerns and culture differ from our own, may challenge our assumption that we know what injustice is and may correct our inherent focus on the injustices that impact us directly. Honest engagement with these texts may force us to recognize the ways our own vision of redemption is too narrow. A biblical salvation theology can contribute constructively to the task of feminist theology by orienting us to the liberative concerns of others besides ourselves.

But the conversation is not one-directional. Biblical salvation texts may broaden our sense of what it means to hope for the cosmos's redemption, not least in the brokenness of female-male relationships. In the same way, insights from our own time may help us read these texts better. Of particular interest for this essay are ideas from feminist theory about how people know and learn, including attention to experience, emotion, and embodied ways of knowing.

First, feminists have insisted that describing human experience in generic terms privileges male experience.[9] Claiming that individual, human, lived experience is an important part of how we know and learn, feminist theologians have urged that "women name their experiences and identify experiences as loci of theological practice."[10] This idea offers a helpful way to read texts theologically. That is, we might read texts not solely for the truth claims we can extract from them. Instead, we might consider the experience they present a reader. Such an experience-oriented approach may offer insights that add to what we gain from reading for ideas.

Second, feminist writing has quite a lot to say about "real bodies, lived lives."[11] The body is central to feminist work on gender-based violence, and feminists are interested in ways discourses of power use women's bodies as symbols.[12] Since we can know our experiences only through lives lived in our bodies, experience and embodiment belong together. Both are ways of knowing that honor the individual's perceptions. If the body is an essential part of how we know, it makes sense to attend to this theme while reading texts, to look for the ways the text uses body imagery to make its truth claims, and to note the ways bodies appear when hierarchy and power are at stake.[13] The body gives shape and boundaries to human truths.

Third, emotion is increasingly regarded as a reliable source of knowledge. It is an element of truthful perception and an important consideration in ethical discussions. Philosopher Martha Nussbaum has emphasized the important place of emotions as both "bodily" and "suffused with intelligence and discernment."[14] She argues that our emotions are essential to ethical decision making since they indicate how important something is to us and register our "imperfect control" and our "vulnerability."[15] Reading texts while valuing emotion means paying attention to the emotions they describe and those they provoke in us, reading with fuller appreciation of the ethics a text calls for rather than simply drawing out of them ethical "principles to be grasped by the detached intellect."[16] Reading emotional texts as emotional beings valorizes the place of emotion in human knowing and helps us understand the vision of flourishing these texts offer.

In what follows, I will read Isa 51:9–52:12 and Ps 62, asking how attention to experience, embodiment, and emotion might help us better understand the vision of salvation offered by each. Applying approaches championed by feminist scholars may allow us to encounter these texts more fully, helping us see their revelatory and liberating message more clearly. The aim is not to impose experiential, bodily, and emotional knowing on texts that are devoid of these qualities. Rather, selection of these elements of feminist discourse has been driven by the observation that the texts themselves embody these motifs.

In order to aim for honest engagement between ancient texts and contemporary reader, it will be necessary to name points of challenge that these texts present. Yet, holding the biblical text as revelatory, I find myself more willing to conclude that contemporary theories are insufficient than to reach the same conclusion about the biblical text.[17] I strive for a reading that holds these commitments together.

Salvation in Isaiah 51:9–52:12: A Cosmic Battle Cry

Isaiah 51:9–52:12 depicts salvation in a profoundly emotional and heavily embodied way. The body language and emotional streams of the "rebuking consolation" overturn the way the implied audience addresses the LORD.[18] In doing so, the poem dramatically shifts expectations of what divine deliverance looks like. It guides the audience to see salvation not as something that God must wrestle away from an equally strong adversary. Instead, salvation is easily within the LORD's power and in fact is already accomplished. The contest in the passage is not between the LORD and the oppressor but between the people and their God. The question is not whether salvation can be achieved but whether the people can perceive and rejoice in it.

The passage begins with an urgent cry. Probably speaking for the audience, the prophet calls out for salvation with a doubled petition ("Arise, arise" [v. 9]). This opening plea is a call to battle. The sound of the words "arise, arise" ('uri, 'uri) may imitate a horn calling soldiers to fight (e.g., Josh 6:5; Ezek 7:14). It echoes the call to Deborah, ancient Israel's warrioress-deliverer, who is addressed in precisely these words (Judg 5:12). But this battle is no ordinary one. The call to arms invokes the aid of a cosmic deliverer, as becomes clear when the voice continues by recalling divine deeds of the ancient past. The poem mixes images of ancient creation myths and the exodus from Egypt, depicting the divine deliverer as "hewer of Rahab," "piercer of the sea monster," and "parcher of the sea" (vv. 9-10). Through these titles, the voice speaks of divine deliverance that is violent and militaristic.

The battle cry addresses its cosmic deliverer in a strikingly embodied, gendered way: "Arise, arise, wear strength, O forearm of the LORD" (v. 9). The body image "forearm of the LORD" is a common phrase for divine might in the Hebrew Bible (e.g., Exod 6:6; 15:16; Deut 4:34; 26:8; 1 Kgs 8:42; Ps 79:11). However, this poem develops this common phrase through personification, through addressing the forearm (zeroa', a feminine noun) directly as a hearing, acting figure. Twice the voice asks, "Are you not she" (vv. 9, 10) who claimed the divine victories of the past?[19] These pronouns are not merely an accident of grammar. Rather, they draw attention to the forearm's personification, which continues to merit personal address throughout verses 9 and 10. More importantly, verse 12 responds to the feminine personification by reversing the gender when the divine voice begins speaking. To the battle cry that implored the divine forearm to arise, the divine voice replies, "I, I am he, your comforter" (v. 12).

Through emotional and embodied motifs, the divine response will further challenge the audience's perception of their situation. The emphatic declaration, "I, I am he, your comforter," continues with the rhetorical question, "Who are you?" (v. 12). Providing the answer immediately, the divine voice tells the audience who they are: they are those who fear human beings and forget the LORD. Through repeated references, the divine speaker emphasizes the audience's misplaced fearfulness, explicitly contrasting the human beings that the audience fears with the divine deliverer. The human is destined to die and be buried ("To the grass he will be given" [v. 12]). The LORD, on the other hand, is the cosmic creator, "the stretcher of the heavens" (v. 13) and "the stirrer of the sea" (v. 15). Thus, the divine response reinterprets the audience's situation: what they need is not a cosmic warrior's deliverance but recognition of the oppressor's mortality. The LORD replaces the warrior motif with that of divine comforter. The imagery of the cosmic creator remains, but the divine voice denies that what is needed now is such a cosmic battle.

The divine voice also redirects the feminine personification: it is not now the divine deliverer who is feminine but the recipient of salvation, Zion herself. This reversal is clearest when the divine voice perfectly repeats the opening address, "Arise, arise, wear strength" (52:1), addressing this command instead to Zion. Even in the first address to Lady Zion in 51:17, which seems quite different in translation, the audience's plea is recalled. "Stir yourself, stir yourself! Stand up, O Jerusalem" employs the same verb in the reflexive form, insisting that Jerusalem do for herself what she was demanding of the divine forearm.

Zion's body is important to Isa 51:9–52:12's depiction of salvation, as she is told first to stir herself and to stand up (51:17), and then to shake the dust from herself, to stand, and to "loosen the bonds of [her] neck" (52:2). This new bodily posture, with its upward movement, contrasts explicitly with Zion's prior state. She had been drunk, staggering (51:17), and in need of someone to "seize her by the hand" (v. 18). Her "hand" is both what she needs someone to hold and what holds the "cup of staggering," which is to be removed (v. 22). Her oppressors had commanded that she "bow down" her "throat" (v. 23) and that she make her back "like the ground" (v. 23) for them. Zion's oppressors had brought her low, but now she is commanded to arise.

Although this passage uses body language for both the deliverer and the deliveree, it minimizes the bodies of those from whom deliverance is achieved. The divine voice asks the audience why they fear human oppressors, why they "fear a man (he will die), and the son of a human (he will be made grass)" (51:12). This body, which will be buried and decay, is not named but passed over, reinforcing the divine voice's claim that it is ultimately of no account. Likewise, when the LORD describes the violence done to Zion, the enemies' bodies are implied. But what the oppressors do, vaguely and undescriptively, is to "pass over" (v. 23). Their "hand" is the place the cup will go when taken from Zion's (v. 23). They are "uncircumcised and unclean" (52:1). In each case the focus is on Zion's body and the overturning of her complaint.

Though the divine voice rejects the battle cry, it does not leave the realm of violence entirely. The battle is here described not as impending and cosmic but as a past battle in which Zion has suffered defeat. The metaphors describing this past battle are mixed. What we see is not the divine warrior consistently fighting for Jerusalem's salvation. Instead, we see a mixture of cosmic creation (51:16), divine rage (vv. 17, 20), staggering drunkenness (vv. 17, 21), and trampling by human oppressors (vv. 19, 23). This jumble of debilitating conditions and glimpses of liberation mirrors the audience's apparent misapprehension of the situation. It is not completely clear whether they need deliverance from oppressors or from the LORD's own rage. Both seem to intermingle. Yet both have receded into the past. In this way, the poem reinforces its message, showing that the relationship between deliverer and deliveree is far from tranquil.

After commanding Zion to rise up and be clothed, the divine voice continues shifting the audience's focus to recognize that the conflict has ended. The invitation to shake off defeat, to "wear strength," parallels the command to "wear garments of beauty" (52:1). These words concerning Jerusalem's clothing recall the people's opening cry, in which they expressed hope that through divine deliverance they might wear elation (51:11). The transformation of Jerusalem's beleaguered position to one of standing, freed from dust and bondage (52:2), is treated as having been accomplished already; the poem envisions no further struggle. Deliverance comes not as the violence envisioned in the people's invocation of the "piercer of the sea monster" (51:9) but as the removal of a cup from Jerusalem's hand. Since the divine speaker occupies an entirely different realm of power than the human oppressor, salvation is not a cosmic battle between equal powers but a cosmic mismatch, as easy for the "stretcher of the heavens" (v. 13) as transferring a cup from one hand to another. All that remains is for Jerusalem to see, rejoice, and act.

The message that salvation has been accomplished employs further bodily attributes in the heavily emotional closing lines, extolling the "beautiful" feet of salvation's messenger (52:7) and drawing attention to the watchmen's voices and eyes (vv. 8-9). Even the waste places have voices, crying out in joy (v. 9). The response to this good news is embodied as well. The people are commanded to "turn away," to "go out," and not to touch anything unclean (vv. 11-12), as they carry the LORD's vessels. These activities call the audience to enact the passage's emotions, moving them from fear to rejoicing.

Body language clearly plays a key role in meaning-making in this text and is intimately connected to its portrayal of salvation desired, received, and realized. Such bodily imagery grounds this text's vision of salvation in concrete reality. Salvation is not an abstract principle, far off and ephemeral, but realizable. It happens to "real bodies, lived lives," even when they are portrayed in idealized, representative form.[20]

As noted earlier, feminist writing reminds us that the body has been the site of gender-based violence and has been used symbolically to reinforce difference, distinction, and hierarchy. For this reason it is appropriate to consider how the body imagery in the Isaiah text's proclamation of salvation relates to contemporary concerns.

Both the personified divine forearm and Lady Zion participate in violent imagery, though in dramatically different ways. As the personified victim of warfare's violence, Lady Zion fulfills certain gender stereotypes present in both ancient and modern understandings, appearing as a vulnerable war victim in need of a masculine deliverer.[21] She is trampled and brought low, and she needs a comforter. The source of the violence that has befallen her is mixed: she is victim both of the LORD's "cup of rage" (51:17) and of the invasion of unclean and uncircumcised oppressors (51:23–52:1). Her deliverance and salvation are the responsibility of a masculine figure, the one who proclaims, "I, I am he, your comforter" (51:12). But the deliverer and the afflicter overlap: violence is based in the deliverer's own rage, a rage far more fearsome than any human anger. Treating the divine deliverer both as the source of violence and as the one who delivers Zion concentrates agency in the LORD, on whom the text confers masculine gender.

Yet the opening calls to the "forearm of the LORD," addressed as "she," may undermine the straightforward correlation of violence and gender stereotypes in this text, since "she" is a violent agent. The anticipated salvation involves bloodshed, the vanquishing of cosmic foes through brute force. The call to the forearm uses mythological imagery from ancient Near Eastern warrior goddess traditions,[22] and it offers a portrait of divine deliverance that transgresses the common association of violence with masculinity, both within the biblical tradition and in the imagination of modern readers. Indeed, feminine warriors occupy a special place in cross-cultural imagination, from the warrior heroine Deborah in Judges to mythic figures such as Mulan in China and Queen Maeve of Ireland, to historical figures such as Joan of Arc and Countess Markievicz. The fact that the warrior is a woman merits special comment in the traditions (e.g., Judg 4:9), and at times it results in remarkable behavior (e.g., Joan of Arc's and Mulan's masculine dress to conceal that they are female) or exceptional treatment by their enemies (e.g., Countess Markievicz's reprieve from execution).[23]

The address to the feminized "forearm of the LORD" seems at least initially to provoke just such a reaction within the Isaiah text. As Jeremy Hutton has argued, with its reliance on Near Eastern myths, the text subverts the feminine gender designation.[24] This usage creates tension within the text when, unlike the deliverer the people invoke, Zion's savior is emphatically a "he" (51:12). The divine speaker's "correction" reinforces the sense that addressing God in warrior goddess terms violates Israel's dominant theology. Yet when the passage concludes with rejoicing over salvation, the divine forearm returns: "The LORD has bared the forearm of his holiness before the eyes of all the nations. All the ends of the earth have seen the salvation of our God" (52:10). Mention of the forearm, no longer personified, nonetheless points back to the people's opening plea. Thus, the overall sweep of the passage makes it difficult to read the divine voice's rejection of the opening invocation as entirely concerned with assigning both violence and agency to masculinity. Rather, it rejects the audience's misplaced fear. In addition, the complicated picture of divine violent activity mixes masculine and feminine images: the divine forearm frames the passage as a whole, and after the repeated address to the forearm as "she," its reappearance hardly seems gender neutral. Instead, it reintroduces an already established feminine motif for divine deliverance. This mixing of gender motifs shares in the general phenomenon that Corrine Carvalho describes in her analysis of divine violence in prophetic texts; she notes, "The divine warrior is not like a human one: acting as both god and goddess, yet not fulfilling either gender expectations fully. . . . This gender-bending . . . subverts the very binary opposites on which most analyses of violence flounder . . . [and] reveal[s] how the divine nature is beyond human categories of appropriate behavior."[25] Thus, whether feminists should laud or condemn the violent female imagery of this text is perhaps beside the point. The text does not so much offer female violence as either a response to or an imitation of male violence. Instead, it juxtaposes male and female imagery for the divine deliverer, complicating human attempts to claim the right to imitate divine violence, since it places agency for salvation well outside the human sphere. In addition, the text's complication of gender stereotypes should remind readers that men as well as women suffer from cruelty, war, and oppression. The relationships among agency, gender, and violence are not as simple as our common cultural stereotypes might lead us to believe.

The passage's body imagery also raises the matter of boundaries for contemporary readers. The female body continues to be used to reinforce national and ethnic identities, as recent Irish feminist theory, for example, has shown. When a nation is personified as a female, as is common in Western culture generally, this cultural metaphor gives femininity political import.[26] The female body, and particularly its reproductive functions, may be used to mark and protect the borderlines of ethnic identity.[27]

Certainly, scholars who have discussed the Zion personification in Second Isaiah have considered the question of boundaries, of whom the image includes and excludes. In Isa 51–52, personified Zion is the recipient of salvation. Thus, salvation is extended to all included within the Zion image—that is, "his people" (52:9). This salvation is witnessed by the "ends of the earth" (52:10), but it is not said to be extended to them. Carol Newsom has pointed out that Second Isaiah uses Judean speech but does not specifically refer to the people who remained in Judah. She has observed that "omitting separate reference to the Judahite population implicitly merges them into the figure of personified Zion."[28] The metaphorical announcement of salvation for Zion, which involves the return of her "children" (e.g., Isa 49:19-23), represents salvation, and those to be included in it, along ethnic boundary lines. Zion's female personification allows her reproductive role to include some (i.e., Judeans and Judean exiles), but not others (i.e., other nations), in the salvation announced to her. We should not be surprised to realize that an ancient Israelite text addressed to exiles draws ethnic boundary lines around the deliverance it anticipates. However, it should caution us about the use we make of such metaphorical descriptions in our own societies. Recipients of liberation cannot be simply united as the daughters and sons of a personified figure without excluding many, whether this is the intended effect or not.

Isaiah 51:9–52:12 conveys strong emotions around the experience of salvation, emphasizing the fear as well as the exuberance that accompanies fear's rejection. Exultation, rejoicing, and crying out with joy contrast with rage, wrath, anger, and fear. Salvation comes because the LORD has turned away from wrath and resolves to comfort Zion. This movement from fear to joy underscores the passage's claims that salvation is urgently needed, that the divinely proclaimed deliverance is real, and that it is something the audience cannot accomplish for themselves. If Nussbaum is right that our emotions reflect the importance we attach to situations and to our inability to control them, then Isaiah's heavily emotional depiction of salvation is more than appropriate. Salvation needed, and salvation received, inspired strong feelings for Isaiah's original audience, as they do for contemporary readers. Many situations in our world demand deliverance and rightly ought to produce intense emotional responses. This passage's vivid portrayal of emotions resonates with the common experience of human yearning and provokes empathy in contemporary readers, confronting us with emotions we know today, and offering words and images to express our own responses to salvation needed, offered, and experienced.

Salvation in Psalm 62:
An Encounter with the Emotions of Trust

In an entirely different emotional key, Ps 62 presents calm, settled trust. It invites the hearer to imagine a world where salvation is the absence of disorder and strife, where God's reliable strength is the antidote to any perception of injustice or oppression, where God's secure righteousness gives peace: salvation from fear, distress, and struggle.

The psalm is calm but certainly not unemotional. It knows the vulnerability of human existence, but it sets that recognition alongside an overwhelming assurance of secure trust. For the psalmist the LORD is both the source of salvation and salvation itself.

Psalm 62 is poetic tidiness itself, exhibiting an aesthetics of certainty. The psalm's twelve verses are neatly divided by a refrain that states the psalmist's trust in divine salvation (vv. 1-2, 5-6). Alongside these repeated expressions of trust stand two short sections addressed first to the psalmist's enemies (vv. 3-4) and then to the psalmist's apparent audience (vv. 8-10). These two sections point out the fleeting nature of human oppression and reinforce the theme of the refrain. The psalm's final verses, 11-12, return to the refrain's theme, pointing to divine strength as certain. The psalm's orderly structure supports the psalmist's claim to have found security in divine salvation and adds rhetorical weight to the appeal to its audience to do the same.

The psalm is unified by a single personal voice speaking throughout, testifying to dependence on God's salvation (vv. 1-2, 5-7) and inviting others to take the same position of trust (v. 8). Throughout, the psalmist refers to God as "my salvation" (vv. 1, 2, 6, 7), indicating an intensely personal experience of deliverance, out of which the speaker's claims grow. This element of testimony contributes to the experience of trust the psalm offers. Such first-person speech invites the audience to make the poem's speech their own. The first-person yet unspecified speaker opens the possibility that hearers (urged to "trust in him at every time . . . pour out your heart before him" [v. 8]) might choose to speak these words themselves, thus learning, as the psalmist had, to call God "my salvation."

The psalmist's refrain in verses 1-2 and 5-6 introduces and reiterates the psalm's key themes. Each verse begins with the Hebrew particle 'akh, a term that can convey either certainty ("surely") or limitation ("alone"). As a result, English translations differ. Some translate the verses, "For God alone

my soul waits in silence" (NRSV; ASV, JPS, NAS, and NIV are similar).
Others render these verses: "Truly my soul waiteth upon God" (KJV; TNK
is similar). The particle appears twice more in the psalm, and each time it
conveys certainty about the description the psalmist gives of other human
beings (vv. 4, 9). Each time, the particle begins a poetic line, giving the whole
psalm a repeated emphasis on the certainty of the psalmist's claims. With
its urgings to look only to God and not to human beings or human schemes,
the psalm as a whole conveys that the LORD alone is the psalmist's salvation. The refrain, with its initial 'akh, seems to carry both meanings: the
psalmist is *certain* that God *alone* is salvation.

The refrain also captures two key motifs: stillness and refuge. In the
description of the psalmist's own activity and in the primary metaphors
employed for God, the psalmist makes the point that security is the benefit
of trusting in divine salvation. The psalmist waits for God in stillness (vv. 1,
5), employing the rare word *dumiyah*. It seems clear in some cases that the
word means "silence" (e.g., Ps 39:2). However, as James L. Mays points out,
it cannot mean silence here, since the psalmist will go on to encourage others to pour their hearts out to God (v. 8).[29] It seems best to regard the term
as conveying "an inner stillness that comes with yielding all fears and anxieties and insecurities to God in an act of trust."[30]

The psalm's primary metaphors for both people and God convey this
secure stillness as well. The poem is dominated by the theme of refuge.
The refrain emphasizes these converging metaphors of refuge and security. The LORD, who is salvation itself in the psalm, is extolled throughout by use of physical, solid, persistently inorganic language: "rock" is the
primary and recurrent image of salvation (vv. 2, 6, 7), and the LORD is
"stronghold" and "refuge" (vv. 7, 8) as well. Neither God nor humans are
said to move in the psalm, but they seem to be stationary. The actions
that do occur are passive: being "crushed" (v. 3), being "shaken" (vv. 2, 6),
and being "fooled" (v. 10). When the psalmist discusses human activities,
these tend to involve their voices rather than their bodies. People "shout"
(v. 3); "take counsel," "bless," and "curse" (v. 4); and are urged to "pour out
[their] hearts" (v. 8). Even the enemies' "leaning" and "toppling" (v. 3) are
more characteristics than activities. Divine activity is also fairly limited: it
includes speaking (v. 11) and repaying (v. 12).

Building metaphors dominate (e.g., "stronghold" [vv. 2, 6]; "refuge"
[v. 6]), with stability and security their primary attributes. This edifice of
trust reinforces the psalmist's claim that God is salvation itself and that

security comes from trust in the LORD. The divine attributes of stability and security contrast with the ephemeral, fleeting nature of human being (v. 9)—a perspective shared with the Isaiah passage. The body language that does appear in the psalm details the parts of the wicked that are involved in oppressing the psalmist, their "mouths" and their "inward parts" (v. 4). The contrast between divine dependability and human corruption and deterioration conveys the unchangeability of the LORD's salvation, over against the unreliability of human beings.[31]

If the Isaiah poem and the psalm share a vision of the LORD's salvation as overwhelmingly distinct from human transience, they employ bodily imagery in dramatically different ways to underscore this point. While the Isaiah poem shifts the embodiment image from the LORD to Zion and argues that the audience's fears are misplaced, the psalm employs embodied images minimally—and primarily for the oppressors, whose bodies were passed over in the Isaiah text. Though they present very different imagery, both passages assert the deity's superiority over oppressors.

Ironically, the more "peaceful" psalm ties the divine presence to martial imagery more directly than does the Isaiah passage. Psalm 62's inanimate images are military defenses, "stronghold" and "refuge." The struggle remains, and the psalmist emphasizes experiencing salvation as leaving the struggle in God's hands. Only the defensive refuge metaphors point to the struggle's important place in the psalmist's experience.

While the peacefulness of the psalm may sit more comfortably with feminist readers than the initial violence of the Isaiah passage, its emphasis on stillness merits examination. Feminist scholars have quite rightly objected to societal structures that call for female silence or submission, and feminist focus on women's stories and experiences has encouraged women to speak up. Victims of abuse, for instance, are encouraged to break their silence for the sake of justice and for their own flourishing.

Does a biblical text that associates salvation with waiting for God in silence run counter to such liberative aims? As I have argued already, I do not think the psalm actually commends silence of this sort. A psalmist who both speaks in the first person and urges hearers to pour out their hearts to God is certainly not advocating passive silence and submission. Rather, in commending stillness, the psalmist conveys surrendering oneself without anxiety to the deliverer's care, expecting intervention.

Conclusion: Reading the Texts Together

The two texts offer readers different emotional experiences. Emotions play a central role in the way these texts make meaning and in the way we process and evaluate that meaning. Since these texts rhetorically invoke, inspire, and engage emotions, our own readerly emotions, embedded as they are in our own historical and social locations, are relevant for considering the texts' import and for appropriating their message of salvation.

The psalm presents a testimony of trust, expressing reassurance, security, and peace, and inviting hearers to join the psalmist in those registers. The psalmist associates salvation with the release of fear. The Isaiah passage shares in this release but characterizes both the fear and the expected exuberance that accompanies fear's rejection far more vigorously and viscerally. Yet despite their differences in tone, the two poems depict salvation itself in strikingly similar ways. For both of them, salvation comes from God alone. Neither text places agency in the human realm. In fact, the most nearly parallel lines between the two texts appear in the insistence on the fleeting lives of human oppressors in contrast to divine stability (Isa 51:12-13; Ps 62:9). The texts also share awareness of real human struggles, often involving physical violence, from which deliverance is needed. The turbulent emotions of the Isaiah text appeal to an audience embroiled in turmoil, though the message is that salvation comes not from their own struggle but from God. By contrast, the psalm, with its transparently militaristic metaphors for the LORD as defense and refuge, places the psalmist's testimony after the struggle and its emotional turmoil have ended. The psalm's peacefulness and trust, and the orderly and controlled way trust is expressed, bear witness to strife that has already been left in God's hands.

For both of these texts, salvation is a struggle against oppression, a struggle that takes violent form, though the violence is not part of the human task. The texts offer an experience that transforms the audience's perspective, removing their struggle to the divine realm. Both texts portray the human role as calling the LORD's attention to the need for deliverance. While the Isaiah text rebukes the audience's perceptions, it does not reject the plea for salvation itself. Similarly, the psalm urges others to pour out their hearts before the LORD. Both texts hold together the human experience of crying out in need and expectation with the perception that salvation is God's doing. These texts offer a vision of embodied salvation that may transform readers' lived experience. Their vision of salvation is emotional, meeting readers where what is central to well-being intersects with human "vulnerability and imperfect control."[32]

This essay began with the claim that salvation theology is deeply rooted in the brokenness of human experience. These texts offer a vision of salvation that does not treat that aspect of human living lightly. They demonstrate that human bodies and lived experience matter a great deal, that we feel profoundly the pain of oppression and injustice. They acknowledge that overcoming this brokenness is an immense struggle, one worthy of battle metaphors. They insist that only God can overturn human brokenness. For people committed to living a biblical vision of justice and freedom, these poems demand two things:[33] first, that we allow their emotional expressions, and similar testimonies from our own times, to shape our own emotions, creating in us a desperate longing for deliverance; and second, that we take that desperate longing to God, the only one who can deliver us from our brokenness.

Though God alone saves, these texts do not call for human passivity in the face of real-world injustice. Zion is told to rise up and shake off her oppression (Isa 52:2); the people are commanded to enact their deliverance (v. 11); and the psalmist complains not only to God but to the oppressors themselves (Ps 62: 4). Salvation dawns at the mysterious meeting point of divine deliverance and human response.

For Further Reading

Carvalho, Corrine. "The Beauty of the Bloody God: The Divine Warrior in Prophetic Literature." Pages 131–52 in *Aesthetics of Violence in the Prophets*. Edited by Chris Franke and Julia M. O'Brien. London: T&T Clark, 2010.

Davis, Kathy. "Embodying Theory: Beyond Modernist and Postmodernist Readings of the Body." Pages 1–23 in *Embodied Practices: Feminist Perspectives on the Body*. Edited by Kathy Davis. London: Sage, 1997.

Maier, Christl M. *Daughter Zion, Mother Zion: Gender, Space and the Sacred in Ancient Israel*. Minneapolis: Fortress, 2008.

Meaney, Gerardine. *Gender, Ireland, and Cultural Change: Race, Sex, and Nation*. London: Routledge, 2010.

Nussbaum, Martha C. *Upheavals of Thought: The Intelligence of Emotions*. Cambridge: Cambridge University Press, 2001.

Tamez, Elsa. "Women's Rereading of the Bible." Pages 48–58 in *Voices from the Margin: Interpreting the Bible in the Third World*. Edited by R. S. Sugirtharajah. London: SPCK, 1995.

CHAPTER 6

READING PSALM 146 IN THE WILD
A Feminist Biblical Theology of Praise

Jacqueline E. Lapsley

The Psalter is a microcosm of our life with God. As a human response to God's actions in and for the world, the Psalter lays before God expressions of deepest grief and profoundest joy, registering sorrow, anger, bitterness, recrimination, and bafflement but also wonder, awe, gratitude, and, ultimately and definitively, praise. Its arc moves, somewhat like Beethoven's Moonlight Sonata, from a predominantly mournful tone to one of untrammeled doxology. One can read one psalm alone, or a few together, and find a wide variety of human experiences. But one is always reading or hearing these individual psalms in the context of the whole Psalter, which provides the frame within which all such expression occurs. With the Psalter, human beings are always moving—sometimes dancing, sometimes slouching—toward praise of God.[1]

Feminist and womanist theologies have excelled at critical analysis of patriarchy, both in the Bible and in the culture. The harvest of feminist and womanist theologies is prodigious: crucially, they have exposed androcentric modes of discourse that masquerade as gender neutral, and so have transformed theological disciplines. One important outcome of feminist biblical interpretation of the Psalms in particular has been to surface and interrogate the Psalter's binary worldview. Like wisdom literature, the Psalms tend to divide the world between the righteous and the wicked. This division has pernicious consequences for interpretation because we do not live in that bifurcated world. (In fact, ancient thinkers also questioned whether the world could be divided in that way.) It does not take too much experience of life to realize that "good" and "evil" are intertwined at every turn, including within human beings themselves. The negative effects of androcentric biblical interpretation on women, men, other animals, and the rest of creation will never be completely eradicated. Yet feminist reflection has achieved much, and can accomplish more, in exposing the fallacies of androcentric thought so that church and world may reflect more of the fullness of God's grace.

Yet, as vital as it is, critical reflection is not the only task of feminist theologies. Feminist resources must also be brought to bear on the constructive task of rearticulating biblical theology. In what follows, I will suggest that feminist thinking illumines the Psalms in important ways, opening up more fully what it means to praise God. A feminist lens emphasizes that praise entails the whole self; it eschews fragmentation. It decenters human endeavor as the focus of our trust, instead revealing an intimately connected created order of which humans are a part but not the center. Thus, our trust rests in God alone. Furthermore, when appropriately directed toward God, praise is a performative act—it brings about the flourishing of the world. And a feminist lens highlights the justice-loving character of God as one who longs for the world to thrive.

The main focus of this essay is a reading of Ps 146, the first of the last five hymns of praise that close the Psalter. This psalm is a good subject for this study not only due to its position as the first of the doxological hymns that form the grand finale of the Psalter but also because it calls explicitly upon humanity to praise God and makes significant claims about the character of this God who deserves praise.

In addition, I will place Ps 146 in dialogue with Pss 104 and 148, two psalms that contextualize humanity within the much larger frame of creation as a whole. Listening in on a textual conversation among these psalms enriches a feminist interpretation of all three as well as enriches our understanding of what it means to praise God in the present context of ecological crisis. Psalm 104 is a lengthy hymn of praise to God as creator and sustainer of the diverse works of creation. Psalm 148, on the other hand, expands the scope of praise to creation as a whole and points toward the end of the Psalter, where "everything that breathes" praises God. Both Pss 104 and 148 include human beings as part of the created order, but neither allows them a central position of power within it. When read with Ps 146, therefore, they reveal that human beings as praising creatures must be understood as embedded within the larger created world, which also gives praise to God in its own way. Engaging these additional psalms widens the scope of inquiry about the significance of praise beyond humanity.

I will turn first to Pss 104 and 148. With the concerns of these psalms in mind, I will then examine Ps 146 in some detail. Finally, I will step back to consider these psalms from a wider feminist perspective to see how they might help feminist theology to reclaim praise as a meaningful category.

Psalms 104 and 148 in Conversation with Psalm 146

Although one senses appreciation of the created world around the edges, the perception of the cosmos in Ps 146 tends toward the anthropocentric. Psalms 104 and 148 widen the vision of praise to the created world in which human beings live, move, and have their being. This broader view has long been a central feature of feminist thought and, indeed, is one of the key contributions feminism makes to theology.

Psalm 104 begins, "Bless the LORD, O my soul."[2] This opening call to thanksgiving resonates with that of its companion, Ps 103, as well as that of Ps 146. Psalm 104 begins with light, which not only is created by God but constitutes part of the divine being ("the one clothing self with light as a garment" [v. 2a]). From there the psalm moves to the creation of heaven, earth, sea, and all creatures that inhabit this world. Creation's purposiveness appears as an undercurrent throughout the psalm. For example, as Patrick Miller notes, "darkness is created to give time for animals to hunt their prey, and the springs of water come forth to provide water for them."[3] This purposiveness supports an ethic of flourishing: God creates all creatures with the intent that each thrives in a way appropriate to its kind. Furthermore, creation in Ps 104 is marked by beauty and pleasure, witnessed by sudden eruptions of praise such as, "O LORD, how many are your works!" (v. 24). Psalm 104 emphatically proclaims that creation is not an object with "resources" to be exploited. Its vision counters the strongly instrumental ethic of traditional theologies and ideologies that see the value of creation as constituted by its usefulness to human beings. Humanity does not dominate this world but fits as one element within it.

This evocation of creation as the context of praise is unsentimental. Psalm 104 provides a beautiful portrait of nature, but violence and death are nonetheless present, as verse 21 makes clear: "The young lions roar for prey, and seek their food from God." In her discussion of Song of Songs,

Elaine James speaks of the danger of sentimentalizing creation, a problem in some feminist theologies and some forms of environmental feminism (ecofeminism): "Any account of nature in the Song must take such elements [violence and conflict as threats to flourishing] seriously or risk sounding rather sentimental and superfluous. This is the problem to which many ecological and ecofeminist projects succumb: they are romantic and idealistic, not taking into account Darwinistic competition and the reality that life—human life, animal life, biotic life—is only possible through death."[4] It is this violent, conflictual creation—with violent, conflictual human beings in it—that nevertheless offers its praise to God.

If the great doxological coda that is Pss 146–150 begins with humanity praising God, it ends with "everything that breathes" joining in the praise (150:6), suggesting that a much more inclusive vision of a praising community—all creation, not just human beings—finally reigns. A brief look at Ps 148 will assist in fleshing out the scope of praise in this five-psalm coda. In Ps 148:1-6, all the cosmic entities that were created in the beginning and given their boundaries and assignments, as it were (sun, moon, stars, angels, etc.), are exhorted to join in praise of God. In verses 7-10, the focus shifts downward to the earthly realm, where all creatures in the sea, on the earth (both wild and domestic), and flying in the sky; the earth itself with its vegetation; and even the various weather forces are commanded to praise. Verses 11-12 zoom in more precisely still to cover humanity of all types from kings to "all peoples," young men and young women, the oldest, and the youngest.

One may no doubt assign various meanings to such a structure, but the fact that the nonhuman created entities of the cosmos begin the psalm and constitute six verses, followed by four verses on the earthly realm, followed by only two on human beings, suggests that humanity is not the apex of the psalm but rather only one small element in a much larger world, as in Ps 104. Psalm 148 expands the vision of praise offered by Ps 146 from one that is anthropocentric to one that encompasses all of creation. This vision subtly decenters humanity, situating us among other creatures, nestled in creation as the structure of the psalm suggests, but with no evident priority.

The word "all" recurs frequently in Ps 148: twice in verses 2, 9, and 11, and once each in verses 7, 10, and 14, for a patterned repetition occurring a total of nine times. These repetitions audibly flood hearers: the vocation for everything (e.g., "fire and hail") and everyone (e.g., "all wild and tamed beasts") is praise of the creator. As William P. Brown rightly observes, "These psalms [psalms as praise] profile the human as *Homo laudans*, 'the praising human,' and in praise the full identity of the human self is reached."[5] Yet it is the vocation of the rest of creation also, not just humanity. The whole end of the Psalter unrelentingly presses for unified praise by the entire created order, with its last line discharging a final exhortation: "Let all that breathes praise the LORD. Hallelujah!" (Ps 150:6). These psalms, together with Ps 104 and others, reveal how misguided the classic anthropocentrism of the Judeo-Christian traditions truly is.

Praise and Trust in the LORD, Not Human Beings: Psalm 146:1-5

With the wider all-creation framework provided by Pss 104 and 148 and the last line of the Psalter, we now turn to Ps 146:

Praise the LORD!
   Praise the LORD, O my soul!
I will praise the LORD with my life;
   I will sing praises to my God as long as I live.

Do not put trust in elites,
   in mortals in whom there is no deliverance.
Their spirit goes forth, then returns to the earth.
   On that day their plans perish.

Happy are those whose help is the God of Jacob,
   whose hope is in the LORD their God,
maker of heaven and earth,
   the sea, and all that is in them;
who keeps faith forever;
   who executes justice for the oppressed;
   who gives food to the hungry.

The LORD liberates prisoners;
   the LORD opens the eyes of the blind.
The LORD raises those who are bowed down;
   the LORD loves the righteous.
The LORD watches over immigrants;
   orphan and the widow he upholds,
   but makes crooked the path of the wicked.

The LORD will reign forever,
   your God, O Zion, for all generations.
   Praise the LORD!

The psalm calls upon human beings to praise God with an implicit twofold argument: first, that hearers have *over*estimated the power of human beings to save and, second, that hearers have *under*estimated God's power to save. The psalm begins—as do all of the final five psalms—with a burst of joy that is both command to praise and act of praise itself. "Praise the LORD, O my soul" (*nephesh*, meaning "entire being" [146:1]) is an unusual command in a psalm, but it echoes similar calls to the soul to "bless the LORD" that frame both Ps 103 (vv. 1, 22) and Ps 104 (vv. 1, 35).

Significantly, each of the five final praise psalms begins by exhorting the whole self to praise. The call to praise properly orients both speaker and hearers, helping them to adopt an appropriate posture of praise not only as a practice, not only as an idea, but with their entire self (*nephesh*). Verse 2 adds to the holistic dimension by describing the timespan of praise as the psalmist's full life: "I will praise the LORD with my life; I will sing praises to my God as long as I live" (cf. 104:33). The whole self praises for the whole life—the emphasis is on completeness of both time and being.

For the psalmist, being alive means praising God, and death means inability to praise God any longer. While not writing from a feminist perspective, Erich Zenger identifies a claim in the psalm important for a feminist reading: "Those who live their lives *as* life owed to God are in a sense living praise of YHWH—and thus counterimages to those who found their lives on mortal human beings."[6] In other words, praise of God is *holistic*—one is to praise God with one's entire being, without compartmentalizing the spiritual from the mundane or from the political. All of our decisions (how we choose to live: how we eat, what we buy, etc.) form our praise of God. Many feminist and womanist thinkers are critical of mainstream theologies and ideologies that have fragmented and objectified important aspects of reality to the detriment of people, animals, and the environment. Psalm 146 rejects such fragmentation; true praise involves our whole selves. When such praise is expressed in word and deed, the whole creation flourishes.

In verses 3-4, the issue turns upon whom to trust:

> Do not put trust in elites [*nedivim*],
> > in mortals [*ben-'adam*] in whom there is no deliverance.
> Their spirit goes forth, then returns to the earth.
> > On that day their plans perish.

The puzzle here is that *nedivim* ("elites," signifying those wielding power, sometimes translated as "rulers" or "the great") is not obviously a parallel term for *ben-'adam* ("mortals"), as we would expect. Is the psalmist warning the hearer not to trust in elites in particular, with "mortals" thrown in for an unbalanced parallelism? Or is the warning a more general one, as verse 4 suggests, that one should not place trust in any human being because they are all finite and because even their well-intentioned plans come to an end at their deaths?

Interpreters, no doubt influenced by their own contexts, have understood the verses in both senses. Augustine, for example, thought the *nedivim* might be pagans who threaten believers' faith in the one true God.[7] Twentieth-century biblical critics tended to discount "elites" as a translation for *nedivim*, saying that the psalmist was not really talking about the special problems encountered when one trusts the powerful instead of God, but rather was setting the two terms—*nedivim* and *ben-'adam*—in parallel to each other. One scholar suggests that *nedivim* and *ben-'adam* be taken as a merism referring to all humanity, both the high and the lowly.[8] The idea here is that *all* human leaders are unfit for trust because they all die. It is their finitude that makes them untrustworthy, not the fact that they are corrupted by power.

Unfortunately, the word translated as "their plans" in verse 4 occurs only once in Scripture, so its uncertain meaning only clouds the picture further. Are these the devious, oppressive plans of the powerful elites, which come to naught at their deaths? Or simply the ordinary plans of ordinary human beings that finally shrivel into nothing? Or perhaps they are not ordinary plans but the excellent ideas of the well intended, which will return to dust along with those who dreamed them up.

But the choice of *nedivim*, "elites," should not be discounted as a mere rhetorical device designating all humanity. Especially since the LORD is described in verses 5-9 as deliverer of the oppressed, the presence of *nedivim* in verse 3 does not seem casual. Psalm 118:9 ("It is better to take refuge in the LORD than to trust in elites [*nedivim*]") suggests that a mistrust of elites *in particular* is culturally alive. This idea, if not the precise language, is apparent in other texts as well (cf. in particular Ps 146:3-4).[9] Ultimately, however, the question resists resolution. The psalm, perhaps intentionally, does not force us to decide between the two possibilities. Elites who wield power for their own gains cannot be trusted, and this foreshadows the rest of the psalm in verses 5-9 where injustice and oppression are brought to the fore. Yet even those who act in good faith offer no ultimate deliverance, because the best intentioned among them are but transitory and their plans come to naught.

As one cannot always determine the good or bad motivations driving other people's projects and plans, so it is with the "plans" in verse 4. Indeed, as often as not, our own motivations are not entirely known to ourselves, no matter how high-minded our intentions appear, since we are often driven by unconscious forces that do not rise to the level of self-reflection. The ambiguity of the psalmist's words indexes the ambiguity of human motivation. The psalmist foregrounds the unreliability of human systems: whether well intentioned or not, they cannot be trusted for deliverance.

All forms of human power are ultimately rejected for all of these reasons—because they are often corrupt, because we cannot always discern whether they are corrupt, and, finally, because they are always finite, even when not corrupt. Thus, in affirming the reasons for divine royal rule, the psalm is more subtle than many interpreters allow. Only God deserves our trust and praise.

A major shift takes place in verse 5, as the psalm turns to a description of the one who can be trusted, God. Unlike the misguided soul who trusts in human beings, whether ordinary mortals or elites, the one who trusts in God is "happy" or "flourishing" or, in the traditional phrasing, "blessed."[10] Most commentators observe not only the sapiential flavor of the psalm but also the way its explicitly instructional tone evokes Ps 1. Where Ps 1 sets forth the two paths that human beings might take—that of the righteous and that of the wicked—Ps 146 presents the two options for trust and implies that the "righteous" trust in God, whereas the "wicked" do not. Psalm 1 provides a "reader's guide" for the Psalter, a way of reading the Psalter as torah, whereas Ps 146 comes at the beginning of the conclusion of the Psalter—a fitting summary of the Psalter's great themes.[11]

The Character of God: Psalm 146:6-9

In the remainder of the psalm, in a series of ten participles (vv. 6-9b) and two finite verbs (9c-10), the speaker presents evidence of God's trustworthiness. In describing God's character, the psalmist draws heavily on Israelite traditions, so much so that the psalm functions as a summary of Israel's core proclamation about God.[12] This centerpiece of the psalm draws broadly on Israelite confessions of God as creator and redeemer. Here the LORD

- is maker of heaven and earth (v. 6a; cf. Gen 1:1; Pss 115:15; 121:2);
- keeps faith (v. 6b; cf. Exod 34:6);
- executes justice for the oppressed (v. 7a; a summary of more specific actions expressed in, e.g., Deut 10:18, Ps 9:5);[13]

- ✦ feeds the hungry (v. 7b; cf. Deut 10:18; Ps 107:9; Isa 58:7);
- ✦ frees the prisoners (v. 7c; cf. Isa 58:6; 61:1);
- ✦ gives sight to the blind (v. 8a; cf. Isa 29:18; 35:5; 42:7);
- ✦ raises up those bowed down (v. 8b; cf. Ps 145:14);
- ✦ loves the righteous (v. 8c; cf. Pss 11:7; 37:28); and
- ✦ watches over the stranger/immigrant and lifts the orphan and the widow (v. 9; cf. Lev 24:22; Num 15:16; Deut 10:18; 27:19; Jer 7:6; 22:3; Ezek 22:7).

The psalmist draws from a remarkable array of traditions to evoke the essential character of God.

The language of "immigrant," "orphan," and "widow" in verse 9 particularizes the more general term "oppressed" in verse 7.[14] The psalmist's concern with the oppressed is not entirely disinterested, for in the Psalter the oppressed are frequently identified with "the righteous" (e.g., Pss 34:19; 119:121). This identification reframes the psalm's perspective: though God's reign is not always apparent on earth, and the righteous are oppressed in various ways, the trajectory of God's reign stretches from earth's beginning to the eschatological horizon.[15] Rev. Dr. Martin Luther King Jr. made famous a remark that shares resonances with the wisdom tradition: "The arc of the moral universe is long, but it bends toward justice."[16] Carol Newsom's account of the wisdom perspective underlying such thinking is illuminating:

> The resilient, enduring quality of good derives from its participation in the structures of creation itself, whereas evil, no matter how powerful and vital it appears, is actually fragile and subject to disintegration because it has no root in that order of creation (e.g., Psalm 1). This contrast between the enduring and the ephemeral contains no denial of the existence of evil; it betrays no curiosity about its origin.[17]

Like Ps 1, Ps 146 perceives the world as one in which God reigns and acts to deliver those oppressed by the wicked. The fact that this reality may not always be apparent is painful, but it does not ultimately contradict that reality. Appearances are deceiving.

Verse 9 asserts, "The LORD . . . makes crooked the path of the wicked." In a psalm that otherwise focuses on God's positive acts, this colon often makes modern Western hearers uncomfortable. The psalm's treating the "wicked" as "other" confounds our preference for an inclusive Psalter that blesses all. Yet, as just war theorists and even some pacifists argue, making the path of the wicked a torturous one is necessary to executing justice, feeding the hungry, and carrying out all the other justice-affirming actions of the psalm's central section. The psalm presumes the presence and activity of the wicked. For justice to prevail, therefore, their actions must be interrupted, interfered with, "made crooked."

When thinking about the Psalms' language about the wicked, two issues need to be untangled. First, as I mentioned earlier, the division of the world into two camps, "the righteous" and "the wicked," does not accord with current understandings of human nature. At the same time, we should take seriously the psalmist's desire for God to disrupt the plans, schemes, and behaviors of those who thwart justice and actively prevent others' flourishing. We need not label them "wicked" to agree that such activities should stop. Given human nature, we too sometimes find ourselves, perhaps unintentionally and/or through participation in systems of which we are unaware, denying others' ability to flourish. This complicity is especially true of the ways in which we, the privileged, participate in, and are subject to, the principalities and powers. The categories of "wicked" and "righteous" are slippery indeed, but in many ways real.

Time and Community: Psalm 146:10

Though the psalm seems to appeal to Zion as its intended addressee at the end (v. 10), it is correctly understood to address a broader audience. As evidence, one notes that it shares significant themes with Isaiah 40–55, with its overarching attention to the nations and the world in general. Both proclaim God's liberation from captivity. In both, God rules by overthrowing the oppressor and by freeing the oppressed, acting in accord with the divine justice that God established in creation. So, as one scholar concludes, "both the call to praise in the framing 'hallelujah' cries and the beatitude in verse 5 are directed not to Israel alone but to all nations."[18] It makes sense for the beginning of the final praise coda of Pss 146–150 to appeal to all nations since as the coda swells to its fullest expression, and sounds its final note (150:6), it appeals to "all creatures" to praise the LORD.

The appeal to all nations may be viewed as mere sentiment or, worse, as "political correctness." Yet this broader reach should be taken seriously as a theological claim especially in our current context, in which nationalism foments violent conflict and in which too few people understand that human flourishing depends on the flourishing of all creatures. Psalm 146 thus helps draw the themes of the whole Psalter together in an expression of justice: the songs and prayers that form the Psalter both *give voice* to

God's will for justice in all creation and *participate in* realizing justice for all.[19] Some feminist theologies, at least, rightly underscore the importance of justice for all as a theme and, as will be discussed below, stress humanity's embeddedness within a wider ecological ethic.

The last line of the psalm (v. 10) establishes both the unending time frame of God's rule and the breadth of the audience intended. God reigns "forever" and "for all generations"—and at last the psalm specifies the more focused addressee: Zion. The psalm ends as it began, with a call to praise God. It is not only individuals who are called to praise, but the entire community (in this context, "all nations"). Indeed, the word translated as "Praise the LORD" (hallelujah) is grammatically plural—it means "All y'all praise the LORD."

Feminist scholars have not been the only interpreters to point out the Hebrew Scriptures' emphasis on community, but feminist theologies bring this to the fore in particularly compelling and convicting ways. The Latin American feminist theologian Ivone Gebara, for example, writes her theology while living with those struggling with severe poverty; she does theology "between noise and garbage."[20] She speaks without sentimentality of what it means to praise God from such a place. The communal orientation of this psalm and so many others, brought into focus through a feminist lens, reveals the inadequacy of the individualizing tendencies in modern interpretation and underscores the communal theology of Gebara and other feminist theologians. One flourishes by living among those for whom flourishing does not come easily, and by participating in the flourishing of those to whom it does not come easily.

In sum, a feminist lens on Ps 146 reveals a number of important features. First, self-compartmentalization (disconnecting actions from beliefs, promoting the objectification of the created world around us—in short, the reigning way of being in the post-Enlightenment West) is antithetical to the psalmist's call to praise with the whole self (*nephesh*). Second, human endeavors, while potentially useful in furthering God's intention for a flourishing creation, can never be the object of our trust, both because they are often corrupt and because they are as ephemeral as the people who generate them. Thus, even feminist theology is only a tool to aid us in understanding our world better and to act on that understanding: our trust can only rest in God. Third, all creation is called to praise God. The act of praise both expresses the intimacy of our relation to God and, in and of itself, activates flourishing within the world and flourishing for the world. Finally, God's desire that the whole creation thrive is revealed in the central verses of the psalm. Divine passion for justice flows out of the character of God, who cannot but long for a just and verdant world.

Reading Psalm 146 through a Feminist Lens

Psalm 146 makes the clear distinction between trust in God and trust in human systems. For us, those systems are riddled by patriarchy and environmental degradation. The psalm affirms that praise of, and trust in, God alone relativizes praise of, and trust in, lesser entities (e.g., government entities, the economy, etc.), which are subject to sin. So praise, reflecting that trust, is the primary posture of humanity toward deity. But the problem with praise from a feminist viewpoint is hinted at by the word "posture," which may connote a mere attitude, perhaps with a glaze of superficiality. Praise often seems to mean precisely that: a posture, and a passive one to boot. And a feminist perspective cannot tolerate a passive response of praise because it values the embodied and the holistic. For feminist theologians, life is lived as praise of God, and such a life provides a robust alternative to grounding life in human beings and their systems. As Patricia Tull observes, "Dependence on other gods, or goods, is not a measure of confidence, but of restlessness, a fruitless search for satisfaction elsewhere than in God."[21] The psalm's robust understanding of praise nourishes feminist theology's own rich conception.

But we can go further: praise of God from a feminist perspective involves active participation in human and environmental *flourishing*. Chris Cuomo is an ecological feminist who draws on Aristotelian tradition, shaping it to feminist concerns. For Cuomo, the concept of "flourishing" is large enough to encompass both the human and the nonhuman (as opposed to a strictly anthropocentric conception) without sentimentalizing the natural world or humanity's relationship to it. "Flourishing," for Cuomo, refers to that which promotes the integrity, stability, and beauty of both human and nonhuman communities.[22] Such flourishing will look different for each "community" within creation, but the crucial feature of her ecological feminism is that all such flourishing requires the flourishing of the others. The emphasis in such an ethic is on assessing "actions, practices, institutions, attitudes, and values in terms of their impact on ecological and human flourishing."[23]

As an interpretive lens, an ethic of flourishing both validates and helps explain the Psalter's frequent attention to "the wicked." At first glance one might be inclined to lop off the last half of verse 146:9—for example, the assertion (embarrassing to modern sensibilities) that God brings the way

of the wicked to ruin. But we should not be so quick to pass over this statement. First, to excise such thoughts neuters the psalms of their power, so
that they become expressions of mere sentiment. But second, if we are honest, we stand alongside the psalmist in desiring that the way of the wicked
be thwarted. There are plenty of individuals and institutions engaging in
terrible acts around the world, knowingly destroying both human and nonhuman life. Systemic ills, mixed motives, and ignorance also destroy human
and nonhuman life, often unknowingly. The oppressed might well desire
that God more aggressively "make crooked" the way of the wicked. Such
an expression is in keeping with an ethic of flourishing for both human and
nonhuman communities.

Yet the division of the world into righteous and wicked *people* that characterizes so many psalms—as though persons embodied these characteristics in some binary way—has been subject to justifiable feminist critique
for reifying patriarchal power dynamics and as failing to reflect the lived
experience of women (and men). As Gebara observes:

> What we call evil is here, in this place, just as much as what we call good,
> intermingled in the daily life of our cultures, our choices, and our refus-
> als. We feel that it is impossible to make a clear separation between good
> and evil. Just as when women mix ingredients for a soup or a pie, we
> clearly know good and evil to be inextricably present and commingled in
> our own bodies.[24]

This is a very different account of good and evil from the one Newsom
provides of the sapiential perception of the world—a world in which evil
is understood as ultimately fragile and ephemeral, though still vividly
present—reflected in the speeches of Job's friends and in many psalms. Of
course, binary systems in general have been subject to considerable feminist
critique and, indeed, postmodern critique more broadly. As an ecofeminist,
Gebara rejects a theology of binaries and instead posits "an understanding
of the human person . . . in a *network of relationships.* . . . To be is to *be related*;
shaping the quality of those relations is the critical ethical task."[25]

The clearly binary worldview underlying the psalms we have examined
is mitigated by the ways in which the differences in emphasis of each psalm,
when put in dialogue with one another, contribute to a more relational
understanding of being in the world than has been historically dominant.
Psalm 146 draws on a wide swath of biblical traditions, many of which
require active human engagement in the upholding of justice. Executing
justice for widows, orphans, and the oppressed requires human action, after

all. Thus, praise of God in Ps 146 entails active human participation in facilitating the flourishing of the whole world.

There is another point to be made here as well: while the binary worldview of the psalms—that people are either wicked *or* righteous and that wickedness can always be clearly distinguished from righteousness—cannot be affirmed, another conviction of the psalms, that God will *ultimately* have God's way with the world despite the apparent strength of evil, can be an important claim in feminist theology as well. This conviction, so deeply rooted in Scripture, is the ultimate source of King's famous affirmation cited above: "The arc of the moral universe is long, but it bends toward justice."

In sum, the psalms examined here, when seen through an ecologically sensitive feminist lens, turn the pervasive Western understanding of the world inherited from the Enlightenment on its head. Human beings are not at the center of the world, with the rest of creation as "resources" for their use. Rather, human beings possess authentic self-knowledge only when they understand their embeddedness within, and interconnectedness to, creation as a whole. As Aldo Leopold observed: "We abuse the land because we regard it as a commodity belonging to us. When we see land as a community to which we belong, we may begin to use it with love and respect."[26] The church, when shaped by Scripture, can be a sign of God's ongoing creative power and a source of blessing for the wider creation. Our hope lies not in ourselves but in God. A life saturated in praise to this God both flourishes and enables the flourishing of others.

For Further Reading

Brown, William P. *Psalms*. Interpreting Biblical Texts Series. Nashville: Abingdon, 2010.

Cuomo, Chris J. *Feminism and Ecological Communities: An Ethic of Flourishing*. London: Routledge, 1998.

Gebara, Ivone. *Out of the Depths: Women's Experience of Evil and Salvation*. Translated by Ann Patrick Ware. Minneapolis: Fortress, 2002.

CHAPTER 7

WOMAN WISDOM AND HER FRIENDS
A Feminist Biblical Theology of Justice

Anne W. Stewart

What is justice? Its very definition is fraught with conflict—justice *for whom* and *by what standards?* At stake in this conversation are the values by which justice is measured. As Michael J. Sandel asserts, "Justice is inescapably judgmental. . . . Justice is not only about the right way to distribute things. It is also about the right way to value things."[1] The values inherent in definitions of justice are made evident by the many brands of justice common to contemporary discourse: social justice, racial justice, gender justice, global justice, environmental justice, food justice, and the like. Implicit within this myriad of designations are different conceptions of what society should value as well as the means by which such values should be promoted.

Ancient Israel did not employ these categorical designations within its concept of justice. But the Hebrew Bible does reflect diverse witnesses to the nature of justice and its purpose in the moral order. The Hebrew term *mishpat*, which can mean both "justice" and "judgment," is frequently paired with the term for righteousness, *tsedaqah*. In fact, the two terms are often invoked as a hendiadys to express a singular concept. In Ps 99:4, for example, the terms describe God's praiseworthy administrative work: "Mighty King, lover of justice, you have established equity, you have executed *righteous judgment* [*mishpat utsedaqah*, lit. 'judgment/justice and righteousness'] in Jacob." Yet even as justice and righteousness are inextricably linked across the biblical

canon, they are given different emphases in particular traditions, expressing subtle, though quite significant, variations. For this reason, one cannot
appeal to the Bible as a univocal arbiter of justice any more than one can call
upon justice itself as a singular concept.

The Hebrew Bible offers a generative source of ethical reflection for
contemporary audiences who continue to debate the nature of justice. In
fact, the Bible is a particularly interesting conversation partner for feminist thinkers who are concerned with gender justice in its myriad forms,
even as feminists critique some notions of justice found in the Bible. Three
distinct traditions within the Bible—psalms, prophets, and wisdom—offer
both constructive and problematic notions of justice for feminist interpreters. Each tradition poses the questions of justice (justice for whom, by what
standards?), and each provides an answer that is constructive for feminist
thinkers who are also asking these questions. This essay will briefly survey
the contours of justice as found in psalms, prophets, and wisdom, while
offering ways in which feminist interpreters might converse with each tradition, both to draw helpful insight and to offer critique.

Justice and the Psalms

Within the Psalms, justice is the domain of YHWH. It is closely connected to God's role as cosmic king. As Ps 89:14 proclaims in praise of God,
"Righteousness and justice are the foundation of your throne." The Psalms
frequently appeal to God's justice when requesting both punishment of enemies and deliverance from personal travails. In this respect, God's capacity
to deliver justice has not only a compassionate but also a violent dimension:
God as cosmic king and judge is able to ruin or destroy wicked oppressors
of the lowly. Psalm 7, for example, describing God sitting in judgment over
the world, declares: "God is a righteous judge, and a God who has indig-
nation every day. If one does not repent, God will whet his sword; he has
bent and strung his bow; he has prepared his deadly weapons, making his
arrows fiery shafts" (Ps 7:11-13). Here, as elsewhere in the Psalter, YHWH
as divine judge is also the cosmic warrior. Psalm 97 likewise connects God's
sense of justice to God's might on a cosmic scale:

> YHWH is king! Let the earth rejoice;
>   let the many coastlands be glad!
> Clouds and thick darkness are all around him;
>   righteousness and justice are the foundation of his throne.

Fire goes before him,
  and consumes his adversaries on every side.
His lightnings light up the world;
  the earth sees and trembles.
The mountains melt like wax before YHWH,
  before the Lord of all the earth. (Ps 97:1-5)

Fire, lightning, and fearsome sovereignty are an expression of God's role as just judge and king.

God's justice is expressed in the Psalms as divine compassion for vulnerable people, including the poor, oppressed, widows, orphans, and strangers. Psalm 10, for example, contrasts God's nature with that of the wicked, who oppress the helpless and prey upon the poor: "O YHWH, you will hear the desire of the meek; you will strengthen their heart, you will incline your ear to do justice for the orphan and the oppressed, so that those from earth may strike terror no more" (vv. 17-18). Similarly, Ps 103, which states that God "does righteousness and justice to all the oppressed" (v. 6 AT), is filled with images of God as a merciful and compassionate deity who "forgives all your iniquity, who heals all your diseases, who redeems your life from the Pit, who crowns you with steadfast love and mercy, who satisfies you with good as long as you live" (vv. 3-5).

The Psalms frequently invoke God's justice both as comfort and as might, simultaneously bringing relief from a supplicant's distress and punishing one's enemies. Divine justice aids the oppressed because it has the ability to overturn earthly powers, as in Ps 10: "The helpless commit themselves to you; you have been the helper of the orphan. Break the arm of the wicked and evildoers; seek out their wickedness until you find none. YHWH is king forever and ever; the nations shall perish from his land" (vv. 14b-16).

In the Psalms, God's cosmic kingship serves as a model for human justice. Psalm 72 provides one of the most elaborate treatments of the multifaceted dimensions of just rule. The psalm invokes God's own brand of justice, praying that the human king might judge with righteousness, defend the poor, and subdue those who oppress. Its two opening lines use a chiastic structure to highlight this model, proclaiming: "Give the king your *justice*, O God, and your *righteousness* to a king's son. May he judge your people with *righteousness* and your poor with *justice*" (vv. 1-2 [emphasis added]). The inverted repetition of justice and righteousness establishes the parameters of the monarch's rule, which the psalm develops as the poem continues. Verse 4 emphasizes the ruler's responsibility toward the poor with a triplet line: "May he defend the cause of [literally, 'may he judge'] the poor of the people, give deliverance to the needy, and crush the oppressor"—language recalling YHWH's own activity as cosmic king (cf. Pss 12:6; 69:32-33; 82:1-4; 113:5-8).

Unlike YHWH the divine king, the human king is not figured as a cosmic warrior. Contrasting markedly with psalms that celebrate God's violent triumph over enemies, Ps 72 shows remarkable restraint in describing the means by which the king redeems the poor and defends their cause. It highlights not what the king will do to the oppressors but what his rule will mean for the oppressed and, in fact, for the whole earth. Following the entreaty that the king deliver the needy and crush the oppressor (v. 4), the psalm's gaze turns toward the whole cosmos, employing creation imagery to describe the implications of the king's acts. They will be like nourishing showers upon the ground, causing the righteous to sprout up like plants (vv. 6-7); and peace will endure as long as the moon does (v. 7b). With this language, the psalm envisions an everlasting reign that stretches to the world's horizons.

Foreign nations are implicated in this cosmic vision. While their subordination to the monarch is clear, in this respect as well the psalm shows restraint. The nations will bow before the king and pay homage to him with tribute (v. 9). Yet the human king is revered by the nations not for his show of force but rather for his unbridled compassion: "May all kings fall down before him, all nations give him service. For he delivers the needy when they call, the poor, and those who have no helper" (vv. 11-12). Verse 12 is the linchpin of the psalm, providing the substance of the sovereign's character as just ruler. The psalm indicates that one wins respect not for military might but for defense of the helpless. Furthermore, while many interpret the clause as a rationale for YHWH's favor upon the king, in its immediate literary context it is linked to the nations' obeisance.[2] Strikingly, the human king wins fealty from his adversaries through his redemption of the lowly.

The psalm also raises some troubling questions from the perspective of justice as it espouses royal ideology. The psalm leads one to ask, once again, justice *for whom*, and *by what standards?* In the psalmist's vision, justice is grounded in the justice of YHWH. The psalm opens with an invocation that God give divine justice to the king, and in the psalm's depiction, the primary standard of justice is concern for the poor of society. However, this psalm does not proclaim a completely egalitarian vision. It does not call for a radical abolishment of class distinction, but instead it is grounded in a hierarchical relationship of the sovereign over those whom he protects and the foreign nations. Furthermore, this vision is not necessarily a gender-neutral one. As Phyllis A. Bird has argued, references to the "poor" in the Hebrew Bible are often specific to poor *males*.[3] In this sense, Ps 72 may have limited applicability to issues of gender justice in particular, for its vision of justice has a different scope.

Nevertheless, the Psalms provide an interesting point of reference for feminist reflections particularly because these texts make appeal to a range of oppressed groups as the cornerstone of justice. Within the Psalms, justice is largely about social transformation. The exercise of justice renders protection and relief to the powerless: the poor, the widow, the orphan, the stranger. It is about redressing the abuse of power by those who hold these groups captive or perpetuate their condition. At the same time, psalmic justice is inextricably tied to a model of kingship that many feminist interpreters may find deeply troubling. YHWH is the cosmic guarantor of justice, which is rooted in a sovereignty that is secured by often violent demonstrations of power. In this sense, justice within the Psalms is not about an eradication of power imbalance per se but rather about a confession of trust in the ultimate power of YHWH.

Justice and the Prophets

While justice in the Psalms largely focuses on God's role, for most of the prophets justice is something that humans do—or, more frequently, fail to do. It encompasses particular actions, especially on behalf of the weak in society. In Isa 1:17, for example, the divine oracle commands: "Learn to do good; seek justice, rescue the oppressed, defend the orphan, plead for the widow." Jeremiah 22:3 similarly proclaims: "Act with justice and righteousness, and deliver from the hand of the oppressor anyone who has been robbed. And do no wrong or violence to the alien, the orphan, and the widow, or shed innocent blood in this place." Justice's demands are established by God's own activity (see, e.g., Jer 9:24). Failure to do justice earns God's rebuke (see, e.g., Jer 21:12).

Israelite prophets often stood on the periphery of political or religious power. From this position they frequently invoked justice to condemn prevailing social forces. Micah saw a profound discrepancy between the rhetoric of princes and prophets and their violent, exploitative actions:

> Listen, you heads of Jacob
> > and rulers of the house of Israel!
> Should you not know justice?—
> > you who hate the good and love the evil,
> who tear the skin off my people,
> > and the flesh off their bones . . .
>
> Thus says YHWH concerning the prophets
> > who lead my people astray,
> who cry "Peace"
> when they have something to eat,
> but declare war against those
> > who put nothing into their mouths. (Mic 3:1-2, 5)

Prophetic calls for justice thus encompass sharp scrutiny of the exercise of power.

Furthermore, the prophets depict the pursuit of justice not as impartial judgment but as impassioned advocacy. Micah issues exhortations expressing outrage and dismay, characterized by deep anger and grief over the cry of the dispossessed. He objects to practices that violate the security of weaker members of society, and he castigates leaders who use their power to violate others. For Micah, the misguided emotions of the leaders reflect their inability to be agents of justice; they love evil and hate the good (Mic 3:2).

The Israelite prophets' role as chief critics of the structures of power provides a compelling model for feminist thought insofar as it stresses the goal of social and political transformation. For the prophets, the stakes of justice are nothing less than fundamental disruption of prevailing forces of oppression, exploitation, and corruption. Justice is less a concept to be discussed or a confession of the divine character than it is a program to be enacted. If for the Psalms the court of justice is situated in the heavenly realm, for the prophets it is grounded in the public domain of human interaction.

Consequently, the prophets place more emphasis on the human condition than on the maintenance of social or legal norms. As Abraham J. Heschel insists, justice for the prophets is important not for its own sake but for the benefit it brings to humanity: "Justice exists in relation to a person, and is something done by a person. An act of injustice is condemned, not because the law is broken, but because a person has been hurt. What is the image of a person? A person is a being whose anguish may reach the heart of God."[4] In this respect, the prophetic conception of justice may be of greatest value to feminist interpreters since it nurtures a vision capable of attending to the particularity of the human person. As feminist thinkers advocate for a gender justice that recognizes women's full humanity, they may draw inspiration from prophets who insist that God hears the anguish of all people, including and especially women and those whom the social structures of power may neglect.

In fact, within the book of Micah, women are in essence a barometer of justice. In Mic 2:9-10 and elsewhere, the vulnerable position of women and children is one measure of societal injustice ("The women of my people you drive out from their pleasant houses; from their young children you take away my glory forever" [v. 9]). Mistreatment of women leads to erosive self-destruction (v. 10). Indeed, endangering women's security has repercussions for a society's security.

Women also serve as a symbol of the judgment and hope of divine justice. The city Zion (Jerusalem) is personified as a woman. In the oracle in Mic 4, the divine voice proclaims to Jerusalem:

> Now why do you cry aloud?
>   Is there no king in you?
> Has your counselor perished,
>   that pangs have seized you like a woman in labor?
> Writhe and groan, O daughter Zion,
>   like a woman in labor;
> for now you shall go forth from the city
>   and camp in the open country;
>   you shall go to Babylon.
> There you shall be rescued,
>   there YHWH will redeem you
>   from the hands of your enemies. (vv. 9-10)

This image is at once both problematic and compelling. In a troubling way, the birthing process is likened to punishment and alienation, and the woman is figured as one in need of guardianship and protection. At the same time, the metaphor celebrates the female body's ability to bring forth new life. In chapter 5, birth imagery is linked to the promise of restoration (see esp. Mic 5:3). The female figure links pain and possibility, turning the experience of suffering into one of regeneration. Here labor and birth signify the complexity of divine justice: though it originates from a dangerous and distressing process, it finally results not in death but in life.

In the prophetic tradition at large, the metaphorical nature of the prophets' language may prove most problematic to feminist interpreters. In particular, the images of marriage and promiscuous women that are used to describe the relationship between YHWH and Israel are deeply disturbing and leave a violent legacy of discourse surrounding power and justice. The book of Hosea, for example, develops an extended metaphor of a marriage between Hosea and Gomer, a wife of "whoredom" or promiscuity (1:2), as a cipher for Israel's failure to maintain loyalty to YHWH. Throughout the poem in Hos 2 that describes God's relationship with Israel, this metaphor is developed with evocative imagery depicting the husband's violent and abusive retribution, saying, for instance, "I will strip her naked and expose her as in the day she was born, and make her like a wilderness, and turn her into a parched land, and kill her with thirst" (v. 3). The oracle goes on to describe a period of restoration in which the husband will show compassion to the woman, a movement troublingly similar to cycles of domestic violence.[5] It closes with YHWH pledging: "I will take you for my wife in righteousness and in justice, in steadfast love and in mercy. I will take you for my wife in faithfulness; and you shall know YHWH" (vv. 19-20). Following the lengthy description of the wife's violent punishment and sexual humiliation at YHWH's hands, this invocation of righteousness and justice as a seal of the marriage covenant is problematic. Indeed, justice within Hosea, as in the prophetic tradition at large, is a morally complex concept, invoking an ethic of mercy and compassion but also describing YHWH's moral outrage in a manner that carries extremely violent implications for women. The prophets thus offer a mixed legacy to feminist conceptions of justice. They emphasize the necessity of social transformation, yet their rhetoric stresses this imperative with language that is highly troubling, even dangerous, for women.

Justice and the Wisdom Tradition

The notion of justice within the book of Proverbs rests on certain assumptions about the nature of order in the cosmos. In the minds of the sages, justice ultimately comes from God and reflects the divinely ordered world. Proverbs 16:11 states, "The scales of justice belong to YHWH; he made all of the weights in the bag" (author's trans.). Similarly, Prov 11:1 proclaims, "A false balance is an abomination to YHWH, but an accurate weight is his delight." Both sayings reflect the sages' perceptions about order. The reliability of weights and measures represents the reliability of order in the cosmos at large. Moreover, it is God who calibrates the scales; God both instills and maintains justice in the world. Proverbs 2:8 insists that God is "guarding the paths of justice and preserving the way of his faithful ones." Proverbs 29:26 states, "Many seek the favor of a ruler, but it is from YHWH that one gets justice." In this respect, Proverbs provides an interesting contrast to the ideology of justice in many psalms, which often highlight the divine king as justice's prime agent. While certain sayings in Proverbs associate kingship with the maintenance of justice (see 16:10, 13; 20:8, 26; 29:4), on the whole the book associates justice more closely with order established by God, which is not as deeply connected with kingship, either human or divine.

Even as justice ultimately comes from God, according to the sages, humans also have a profound role to play: through exercising justice, humans help maintain order in the cosmos. Consequently, justice is central to the pedagogical goal of the book. Its prologue defines its aim, in part, as promoting justice. Its purpose is "for gaining instruction in wise dealing, righteousness, justice, and equity" (1:3). Achieving this end involves calibrating one's moral sensibilities to see the structures of order at work and to promote them actively since advancing justice serves the health of the community. For example, 24:23b-25 says,

> Partiality in judging is not good.
> Whoever says to the wicked, "You are innocent,"
>   will be cursed by peoples, abhorred by nations;
> but those who rebuke the wicked will have delight,
>   and a good blessing will come upon them.

In this sense, the righteous are those who not only recognize the structures of justice rightly but also delight in just activity, since "doing justice brings joy to the righteous but terror to evildoers" (21:15, author's trans.). Conversely, the wicked are those who obstruct justice, as in 17:23: "The wicked accept a bribe to subvert the ways of justice" (author's trans.). Showing their serious moral malformation, the wicked may even take delight in injustice (19:28).

The promotion of justice requires right understanding of the world, which for the sages is grounded in a claim about the divinely structured cosmos. Since the sages' worldview is largely hierarchical and patriarchal, many feminists have found them a fairly distasteful source for reflections about the nature of order.[6] Nonetheless, the broader point that justice requires the capacity to assess the deep structures of order may provide a helpful

connection to feminist notions of justice, which likewise assess social structures. One of the primary dilemmas for feminist politics is the problem of
"false consciousness," the idea that women may not challenge male privilege
because other women, having been socialized to accept such structures, do
not perceive gender injustice in the same way. To a certain extent, this is
similar to the way Proverbs diagnoses the problem of injustice, for promoting justice requires having the right analytical tools—that is, the capacity to
understand the deep structures of the cosmos and to measure reality accordingly. While feminist interpreters may quarrel with the sages of Proverbs
about the nature of the structures discernible in the world, they may in fact
share the goal of cultivating the critical capacities to see the world through
the lens of justice as right order.

Within the Israelite wisdom tradition, the nature of justice is highly
contested. Conflicting ideologies of justice are most apparent in the book of
Job. The dialogue between Job and his friends concerns fundamental questions about the nature of justice and its relation to the divine, as well as
whether or not a just order can even be perceived. For Job, the paradigmatic
righteous person, great personal loss and travail lead to radical questioning
of the foundations of justice. The issue is encapsulated in Job's piercing cry:
"God has put me in the wrong, and closed his net around me. Even when I
cry out 'Violence!' I am not answered; I call aloud, but there is no justice"
(19:6-7). Job's friends, in contrast, insist on justice's reliability and profess
confidence in God as a righteous arbiter. Bildad, for example, protests Job's
words, saying: "Does God twist justice? Or does the Almighty pervert the
right?" (8:3). Such a proposition is unimaginable to Job's friends, for whom
justice conveys reliable, equitable retribution. As Elihu explains,

> Far be it from God that he should do wickedness,
>   and from the Almighty that he should do wrong.
> For according to their deeds he will repay them,
>   and according to their ways he will make it befall them.
> Of a truth, God will not do wickedly,
>   and the Almighty will not pervert justice. (34:10-12)

As different notions of justice interact throughout the book, they lead
not to a resolution but to an expanded conception of justice that is more
than the sum of the individual perspectives. As Carol Newsom has argued
at length, the book of Job presents a dialogic sense of truth, which exists at
the intersection of multiple voices and is always unable to be finalized. She
explains:

The notion that there is a deep structure of justice at the heart of existence must interact with the idea of the arbitrariness or hostility of the divine, be complicated by considerations of temporality, engage the epistemological claims of direct observation and the limits of human reason, and so forth.[7]

Justice often has a legal tone in the book of Job, which frequently employs metaphors pertaining to the courtroom. Job proclaims that the scales of justice are skewed toward the divine since God "is not a mortal as I am, that I might answer him, that we should come to trial together" (Job 9:32). Since it is impossible for a human to enter into a fair trial with God, Job says, there is a fundamental inequity in the moral order of the cosmos. In effect, in the courtroom Job envisions, God is defendant, judge, and jury, making impossible an impartial trial.

Job's legal metaphor subtly reframes and critiques the notion of divine justice commonly found in psalms where, within the context of hymnic praise, divine violence is associated with God as victor over chaos, defender of the oppressed, and redeemer from danger, all in an effort to celebrate God's mighty power. When Job protests, "Though I am innocent, I cannot answer" (9:15), he questions the praiseworthiness of God's might. Newsom observes, "By this means, the immense alterity between God and humans, which is lifted up by Eliphaz and which is a reassuring feature in the divine warrior hymns, appears as disturbing and morally troubling when reframed in a forensic context."[8] In this way, the book itself offers a practicum in the contestation of justice. For the wisdom tradition as a whole, the questions of justice are largely about the maintenance of order in the world. Yet there is vibrant debate about the nature of that order and its reliability, an issue that is also at the heart of feminist reflections on justice.

Woman Wisdom and the Nature of Justice

While there are different conceptions of justice among the traditions in the Hebrew Bible, they share a notion that justice is not an abstract concept but is embodied, whether in the deity or in the community. Justice takes concrete expression in the actions, ideals, and emotions of sovereigns, prophets, and students of wisdom. In this sense, one of the most fruitful conceptions of justice for feminist interpreters occurs in the book of Proverbs, where justice is embodied in personified woman Wisdom. This portrait provides a striking counterpoint to the psalmic image of the divine king and warrior. By way of conclusion, we will examine the poetic speech of personified

Wisdom in Prov 8. This extended poem offers a particular kind of instruction that appeals to her desirability and grounds her authority in her relationship to YHWH.

Central to Wisdom's vision of justice is the capacity to discern, to measure the moral world accurately. She implores her students to acquire facul-
ties of discernment: "Learn shrewdness, you simpletons! And fools—gain
sense!" (Prov 8:5, author's trans.). Her directive "gain sense!"—in Hebrew,
"to make the heart understand"—implies a holistic task of mind, emotion,
and sense perception, and the tutorial comes from Wisdom herself. "My
mouth will utter truth," she cries,

> wickedness is an abomination to my lips.
> All the words of my mouth are righteous;
>   there is nothing twisted or crooked in them.
> They are all straight [or: plumb] to one who understands
>   and right to those who find knowledge. (vv. 7-9)

With this language, Wisdom figures discernment as an act of measure-
ment. Straightness, or uprightness, denotes an attribute of order as well as
the ability to speak and act to promote order, rather than using crooked or
twisted speech. Wisdom not only acts in accord with such order but also
grants her students the ability to discern it (v. 9). Her words are "plumb," a
term often used metaphorically to describe something that is straightforward or true (cf. Prov 24:26; 2 Sam 15:3; Isa 26:10; 57:2; Amos 3:10). This
language gives Wisdom's words an aesthetic dimension; they are "high" and
"straight," neither "twisted" nor "crooked." A wise person can discern the
correct measurements of her words. That is, to discern and promote justice,
one's scales must be correctly calibrated. Cultivating discernment is about
acquiring accurate perceptions of the world.

Wisdom declares that "insight and might" belong to her (v. 14). This
language may seem to resemble the monarchical imagery of the Psalms,
but Wisdom's might is a profoundly different show of force. Rather than a
martial display, Wisdom's might is an intellectual, ethical capacity. Accordingly, her figure offers a striking model for earthly rulers. She declares,
"With me, rulers reign, leaders decree righteousness. With me, princes
rule, nobles and all judges of righteousness" (vv. 15-16, author's trans.).
What does it mean to reign by Wisdom? She exercises discernment and
promotes just order not by violent acts of retribution but with right speech
(vv. 6-8), acts of love (v. 17), and abundant beneficence (vv. 18-21). Wisdom
proclaims that she walks in the pathways of righteousness and justice to

endow all who love her, filling their storehouses (vv. 20-21). Embodied in woman Wisdom, the way of justice is thus desirable. It offers prosperity, fruitfulness, and flourishing life to those who follow in Wisdom's ways. She proclaims, "Take my discipline! Not money! And knowledge above choice gold! For Wisdom is better than jewels; no delights can equal her" (vv. 10-11, author's trans.).

Within this poem, the purview of human life cannot be separated from the horizon of creation. Situated in the middle of the poem is a series of images in which Wisdom recalls the world's creation. This is not an interlude unrelated to the instructions that precede and follow it. Rather, creation imagery both grows out of her instruction and is its foundation. Wisdom and her justice lead to flourishing—not only the flourishing of human life, but the flourishing of all creation.

In fact, in her relationship to YHWH and to creation, Wisdom offers a striking counterpoint to the image of the divine warrior. She participates with God in the activity of creation and witnesses to the formation of the cosmos (vv. 22-31). In this capacity, she is characterized not by violent power but by playful delight. She describes herself as YHWH's childlike companion, experiencing the unfolding creation with wonder:

> When he established the heavens, I was there;
> > when he inscribed the horizon upon the deep,
> when he made firm the clouds above,
> > when he strengthened the fountains of the deep,
> when he set the bounds of the sea
> > that the waters would not cross his command,
> when he inscribed the foundations of the earth,
> > I was there beside him growing up,[9]
> I was a daily delight,
> > playing before him all the time,
> playing in his inhabited earth
> > and delighting in humanity. (vv. 27-31, author's trans.)

This poetic litany artfully highlights the priority of Wisdom as YHWH's confidante in creation. The section's final two lines employ a chiastic structure to underscore Wisdom's playful persona: she is a *delight* who *plays* before YHWH, *playing* and *delighting* in humanity. The chiasmus binds these lines together, pointing to Wisdom's connections with YHWH and humanity, delighting YHWH as she herself delights in YHWH's world.[10] In this sense, as William P. Brown notes, "Yahweh and creation are bound together by Wisdom's elation, by a celebration of Yahweh's creative activity through Wisdom's recreative response."[11]

Wisdom's play is a richly generative vision of justice in the cosmos, where order is reflected in Wisdom's own wonder and celebration of creative activity. Wisdom points toward joy, delight, and life as the ultimate ends of justice. Her vision promotes the flourishing of humanity and all creation. Wisdom's final cry as the poem closes points to the life-giving nature of her counsel: "For whoever finds me finds life and obtains favor from YHWH" (v. 35).

Not only does Wisdom offer a striking contrast to the image of the divine warrior, but she also functions differently from the father in Prov 1–9. Her authority is rooted in her priority: having been created by YHWH before all else, she has even greater longevity than the father whose voice utters most of the instructions in Prov 1–9. Yet she exercises her authority not through the paternal, hierarchical model implicit in the rest of the book but through kinship.[12]

As in the wider wisdom tradition, the notion of justice rests here also on a conviction about order in the cosmos. Yet this image of woman Wisdom as a delightful, desirable, playful beacon of justice helps undermine the more hierarchical order depicted elsewhere in Proverbs. Nor is she the violent aggressor who enforces justice by the sword, as YHWH is figured in other traditions in the Hebrew Bible. Rather, Wisdom's justice leads to life for humanity, indeed for all creation, and she enacts this vision through playing alongside creation. Wisdom as portrayed here provides a generative metaphor for contemporary feminists who are cultivating a conception of justice that challenges certain ideologies.

Conclusion: Justice for Whom?
Justice by What Standards?

When one traverses the Hebrew Bible's major conceptions of justice, the importance of scrutinizing justice becomes apparent. All concepts of justice reflect particular moral imaginations, with their own prevailing ideologies and valuations of virtue. Consequently, justice is inevitably a contested concept, and its analysis requires careful evaluation of implicit ideology. Feminist interpreters find much to critique in notions of justice present in the Hebrew Bible. Yet they must at the same time allow their own conceptions of justice to be scrutinized. In this respect, the Hebrew Bible's diversity of perspectives offers an instructive reference point.

Contemporary conversations about gender justice have many different starting points, including political philosophy, public policy, legal traditions, and theology. Such diverse starting points produce different standards of justice. So do the diverse social locations of women themselves. As Anne Marie Goetz explains, "Women cannot be identified as a coherent group along with other sets of disempowered people such as ethnic minorities or socially excluded immigrants. Gender cuts across these and all other social categories, producing differences of interests—and conceptions of justice— between women."[13] For this reason, it is difficult to speak of a singular concept of justice common to all feminist thinkers and theologians.

Just as justice takes different shapes in various biblical traditions, so it reflects varying commitments among feminist thinkers. Goetz identifies three different definitions of gender justice. One prominent tradition, which is rooted in feminist political philosophy, defines justice in terms of the capabilities required for free and rational choice. Martha C. Nussbaum, for example, aware that in no country are women treated as well as men and that in many countries women lack support for even basic human functions, advocates for a vision of justice that is universal in scope and articulates constitutional principles that provide an essential respect for human dignity.[14] Justice, in this perspective, is about the human capacities that one needs to "form a conception of the good and to engage in critical reflection about the planning of one's own life."[15] On the other hand, the 1999 United Nations Convention on the Elimination of All Forms of Discrimination Against Women (CEDAW) identified the goal of gender justice as the prevention of gender discrimination within the laws and policies of established legal systems. Finally, a contemporary "rights-based" approach to gender justice seeks to establish the basic rights that citizens may expect from the state, acknowledging that power relations affect the outcomes of policy. Some advocates of this mode of justice link rights to the state's promotion of access to resources such as food or information, insisting that the state has a role in identifying vulnerable groups and facilitating their access to resources.[16] In addition to the definitions that Goetz enumerates, gender justice can also be defined in theological terms. Beverly Wildung Harrison, for example, explains that "justice is . . . our central theological image, a metaphor of right relationship, which shapes the telos of good community and serves as the animating passion of the moral life."[17] Even within this cursory survey, justice takes may different forms: human functioning; the absence of discrimination; human rights; and relationship.

Despite this diversity, in some measure each of these conceptions is rooted in a concern with power and its distribution. As Walter J. Houston remarks, the questions of justice are essentially about power: "Who has power, who benefits from it, and who has no power and loses from it?"[18] The question of power, and the degree to which power is vested in social and political institutions in a way that privileges men, is particularly relevant to gender. Central to most notions of feminist thought is a commitment to transform structures that disempower or oppress. The agenda of feminist thought goes beyond diagnosis or description to call for fundamental change. As Ada María Isasi-Díaz insists, "Using the oppression of women as their source and locus, feminist accounts of justice are discourses specific enough to force options and concrete enough to play a central role in devising strategies to bringing about radical social change."[19] In this respect, she argues, feminist accounts of justice privilege women as moral agents, for "feminist accounts of justice are not only about women's rights but also about women's responsibilities; they are about women as moral subjects and agents as well as about the social consequences of personal behaviors and institutional policies."[20]

One of the main critiques of some contemporary constructions of gender justice is that they work for gender equality on a national or international scale in ways that do not significantly impact women's individual lives, particularly when they have little applicability to cultures that privilege kinship or community over individual rights. Naila Kabeer argues that women in Afghanistan and Bangladesh, for example, have a profoundly different understanding of individual rights and citizenship than do Western women. Consequently, those who advocate for gender justice at the level of institutional or constitutional rights touch the lives of women in these societies very little.[21] These women's notions of justice may concern not political emancipation but personal piety and relationships to kinship circles. In other words, women in other parts of the world "might be called to personhood, so to speak, in a different language," as Lila Abu-Lughod concludes.[22] Thus, Kabeer insists that "gender justice surely requires societies that can accommodate these multiple pathways, the pious and the secular, the individual and the collective, without necessarily privileging one or negating the other."[23]

In this respect, the Hebrew Bible offers an instructive collection of texts holding multiple conceptions of justice in conversation. Perhaps one of the Hebrew Bible's signal contributions to gender justice is to stand in productive tension with definitions of justice that prize equality as the highest good and individual autonomy as the chief end. Even as feminist commentators rightly critique the often hierarchical and patriarchal ideology behind biblical texts, these texts also challenge certain points of Western feminist ideology.

Within the Hebrew Bible, equality in and of itself is not necessarily the desired end of justice, and impartiality is not an expressed goal. The Hebrew Bible's notions of justice stand in marked contrast to the image found in Western society of the blindfolded woman holding the scales of justice. As Heschel notes, the figure of the blindfolded virgin conveys a value of rational evaluation and impartial judgment, but it also "conceives of the process of justice as a mechanical process, as if the life of [the person] were devoid of individuality and uniqueness and could be adequately understood in terms of inexorable generalizations."[24] To the contrary, justice in the Hebrew Bible—whether in the form of psalmic praise, prophetic critique, or Wisdom's play—celebrates God's concern for human life, as well as the divine and human prerogative to promote wholeness and flourishing. This end requires a certain partiality that attends to human particularity rather than to the abstraction of political or gendered classes.

A biblical theology of justice provides a different starting point for a gender justice than that of political philosophy or human rights. The theologies of justice in the Hebrew Bible share a cosmic vision that is both partial and, to some degree, hierarchical, grounded in YHWH's ultimate authority over the moral world. Yet this vision remains powerful for feminist reflection precisely because it critiques the distorted power structures of human society. Indeed, from the righteous monarch to the critical prophet to playful Wisdom, the voices of the Hebrew Bible continue to challenge and reframe notions of justice. In doing so, they testify to the value of working for justice alongside a source that is capable of contesting one's own understanding.

For Further Reading

Harrison, Beverly Wildung. *Justice in the Making: Feminist Social Ethics.* Edited by Elizabeth M. Bounds, Pamela K. Brubaker, Jane E. Hicks, Marilyn J. Legge, Rebecca Todd Peters, and Traci C. West. Louisville, Ky.: Westminster John Knox, 2004.

Houston, Walter J. *Justice—The Biblical Challenge.* Biblical Challenges in the Contemporary World. London: Equinox, 2010.

Nardoni, Enrique. *Rise Up, O Judge: A Study of Justice in the Biblical World.* Translated by Seán Charles Martin. Peabody, Mass.: Hendrikson, 2004.

Newsom, Carol A. *The Book of Job: A Contest of Moral Imaginations.* New York: Oxford University Press, 2003.

CHAPTER 8

WHEN ESTHER AND JEZEBEL WRITE
A Feminist Biblical Theology of Authority

*Cameron B. R. Howard**

As a child growing up in the Presbyterian church, I learned that the answer
to the question "Who wrote the Bible?" is "Holy men, who were taught by
the Holy Ghost."[1] That answer echoes two assumptions many readers bring
to their study of the Hebrew Bible. For readers from numerous faith traditions, including my own, the Bible is authoritative because it is thought to be
inspired by the Holy Spirit. Its precepts wield power because they are, in some
fashion, divine. At the same time, most readers assume that men—that is, not
just human beings in general, but, particularly, *male* human beings—wrote the
Bible. There are a few biblical texts for which female authorship seems a distinct
possibility, since they represent a female voice. Much of the poetry in the Song
of Songs, for instance, is written in the first-person speech of the female lover.
Psalm 131:2c, "my soul is like the weaned child that is with me," also implies a
female speaker and therefore possibly a female author. Even so, these glimpses
of female authorship are rare and fleeting, and it is difficult to determine with
any certainty which if any biblical texts were written by women.

Without recourse to women's authorial voices *behind* the text, readers
are left to listen for women's authorial voices *within* the text. Do any female

---

* It is a great joy to present this essay in honor of my teacher Carol Newsom, who, when
asked by strangers about her occupation, will sometimes reply, "I teach reading and writing."

characters in the Hebrew Bible possess scribal authority? In other words, do women in the Bible write? The answer is that only twice does the Hebrew Bible depict women writing: Jezebel writes letters in Ahab's name in order to entrap Naboth (1 Kgs 21:8-9), and Esther writes to establish the festival of Purim (Esth 9:29). Both of these women writers are queens, holding a rare but powerful position of public leadership. Thus, the "scribal" authority held by Jezebel and Esther coincides with their royal authority.

The fact that the women who write are monarchs is consistent with other biblical portraits of leadership. Throughout the Hebrew Bible, leaders write. Moses and Joshua write down the law (Exod 24:4; Deut 31:9; Josh 8:32). Prophets—including Samuel (1 Sam 10:25), Isaiah (Isa 8:1; 30:8), Jeremiah (Jer 30:2; 36:4), and Ezekiel (Ezek 24:2; 37:16)—write or are commanded to write for the sake of symbolism, record keeping, and the investiture of authority. Kings from David (2 Sam 11:14) to Artaxerxes (Ezra 7:11) exercise the power of their office through writing. Even God is a writer, sending a finger over the tablets of the covenant and keeping records in the book of the living (Exod 31:18; Ps 139:16). The written word carries authority within the Bible, and men with authority do the writing. But does anything change when women do the writing?

My study of women's leadership and authority in the Hebrew Bible begins at the point of connection between these two characters: Esther and Jezebel are *women writers*. This essay will explore what they write, how they write, and the authority of their texts. Esther and Jezebel are also *queens*, holding the highest public position of authority available to women in biblical times. Their royal position gives them access to writing, even expectations for it, and their texts are themselves reflections of that royal authority. Esther and Jezebel share other characteristics, too. Neither woman is the primary ruler; instead, each acquires her power and position by marrying the monarch. Both women are foreigners in their royal contexts: Jezebel is the daughter of a Phoenician king and married to Ahab, king of Israel, while Esther is a Jewish woman living in Diaspora who marries the Persian king Ahasuerus. Both are outsiders in their environments.

Despite their many shared characteristics, Jezebel and Esther have dramatically different reputations both within the Bible and throughout Jewish and Christian tradition. In Kings, a book that blames foreign women and their foreign gods for facilitating the collapse of the kingdoms of Israel and Judah, Jezebel is the ultimate villain. She eagerly uses her royal power for apostasy and exploitation. Esther, on the other hand, heroically saves the people of Israel from annihilation in a foreign land. She is portrayed as charming yet humble, reluctant yet courageous. These divergences, coupled with the many points of overlap between the two characters, may inspire ideas that Esther and Jezebel are "foils" for each other, in either intent or effect.[2] However, I hope to draw attention away from the biblical narratives' evaluations of their moral character and toward their participation in the acts of reading and writing. Given their many overlapping circumstances, do Esther and Jezebel write the same kinds of texts in the same ways? What can these two characters tell us together about women's leadership and the power of the written word? Can their writing in any way provide a model for feminist theology today?

I propose that the stories of Jezebel's and Esther's writing demonstrate, each in its own way, that the power of the reader trumps the authority of the writer. In contexts in which the written word tries to claim absolute authority, that authority is persistently destabilized by the presence of the reader, who has the power to interpret, to refrain from acting, or to act in ways not necessarily envisioned by the text itself. Rather than being fixed in a limiting, even oppressive, past, biblical authority continues to be reinterpreted and reshaped into a liberating future.

Literacy and Royal Authority

It is no mere coincidence that the two biblical women writers are also both queens. Literacy was not a widespread, democratized phenomenon in the ancient Near East. In fact, the content of the Hebrew Bible reflects an oral culture as much as it reflects a literate one. Such an assertion may seem counterintuitive, given the continuing importance of the Bible as a sacred text. Yet the world depicted in many parts of the Hebrew Bible is one in which writing and reading are specialized activities for particular circumstances rather than common features of everyday life. Writing might be used for symbolic activity, as when the prophet Ezekiel writes the names Judah and Joseph on two sticks and joins them together to symbolize the unity of the southern and northern kingdoms (Ezek 37:15-28). At Num 5:11-31, writing is used in a ritual to determine the guilt or innocence of a woman accused of adultery. The priest writes curses and washes the writing in the "water of bitterness," which the woman then drinks. The writing imbues the water with magical properties that reveal guilt or innocence.[3] In these examples, the mysterious power of writing outweighs its practical application.

Even in biblical texts that may regard writing as common bureaucracy more than ethereal mystery, orality remains a prominent feature of their context. The Hebrew verb for reading, *qr'*, also means to call, announce, or shout, pointing to the oral underpinnings of the act of reading. Rather than understanding reading as a silent and solitary act, the verb implies a designated reader reading a text aloud to an assembled group. This is precisely the kind of reading Neh 8:3 describes as Ezra reads the law of Moses to the assembled community: "He read [*qr'*] from it facing the square before the Water Gate from early morning until midday, in the presence of the men and the women and those who could understand; and the ears of all the people were attentive to the book of the law." Even if basic literacy were relatively widespread by the postexilic era (a contested notion to be sure), the production of texts was so tedious and expensive that few households would have actually owned scrolls of any sort. The paucity of copies drove the need for oral performance; for a text to be widely received, it would need to be read aloud publicly.

The written record has long been a feature of effective government. In cultures where writing is sparse overall, texts may nonetheless proliferate in service of a bureaucracy. If any sector of society can be said to be thoroughly "literate," government can. The more potent a ruling power of the ancient Near East became, and the more complex its economic systems became, the more it turned to writing for record keeping, correspondence, and other administrative functions. Written texts might also be used for propagandistic purposes, such as memorializing—and publicizing—a king's victories in battle via stelae or other inscriptions. The beginning of the book of Ezra shows Cyrus, king of Persia, issuing an edict allowing the exiled Jews to return to Judah and rebuild the temple there. Ezra 1:1 specifies that the edict of Cyrus is both written down and announced orally: "[H]e sent a herald throughout all his kingdom, and also in a written edict declared." Here the pairing of the written text with its oral pronouncement is made explicit, and the two forms of communication work together to convey the official word throughout Persia's territories.

Both Esther's and Jezebel's texts belong to this public, administrative realm. Their writings are extensions of their royal authority. Their instructions carry weight not simply because they are written down but because monarchic authority stands behind them. The women have access to the materials for writing and to the scribal class for assistance. In fact, it is unclear whether kings and queens would have been literate themselves or whether any mention of a monarch writing must assume the monarch's dictation but a scribe's hand. Inasmuch as literacy was the domain of society's elites, then there is every reason to believe that kings and queens would have been educated to read and write, even if they often availed themselves of the service of scribes.[4] It is also likely that many if not most "regular" Israelites, including and perhaps especially women, would not have been literate beyond the ability to sign their names and recognize basic words. Therefore it is precisely Jezebel and Esther's roles as public figures that enable them to write. They write in a world that is still dominated by orality but that knows of textuality, particularly textuality and literacy as the purview of society's powerful elite.

Esther

Esther as Monarch

Esther's rise to power begins with the dismissal of another queen. When Vashti refuses to appear before the drunken king and his subjects on the seventh day of his latest banquet, the king's advisers become concerned that every wife in Persia, upon hearing of the incident, will likewise despise her husband. Memucan, one such adviser, suggests, "If it pleases the king, let a royal order go out from him, and let it be written among the laws of the Persians and the Medes so that it may not be altered, that Vashti is never again to come before King Ahasuerus; and let the king give her royal position [*malkhut*] to another who is better than she" (Esth 1:19). This scene makes it clear that the position of queen in Persia is not a legislative one. The king, easily suggestible though he may be, has power over the queen, including the power to make laws that Vashti must follow. Even so, the king's power is immediately tenuous; although her refusal comes with significant consequences, Vashti does not obey. The king's response, closely shepherded by his coterie of advisers, is to codify his power over women into an irrevocable decree, to write a text that might remove any distance between his words and women's actions. As Mieke Bal describes, "The first decree, banning Vashti, was meant to fix forever the obedience of wives, hence, male power over women in private and public. In its excessive ambition and fearful defensiveness . . . this intention cannot but fail, and the rest of the story will stage that failure. The submission of women cannot be fixed by writing, the story tells us."[5] Esther's own defiance of the king's law (5:1-2; cf. 4:11) will further demonstrate the futility of the king's actions.

Vashti, like Esther after her, has the title of queen and its accompanying royal status: a profoundly elevated position within the kingdom. In her foundational literary study of the book, Sandra Beth Berg names kingship as a "dominant motif" in Esther and traces that motif through the book. She notes that the use of *malkhut* (adj. "royal" or noun "royalty") is not restricted to the person or possessions of King Ahasuerus but at various times indicates the royal power of either another king, Vashti, or Esther.[6] When the king summons Vashti to his banquet, he wants her to wear her "royal crown" (*keter malkhut*). When he later chooses Esther as Vashti's replacement, "he set the royal crown [*keter malkhut*] on her head and made her queen instead of Vashti" (2:17). Thus, the crown symbolizes the transfer of status from Vashti to Esther.[7]

Even so, it is only later in the story, when Esther dares to approach the king uninvited, that she embraces her royal authority and acts upon it. Esther 5:1a reads, "And so it happened on the third day that *Esther put on royalty* and stood in the inner court of the palace of the king, opposite the king's dwelling" (author's trans.). If this appearance before the king is to parallel Vashti's nonappearance in chapter 1, then Esther should put on her *keter malkhut*, not simply her *malkhut*, which becomes the abstract idea of "royalty" without any other concrete noun (like "crown") for it to modify. Indeed, the verb "put on" (*tilbash*) requires a direct object associated with some sort of clothing or other adornment. One way to account for the apparent omission is to assume haplography here: somewhere in the ancient scribal enterprise of copying this text, a word dropped out. Yet this moment of adornment also marks a pivot point in the narrative, from a time when Esther receives her royal position from Ahasuerus (2:17) to a time when she actively utilizes that authority. When Mordecai challenges Esther to speak up for her people, he tells her, "Perhaps you have come to royal dignity [*lamalkhut*] for just such a time as this" (4:14). As Berg remarks, "The repetition of *mlk* in Esth 5:1 directs our attention to the question of 'kingship'—an issue raised by Mordecai in Esth 4:14, the last occurrence of *malkhut* prior to Esth 5:1. Esther's assumption of her *malkhut* thereby constitutes a suitable response to Mordecai's challenge."[8] This is indeed Esther's time. Notably, the narrative itself refers to Esther by the title "Queen Esther" (*'ester hammalkah*) only after 5:1. Her initial unannounced entrance into the king's inner court marks her embrace of her agency and her authority. At this moment Esther asserts the power afforded her by her royal position, and the narrative affirms her.[9]

Haman's actions toward Esther likewise underscore her authority; though he has an otherwise unrivaled position in the kingdom, he recognizes her superior rank. The king has situated Haman over all his other advisors and instructed all to bow to Haman (3:1-2). When Haman hatches his plot to destroy the Jews, the king also hands over his signet ring, a concrete symbol of the power of the royal office. Haman has the power to write on behalf of the king and thus to enact policies, including his own call for the murder of the Jews. Yet he continues to yearn desperately for royal affirmation. He boasts to his wife and friends, "Even Queen Esther let no one but myself come with the king to the banquet that she prepared. Tomorrow also I am invited by her, together with the king" (5:12). He counts Esther's invitation among the symbols of his favored status, which also include riches, sons, and promotions by the king (5:11). When Esther reveals Haman's plot and character to the king at her second banquet, Haman pleads for his life from Esther, not Ahasuerus, imagining that petitioning the furious king would be fruitless (7:7). Whether Esther ultimately has the power to stop Haman's execution is unclear from the text, as she does not appear to try. Even so, Haman certainly perceives her authority as on par with that of the king, and his interactions with her emphasize her royal position.

Esther as Writer

The developing portraits of royal authority as seen in the book's primary characters subtly comment on the authority of written texts. References to writing and written texts proliferate in the book of Esther as in few other biblical books, beginning with the story's first dramatic scene. Vashti's expulsion from her position coincides with the first mention of a royal order from the king, to be "written among the laws of the Persians and the Medes so that it may not be altered" (Esth 1:19). Writing codifies and reifies a royal command into an immutable law. When Haman wishes to insure the destruction of the Jews, he asks, "Let it be written to destroy them . . ." (3:9, author's trans.). After a law is crafted, it is sent with haste throughout the kingdom. When Ahasuerus institutes a new law in reaction to Vashti's insubordination, he sends "letters to all the royal provinces, to every province in its own script and to every people in its own language, declaring that every man should be master in his own house" (Esth 1:22).[10] Notification of the law is distributed throughout the reaches of the empire by letters sent in the language of every region; writing thus allows for wide distribution of royal mandates, even if they are publicized orally when they arrive at their destinations. The same wide-reaching, multilingual publication also characterizes Haman's edict (3:12). Similarly, when Mordecai issues the counteredict allowing the Jews of Susa to defend themselves against the attacks instigated by Haman, the text advises, "A copy of the writ was to be issued as a decree in every province and published to all peoples, and the Jews were to be ready on that day to take revenge on their enemies" (8:13). Most of the texts described in the book of Esther, including the one Esther writes (9:29), fall into this category of public imperial edict: a text widely distributed with implications for the entire kingdom.

The book of Esther also repeatedly emphasizes the immutability of Persian law. Writing has a long-standing reputation, including within the Bible itself, as a means of securing permanence for a law, an idea, a prophecy, or a story.[11] With that sense of permanence comes authority: a perception that once an idea is written down, it becomes less contestable, less subject to either shifting memories or changing wills. In Esther, the act of writing a rule into the law books renders it unalterable. Marking the law as "irrevocable" seeks to collapse the distance between the text and its enactment; it is an attempt to shut down the act of interpretation. The textuality of Persia, so says the story, sees the king's power, the written text, and the law's implementation as all coequal, instantaneous, and secure: the ultimate manifestation of authorial intent.[12]

Yet Esther herself has already begun to destabilize royal notions of irrevocable law. In what has come to be her signature line, Esther decides, "After that I will go to the king, though it is against the law; and if I perish, I perish" (4:16b). In this moment, Esther becomes a reader. She acknowledges that the king's power is not wholly embodied in the written law. She has the power either to capitulate to its ideas or to imagine something new— namely, that the king might not act in accordance with the law. We have seen above that Esther's decision to enter the king's court uninvited was an assertion of her monarchic power; as she entered the king's palace, she "put on royalty." Even as she avails herself of her power—both her official royal power and that preternatural power that charms eunuchs and kings alike— she destabilizes that power. If the king's law can be disobeyed, her laws can be, too. At the moment of the greatest embrace of royal power is also the greatest disavowal of it.

After Haman is hanged (7:10), the narrative describes the transfer of power from Haman to Esther and Mordecai: "On that day King Ahasuerus gave to Queen Esther the house of Haman, the enemy of the Jews; and

Mordecai came before the king, for Esther had told what he was to her. Then the king took off his signet ring, which he had taken from Haman, and gave it to Mordecai. So Esther set Mordecai over the house of Haman" (8:1-2). At the center of the power transfer is the king's signet ring, in which royal authority and written authority converge. The power that once belonged to Haman now belongs to Mordecai and Esther. In the book of Esther's depiction of the Persian Empire, that power is the power to write. But Esther's own defiance has demonstrated the tenuousness of that power.

The production of texts continues at a quick pace throughout the rest of Esther. Mordecai issues a counteredict to Haman's script (8:9-14) after Ahasuerus declares to him and to Esther, "You may write as you please with regard to the Jews, in the name of the king, and seal it with the king's ring; for an edict written in the name of the king and sealed with the king's ring cannot be revoked" (8:8). The irony is thick; Mordecai and Esther issue a new irrevocable order that, in effect, revokes the first order, thereby illustrating that neither text is in fact irrevocable. Royal, written power continues to be destabilized.

At Esther's request, Ahasuerus issues yet another decree, this one extending the power of the Jews to kill their enemies for another day and ordering the hanging of Haman's ten sons (9:13-15). Then Mordecai and Esther write documents that establish the festival of Purim. Despite the agency Esther has had in the production of many of the foregoing documents, it is only in the last few verses of the book that we encounter her writing directly: "And Queen Esther, daughter of Abihail, wrote with all authority, along with Mordecai the Jew, to establish this second letter of Purim" (9:29, author's trans.). Unlike in the story of Jezebel, the letter Esther writes is not recounted here, but rather the fact and purpose of her having written. When, at Esth 9:32, the practices of Purim are described as having been written, the reader who has journeyed through the book of Esther recognizes their permanence and authority. Though they are not among the laws of the Medes and the Persians, the Purim regulations have nonetheless been irrevocably secured by having been written: "The command of Queen Esther fixed these practices of Purim, and it was recorded in writing" (9:32). Moreover, the weight of Esther's royal authority stands behind them; they should be implemented as much because of who she is as because of what they say. And yet, precisely because they are written, they become subject to interpretation; their power lies with their readers. The text, having been written, becomes at once authoritative and destabilized.

Jezebel

Jezebel's act of writing occurs within the story of Naboth's vineyard in 1 Kgs 21. Like Esther, Jezebel writes from a position of royal authority. Unlike Esther, however, the biblical text never describes her with the title "queen," referring to her instead by name, by the appellation "his [Ahab's] wife," or with a nod to her royal Phoenician parentage. Despite the lack of overt recognition of her title in the text, Jezebel uses her monarchic power even more effectively than her husband Ahab does. When Ahab sulks over Naboth's refusal to sell or trade his vineyard, Jezebel asks Ahab, "Do you now exercise kingship over Israel?" (1 Kgs 21:7a, author's trans.).[13] Her question challenges Ahab's exercise of monarchic control. Inherent in the question is an assumption that kings, by virtue of their title, may take whatever they wish and need not rely on law or custom to dictate their behavior.[14] Samuel's warning that kings *take* (1 Sam 8:11-17) looms over this episode. By not taking Naboth's vineyard outright, Ahab fails to act like a king.[15] When Jezebel orchestrates the seizure of Naboth's vineyard, she embraces the raw power afforded her by her royal position.

In order to deliver the vineyard to Ahab, Jezebel writes. "So she wrote letters in Ahab's name and sealed them with his seal; she sent the letters to the elders and the nobles who lived with Naboth in his city" (1 Kgs 21:8). The seal of the king carries the requisite authority. In fact, if Jezebel were to give her directives orally rather than in writing, perhaps her authority would not be heeded. With Ahab's seal—that is, specifically with a written text—Jezebel's identity is concealed, but her own wishes are communicated. Jezebel must borrow Ahab's titular power, but she supplies all the necessary initiative.

The letters instruct the elders and nobles to find two witnesses to bring a charge of blasphemy and treason against Naboth and then immediately to stone him to death. If securing the false charge is meant to provide a ruse of "due process," it is a disguise easily unmasked. Deuteronomic law's requirement for two witnesses rather than one (Deut 19:15) is fulfilled, but the witnesses are "scoundrels" (lit. "sons of worthlessness"). Jezebel's letters imagine no discussion, no judicial inquiry, no interpretation of the accusation once it has been made: "[S]eat two scoundrels opposite him, and have them bring a charge against him, saying, 'You have cursed God and the king.' Then take him out, and stone him to death" (21:10). It is as if the accusatory utterance is self-executing.

Kings presents the text of Jezebel's letters with a convention used to introduce reported speech: "She wrote in the letters, *saying*." The verb translated here as "saying" (*le'mor*) is often left untranslated since it functions almost like an opening quotation mark. Thus, what follows is meant to be the body of the letter: "Proclaim a fast, and seat Naboth at the head of the assembly; seat two scoundrels opposite him, and have them bring a charge against him, saying, 'You have cursed God and the king.' Then take him out, and stone him to death" (1 Kgs 21:9-10). This is Jezebel's text; within the presentation of Jezebel's story in the Hebrew Bible, this is what Jezebel wrote.

To say that the book of Kings "preserves" the text of Jezebel's letter would be an overstatement. Preservation implies some sort of historical existence, and, barring the unlikely unearthing of some as yet unknown archaeological find, it is impossible to know what part of the story, if any has any grounding in historical fact. Regardless, the inclusion of the text of Jezebel's command produces the rhetorical effect of showing how tightly the implementation of the plan corresponds to its proposal: "The men of his city, the elders and the nobles who lived in his city, did as Jezebel had sent word to them. Just as it was written in the letters that she had sent to them, they proclaimed a fast and seated Naboth at the head of the assembly. The two scoundrels came in and sat opposite him; and the scoundrels brought a charge against Naboth, in the presence of the people, saying, 'Naboth cursed God and the king.' So they took him outside the city, and stoned him to death" (1 Kgs 21:11-13). Their actions correspond word for word with Jezebel's commands in her letter. The text imagines no room for interpretation, no possibility of refusal, no debating the merits of the commands, no weighing their consequences; the men comply without hesitation. In the same way that the scoundrels' accusation is without an interpretive hearing, so too are Jezebel's letters imagined as self-actualizing. While a letter cannot physically kill Naboth without human agency, once it is written, it is as good as enacted; at least, that is what the text would have us believe. Jezebel's letter barely needs a reader at all.

And yet, Jezebel's letter *does* need a reader. No matter how much the text tries to present the death of Naboth as Jezebel's work alone, it could not have happened without the elders' and nobles' reading, interpreting, and acting. In the same way, the scoundrels' accusation must have been read and interpreted, even if Jezebel's letter makes no provision for it and the text of 1 Kings does not acknowledge it. John D. Caputo reminds us,

"The idea of a self-interpreting text makes no sense, since texts are texts only because they operate in the absence of their authors."[16] When Jezebel writes the letters, she releases them from her creative grip and places them into the interpretive grip of their readers. The letters do nothing until they have been read. Compliance, refusal, and every interpretation in between become available; even this most seemingly determined of texts is ultimately indeterminate.

In her 1994 presidential address to the Society of Biblical Literature, Phyllis Trible demonstrated how the interpretive act provides resistance to even the most seemingly intractable texts: in this case, the stories of Jezebel and Elijah in 1 Kgs 17–18.[17] In the tightly crafted narrative, Jezebel and Elijah are antithetical characters in almost every way: "She is female and foreign; he, male and native. She comes from the coastlands; he, from the highlands. She thrives in a sea climate; he, in a desert climate. She belongs to husband and father; he, neither to wife nor father. She embodies royalty; he, prophecy. Both bear theophoric names that unite them in opposition: Jezebel the Baal worshiper and Elijah the YHWH worshiper."[18] As these antitheses play out in the narrative, they deepen, all to further the polemical agenda of demonizing Jezebel. When Elijah is fed by the Sidonian widow, for example, that woman becomes a foil for Jezebel, since the widow is a Phoenician woman who will confess Elijah's God.[19]

Nevertheless, as Trible's analysis shows, the same antithetical parallels that attempt to erase any positive characteristics of Jezebel's character also keep Jezebel ever present, a constant shadow behind and sometimes over Elijah. When Elijah draws attention to the hundreds of prophets who eat at Jezebel's table, he succeeds not only in expressing his disdain but also in illustrating her power: the number of prophets testifies to her "religious zeal"; their presence at her and not Ahab's table "suggests her economic independence as well as her abundant resources."[20] The story of Naboth's vineyard similarly undercuts the narrative's negative portrayal. At the same time Jezebel is antithesis of Elijah and epitome of monarchic ruthlessness, she is also an ideal wife à la Prov 31. Devoted to her husband, "she considers a field and possesses it; with the fruit of her hands she secures a vineyard" (31:16).[21]

The history of interpretation surrounding Jezebel has not looked upon her with favor. Most interpreters have affirmed, to a greater or lesser extent, the narrative's hatred of her.[22] Yet Trible's analysis shows that alternative readings are possible, even for this most reviled of characters and even in a text as polemical as Kings. Like Jezebel herself, the Deuteronomistic authors try to set up one way to read these stories, but everything the narrative tries to communicate about her simultaneously communicates its undoing. The power of the reader persists.

Conclusions

A close look at Esther and Jezebel as women writers does not lead us to an authoritative paradigm describing how women wrote in the ancient Near East, nor does it give us a clear prescription for how women biblical interpreters should write now. Esther and Jezebel write because they have monarchic authority. There is nothing inherently liberating in the fact that these two female biblical characters write; in fact, both women embrace their powerful roles in established imperial modes that perpetuate oppression. Their status as queens gives them the opportunity to write, the means to write, and even the reasons to write. Both queens write in imperatives, communicating the will of their offices to their subjects outside the palace gates. Their texts are neither narrative nor poetic nor revelatory. If we readers come to the Hebrew Bible looking for romantic accounts of women writing breathtaking fiction, poetry, or theology, we must be disappointed.

And yet, both Esther and Jezebel help us see that ancient women, those in the biblical text as well as those behind it, made the most of the power available to them. Though their authority may have been mediated by their husband-kings, "they handled pens and paper and seals; they imagined audiences; they were read."[23] Perhaps when we read the Bible, women—nameless, unnoticed, uncredited women—are *being read*, and we shall never know it. But if their work is lost to the passive voice, ours persists in the active voice: we *read*. Every time we read, we open the possibility that texts long used to silence and oppress can and will be used to liberate. When she chooses to approach the king uninvited, Esther, too, is a reader. She refuses to capitulate to the idea that a text can be read one way alone. The stories of Esther and Jezebel become not just stories about women writing but also stories about women—and men—reading. The act of writing may change the law, but readers as much as writers imbue the text with authority.

The power of the reader gives both hope and responsibility to contemporary readers of this ancient text. Bal writes, "For if reading is the only way to blow life into the dead letter of the text, and if, moreover, reading is a matter of historical importance, then Esther becomes a mirror for the contemporary critic. Like her, exposing the abuse of power, the danger of writing, and the instability of subjectivity, the critic can escape neither the responsibility for her activity nor the encapsulation of that activity in historically diverse, subjectless writing."[24] The Bible is not automatically oppressive or liberating; it requires good readers—many readers, diverse readers—to manifest its multiple meanings.

In a world where the Bible itself continues to be used both to liberate and to oppress, the indeterminacy of the text is actually good news. As Timothy K. Beal describes, "Hope emerges here, on political grounds, in the affirmation not that history is ultimately determined, but that it can never be determined and is always open to subversion, precisely because it cannot contain and control otherness."[25] If we are to ask, "Who wrote the Bible?" we must also ask, "Who is reading the Bible?" The Holy Spirit blows through the reading of these Scriptures, not just the writing of them. In the persistence of that Spirit, there is hope.

For Further Reading

Beach, Eleanor Ferris. *The Jezebel Letters: Religion and Politics in Ninth-Century Israel*. Minneapolis: Fortress, 2005.

Beal, Timothy K. *The Book of Hiding: Gender, Ethnicity, Annihilation, and Esther*. Biblical Limits. London: Routledge, 1997.

Niditch, Susan. *Oral World and Written Word: Ancient Israelite Literature*. Library of Ancient Israel. Louisville, Ky.: Westminster John Knox, 1996.

Schniedewind, William M. *How the Bible Became a Book: The Textualization of Ancient Israel*. Cambridge: Cambridge University Press, 2004.

CHAPTER 9

MIRIAM, MOSES, AND AARON IN NUMBERS 12 AND 20
A Feminist Biblical Theology Concerning Exclusion

Suzanne Boorer

Numbers 12 and 20:1-12 both concern the three leaders of the wilderness generation—Miriam, Moses, and Aaron. At the heart of both lie stories, variously nuanced, involving insider/outsider motifs. Most obviously, in Num 12 Miriam becomes a temporary outsider both physically and socially, whereas Moses, as the speaker of God's word, is portrayed as the ultimate insider. Aaron, who is closely associated with Moses, retains his insider status, despite having acted with Miriam in challenging Moses about his foreign wife, who is another potential outsider. In Num 20:1-12, all three leaders become outsiders in relation to the promised land: Miriam dies outside the land, and Moses and Aaron are told they will be stripped of their leadership roles and will die without entering the land.

This essay will set these two texts in dialogue with each other, taking into account issues regarding the history of the formation of these passages.[1] Whether Num 12 is to be seen as earlier or later than Num 20:1-12 will be considered, as well as how interpretation of these texts, and how various characters' shifts between outsider and insider status, are nuanced, depending on which passage is viewed as a later comment on the other. Setting these texts in a dialogical relationship will yield insights concerning the various nuances in meaning of, and shifts between, the insider/outsider status of these leaders, and the reasons for these. These stories will inform theological reflection regarding issues of power in relation to insider and outsider status, a problem critical for women as well as for others who have found themselves standing outside of circles of power.

Numbers 12:1-16 and Numbers 20:1-12

First I will outline the features of each passage. Numbers 12 is an enigmatic text:

> While they were at Hazeroth, Miriam and Aaron spoke against Moses because of the Cushite woman whom he had married (for he had indeed married a Cushite woman); [2]and they said, "Has the LORD spoken only through Moses? Has he not spoken through us also?" And the LORD heard it. [3]Now the man Moses was very humble, more so than anyone else on the face of the earth. [4]Suddenly the LORD said to Moses, Aaron, and Miriam, "Come out, you three, to the tent of meeting." So the three of them came out. [5]Then the LORD came down in a pillar of cloud, and stood at the entrance of the tent, and called Aaron and Miriam; and they both came forward. [6]And he said, "Hear my words:
>
> > When there are prophets among you,
> >   I the LORD make myself known to them in visions;
> >   I speak to them in dreams.
> > [7]Not so with my servant Moses;
> >   he is entrusted with all my house.
> > [8]With him I speak face to face [lit., 'mouth to mouth,' peh 'el-peh]
> >   —clearly, not in riddles;
> >   and he beholds the form of the LORD.
>
> Why then were you not afraid to speak against my servant Moses?" [9]And the anger of the LORD was kindled against them, and he departed.
>
> [10]When the cloud went away from over the tent, Miriam had become leprous, as white as snow. And Aaron turned towards Miriam and saw that she was leprous. [11]Then Aaron said to Moses, "Oh, my lord, do not punish us for a sin that we have so foolishly committed. [12]Do not let her be like one stillborn, whose flesh is half consumed when it comes out of its mother's womb." [13]And Moses cried to the LORD, "O God, please heal her." [14]But the LORD said to Moses, "If her father had but spit in her face, would she not bear her shame for seven days? Let her be shut out of the camp for seven days, and after that she may be brought in again." [15]So Miriam was shut out of the camp for seven days; and the people did not set out on the march until Miriam had been brought in again. [16]After that the people set out from Hazeroth, and camped in the wilderness of Paran.

The initial challenge to Moses by Miriam[2] and Aaron is two pronged: They "speak against" (*dbr b-*) Moses because of his foreign wife,[3] herself a potential outsider. They challenge Moses' unique status in relation to YHWH's word (emphasized by *raq 'akh*, "only"), claiming that YHWH also "speaks through" (*dbr b-*) them. This is clearly an attempt to gain insider status alongside Moses as speakers of YHWH's word. With Moses' extreme humility duly noted, YHWH, in response, comes down to the tent of meeting outside the camp and, ironically, speaks to Aaron[4] (this time mentioned first) and Miriam, but not Moses, though he is present. YHWH asserts that, in contrast to any prophet with whom YHWH communicates in a vision or a dream, with Moses the servant who is entrusted with[5] all his house, YHWH speaks (*dbr b-*) clearly, indeed "mouth to mouth" (*peh 'el-peh*). Moses is, therefore, the insider par excellence in relation to YHWH's word, against which Aaron and Miriam should have been afraid to speak. YHWH's anger against Aaron and Miriam results, with YHWH's departure (repeated twice in vv. 9, 10), in Miriam's becoming leprous "like snow."[6] Thereby, Miriam is shown to be an outsider, both physically and in relation to any status to which she might have aspired as spokesperson for YHWH. Aaron escapes this punishment, even though he was complicit with Miriam in sin and was, like her, the object of YHWH's rebuttal and anger. Unlike Miriam, he does not become an outsider. For the modern reader, the unfairness of this clearly becomes a feminist issue.[7]

In interceding with Moses for Miriam, Aaron now subordinates himself to Moses, addressing him as "my lord." By his submissive association with Moses, he reinforces his insider status, which in challenging Moses' unique oracular status he had potentially put in doubt. In turn, Moses' intercession for Miriam is effective, reinforcing his insider status as the prophet par excellence. As a result, Miriam's extreme outsider status, pictured in Aaron's petition to Moses in terms of a dead fetus ("one stillborn"), is tempered, but her shame and temporary exclusion from the camp still mark her as an outsider for seven days.

There are tensions in Num 12 that have led some scholars to view it as having originally been two stories joined together: an earlier one concerning Miriam's objections to Moses' foreign wife (basically, vv. 1, 10-15) and a later one concerning Moses' oracular status (basically, vv. 2-9). The subject of the foreign wife seems simply to fade out, with no reference to her in the rest of the text. Verse 2 switches to the issue of oracular speech, to which YHWH's speech responds explicitly. The order of Miriam's and Aaron's

names differs in verses 1 and 5. And although Aaron is complicit with Miriam, and along with her is the object of YHWH's rebuttal and anger, only
Miriam is punished.

Yet there are plenty of signs of unity binding the rather disparate motifs
together. For example, the plural verb in verse 2 presupposes both Miriam
and Aaron. Aaron's acknowledgment of guilt with Miriam in verse 11 refers
back to verse 1. And the repetition of the expression *dbr b-* in verses 1, 2,
6, and 8, with its varying nuances, seems to play a unifying role.[8] For these
reasons we will treat the chapter as a literary unity.[9]

Numbers 20:1-12 also contains tensions. In this case it seems there is an
underlying coherent story to which verses have been added that for the most
part echo Exod 17:1-17, harmonizing two texts that both concern the miracle
of water from the rock. These latter verses in Numbers muddy the waters, so
to speak. So it is the underlying coherent story, comprising Num 20:1, 2, 3b,
4, 6, 7, 8*,[10] 10, 11b, 12,[11] that will form the focus of our discussion and be set
in dialogue with Num 12. Here is the modified passage:

> The Israelites, the whole congregation, came into the wilderness of Zin
> in the first month, and the people stayed in Kadesh. Miriam died there,
> and was buried there.
>
> [2]Now there was no water for the congregation; so they gathered
> together against Moses and against Aaron, [3]. . . and said, "Would that
> we had died when our kindred died before the LORD! [4]Why have you
> brought the assembly of the LORD into this wilderness for us and our
> livestock to die here?" . . . [6]Then Moses and Aaron went away from the
> assembly to the entrance of the tent of meeting; they fell on their faces,
> and the glory of the LORD appeared to them. [7]The LORD spoke to
> Moses, saying: [8]. . . [A]ssemble the congregation, you and your brother
> Aaron, and command [*dbr 'l*] the rock before their eyes to yield its
> water. . . . [10]Moses and Aaron gathered the assembly together before the
> rock, and he said to them, "Listen, you rebels, shall we bring water for
> you out of this rock?" [11]. . . [And] water came out abundantly, and the
> congregation and their livestock drank. [12]But the LORD said to Moses
> and Aaron, "Because you did not trust in me, to show my holiness before
> the eyes of the Israelites, therefore you shall not bring this assembly into
> the land that I have given them."

In this passage, Miriam dies and is buried.[12] The people gather against
Moses and Aaron because there is no water. YHWH appears at the tent
of meeting, within the camp[13] but away from the people, and tells Moses
and Aaron in private to speak to *the rock* before the eyes of the people so

that it will yield its water. Instead, Moses speaks to *the people*, accusing them of being rebels and asking, "Shall *we* bring water for you out of this rock?" Water gushes out of the rock. To the people, who were not privy to YHWH's command to Moses and Aaron, it seems that it is Moses and Aaron that have accomplished this. Consequently, YHWH pronounces judgment on Moses and Aaron, saying that because they did not trust YHWH to show YHWH's holiness before the eyes of the people, they will not lead them into the promised land.[14] So all three wilderness leaders— Miriam, Aaron, and Moses—die as outsiders to the promised land.

Whether Num 12 is perceived as written earlier or later than Num 20:1-12 affects the interpretation of these texts, since whichever passage is viewed as having been inserted later can be interpreted as a comment on the earlier story. The shifting insider/outsider status of the three leaders will differ accordingly. The choice also affects intertextual interpretation: if Num 12 is perceived to be relatively late, a wider range of texts can be drawn on to interpret it than if it is perceived as relatively early.

Traditionally, Num 12 has been seen as earlier than Num 20:1-12, but, more recently, the reverse has been suggested. Coming to a firm decision on this is difficult, particularly since each position operates with different assumptions regarding the composition of texts.[15] In the discussion that follows, I will explore both possibilities.

First Alternative: Numbers 12 as Earlier Than Numbers 20:1-12

If Num 12 is seen as earlier than Num 20:1-12, what interpretive nuances emerge? In this case, the parallel texts traditionally seen as earlier than or contemporary with Num 12 are as follows:

+ Exod 33:7-11, which describes Moses' practice of consulting with God at the tent of meeting;
+ Exod 4:16 and 15:20, which refer to Aaron's and Miriam's leadership roles, he as Moses' "mouth," and she as a prophet;
+ Exod 32, the story of the golden calf; and
+ Num 11:14-17, 24b-30, the story of the appointing of seventy elders to assist Moses in leadership.

These texts, like Num 12, are all non-Priestly and traditionally seen as earlier than the Priestly texts such as Num 20:1-12. When Num 12 is interpreted in light of these texts, prophetic motifs in particular are highlighted and nuanced.

First, the tent of meeting outside the camp, as the place to which YHWH comes down to speak in Num 12:4-5, is highlighted, since this an important motif also in Exod 33:7-9 and Num 11:16, 17, 25. That YHWH speaks only to Moses in these latter passages, but to Aaron and Miriam in Num 12:4-5, sharpens the inherent irony of Miriam's and Aaron's assertion that YHWH speaks also through them. However, YHWH's disappearance after speaking to them in Num 12:10 has no parallel in the other two episodes. Its explicit link with the appearance of Miriam's leprosy suggests that YHWH cannot be in proximity to someone with this disease.

Second, the expression of Moses' unique oracular status and relationship with YHWH, who speaks to Moses "mouth to mouth," is highlighted in light of the reference to YHWH's speaking to Moses "face to face" (*panim 'el-panim*) in Exod 33:11.[16] Although similar in meaning, "mouth to mouth" accentuates the direct speech between YHWH and Moses, ensuring that Moses' words are precisely YHWH's,[17] not the indirect revelation other prophets receive.

Third, if the story is read in light of Exod 4:16 and 15:20, it is Aaron's and Miriam's roles as prophets that underlie their claims that YHWH has spoken through them: in Exod 15:20 Miriam is called a "prophetess," and in Exod 4:16 Aaron is to serve as Moses' "mouth"—which interplays with YHWH's "mouth to mouth" speaking with Moses in Num 12:8. However, given that in Exod 4:16 Moses is to serve as God to Aaron, it is clear that in seeking to claim equal status with Moses in Num 12:2, Aaron has overstepped the boundaries of his position. Accordingly, in confessing their sin, Aaron reverts to his subordinate role, treating Moses as God by interceding with him and addressing him as "my lord." Moses then demonstrates his special prophetic status by successfully interceding with God. Therefore, when situated in relation to these texts, Num 12 appears concerned with conflict among prophets.

Fourth, prophetic motifs within Num 12 are further highlighted when it is interpreted in relation to Num 11:14-17, 24b-30. There, Moses' prophetic spirit is shared with others, and Moses expresses the wish that all YHWH's people would be prophets (11:29). Such a wish on Moses' part makes the question of Miriam and Aaron in Num 12:2 more understandable. But Num 12 goes on to correct the possible implication of Num 11 that others might be on an equal footing with Moses. Moreover, Miriam's leprosy, when set in relation to these texts, is not particularly highlighted, since the Priestly laws in Lev 13–14 would not yet have become part of the pentateuchal account. Rather, what comes to the fore is her exclusion from the camp, likened to the shame of a daughter whose father had spat on her. Miriam's exclusion is related to her claim in verse 2 that YHWH speaks through her and that she is a prophet on par with Moses.[18]

Finally, Exod 32 could be used to help illuminate the inequity of Aaron's lack of punishment in Num 12. In both stories Aaron sins and is called to account but is not punished, though others are (the people in Exod 32, Miriam in Num 12). In Num 12, he at least admits his sin, which he does not in Exod 32. Escaping punishment twice, Aaron continues, inexplicitly, to live a charmed life.

In terms of insider/outsider motifs, what is primarily highlighted is Moses as the prophet par excellence who is uniquely an insider because of his special relationship with God. His speech is God's speech, and only he can intercede with God. Aaron is an ambiguous figure. Though complicit with Miriam, he is not punished with outsider status. Rather, he reverts to his proper subordinate role, treating Moses like God. Miriam is the outsider, punished and situated outside the camp for a period of time for seeking to make herself equal to Moses.

Ironically, YHWH's intermittent appearance occurs at the tent of meeting outside the camp, where Miriam in her punishment is situated. Yet since the text makes quite clear that YHWH has withdrawn from her, it cannot be said that Miriam is closer to YHWH outside the camp. Rather, it could be argued that the symbolism of being outside the camp, for YHWH on the one hand and for Miriam on the other, is completely opposite: the location preserves God's transcendence and separation from the day-to-day existence of the people, while for Miriam it signifies shame and social isolation.

Numbers 20:1-12 as a Comment on Numbers 12

Setting Num 12, nuanced in this way, in dialogue with Num 20:1-12, perceived as later, reveals the following:

The features common to the two texts, interpreted in this way, are the appearance of YHWH in relation to the tent of meeting in order to speak (Num 20:6; see 12:4-5), and the relationship between YHWH's speech and Moses' speech (Num 20:7-8a*, 10; see 12:8).

In Num 20:6, YHWH appears at the tent of meeting (here inside the camp, as in all Priestly texts, but away from the assembly) to speak to Moses, with Aaron present, whereas in Num 12:4-5, YHWH appears at the tent of meeting outside the camp to speak with Aaron and Miriam, with

Moses present. In stark contrast to YHWH's claim of speaking with Moses "mouth to mouth" in Num 12:8, implying that Moses' words are inevitably YHWH's, YHWH's instructions to Moses and Aaron in Num 20:8 are disobeyed by Moses: instead of speaking to *the rock* to yield its water, he speaks to *the people*, calling them rebels and saying, "Shall *we* bring water for you out of this rock?" Moses' words are certainly not YHWH's words here. Moses, the prophet par excellence of Num 12, has disobeyed YHWH precisely in relation to the words he speaks.

Not only this, but the content of Moses' words shows that Moses, who with his "we" includes Aaron, is indeed usurping YHWH's place, pointing to himself and Aaron as the water's source. Since the people were not privy to YHWH's command, which was given privately to Moses and Aaron, they would have attributed to them the water that appears from the rock. Moses, the prophet par excellence with whom YHWH speaks mouth to mouth, has now not only disobeyed YHWH but sought to elevate himself even higher than his status as YHWH's confidant, usurping the very role of YHWH. In so doing he acts in stark contrast to his description in Num 12:3 as extremely humble. Aaron and Miriam had tried to elevate their statuses as prophets. But Moses' sin is worse, for he seeks not only to be equal to, but to replace, YHWH.

Accordingly, this sin is described in Num 20:12 as not trusting in (*'mn, hiphil*) YHWH to show YHWH's holiness before the people. This plays on, and negates, YHWH's description of Moses as "entrusted with [*'mn b-, niphal*] all my house" in Num 12:7. In Num 20:1-2, Moses attacks the people—accusing them of being rebels in his own words, not in words that have come from YHWH—and presents himself and Aaron to them as performing the very role of YHWH. Correspondingly, Moses is stripped of his leadership role, no longer entrusted with guiding the people into the promised land. The punishment fits the crime. The picture of Moses in Num 12 as the humble prophet par excellence and servant of YHWH, entrusted with guiding YHWH's people, is entirely reversed in Num 20:1-2.

Aaron continues his self-subordination to Moses in Num 20:1-2. This choice is a positive thing in Num 12. But as a figure subordinated to Moses in Num 20:1-2, Aaron is by default caught in Moses' sin and is therefore included in YHWH's accusation. Aaron, once complicit with Miriam in trying to elevate their prophetic statuses as equal to that of Moses, now becomes complicit with Moses in a greater sin than his initial one—that is, Moses' elevating his status above YHWH's. Accordingly, Aaron receives the same punishment as Moses: he will not lead the people into the promised land but will die outside it. The sin of Moses and Aaron in Num 20:1-12 is worse than that of Miriam and Aaron in Num 12; therefore, their punishment, the stripping of their leadership and death outside the land, is worse than that of Miriam's temporary exclusion from the camp. However, since Miriam's death is announced in this same chapter, it is clear that Miriam's exclusion from the camp foreshadowed her death in the wilderness outside the land, along with the deaths of Moses and Aaron.

In terms of insider/outsider motifs, when Num 20:1-12 is seen as later than Num 12 and a comment on it, Moses the insider par excellence, as prophet and leader of the people, becomes the opposite, the outsider par excellence, losing his leadership role and dying outside the promised land. Aaron, initially a potential outsider, becomes an insider subordinated to Moses. Ironically, this leads him to become an outsider with Moses, sharing Moses' fate outside the land. Miriam's exclusion from the camp, even though temporary, is a proleptic symbol of her outsider status, which is completed when she dies outside the land.

Second Alternative: Numbers 12 as Perceived as
Later Than Numbers 20:1-12

If Num 12 is seen as later than Num 20:1-12, other interpretive nuances emerge. A wider group of parallel texts can be drawn in to illuminate Num 12. Besides those mentioned earlier, we can now include some later passages that bring out new dimensions over and above the features already highlighted, whose insights will be presupposed in the discussion that follows:

- Deut 34:10, which describes Moses as the incomparable prophet, whom YHWH knows face to face;
- Deut 7:3 and Ezra 9–10, two passages prohibiting marriage to foreign women;
- Num 26:59 and 1 Chr 6:3, which explicitly portray Moses, Aaron, and Miriam as siblings;
- Exod 7:1; Exod 28–29; and Lev 8, three Priestly texts concerning Aaron's role and title; and
- Lev 13–14 (esp. 13:4-5, 46; 14:8), Priestly laws concerning skin diseases.

These texts are thought to be either Priestly (as is Num 20:1-12) or later than the Priestly material (that is, post-Priestly). Interpreted alongside of Num 12, they suggest the following.

First, Deut 34:10, speaking of Moses' incomparability, underscores the motif of Moses as the prophet par excellence.

Second, in light of Deut 7:3 and Ezra 9–10, which prohibit marriage to foreign women, the objection of Miriam and Aaron to Moses' Cushite wife comes into sharp relief.[19] Over against the stance portrayed in these other passages, Moses' marriage here legitimates such marriages in the strongest terms. Her status is further reinforced through Miriam's punishment for opposing her, in which Miriam becomes the outsider instead.

Third, the portrayal of Moses, Aaron, and Miriam as siblings in Num 26:59 and 1 Chr 6:3 adds yet another dimension to the interpretation of Num 12.[20] This allows for a further interpretation of the motivation for Miriam and Aaron to speak against Moses over his foreign wife (Num 12:1): family conflict and household power relations.

Fourth, Aaron's roles in Exod 7:1 as a prophet to Moses and in Exod 28–29 and Lev 8 as high priest bring further interpretive nuances to light in Num 12. Exodus 7:1 reinforces Aaron's subordinate prophetic role in relation to Moses. But the conflict becomes one between priest and prophet, between Aaron as the high priest and Moses as the prophet par excellence. When Aaron as high priest subordinates himself to Moses in Num 12, his high priestly role is clearly subordinated to the unique prophetic role of Moses.[21] Moreover, Aaron's high priestly role explains why Aaron is not punished with leprosy as Miriam is: it would not do for the high priest to become polluted, not only because he then would be unable to function as a priest (see Lev 22:4), but more importantly because in the Priestly material Aaron is "the paradigmatic priestly figure, the one from whom all priestly lineage descended."[22] Aaron's high priestly role, therefore, protects him from becoming an outsider. (It also sheds light on Aaron's diagnosing Miriam's leprosy, since this was a priestly function.)

Fifth, situating Num 12 in relation to the Priestly purity laws, especially in relation to the laws concerning skin diseases in Lev 13–14, not only brings to light why Aaron escapes the punishment of leprosy but also highlights and brings an added nuance to Miriam's punishment, Aaron's description of her state, and her seven days of exclusion from the camp. Aaron's description of Miriam as a dead fetus images Miriam as polluted in multiple ways—not only in terms of her disease (see Lev 13–14), but in terms of the pollutions of childbirth (see Lev 12) and death (see Num 5:2).[23] According to these laws, Miriam would be excluded from the camp by definition (see Lev 13:46; Num 5:2), the paradigmatic outsider.[24]

In light of the laws in Lev 13–14, Miriam's exclusion for seven days suggests that Moses' intercession heals her leprosy since, according to Lev 14:8, a person who is healed still undergoes seven days of ritual purification before returning to the camp. This further enhances the efficacy of Moses' intercession and therefore his status as the prophet par excellence.

Furthermore, in light of the purity laws in Lev 13–14, the reason for the explicit reference to YHWH's departure becomes clear. The unclean cannot be in geographical proximity to YHWH (the holy God); indeed, this is the reason why those with leprosy are excluded from the camp. However, here we come up against an anomaly. Though the explicit reference to YHWH's appearance at the tent of meeting in Num 12 is outside the camp, the Priestly purity laws of Lev 13–14 assume that YHWH's tent of meeting, signaling divine presence, stands at the center of the camp (see Exod 25–30; 31–35; Num 2). Thus, in Num 12, as interpreted as relatively late, YHWH's presence is both within and outside the camp.[25] YHWH can speak to Aaron and Miriam at the tent of meeting outside the camp (12:5-8), and Moses can speak to God, implicitly within the camp (12:13). Miriam's exclusion from the camp could suggest that she is as close to YHWH outside the camp as those inside are.[26] But the text makes quite clear that Miriam and YHWH are not in each other's vicinity by repeatedly stating that YHWH departed.

In terms of insider/outsider motifs, Moses as the insider is heightened even further, and the efficacy of his intercession clarified. Moses' marriage to the foreign woman has made her, the stereotypical outsider, into an insider. In contrast to the foreign wife, Moses' sister Miriam becomes the outsider in a heightened way through both exclusion from the camp and leprosy described as triple pollution. Aaron the high priest, despite his actions, cannot become an outsider like Miriam, for he cannot become unclean.

Numbers 12 as a Comment on Numbers 20:1-12

Seeing Num 12, nuanced in this way, as later commentary on Num 20:1-12 reveals the following insights:

Numbers 12 reinstates Moses as the prophet par excellence, whose words are the very words of God. The Moses who did not speak as YHWH commanded him at the edge of the land is now the incomparable prophet to whom YHWH speaks "mouth to mouth," whose words are only YHWH's words. The Moses who did not trust in YHWH is now YHWH's servant who is "entrusted with all my house" (12:7). The Moses who attacked the people as rebels is responsible for the people's care. The Moses who tried to usurp YHWH's role is humbler than anyone else on earth. All the ways in which Moses sinned in Num 20:1-12 are reversed in Num 12, which acts as a corrective.

But why is Num 12 placed where it is, since it might be expected that, as such, it would come sequentially after Num 20:1-12? Its placement shortly after the Sinai material in which YHWH gives the laws through Moses is significant. It ensures that these laws, given through the incomparable prophet Moses, are seen as YHWH's very words. In this way Num 12 serves to legitimate the high authority of the Sinai laws. The fact that Moses will die outside the land because of his failings at the land's edge does not negate either his unique role as the conduit of YHWH's words at Sinai or his leadership in the wilderness up to the incident of Num 20:1-12. Moses is still YHWH's trusted leader throughout the paradigmatic period of the wilderness. Moreover, Num 12 uses Moses' elevated status to defend the practice of marriage to foreign women, nullifying the position of those who prohibit exogamy.

Like Moses, Aaron is put in a more positive light when Num 12 is seen as a comment on Num 20:1-12 and his role as high priest is reasserted. In Num 20:1-12, Aaron was implicated in Moses' sin. YHWH's accusation in Num 20:1-12 includes failing to show YHWH's holiness before the Israelites (by usurping YHWH's place)—the ultimate sin for Aaron as high priest. But Aaron's questioning of Moses' unique prophetic status in Num 12, and his assertion of his own credentials as one through whom YHWH speaks separately from Moses (the one bringing Aaron down by not speaking YHWH's words), read as a positive initiative. Such a reading may provide a further explanation, over and above his high priestly status, for his not being punished along with Miriam. However, since Num 12 then goes on to support Moses as the incomparable prophet over against Aaron and Miriam, Aaron confesses his sin and reverts to his subordinated role as one who speaks YHWH's words as channeled through Moses (Exod 7:1). In this way Aaron's priestly role is subordinate to Moses', and his words are not his own but YHWH's words through Moses. His figure is thus somewhat redeemed in relation to Num 20:1-12: he is not punished, and his standing as founding high priest is maintained, since he receives this authority from Moses. Like Moses, he will die outside the promised land. But with the insertion of Num 12, his role as founding high priest in the wilderness at

Sinai is not negated, for he comes to stand in solidarity, albeit in a subservient position, with Moses as prophet par excellence.[27]

Miriam, however, is not redeemed. In Num 20:1, Miriam dies at Kadesh (*qdsh*), a word play on the verb *qdsh* (meaning "show holiness") in Num 20:12. Miriam's death is therefore associated with holiness, but in this context this connotes the divine holiness that Moses and Aaron did not manifest when they tried to usurp YHWH's role. But, in Num 12 as a later comment on this, it is not Moses and Aaron whose fate is associated with pollution but Miriam. Her triple pollution represents an ironic play on the place of her death at Kadesh, the place of holiness:[28] the one who died at Kadesh, not complicit in Moses' and Aaron's sins, now becomes unholy in Num 12. Her aspiration to Moses' prophetic status in Num 12 is not as heinous as Moses' aspiration in 20:1-12 to usurp YHWH. Yet it is Miriam, not Moses or Aaron, who becomes unholy and unclean, foreshadowing her death outside the land. It takes far less of a sin for Miriam to become an outsider to the promised land than it did for Moses and Aaron. Though Moses and Aaron are redeemed in Num 12 as the prophet par excellence and founding high priest respectively, no insider status is given to Miriam, only a foretaste of her death outside the land. Her healing and reentry are only a temporary reprieve.

In terms of insider/outsider motifs, then, when Num 12 is seen as a later comment on 20:1-12, the following picture emerges: Moses is redeemed from being an outsider to the promised land to being the insider par excellence for the wilderness period. Aaron also is redeemed from being an outsider to the promised land to being an insider as founding high priest of the wilderness period. Thus, Moses the incomparable prophet and Aaron— Moses' prophet and founding high priest—are the insiders par excellence of the paradigmatic wilderness period that encapsulates the Sinai laws and the blueprint for the tabernacle and its cult. Their eventual exclusion does not diminish this. Moses' foreign wife is also legitimated as an insider by association with Moses. In contrast, however, Miriam becomes the paradigmatic outsider, not only dying outside the land, but deprived of leadership in the wilderness, the figure whose pollution and exclusion from the camp foreshadow her death, which takes place, ironically, at Kadesh.

The Present Text

If we return to the final text, the interpretive nuances of Num 12 are the same as those that emerged in analyzing it as a relatively late text.[29] But in contrast, Num 20:1-12 now occurs after Num 12 in the narrative sequence. Read in this way, Moses as the prophet par excellence and, after a hiccup, Aaron his subordinate and founding high priest are the paradigmatic leaders and insiders of the wilderness era, through whom the Sinai laws, the very words of YHWH, are communicated. But they later lose their leadership status and die as outsiders precisely through reneging on the very things that made them incomparable. Moses' foreign wife retains her insider status, since his later sins have nothing to do with intermarriage. Finally, Miriam is the consummate outsider, denied any paradigmatic leadership in the wilderness. Though as sister of Moses and Aaron she attempts insider status, this becomes an explanation for her eventual death outside the land, foreshadowed graphically by her multiple pollution and temporary exclusion from the camp.

Conclusion

Our exploration of Num 12 in dialogue with 20:1-12 has resulted in various perspectives on what it means to be insiders and outsiders, along with various reasons for shifting in status. For Moses, to be an insider means having been chosen by God to be the prophet par excellence, to speak the very words of God, and thereby to exercise leadership over the people and to be an effective intercessor. He is an insider only while he obeys this vocation. Choosing insider status is not within his power; but he can and does play a role in effecting outsider status. In not witnessing to God, in not leading the people correctly, he can have no leadership role, he can have no insider role in relation to the land era, and he dies outside the promised land.

Aaron's insider status as secondary leader subordinate to Moses depends almost entirely on Moses' insider status. Even when he rebels against Moses, Aaron's insider status is somewhat protected, and he remains able to resume his insider role. But Aaron's subordination to Moses is a two-edged sword: Aaron's fate is ultimately not in his own hands. When Moses sins and becomes an outsider, so does Aaron. Aaron's fate is that of Moses: an insider for the wilderness era, he has no leadership role later but will die outside the land.

Moses' foreign wife, though potentially an outsider, gains her insider status by association with Moses. She is accepted legally and socially into the Israelite community. As such, she becomes a symbol of hope for foreign wives, justifying their marriages to Israelites and their inclusion in the Israelite community. There is no suggestion in these texts that her insider status is threatened; it is not negated by Moses' disobedience and loss of leadership.

Miriam, however, is the consummate outsider. No matter from which angle these texts are explored, she at no point has explicit insider status. Although it might possibly be implied that, at least initially, she enjoys some sort of insider status either as prophet or as sister to Moses, she quickly becomes the outsider par excellence by rebelling against Moses just as Aaron did. Not only is she robbed of any leadership role whatsoever, but she becomes a social outcast, shut out of the camp, shamed and polluted, isolated from God and the cultic community, and associated with the realm of death. Her death then excludes her from the promised land. Any temporary reprieve from her isolation depends on Moses' intercession.

A hierarchy of power underlies insider and outsider status in these Numbers texts. God ultimately possesses all the power and can be present both inside and outside the camp. Of the human characters, Moses has the most power: although God determines his insider status, he can effect his outsider status depending on whether he subordinates himself to God. Aaron's standing and that of the foreign wife are dependent on Moses; they cannot determine their insider or outsider statuses. Miriam stands at the bottom of the hierarchical heap. It appears that in her potential power as prophetess, she flew too close to Moses' flame. Her threat is effectively annihilated.

The feminist implications are clear. In a patriarchal world, women are liable to turn against women as Miriam turns against Moses' foreign wife. Often women who seek a leadership role are denied it and denied it for lesser faults than those committed by men, who do not reap the same consequences. Miriam's bid for equal status is not on par with Moses' sin of trying to play God, yet she reaps a more multifaceted and more complete punishment. Aaron, though complicit with Miriam in wanting equal status with Moses and though rebuked by God, is not punished as she is. Can Miriam's bid for empowerment and leadership be called a fault at all?

In short, Num 12 frowns upon female leadership and the empowerment and prophetic voice of women. These stories reflect the disadvantages for any who are low in the hierarchy of power and dependent on those with more power, as many women are in patriarchal societies today.

How can these texts help women reflect theologically on insider and outsider status? Though difficult, these stories can mirror back to us current societal conditions regarding power relations in general and between genders, especially concerning leadership, providing insight into these dynamics and helping articulate them. Just as Num 12 and 20:1-12 dialogue and conflict with each other in various ways, so too these texts can be dialogue partners for us, helping us clarify what we think about power, leadership, and women's roles. In particular, God's depiction at the top of the hierarchy, seemingly on the side of male power and authority, may inspire us to formulate different views of God and of how society and its leadership should operate. In dialogue with these stories, and in reaction to them, alternative views of God and power relations may arise not only from our experiences and reflections but through attention to other biblical texts and traditions that contradict these. For example, Huldah the prophetess is given a voice in her own right, as speaking the word of God (2 Kgs 22:14-20; 2 Chr 34:22-28). The woman of strength in Prov 31:10-31 breaks free of hierarchies of patriarchal power, as seen in the call to praise her in her own right at the very center of male power, at the city gates.[30] Through dialogue with these more positive texts, but also with the difficult ones considered here and elsewhere, we can articulate our theologies of gender relations and of power.

For Further Reading

Barton, Mukti. "The Skin of Miriam Became as White as Snow: The Bible, Western Feminism, and Colour Politics." *Feminist Theology* (2001): 68–80.

Burns, Rita J. *Has the Lord Indeed Spoken Only through Moses? A Study of the Biblical Portrait of Miriam.* Atlanta: Scholars Press, 1987.

Camp, Claudia V. *Wise, Strange and Holy: The Strange Woman and the Making of the Bible.* JSOTSup 320. Sheffield: Sheffield Academic, 2000.

Fischer, Imtraud. "The Authority of Miriam: A Feminist Reading of Numbers 12 Prompted by Jewish Interpretation." Pages 159–73 in *Exodus and Deuteronomy.* Edited by Athalaya Brenner and Carole Fontaine. 2nd series. Sheffield: Sheffield Academic, 2000.

Gafney, Wilda. *Daughters of Miriam: Women Prophets in Ancient Israel.* Minneapolis: Fortress, 2008.

Kramer, Phyllis S. "Miriam." Pages 104–33 in *Exodus and Deuteronomy.* Edited by Athalaya Brenner and Carole Fontaine. 2nd series. Sheffield: Sheffield Academic, 2000.

Sadler, Rodney. *Can a Cushite Change His Skin? An Examination of Race, Ethnicity, and Othering in the Hebrew Bible*. New York: T&T Clark, 2005.

Sakenfeld, Katharine. "Numbers." Pages 79–87 in *Women's Bible Commentary*. Edited by Carol A. Newsom, Sharon Ringe, and Jacqueline Lapsley. Louisville, Ky.: Westminster John Knox, 2012.

Trible, Phyllis. "Subversive Justice: Tracing the Miriamic Traditions." Pages 99–109 in *Justice and the Holy: Essays in Honor of Walter Harrelson*. Edited by Douglas Knight and Peter Paris. Atlanta: Scholars Press, 1989.

CHAPTER 10

BE KIND TO STRANGERS, BUT KILL THE CANAANITES
A Feminist Biblical Theology of the Other

Julie Galambush

Deuteronomy 20:16-17 is one of several biblical texts in which the Israelites are commanded by God to exterminate the native residents of Canaan: "But as for the towns of these peoples that the LORD your God is giving you as an inheritance, you must not let anything that breathes remain alive. You shall annihilate them." Elsewhere, and even more frequently, the Israelites are instructed to love and protect resident aliens with whom they will share that land: "When an alien resides with you in your land, you shall not oppress the alien. The alien who resides with you shall be to you as the citizen among you; you shall love the alien as yourself, for you were aliens in the land of Egypt: I am the LORD your God" (Lev 19:33-34).

These two commandments might well be said to represent the best and the worst of the Western religious heritage: a mandate to champion the rights of the oppressed "other," and a mandate to eliminate the other in the name of God. Each of these commandments is presented as an essential aspect of Israel's relationship with others.

The commandments in question occur in the books of Exodus, Leviticus, Numbers, and Deuteronomy, books in which Israel receives instructions on how to enter and live in the land. As reported in the text, the commandments are not technically contradictory: Israel is to slaughter all of the land's *current* residents; once it has done so, it is to protect the rights of all non-Israelites

who reside there. The only scenario making sense of the two sets of commandments is sequential: the Israelites first slaughter all non-Israelites,
then occupy the land and welcome the non-Israelites wishing to live there
subsequently. Thus, the juxtaposition of the two commandments does make
a kind of logical sense. But even if the two sets of commandments regarding the other can be rationalized as sequential actions and attitudes—first
hate and then love the other—the combination makes little sense to most
contemporary readers. This essay seeks to develop a plausible model to
explain why biblical editors might have built such powerful and contradictory messages into the text, and to reflect on how contemporary readers
might respond to this legacy.

Israel (and YHWH) as "Others" in the Promised Land

Biblical Israel has its origins in YHWH's promise of the land. Long before
the covenant at Sinai, YHWH promises Abraham a land in which his offspring will become a mighty nation (Gen 12:7). From the outset, Abraham
is told that this land already belongs to someone else: it is "the land of the
Kenites, the Kenizzites, the Kadmonites, the Hittites, the Perizzites, the
Rephaim, the Amorites, the Canaanites, the Girgashites, and the Jebusites"
(Gen 15:18-21). By introducing the land as the land of *other* peoples, the narrator posits land ownership as a problematic category: On the one hand, the
land is granted by divine fiat; on the other hand, whose land is it, really? Near
Eastern peoples typically saw each land as belonging to the god of that land.
Thus, Moab was the land of Chemosh, and Babylon the land of Marduk.[1]
Here, however, the land is introduced only in terms of the people who inhabit
it; their gods are apparently not relevant. The narrative says nothing about
other gods or about YHWH's prior relationship to Terah and his family,
but one might imagine YHWH as the family god of Terah, since he appears
to Abram immediately following Terah's death with instructions concerning
the family's future, and because Abram, unlike Moses in Exod 3, expresses no
confusion over which god he is addressing.[2] Whatever YHWH's status, he is
not presented as the patron god over "the land of the Kenites, the Kenizzites,
the Kadmonites, the Hittites, the Perizzites, the Rephaim, the Amorites, the
Canaanites, the Girgashites, and the Jebusites." Rather, both Abram and his
god are portrayed as outsiders. Did the land of Canaan already have a high
god? Does YHWH anticipate serving as only the patron god of Abram's

family or as high god over the entire land? The narrative does not address these questions at this stage.

Abram enters the land and soon receives another word from YHWH: that his descendants will be "aliens [*gerim*] in a land that is not theirs, and shall be slaves there, and they shall be oppressed for four hundred years," but that YHWH will bring them out, giving them the land in which Abram now lives as a *ger* (Gen 15:12-16). Thus, not only will Abram himself continue to be a transient; his descendants will continue to live as aliens even outside the land. Even as the narrative reiterates the promise of the land, it seemingly goes out of its way to stress that Abram and his descendants will maintain the status of aliens. This four-hundred-year separation between people and land highlights a peculiarity of the biblical narrative: that YHWH, Israel, and Canaan are presented not as a primordial unity but as construct. The unity of people, god, and land must be constructed over the course of the narrative or, in the terms of that narrative, over centuries.

YHWH's prediction is fulfilled, of course, and after a short stay in the land Abraham's descendants migrate to Egypt, where they are enslaved before being delivered by "the god of their ancestors," YHWH. At this point, however, the people are so estranged from their roots that when YHWH tells Moses to inform the people, "The god of your ancestors has sent me to you," Moses asks, "If I come to the people of Israel and say to them, 'The God of your ancestors has sent me to you,' and they ask me, 'What is his name?' what shall I say to them?" (Exod 3:13). Although it is possible that Moses alone does not know Israel's god, and that the people ask the god's name in order to test him, the overall arc of the narrative suggests that YHWH has become an unknown god (see, e.g., 5:2; 6:7; 14:31). Only as the people move from slavery to possession does YHWH move from being, first, a familial deity (the god of the ancestors), then a forgotten and apparently powerless one, and finally the patron god of both the people and the land.[3]

Remarkably, although YHWH has repeatedly promised the land of Canaan to Israel, he has never claimed that the land is inherently his to give. Only with the crossing of the sea in Exod 14–15 does the "landless" YHWH take on the identity of a high god—that is, a god who rules both a people and a land. In Exod 15, having defeated the gods and king of Egypt, YHWH is proclaimed not only king over his people but also ruler over their *land*. According to Exod 15:13-18, YHWH has already led his people to his "holy abode" and "planted" them on his holy mountain—that is, the Temple Mount in Jerusalem. In fact, only with the Sinai covenant of Exod 19–24 does YHWH begin to speak of Canaan as his own possession. Similarly, only after the exodus will the Israelites themselves cease to be aliens, taking exclusive possession of the land by exterminating its indigenous inhabitants. The exodus and ensuing conquest will "normalize" the relationship between YHWH, Israel, and land.

YHWH's status as an outsider god is easily obscured both by his repeated promises to give Israel the land and, later, by his explicit claim to it. In Leviticus the Israelites are told, "The land shall not be sold in perpetuity, for the land is mine; with me you are but aliens [gerim] and tenants" (25:23). The Psalms regularly acknowledge YHWH as the owner of his land (Pss 10:16; 85:1), though they sometimes carry a reminder that the land is "the mountain that his right hand had won" (78:54)—that is, it was not always YHWH's. Thus, while the narrative repeatedly affirms YHWH's ability to give the land of Canaan to Israel, the land is not presented as inherently his. Like his people, YHWH also must conquer it.

The biblical authors' attitudes toward the land and its ownership are thus profoundly mixed. In many cases they reflect a culturally typical understanding of the land as belonging to (its) god and of the people as tenants or as possessions of the divine landowner: "[W]e are the people of his pasture, and the sheep of his hand" (Ps 95:7). That is, YHWH, his land, and his people are indeed the package deal seen throughout the ancient Near East. Elsewhere, however, the biblical narrative departs from this default arrangement by positing a time when the unit "land-god-people" had yet to be established for Israel. Although it is difficult for modern people to grasp the oddness of Israel's relationship to the land as portrayed in the Bible, the rhetorical work of establishing the unity of god, land, and people motivates a great deal of the primary history in Genesis–2 Kings.

Confirming the idea that YHWH arrives only belatedly in the promised land are the many places in which YHWH is said to have a home outside the land. Both Deut 33:2 and Judg 5:4 report that YHWH arrived from Seir, in Edom, while Deut 33:2 and Hab 3:3 report that YHWH came forth from Paran, an area in the eastern Sinai Peninsula. Indeed, YHWH "shone forth" from Paran (Deut 33:2), a phrase evoking the divine warrior going forth from his sanctuary.[4] The Habakkuk text associates Paran with Teman, another site apparently located in Edom. Finally, and most strikingly, throughout the Hebrew Bible YHWH is associated with Sinai and Horeb, the two names given to "the mountain of God/YHWH."[5] YHWH's "original" holy mountain remains outside the land that will become his possession, as both Sinai and Horeb are described as being to the south, either in Midian (Exod 2:16) or west of Midian, in the Sinai Peninsula. In fact, Ps 68:17, in celebrating the exodus and conquest, notes unselfconsciously that "[w]ith mighty chariotry, twice ten thousand, thousands upon thousands, YHWH came from Sinai into the holy place." Like Israel itself, Israel's god was a late arrival in the land.[6]

This puzzle over the relationship between god and people with the land is compounded by YHWH's commandment that in order to inherit the land, Israel must exterminate the native inhabitants.[7] The idea of a god rejecting, ejecting, or even exterminating his own people has ample precedent in ancient Near Eastern tradition; peoples regularly understood their own defeat and/or exile as the result of their god's anger against them.[8] Here, however, a foreign god casts out or destroys the natives in order to bring in an outside population. One wonders, why does YHWH not want his people in his own land, presumably somewhere in the vicinity of Sinai or Seir? Or, if he has decided to dwell in Canaan, why does he not make the Canaanites his people? Ancient Near Eastern kings regularly conquered new peoples and made them "theirs." The biblical narrative, by contrast, proposes a highly anomalous scenario: a god from the south adopts a people from the east (Ur of the Chaldees), promising them a land that belongs to neither of them.[9]

Although the texts vary as to whether a complete genocide is either commanded or carried out (see, e.g., Josh 13:1; Judg 1–2), Josh 11 affirms that, with the sole exceptions of Rahab's family and the Gibeonites, Joshua completed the job. Following a repetitive litany in which Joshua "put to the sword all who were in [*town name here*], utterly destroying them [so that] there was no one left who breathed" (v. 11, etc.), the narrator concludes that "Joshua took the whole land, according to all that the LORD had spoken to Moses; and Joshua gave it as an inheritance to Israel according to their tribal allotments. And the land had rest from war."[10]

Israelites and Canaanites: Inventing Otherness

Israel's status as "other" than the native inhabitants of the land is central to the biblical narrative. Yet contemporary scholars widely agree that the Israelites did not, in fact, arrive as outsiders taking the land by force. Rather, Israel emerged from within the thirteenth-century BCE population of Canaan. This radically different paradigm eliminates the question of why Israel and its god had such an unusual relationship to the land and its inhabitants, and it instead raises the question of why, if the Israelites were themselves Canaanites, they portrayed themselves as outsiders who destroyed the native population upon their arrival.

Several key pieces of evidence support the likelihood that Israel originated from among the inhabitants of thirteenth-century BCE Canaan.[11] First, we have no direct evidence either of Israel's bondage in Egypt or of the exodus or of a large (or even small) group of people wandering the desert or living at Kadesh Barnea, where the narrative has Israel spending thirty-eight years. Second, though scholars have spent generations trying to match the destruction seen at archaeological sites in the land with the biblical conquest accounts, most have agreed that no meaningful correlation can be drawn and, importantly, no new material culture appears in the land during any of the periods that have been posited for the conquest.[12] These and other factors have led researchers to conclude that at least the majority (and perhaps all) of Israel emerged from within the native population. The Israelites did not exterminate the Canaanites but were themselves Canaanites. Scholars theorize that Israel was formed from among the lower classes in Canaan during a period of social upheaval in the late thirteenth century BCE throughout the eastern Mediterranean, caused among other factors by region-wide drought and ensuing famine and raiding.[13] In particular, pastoralists who had a symbiotic relationship with farmers and manufacturers, finding that they could no longer trade for basic necessities, left the lowlands and formed small communities in the central hill country. Archaeologists have found new settlements in this period by groups sharing the material culture common to the rest of Canaan. We know little of the ideology of these communities, but at some point they took the name "Isra-el," a name that associates them with El, the creator god of the Canaanites. They also, presumably at a later date, took a god named YHWH as their high god, perhaps as a result of immigration by YHWH-worshipers from the south who had joined the hill-country community. Eventually—probably by the late tenth century BCE—the highland group known as Israel gained control over much of the territory previously controlled by other groups within Canaan.[14]

The establishment of new communities in the hill country meant perforce the establishment of a new identity. While these communities may or may not have espoused the egalitarian ethos often attributed to them, they clearly stood outside the old system of the Canaanite city-states. It is therefore reasonable that the network of new communities would identify themselves as separate from the proud cities that had long included (and, in some cases, oppressed) them at their peripheries. Israel's view of itself as "not Canaan" thus comes as no surprise. Moreover, its adoption of a new, apparently non-Canaanite, high god would add to the sense that Israel had been divinely "chosen" as a new people, apart from and superior to "the Canaanites."

Israel's identity as "not Canaan" or even "anti-Canaan" does not, however, explain either the biblical command to exterminate the native peoples of Canaan or the clearly inaccurate claim that they had arrived as conquering outsiders under Joshua. Rather, the image of Israel marching in, newly liberated from a foreign land and claiming the land in the name of YHWH, seems to reflect the realities of a much later period, possibly as late as the fifth century BCE.

Crucial to understanding the biblical description of Israelites and Canaanites is a division within Israel itself over the status of the god YHWH. Although it is unknown how or when YHWH was introduced into Israelite worship, he seems to have been widely accepted as Israel's high god as early as the ninth century BCE.[15] "Traditional" Israelite religion seems to have followed the Canaanite model in which the high god (in this case, YHWH) was worshiped along with a divine consort and an attendant divine council, as reflected by texts such as 1 Kgs 22:19 and Job 1:6.[16] At some point, however, a group of Israelites, apparently members of the upper classes, came to believe Israel should worship YHWH alone. This "YHWH alone party" would ultimately be the group largely responsible for writing and editing the Bible.[17] For this reason, the Bible reflects a situation in which most Israelites, most of the time, are described as "straying" from worship of YHWH alone, in that they continued to worship traditional Canaanite gods, even if they also worshiped YHWH as Israel's patron. This division, between those who incorporate YHWH into the traditional system of Canaanite gods and those who reject all gods but YHWH, helps explain the Bible's absolute vituperation against everything Canaanite: in the eyes of the authors, the gods of Canaan were not Israelite gods but foreign gods whose worship defied YHWH's commands and defiled Israel. If Israel had come into being by defining itself as "not Canaan," then Israelites who included the Canaanite gods in their worship were considered, in effect, no better than Canaanites. Although the call to worship YHWH alone apparently predates the Babylonian exile, the biblical narratives celebrating the suppression of Canaan and the extinction of the Canaanites were probably written after the exile, when the descendants of the "YHWH alone party" reentered the land.

The Biblical Authors as "Others" in the Land

When the Babylonian army burned Jerusalem and its temple in the early sixth century BCE, they took Judeans, including its rulers and many from the elite classes, into exile in Babylonia. These exiles, probably representing less than half the population of Judah, included substantial numbers of those advocating the sole worship of YHWH. When the descendants of these exiles returned under Persian sponsorship, they undertook the writing of a comprehensive history of Israel as an attempt to create a functional and integrative cultural memory. Members of a previously hegemonic class, themselves born and raised in Babylonia, now entered the land as outsiders.[18] Meanwhile, the Judeans who had remained in the land continued to practice the "traditional" religion in which YHWH presided over a pantheon of other deities. In its postexilic form, the Genesis–2 Kings narrative symbolically prefigures the return of the exiles, who enter the land of their ancestors, championing the worship of YHWH alone in opposition to the "Canaanite" religion of the current inhabitants.[19]

If we approach the biblical narrative as the product of an elite class struggling to validate both its theological position (YHWH alone) and its claim to hegemony in the land, then the "genocide" texts can be understood as a tool assuring the returnees that they are YHWH's chosen people, entering the land under divine mandate. Like Abraham, they are called to leave Mesopotamia for a land they have never seen; like Moses, they follow a god who has apparently been weak, without land or temple up to this point; and like Joshua, they are called to reject the ways of the land's current occupants. The command to exterminate the Canaanites "so that they may not teach you to do all the abhorrent things that they do for their gods" (Deut 20:18) implicitly directs the returnees to reject the religious practices of the land's current residents, who worship YHWH along with other traditional Israelite/Canaanite gods. The fantasy of a past in which an Israel loyal to YHWH alone overcame everyone in its path amounts to a claim that YHWH has chosen the returnees (or perhaps the returnees plus those who, like Rahab in Josh 2, recognize their God-given authority) to rule over the people in the land. The narratives of return, particularly those in Ezra and Nehemiah, support this impression, portraying the returnees under Persian sponsorship taking charge of a new state, centered on the Torah and on Jerusalem, in which only the returnees count as "Israel."[20]

Daniel Smith-Christopher has argued that those returning from Babylon suffered both the memory of their ancestors' displacement and the reality of their own.[21] The conquest narrative, then, supports their attempt to cope with displacement, both cultural and geographic. Despite Persian sponsorship, the returning community faced the significant challenge of convincing both themselves and the larger population that they represented not a rejected or even "foreign" version of Israel but rather normative Israel. Whatever cognitive dissonance they might have experienced as exiles, return to a land populated by a majority whom they had ideologically rejected would have created tremendous isolation as well as yet another challenge to their communal identity. In such a context, the conquest narratives, essentially a fantasy of unbridled power exercised under divine mandate, would have accomplished significant cultural work. If Israel's repossession of the land was the will of its patron god, then the returnees' entry is changed from a story of mere survival to one of triumph.[22] The exodus as backstory to the story of return from exile roots the returnees' experience in a formative past; their experience as outsiders positions them as the next heroes in an ongoing cultural narrative.

The *Ger*: Common Ground in the Land

Having proposed a scenario in which the Bible's virulent opposition to the Canaanites reflects a combination of Israel's own Canaanite roots and the returning community's rejection of Israelite polytheism, we turn to the Bible's more gracious side: the laws governing the treatment of the *ger*, the non-Israelite living under Israelite law in the land. Here we address the paradox with which we began—namely, the juxtaposition of the command to kill all non-Israelites upon entering the promised land (and the texts announcing that Israel fulfilled this commandment), with laws protecting the rights of the land's resident aliens. The juxtaposition of the two paradigms—one in which Canaanites (with the exception of those who remain in the land as a "snare," tempting Israel into idolatry) are chased out or slaughtered, and one in which non-Israelites are given protected status—is fraught with difficulties. Historically, the presence of "non-Israelites" in the land is hardly surprising, given Israel's origin as a subset within the larger Canaanite culture. Moreover, every land seems to have had its share of resident aliens and laws governing their rights and responsibilities.[23]

The word *ger* appears regularly throughout the Torah, Joshua, Psalms, and latter prophets, and only occasionally in Samuel, Kings, or Chronicles. It appears most frequently in contexts legislating or otherwise demanding social justice. All the law codes of the Torah command justice for the *ger* (Exod 22:21; Deut 24:17; etc.), with some calling for "one law for the native and for the stranger who sojourns among you" (Exod 12:49; cf. Lev 24:22).[24] Prophetic texts reflect the obverse of the legal corpus, condemning those who abuse or withhold justice from the *ger* (Ezek 22:29; Mal 3:5). But what, specifically, was a *ger*? The term seems to have had a fairly wide range of meaning within the general category of immigrant, noncitizen, or temporary resident. Thus, the *ger* is most regularly contrasted with *ezrakh*, generally understood as the Israelite (e.g., in Exod 12:48, 49; Lev 16:29).

In addition to being a noncitizen, the *ger* is, by definition, landless. Thus, Abraham calls attention to his status as a *ger* when trying to obtain a burial site for Sarah (Gen 23:4). Being (only) a *ger*, he owns no land—a circumstance that makes burial difficult. The Hittites call Abraham "a great prince" among them, apparently suggesting that they consider him "more than a *ger*," and allow him to buy a cave in which to bury Sarah.[25] The fact that the *ger* is always landless (regardless of how long he or his descendants inhabit the land) suggests that the *ger* is never considered an Israelite.[26] Because each of the twelve tribes has inalienable possession of its portion of the land, the tribeless *ger* remains landless, regardless of his status in the community.[27] Leviticus 17 specifies that the *ger* must not only observe the civil code but also be circumcised and participate in rituals of purification.[28] In this regard, the Septuagint passages that translate *ger* with *proselytos* capture the *ger*'s integration into the Israelite polity far better than the English "alien." Leviticus 25:35 indirectly illustrates the quasi-insider status of the *ger*: "If your brother becomes poor, and cannot maintain himself with you, you shall maintain him; as a *ger* and a sojourner he shall live with you" (RSV). In this case your brother is your equal in everything except that, like a *ger*, he owns no land; you must therefore give him the status of a permanent guest at your house, like the status accorded a *ger* in the land.

The *ger*'s perpetual landlessness explains the laws prohibiting abuse: being landless, the *ger* is generally presumed to be poor. In this regard the *ger* is parallel to the Levite, who likewise owns no land and is regularly singled out as in need of support (Deut 14:29).[29] While landless, however, *gerim* were not necessarily poor: Lev 25:47 gives instructions for what to do "if a *ger* or sojourner with you becomes rich and your brother beside him becomes poor and sells himself to the *ger* or sojourner" (RSV). Ironically, while the *ger* was ineligible for land ownership, he was, within certain constraints, permitted to own Israelites. Like the requirement of circumcision, the right of the *ger* to own Israelite slaves clearly identifies him as a member of the community. Bondage to a *ger* was a legally sanctioned status and not condemned as oppression. On the other hand, the covenant curses of Deuteronomy reflect a belief that, while legally permissible, Israelite subordination to a *ger* represents a reversal of the "natural" order of things. Thus, if the people do not keep the covenant, the *ger* "shall mount above you higher and higher; and you shall come down lower and lower. . . . [H]e shall be the head, and you shall be the tail" (Deut 28:43-44 RSV).

A *ger*, then, was a resident alien who was Israelite in everything except the right to own land and, presumably, biological ancestry. Like the widow, orphan, and Levite, the *ger* is singled out in the Torah and prophets as deserving special protection from injustice. Although the status of the biblical *ger* is not markedly different from that of resident aliens in other ancient Near Eastern legal systems,[30] the Torah grounds its protection of the *ger* in an identity shared between Israelite and *ger*: "You know the heart of an alien, for you were aliens in the land of Egypt" (Exod 23:9). Specifically, support for the *ger* is presented as a byproduct of Israel's own experience of otherness: "The alien who resides with you shall be to you as the citizen among you; you shall love the alien as yourself, for you were aliens in the land of Egypt: I am the LORD your God" (Lev 19:34; cf. Deut 10:19). Thus, while the conquest narrative commands the extermination of the non-Israelite in the land, Israel's slavery prior to the conquest is invoked as a warrant for equal treatment based on social, if not biological, kinship.

Of the two commands—kill the Canaanite, protect the resident alien—the law of the *ger* is by far the more consistent. So-called Canaanites are in some places marked for genocide; in others, expelled from the land; and elsewhere, merely off limits as wives for Israelite men. Laws covering the status and treatment of the *ger*, however, uniformly mandate equal treatment for anyone willing to live like an Israelite, as defined by the biblical authors. We cannot know the extent to which any of the biblical law codes ever served as the law of the land. But like the literary law codes of the surrounding cultures, they are clearly intended to set forth normative positions.[31]

Israel Reimagining Israel

Ehud Ben Zvi has explicated the ways in which the varied corpus of Persian-period biblical texts support the proposition that "exilic Israel equals

Israel."[32] By developing a normative vision in which "all Israel" went into and has now returned from the exile, the biblical authors claimed the exile as the decisive moment in which Israel, as represented by its ruling class, was punished, purged, and re-created. The model in which exodus and conquest, now reenacted by the returnees, establishes Israel's core identity positions the returnees as the authoritative leaders of the new, "postexilic" Israel.

Within the postexilic context, the texts alternately rejecting and supporting the stranger could thus have worked together to further the goals of the returnees. It is significant that the textual warrant for destroying the Canaanites (beyond their mere presence in the land) is to prevent them from "teach[ing] you to do all the abhorrent things that they do for their gods" (Deut 20:18; cf. Exod 34:16). That is, the only thing wrong with Canaanites is that they might make polytheism attractive to Israelites. Even Israelites can be referred to as Canaanites if they worship gods in addition to YHWH.

Ultimately, the category of "Canaanite" emerges as a religious rather than an ethnic one. The category of *ger* is more ambiguous. Neither Israelite nor Canaanite, of indeterminate ethnicity, the *ger* serves as the "model" resident alien, who gladly conforms to the religious laws of the land and therefore shares in its bounty. By prescribing death (or, in some texts, merely rejection) to the Canaanite and support to the *ger*, the biblical authors effectively recast the us-them dichotomy as one based on religion rather than ethnicity. Israelites who worship differently may be condemned as "Canaanites," while the *ger* who accepts the returnees' form of worship shall be "as the Israelite." Ultimately, even the right to reside in the land is decided along ideological rather than ethnic lines.[33] Moreover, texts such as the book of Ruth clearly challenge exclusivity based on ethnicity, demonstrating the vital role of the stranger in the community of Israel. Remarkably, Ezek 47:22 claims that in an ideal future, the *ger* will be given part of the promised land as an inheritance.

As parts of an ongoing process of identity formation for the returning community, the commands to either kill or love the stranger can be read, paradoxically, as complementary rather than contradictory. In light of the exilic experience, the conquest narratives function as a sort of revenge/empowerment fantasy in which trauma is reenacted upon the other in a narrative such as this: "My land was invaded; my people were killed or removed, and my god humiliated; but far from being powerless, my god once led *us* as the conquering army. By returning to the land now (albeit peacefully), we realize the divine mandate to inherit the land." In contrast, laws protecting the *ger* empower the community in an entirely different way. The cultural memories of Abraham coming from Mesopotamia to live as a *ger* in the land, and of Israel as *gerim* in Egypt, tacitly acknowledge the community's sojourn in Babylon and the fact that they "know the heart" of an alien. Now, however, they are citizens and more than citizens; they share the traditional role of kings: protecting the disenfranchised members of society. Texts grounding the law of the *ger* in the experience of exodus-cum-exile transform the returnee community's de facto outsider status into an authoritative warrant, one that mandates not the destruction of the other but the creation of an inclusive society. While the conquest narrative claims divine warrant for the returnees' hegemonic presence in the land, actual laws concerning how to live in that land mandate that justice must have its origins in compassion.

Living with the Text

This resolution of the apparent incongruity presented by the sample texts is, alas, far from satisfying to the modern reader. On the one hand, it may be tempting to claim, as some have done, that the genocide commandments are effectively meaningless, as their only application was to a conquest that never in fact took place; even the return of the exiles was no such bloody invasion. But regardless of their manifest inaccuracy, the conquest narratives continue to hold up the pitiless destruction of an entire population as an ideal. As such, the texts retain the potential to serve as warrants for barbarity.[34] Even the far more appealing commandment to "love the stranger as yourself" originally presumed that the stranger would live according Israel's definition of purity. The text does not hand us a model of true inclusivity. That task continues to belong to all of us.

In a reflection on Deut 21:10–25:19 (parashat *Ki Teitzei*), Rabbi Shira Milgrom suggests that "we are what we remember." Focusing on the command to remember the abuses perpetrated by Amalek, Milgrom points out that not only the texts commanding vengeance but also those instructing us to "love the stranger" direct the reader to define herself via the recollection of pain. Thus, "you know the feelings of the stranger, having yourselves been slaves in the land of Egypt" (NJPS). Milgrom points out the many ways in which the deep memory of pain can "wreak havoc in our lives," as when abused children later become abusers themselves. But, she concludes, although "we are what we remember," we can also choose *how* we remember. We can accept the challenge "to transform our pain into empathy, our fear into courage, and our mourning into joy." In order to transform vulnerability into empathy, however, we "need to remember that we were vulnerable and afraid—so that we will fill our world with healing and blessing."[35]

These texts set before us life and death: a world in which the experience of pain, from Judah's experience of exile to the suffering each of us faces in our lifetimes, can fund either profound bitterness or profound compassion. The text, like an echo of the human heart itself, voices both the childish fantasy of destroying those whom we fear and the mature vision of protecting the dignity of all people. The deep vulnerability reflected in these texts is a legacy shared by the whole human family and, potentially, a warning against its dangers and a promise of its healing power.

Most feminists are aware that when Israel receives the law at Sinai, it is only the men in the congregation who are formally part of the covenant (Exod 19:10, 14-15). Many are also aware that, in Deuteronomy, God broadens the covenant by explicitly including women and children (Deut 29:10-11). It is not, however, only women who are "added into" the covenant. Israel is fully ready to enter the land only when the *full* community is included: "You stand assembled today, all of you, before the LORD your God—the leaders of your tribes, your elders, and your officials, all the men of Israel, your children, your women, and the aliens [*gerim*] who are in your camp . . . to enter into the covenant of the LORD your God" (Deut 29:10-12). The text continues to recognize the "otherness" of the other; it is the definition of "us" that has grown.

For Further Reading

Eisen, Robert. *The Peace and Violence of Judaism: From the Bible to Modern Zionism.* New York: Oxford University Press, 2011.

Hawk, L. Daniel. "The Truth about Conquest: Joshua as History, Narrative, and Scripture." *Interpretation* 66 (2012): 129–40.

Plaskow, Judith. "Transforming the Nature of Community: Toward a Feminist People of Israel." Pages 403–18 in *Women in the Hebrew Bible.* Edited by Alice Bach. New York: Routledge, 1999.

Rivera-Pagán, Luis. "Xenophilia or Xenophobia: Towards a Theology of Migration." *Ecumenical Review* 64 (2012): 575–89.

Chapter 11

RAHAB AND ESTHER IN DISTRESS
A Feminist Biblical Theology of Moral Agency

Sarah J. Melcher

The Canaanite prostitute Rahab and the Israelite Persian queen Esther both confront morally ambiguous choices posed by violent threats to their own lives and those of their families. When faced with the certain victory of the Hebrews over the Canaanites at Jericho, Rahab must decide between safety for her family and loyalty to her Canaanite community. Esther, on the other hand, must choose between survival for her and her family and the continued existence of the greater Israelite community in exile. The moral dilemmas faced by the two women are compelling and engaging. Their stories invite readers to reflect on the nature of these women's moral agency, the complexity of moral decision making, and competing visions of the moral self.

Before we engage with the biblical stories, a preliminary discussion of the concept of moral agency will help to orient us. Following this discussion, I will outline the stories of Rahab and Esther—examining them through the various lenses of moral agency set out below—and finally compare the two stories to draw some conclusions.

Moral agency fits into the general area of character ethics. Lisa Sowle Cahill outlines two models of character ethics: (1) For some ethicists, the individual's long-term, inner disposition is more important than the particular acts that the individual carries out.[1] As Cahill describes it, "Character refers to the long term formation and moral self-expression of the person."

(2) Another model "situates individual moral agency within a community of formation."[2] Through the latter perspective, we examine how an individual pursues "the good" as it is defined by the community.[3] The community decides what "the good" is that it wishes to achieve on behalf of its members, and it forms the conscience of its community members accordingly. In the case of Rahab in Josh 2, the community perspective to which we have access is that of the Israelite community. Since the passage originated among Israelites, the perspectives of the king of Jericho and of his community are not truly available to us. In this case, "the good" that Rahab seeks to achieve is formulated by Israelites. According to M. Daniel Carroll R.,

> This foundational and transcendent good to which all other finite goals (and goods) ultimately should point is not limited to some quantifiable material gain or emotional satisfaction. It is inseparable from the virtues—that is, those dispositions of character, habits of life, and emotional responses that one must possess to embody the good. Lastly, this good must be modeled by exemplars, persons who best embody a commitment to the good and the requisite virtues.[4]

As we shall see, one reading of the Rahab story offers a character with "a commitment to the good and requisite virtues," according to the text's Israelite worldview. However, reading from an imagined Canaanite perspective might suggest that Rahab is a traitor, a collaborator with the enemy, or else an opportunist who opts to side with the likely winners. Though her motives are ambiguous, we will explore a possible interpretation through theories of moral agency. Esther—on the other hand, an Israelite acting on behalf of Israelites as seen from an Israelite perspective—appears as a courageous woman who puts the safety of the Jewish people ahead of her own. Of course, Esther's motives are not entirely clear either. Reading from the vantage point of Haman supporters and Persians can put her in a very different light. She has been criticized by readers for later requesting an extra day of fighting in Susa (Esth 9:13).

The first philosopher that modern people know to have formulated a theory of moral responsibility was Aristotle. In his *Nicomachean Ethics*, Aristotle argued that it is sometimes appropriate to ascribe praise or blame based on an individual's actions or dispositional character.[5] However, a person is regarded as a moral agent, and moral responsibility is ascribed to her or him, only if the individual is capable of decision. For Aristotle, a decision arises from a desire based on the individual's conception of the good. Moral agency and moral responsibility are also dependent on the voluntary nature of the action or disposition.[6]

> According to Aristotle, a voluntary action or trait has two distinctive features. First, there is a control condition: the action or trait must have its origin in the agent. That is, it must be up to the agent whether to perform that action or possess the trait—it cannot be compelled externally. Second, Aristotle proposes an epistemic condition: the agent must be aware of what it is she is doing or bringing about.[7]

An Aristotelian approach to moral agency maintains that an individual is an agent if she or he is aware of "crucial features or consequences" of the behavior and is not being forced into the behavior.[8] John Martin Fischer argues that for an individual to be genuinely free to make a decision and to take an action, that individual must have genuine alternatives from which to choose.[9] In addition, the individual must be the one who selects an action from the alternatives.

Notably, Carol A. Newsom—whom this volume seeks to honor—explored the topic of moral agency in her Presidential Address to the Society of Biblical Literature.[10] According to Newsom, "Three elements form the fundamental grammar of the moral self in the Hebrew Bible: desire, knowledge, and the discipline of submission to external authority."[11] In other words, in the Hebrew Bible the interplay among desire, knowledge, and submission to authority constructs the image of the moral self: "Reliable moral decision making is a project accomplished between the individual and her community as desire and knowledge are both shaped in relation to reliable external authority."[12] Newsom pointed out that different biblical books from different historical contexts evince diverse models of the moral self. Especially important is the relationship between desire and knowledge. When knowledge is relational and communal, external factors become involved in moral decision making. In regard to an external authority, Newsom stated, "This authority may be human (the father and the wise in the wisdom tradition), or it may be divine (God or the Torah of God), but it is a recognition of the fact that the coordination of desire and knowledge is not conceived of as an individual project but is always placed in a collective or social context."[13] As we will see, these themes of desire, knowledge, and submission to external authority are particularly illuminating in the stories of Rahab and Esther, though there are significant contrasts in how the two stories utilize these concepts.

Perhaps the most illuminating theory of moral agency for our purposes here is that articulated by Carol Gilligan in her essay "Remapping the
Moral Domain: New Images of Self in Relationship."[14] Gilligan notes two
voices of moral development: "One voice speaks of connection, not hurt-
ing, care, and response; and one speaks of equality, reciprocity, justice, and
rights. . . . The two moral voices that articulate these visions, thus, denote
different ways of viewing the world."[15] This essay will test Gilligan's delineation of the two voices as the essay explores the ways the visions play out
in the two stories. Gilligan describes the two voices as "two meanings of
the word 'responsibility'—commitment to obligations and responsiveness
in relationships."[16] Her theory of the two voices is based upon research with
human subjects, in some cases asking high school students how they defined
responsibility. Though all of the theories about moral agency mentioned
above are helpful in understanding issues about the moral agency arising
from the juxtaposition of Rahab's story with that of Esther, it is ultimately
Gilligan's delineation of two separate moral visions that facilitates clarity
regarding the two stories and the choices each woman makes. Both stories
aid us in developing a theology of moral agency, and both stories help us to
identify the competing voices of moral agency within ourselves.

As we approach these stories, we will be looking for the two competing
voices of moral agency. Both Rahab and Esther have conflicting loyalties
(corresponding to the two voices Gilligan describes) within themselves, but
in the end each woman will reveal which of the visions will be dominant.
This is in keeping with Gilligan's observations that each human research
subject is capable of embracing either of the two competing visions at any
time, depending on his or her stage of development and the particular circumstances involved. Through a series of studies, Gilligan discovered that
"[a]lthough both voices regularly appeared in conjunction, a tension between
them was suggested by the confusion that marked their intersection and
also by the tendency for one voice to predominate."[17] Both the tension and
the confusion caused by the competing visions will be evident in the narratives of Rahab and Esther, though, in each case, a particular vision will be
dominant. To some extent, the moral agency of both women is subject to
certain constraints because of external pressures, but the two stories may
also embrace conflicting visions of the moral self.

So, in our framework of moral agency, this essay will ask the following
set of questions: What are the competing moral visions in the narratives of
Rahab and Esther, both within each narrative and between the narratives?

Which of the visions predominate? How do the two women resolve the moral conflicts within themselves? Ultimately, what do we as readers learn from the narratives of Rahab and Esther about our own moral agency? How can these stories help us to resolve our own moral conflicts?

This essay is also informed by both postcolonial and feminist biblical criticisms. The question of whether Rahab is a collaborator with the conquering forces, against the community in which she resides, is a fascinating one that has drawn commentary from biblical scholars on several occasions. Musa W. Dube, for instance, as well as Kah-Jin Jeffrey Kuan and Mai-Anh Le Tran, have addressed the narrative of Rahab from a feminist postcolonial perspective.[18] These works demonstrate the value of these approaches for interpreting Josh 2, and this essay will also use their perspectives within the overarching framework of moral agency. Specifically, the postcolonial discussion about the nature of colonial literature is helpful in exploring how the colonizers justify their takeover of land.

The Divine Sanction for Israelite Takeover of the Land

Postcolonial criticism calls for an examination of the use of the written word to impose or reject imperial power, and calls for an examination of the use and control of wealth, particularly land and resources. My focus in this section is on how the colonizers produce literature "justifying why their nation has inherent rights of superiority or divine sanction to impose its political, economic, and social institutions on other nations."[19] Joshua 1 establishes just such a divine sanction for the Israelites' taking the land of Canaan. Examining how this is accomplished will precede our study of Josh 2.

Joshua 1:2 establishes the idea that the land of Canaan is YHWH's divine gift to the Israelites and that Joshua is to begin the takeover by the Hebrew people: "My servant Moses is dead. Now proceed to cross the Jordan, you and all this people, into the land that I am giving to them, to the Israelites." To a religiously based community such as Israel, God's decree that the land shall be theirs is the highest possible sanction for them to possess it by force.[20] Hyperbole about the Israelite right to possess the land is so pronounced that the deity proclaims that "every place that the sole of your foot will tread upon I have given to you, as I promised to Moses" (v. 3). Indeed, verse 4 promises a territory far more vast than what was occupied by Israel at the peak of its power, extending from the Mediterranean Sea through Hittite territory to the Euphrates River. In verse 5, YHWH promises that no one will be able to withstand the might of the Israelites. Their possession of the land is a foregone conclusion, with divine presence to accompany them every step of the way.

God continues to solidify the divine sanction of the Israelite possession of the land by giving instructions to Joshua for apportioning the land to the Israelites (v. 6; "apportion" is the rendering in the Tanakh translation). The Hebrew's *hiphil* (causative) construction is such that "apportion" could be rendered as "cause to inherit" (*tanhil*). The Hebrew idiom is one of permanent possession, furthering the theme of permanent divine gift of the land of Canaan to the Israelites. To ensure success in their ventures, YHWH reminds the Israelites not to deviate from the teaching of Moses in any way (v. 8).

Rhetoric about possession of the land becomes even more heightened in verse 11: "Pass through the camp, and command the people: 'Prepare your provisions; for in three days you are to cross over the Jordan, to go in to take possession of the land that the LORD your God gives you to possess.'" Joshua reminds tribes who have already found land of their obligation to enter into battle with the other Israelites. Joshua 1 clearly establishes the Israelite takeover of Canaan as destined and sanctioned by Israel's deity.

Joshua 2 from a Feminist Postcolonial Perspective

Joshua 2:1 sets the stage for what follows, depicting the Israelites as colonizers who seek to dominate the city of Jericho. Joshua secretly sends two men as spies. This raises the question, If the Israelites' intention is innocent and the inclination to dominate absent, then why send spies, and why send them secretly?[21] The latter half of the verse is sparse in detail, telling the reader simply, "So they went, and entered the house of a prostitute whose name was Rahab, and spent the night there." The verse does not say why the men choose to go to Rahab's house or how they came to spend the night there. Did they have insider information that Rahab was an Israelite sympathizer or that she would be amenable to an Israelite agenda? Of course, there are possible comedic overtones since Rahab is a prostitute, yet the text is virtually silent about their motives. We also learn nothing of Rahab's predisposition toward the spies. No conflict is described, nor does the text indicate that the Israelites had difficulty finding a place to hide. It suggests instead that the Israelites entered Rahab's house easily and were able to spend the night there with relatively little risk.

In depicting the first person we meet from Jericho as a prostitute, the Israelite author, writing from the vantage point of the colonizing group, may have intended to denigrate the Canaanites.[22] Yet Rahab's status changes with her loyalties. Within the context of the Canaanite community and from its perspective, Rahab is a person of low status. As she crosses the boundary from the Canaanite community to the Israelite one, however, she obtains the status of exemplar because she has protected Israelite spies and helped the Israelites conquer the land. Of course, this is an indication of the ambiguity present in the biblical passage regarding her character. Modern readers, far removed from the ancient Israelite context, might well ask whether Rahab ought to be viewed as a collaborator or an opportunist rather than the heroic woman celebrated in the later canonical literature.[23] From a moral perspective, how should her actions be viewed?

As was noted above, literature written by colonizers often attempts to justify the takeover of land and resources, while writers representing those who are colonized challenge that hegemony and promote redistribution of the land and its resources. Certainly a primary focus of the book of Joshua is the drama over gaining control of Canaan's land. The book is particularly interested in documenting the settlement of the land by the Israelites. Indeed, the king of Jericho is told in verse 2 that the men have come expressly "to search out the land." The verb translated as "to search out," *lakhpor*, is used metaphorically here; literally it means "to dig." The term implies that the spies will be "digging in the land" as well as spying it out.[24] The advisors surrounding the king of Jericho see the two Israelite men's activities as threatening, so their presence is reported directly to the top.

Rahab cannot be uninformed regarding the Israelites' intentions, yet she chooses to hide them. The king of Jericho sends a message to Rahab (NRSV and Tanakh render this "sent orders"): "Bring out the men who have come to you" (v. 3). The stated reason is that they have come "to search out the whole land"—in other words, to "dig out" any information about the land that they can find. Verse 4 marks the first occasion of Rahab's acting definitively against her own Canaanite community, lying to the king. She acknowledges that the spies were indeed present in her house but claims that she did not know where they came from.[25]

Rahab's lie is actually fairly elaborate. Though she has taken the precaution to hide them safely in her house, she goes on to describe the time when they supposedly left the city: "And when it was time to close the gate at dark, the men went out. Where they went I do not know. Pursue them quickly, for you can overtake them" (vv. 4-5). Not only will she not give the spies up to her countrymen, but she tries to lead the king's men in another direction, so that they will not come looking for them at her house. Thus is Rahab portrayed not only as a prostitute but as a Canaanite who quickly switches her loyalty to those who come to take the land. According to the biblical text, written from an Israelite perspective, Rahab makes the right choice, choosing the Israelite God and the Israelite agenda. For us as readers, is this a favorable depiction of this Canaanite woman, or is this the depiction of someone who all too easily abandons her loyalties?

Desire, Knowledge, and Submission: Rahab as a Moral Agent

While we lack full access to Rahab's desires, we can make some observations about what she wants to accomplish. In fact, the latter verses in the passage, specifically verses 9-24, help to explain Rahab's behavior, indicating that she feels threatened by the Israelites and that she believes the Israelite story that God has given the land to them and that the Canaanites' dispossession is an inevitable consequence of this divine gift. She states to the Israelite spies on her roof, "I know that the LORD has given you the land, and that dread of you has fallen on us, and that all the inhabitants of the land melt in fear before you" (v. 9). The Israelites' reputation had indeed preceded them: Rahab recites how the Israelite God dried up the Sea of Reeds and how the Israelites utterly destroyed the Amorite kings Sihon and Og. Like other Canaanites, Rahab would like to avoid the utter destruction that had been the fate of the Amorites.

Clearly, one of Rahab's desires is to survive the onslaught. Because of the Israelites' past successes, the people of Jericho live in dread of defeat. Indeed, because of the Hebrew people's military successes, Rahab speaks of God's supremacy: "The LORD your God is indeed God in heaven above and on earth below" (v. 11). The gods of Jericho do not even get honorable mention in Rahab's discourse. At least in her rhetoric and in her behavior toward the spies, she capitulates completely.

I emphasized earlier that a person is considered a moral agent, and moral responsibility is ascribed to him or her, only if the action or disposition is voluntary. To be a moral act by a moral agent, the behavior must originate from inside the person herself, uncoerced by external forces. There is no indication in the story that the spies insist that Rahab transfer her allegiance from the king and people of Jericho to the Hebrew people. However, she clearly sees the Hebrew people as an unavoidable threat: "For we have heard how the LORD dried up the water of the Red Sea before you when you came out of Egypt, and what you did to the two kings of the Amorites that were beyond the Jordan, to Sihon and Og, whom you utterly destroyed. As soon as we heard it, our hearts melted, and there was no courage left in any of us because of you" (vv. 10-11a). The extent to which Rahab's freedom of choice is constrained is not immediately clear. Reflecting the narrator's anticipation of Jericho's fall, for the sake of survival, Rahab decides to accept what she sees as inevitable and to create the best outcome she can.

Rahab's desire becomes clear in the deal she proposes to the spies: "Now then, since I have dealt kindly with you, swear to me by the LORD that you in turn will deal kindly with my family. Give me a sign of good faith that you will spare my father and mother, my brothers and sisters, and all who belong to them, and deliver our lives from death" (vv. 12-13). In spite of the intimidation factor (or perhaps because of it), Rahab negotiates to save her family. In fact, the spies suggest that Rahab herself is a moral force to be reckoned with, pursuing her desire assertively—twice they state that she made them swear to an oath: "We will be released from this oath that you have *made us swear* to you" (v. 17); and "if you tell this business of ours, then we shall be released from this oath that you *made us swear*" (v. 20). Another feature helping portray Rahab as a decisive person whose actions may be crucial to the Israelites' success, and even a pivotal character worth remembering, is the fact that she is named, while the spies are not.[26]

Where knowledge is concerned, it is possible, even if the spies' speech contains noticeable linguistic differences, that Rahab did not at first know who they were or where they came from. Perhaps they came initially as customers. By verse 3, however, Rahab has learned that they are spies, and she can no longer feign innocence. She hides them knowing full well who they are, risking harsh retaliation from the king's men, perhaps execution.[27] Her actions from this point on—hiding the men on the roof under flax, lying and misleading the king's men—cannot be construed as proceeding from lack of knowledge. The spies pose no immediate threat and are at her mercy. A quiet word to the king's men could have resulted in their capture and execution. Yet Rahab decides to protect the spies.

Because of her knowledge of the Hebrew people's earlier military exploits, Rahab makes the spies swear to a mutually beneficial agreement. She claims that she has shown them loyalty, and she assertively pursues her desire to save herself and her family. Apparently believing that the Israelites' success is due to their God's support (v. 11), she requires them to swear by the God of Israel to save her and her family. For Rahab, that is enough of a sign.

The spies return to Joshua with renewed confidence that God has given them the land. Rahab's words have given the spies a confidence that is echoed in their own speech to Joshua. They note that the people of Jericho melt in fear before the Israelites. Rahab has convinced them that God has given them the land and that, because of their debilitating fear, the Canaanites will offer no significant resistance.

Newsom suggests that "the discipline of submission to external authority" is one of the elements forming "the fundamental grammar of the moral self" in Hebrew Bible texts. Rahab rebels against external authority, at least from the perspective of her Canaanite community. She openly and deliberately defies the king of Jericho and collaborates with the enemy. Yet from the perspective of the Israelite writers of Josh 2, Rahab is a loyal person who respects the authority of the God of Israel, exhibiting loyalty to a new community of her own choosing. In her behavior, likewise, Rahab extends great courtesy to God's people, declaring God's sovereign authority: "The LORD your God is indeed God in heaven above and on earth below" (v. 11). In this sense she submits to the authority of the Israelites and their God.

Yet, most significantly from the viewpoint of loyalty, Rahab gives first priority to her primary relationships. By pushing for an agreement to protect her family, Rahab shows moral agency and responsibility similar to one of the two types described by Gilligan:

> The values of justice and autonomy, presupposed in current theories of human growth and incorporated into definitions of morality and self, imply a view of the individual as separate and of relationships as either hierarchical or contractual, bound by the alternatives of constraint and cooperation. In contrast, the values of care and connection, salient in women's thinking, imply a view of self and other as interdependent and of relationships as networks created and sustained by attention and response.[28]

The Bible itself evaluates Rahab's actions in relation to Israel's benefit. Joshua 6:25 simply states that Joshua spares Rahab and her family because she hid the spies. Hebrews 11:31 implies that she was obedient because "she had received the spies in peace." James 2:25 declares that Rahab was justified by her works. Nevertheless, the decisions made and actions taken by Rahab fit the model of moral agency that stresses care and connection. She is attentive to the connection with her family members and responds to the threat of Israelite takeover by protecting the people to whom she is in closest relationship.

Rahab in Dialogue with Esther

I originally thought Rahab and Esther would be good biblical characters to place in dialogue because they seemed to share the role of "collaborator." Certainly they shared the position of women characters who are personally threatened and whose communities are also threatened. Though they act in very different ways, each must negotiate the difficult situation of foreign hegemony. Each must use careful strategy to survive and to save lives in precarious circumstances.

Of course, there are significant differences between the two characters. While as a prostitute Rahab stands on a lower step of the social ladder, Esther is crowned queen of Persia by King Ahasuerus (Esth 2:17), who hosts a banquet in her honor and invites all the officials and ministers (v. 18). At the same time, Esther comes from a disadvantaged community, a fact that is underscored in Mordecai's asking Esther to keep her ethnic identity a secret (2:10, 20). The disadvantage is severely compounded when Haman plots to destroy all the Jews in King Ahasuerus' empire (3:6). Because of his extraordinary influence with the king, Haman is able to arrange for a royal edict that the Jews will be destroyed on the thirteenth day of the twelfth month of Adar (3:13-14).

Esther has been accustomed to following Mordecai's guidance since he raised her after her parents' death. Mordecai applies all the pressure he can through his statement in 4:14: "For if you keep silence at such a time as this, relief and deliverance will rise for the Jews from another quarter, but you and your father's family will perish. Who knows? Perhaps you have come to royal dignity for just such a time as this." Mordecai appeals to Esther's special status as the king's favorite to ask her to intervene to save both her family and her people. He also tells Esther that her status as queen will not protect her from annihilation. Perhaps the greatest pressure that Mordecai exerts on Esther is to suggest that she had been destined to become queen in order to deliver her people. His phrasing, though subtle, suggests that divine providence may have been at work in her rise to royal status, or at least that she has been fortunate and that the Jews are lucky that she occupies such an advantageous position.[29] Esther's inclination, as reflected in her childhood formation by Mordecai, is to follow Mordecai's lead, but there are subtle external pressures to deal with in addition to her predisposition to obey her cousin, as his admonition to hide her Jewish identity hints (2:20). As she points out to Mordecai, seeking to influence Ahasuerus involves significant personal risk (4:11): "All the king's servants and the people of the king's provinces know that if any man or woman goes to the king inside the inner court without being called, there is but one law—all alike are to be put to death. Only if the king holds out the golden scepter to someone, may that person live. I myself have not been called to come in to the king for thirty days."

These passages, as well as subsequent verses, suggest that there are significant outside forces that constrain Esther's making a free, independent choice as a moral agent. Esther asks her cousin to have the Jews fast for three days, indicating that she and her maidservants will also fast. Finally, she announces that she will intercede with Ahasuerus, saying, "If I perish, I perish" (4:16).

As the next chapter relates, Esther's actions show even more careful strategizing than Rahab's. Her fear of execution for approaching the king unbidden is quickly put to rest when he sees her, holds out the golden scepter, and indicates that he will agree to any request, up to half his kingdom. Yet despite this reassurance, Esther proceeds very cautiously indeed. Since Haman occupies a powerful position, to speak overtly against him would be a mistake. She has to present her case for the Jewish people in the most persuasive way. Her two banquets serve to convince Haman that he is safe with her. But Esther's deft handling places her in the best possible light in the king's eyes and Haman in the worst. As a result, the king perceives Haman's treason, has him executed, and has an edict issued to counteract Haman's proclamation condemning the Jews. At the end of the story, the tables are turned, and the Jews are able, through divine edict, to attack and kill those who threatened their lives. Esther was a primary catalyst for this turn of events. Esther's desire is to save her community, her fellow Jews. Because of Mordecai's intervention, she had good knowledge of the threat to her people. Though she is initially conflicted, Esther decides to submit to the authority of her community, the community of her moral formation, especially the authority of her cousin Mordecai.

Both Rahab and Esther are forced to negotiate difficult and dangerous situations. They both face terrible consequences if their strategies fail. Both are strongly influenced by external forces that constrict their freedom of choice. Rahab's strategy is not as elaborate or as drawn out as Esther's. Yet in both cases, their own lives and the lives of family members are at stake.

Although it is not entirely clear how much knowledge is available, Rahab seems to know of the Israelites' military successes, even against countries outside of her usual purview. She also has sufficient knowledge of the city gate's operations and the surrounding geography to come up with a workable plan. Esther appears to know how to present herself at the royal court and is, thanks to Mordecai, reasonably well informed about the threat to her people. Mordecai himself seems to possess a great deal of knowledge about the affairs of the kingdom, both inside and outside the court, so Esther has a very capable advisor.

Esther's desire to save both her family and her people is very clear. She is willing to put her own life at risk in order to do so. In the end, she achieves her desires. Rahab's desires to save herself and her family are similarly transparent, and she too achieves that end. An interesting contrast is that while Rahab is placed at risk by circumstance, the circumstantial risk to Esther is unclear both to her and to us, Mordecai's warning notwithstanding. Had she decided to keep her ancestry secret, she might have remained safe. This makes her stepping forward as a Jew an act of courage on par with Rahab's choice to collude with the Israelites to save her family.

To a certain extent, both women submit to the authority of the empire. Rahab submits to the incipient Israelite empire and to the authority of Israel's God. Esther finds a skillful way to navigate within the empire. While she defers to Mordecai, whether she also submits to the God of her ancestors remains ambiguous.

The primary difference between Rahab and Esther lies in their submission to the authority of their respective communities. Esther submits deeply to the community that formed her. Though she assimilates successfully to the royal court of Ahasuerus and negotiates well with the empire's representatives, she is utterly faithful to the Jewish community and, in fact, achieves her community's acceptance within the broader society. Rahab, on the other hand, submits utterly to the Israelite community and to its God, embracing a new community and rejecting her own Jericho community and its gods.

What These Narratives Suggest about Our Own Moral Agency

What insights do these stories offer to the person today who wrestles with moral decisions? Rahab's story may discourage hasty judgments about the moral agency of others. My initial reaction to Rahab was to dismiss her sense of moral commitment as inadequate. I was troubled by the apparent ease with which she abandoned her Jericho community and the king. But Gilligan's essay reveals Rahab as a moral agent who puts her primary relationships first—that is, her close relationships with family members. Viewing Israelite victory as inevitable, she makes the best choice available to protect her family from harm, even when it means abandoning the town where she plied her trade. Her story clarifies the limits of moral agency when every choice available is a tragic one.

Esther, on the other hand, represents the other pole in Gilligan's two models of moral agency. She decides in favor of detachment, of "equality, reciprocity, justice, and rights."[30] Rather than making relationships and connection her primary concerns, Esther risks these relationships, as well as her own safety, in order to pursue a just outcome for the Jewish people. She embraces a different vision of moral agency than that reflected by Rahab. If Esther had put primary relationships in the foreground, she might have chosen to reveal her Jewish identity only to her husband the king and have asked him to make an exception for herself and Mordecai. However, Esther risks both her own safety and her relationship with her husband, King Ahasuerus, choosing to emphasize the innocence of the Jewish people and to save them from massacre.

All of us must wrestle with moral decisions within constrained choices, and as Gilligan points out, each of us has the two different models imbedded in the self and can be pulled either way:

> As in the ambiguous figure which can be perceived alternatively as a vase or two faces, there appear to be two ways of perceiving self in relation to others, both grounded in reality, but each imposing on that reality a different organization. But, as with the perception of the ambiguous figure, when one configuration of self emerges, the other seems to temporarily vanish.[31]

Depending upon the constraints we face when making difficult decisions, we may opt for the relationship model or the justice model. The fully developed moral self is capable of moving in either direction or in a combination of the two. Rahab and Esther teach us that our choices may be limited by our circumstances and that we may also feel pulled in certain directions because of our own moral formation. The two stories certainly point to the complexities involved.

Rahab opts for her family, following a treacherous path to bring loved ones to safety, proving a faithful provider for those who counted on her advocacy. Her family subsequently contributes to the growth of the Israelite people. Esther risks sacrificing relationships, and life itself, to achieve just ends, shrewdly calculating her enemy's self-destruction. These women—acting in a life-threatening, violent world—nevertheless claim moral agency in the full sense of the phrase. When faced with difficult choices, both weigh their options and take decisive action. Their stories suggest that moral decision making is more complex than it first appears and that any decision may involve painful and even tragic trade-offs. In the end, choices are best made through careful discernment, with full knowledge of the moral vision one's actions promote. The Israelite community deemed these women's exploits worth retelling and preserved their stories for future generations. We are fortunate that they were preserved for our consideration.

For Further Reading

Aristotle. *Aristotle's Nicomachean Ethics*. Translated by Robert C. Bartlett and Susan D. Collins. Chicago: University of Chicago Press, 2011.

Cahill, Lisa Sowle. "Christian Character, Biblical Community, and Human Values." Pages 3–17 in *Character and Scripture: Moral Formation, Community, and Biblical Interpretation*. Edited by W. P. Brown. Grand Rapids: Eerdmans, 2002.

Carroll R., M. Daniel. "He Has Told You What Is Good: Moral Formation in Micah." Pages 103–18 in *Character Ethics and the Old Testament: Moral Dimensions of Scripture*. Edited by M. Daniel Carroll R. and Jacqueline E. Lapsley. Louisville, Ky.: Westminster John Knox, 2007.

Eshleman, Andrew. "Moral Responsibility." In *Stanford Encyclopedia of Philosophy*. Winter 2009 ed. Edited by Edward N. Zalta. http://plato.stanford.edu/archives/win2009/entries/moral-responsibility/.

Fischer, John Martin. "Recent Work on Moral Responsibility." *Ethics* 110 (1999): 93–139.

Kuan, Kah-Jin Jeffrey, and Mai-Anh Le Tran. "Reading Race Reading Rahab: A 'Broad' Asian American Reading of a 'Broad' Other." Pages 27–44 in *Postcolonial Interventions*. Edited by T. B. Liew. The Bible in the Modern World 23. Sheffield: Sheffield Phoenix, 2009.

Newsom, Carol A. "Models of the Moral Self: Hebrew Bible and Second Temple Judaism." *JBL* 131 (2012): 5–25.

CHAPTER 12

THE TRAUMATIZED "I" IN PSALM 102
A Feminist Biblical Theology of Suffering

Amy C. Cottrill[*]

Introduction

Encounters with violence live on in bodies long after visible wounds have healed. As a nation at war, the United States is currently confronting the return of soldiers who experience posttraumatic stress disorder (PTSD), displaying symptoms such as depression, hyperarousal, panic, suicidal tendencies, and violent outbursts. General George Casey, the chief of staff of the U.S. Army from 2007 to 2011, called PTSD "the defining military health issue of our era."[1]

Of course, it is not only soldiers who encounter violence, and the consequences of violence are not just a military issue. It is also one of deep theological urgency for all who have experienced trauma, military or otherwise, and for the communities in which they live. Those who study trauma are increasingly clear: when we experience extreme suffering and stress, it may affect us

[*] I feel privileged to offer this essay in honor of Carol Newsom, who has been such a tremendous and valued influence in my intellectual and professional life. Her career is marked by thoughtful consideration of issues of agency, selfhood, and feminism, and her generative scholarly contributions continue to inform my own efforts. I am grateful beyond measure for her generous attention to her students and to her own scholarship that has shaped the theological imagination of so many.

in ways that escape cognitive awareness but that nonetheless register significantly in our bodies.

Recently, theology informed by trauma studies has contributed to the ways we think not only about the moments in which people experience suffering but also about the embodied "open wound" that remains long after.[2] As communities of human beings with bodies, we have a critical need to use the resources at our disposal to help us think, speak, and act in ways that foster empowerment and healing for those who live with the wounds of trauma. The questions guiding my inquiry into these matters are these: How are suffering and trauma imagined and addressed within the Hebrew Bible? What resources does the Hebrew Bible offer to individuals and communities who suffer and experience trauma? How might feminist theologians, scholars, and lay people critique, affirm, and creatively appropriate those biblical resources today?

Feminist theology has much to offer our communities as we struggle to confront the embodied suffering in our midst. It is no surprise that the body has emerged as an important element of feminist theological thought. The female body has been maligned, blamed, abused, scorned, raped, ignored, controlled, silenced, and diminished. Much of this treatment has been supported and informed by Western philosophical and religious teachings that have marginalized the body as a source of authoritative intelligence, positing the idea of a dualistic self that privileges the rational (male) mind over the emotional (female) body. As this flawed paradigm begins to shift, we are challenged to create methodologies that foster thoughtful consideration of all kinds of human experience and to integrate what have been inaccurately conceived as the separate categories of mind and body. The following question will help us bring the body into theological focus: What does it mean to interpret experience from an enfleshed perspective, one that assumes that the embodied self has important information to offer, information that should be of value to God and to one's community? Embedded in this important question are a number of issues for feminist thinkers, issues related to concepts of selfhood, agency, power, the authority of emotion and feeling, and the challenge of reconstructing relationships with community and God after a traumatic experience.

Fortunately, the lament psalms offer concrete examples of embodied theological expression that we can use when navigating trauma and suffering. Strikingly, these laments often include descriptive accounts of the psalmist's own bodily experience. The anguished body of Ps 22 is one example among many:[3]

> Like water poured out,
>> all my bones separate from each other.
> My heart is like wax,
>> melting within my bowels. (Ps 22:14)[4]

To be sure, in these laments the suffering body is portrayed within the patriarchal structures of ancient culture. These patriarchal assumptions rankle feminists today. Yet the laments also offer an indispensable model for expressing suffering, a mode of communication that is at once authoritative for the psalmist, valued by God, and redemptive for the community. The Psalms do not reflect the mind/body dualism that has been so detrimental to our embodied lives. They may therefore assist us in facilitating healing among those who experience trauma and suffering. Simply put, because the body matters in the laments, they offer a way to envision embodied selfhood.

After briefly exploring the hermeneutical lens through which I read the Psalms, I will analyze one psalm in particular. Psalm 102 provides feminist thinkers with an embodied mode of address to God and community in the context of ongoing suffering and trauma. I will use the interpretive tools of feminist theology and trauma theory to see the experience of the body as theologically authoritative and will privilege the body's particular kind of knowledge. Therefore, my analysis of Ps 102 relies upon theological considerations of the experience of trauma, especially the ways that individual and communal trauma—both depicted in this psalm—are experienced through the body.

Theologians have often addressed the issue of suffering through theodicy, asking how we can reconcile the goodness of God with the experience of evil and suffering in the world. Yet, like many people today, this psalmist is far more interested in how one *lives* with the open wounds of trauma, how one remains in the world after an encounter with overwhelming suffering, than in how one answers the theodicy question. Reading with the psalmist provides a vital theological resource for those who suffer and for those who live in community with them.

A Hermeneutic of Creative Resiliency

The Psalms have long been enormously important in the liturgical and devotional lives of Jewish and Christian women. Yet, within the vast literature of Psalms scholarship, the footprint of feminism is shallow. What has been written thus far can be grouped into two categories: treatments character-ized by a hermeneutic of suspicion, and those characterized by a hermeneu-tic of retrieval.[5] Both types of interpretation have yielded important insights into the worldview and assumptions of the Psalms. Treatments typified by a hermeneutics of suspicion describe psalms as deeply embedded in the patriarchal world from which they emerged.[6] This worldview is evident in Ps 109:6-20, for instance, which reflects the privileged values of patriarchal culture. The psalm calls for obliteration of the enemy's community standing, honor, property, family connection, and public reputation. It reflects a culture of masculine warfare and reinforces androcentric notions of social honor and shame. In contrast, recuperative feminist treatments of the Psalms, employ-ing a hermeneutic of retrieval, have explored female metaphors and images of God, the possibility of female authorship of some of the prayers, and the dialogic nature of the lament psalms, which include subversive voices that challenge powerful, official, and exclusive theological messages.[7]

Combining a hermeneutic of suspicion with a hermeneutic of retrieval can provide an effective and empowering method of reading the laments through a feminist lens. Just as others in the past who have not found them-selves directly addressed by the Bible have nevertheless found ways to read it, we feminists can likewise employ creative resiliency to read the laments without abandoning our critical thinking. A hermeneutic of creative resil-iency need not ignore the deeply patriarchal nature of the psalms. Rather, employing such an approach may enable readers fully to acknowledge the context in which the rhetoric of the laments was formed, while also recog-nizing the texts' potential to reach far beyond their originating contexts. The effects of particular textual interpretations are as significant as the his-torical and ideological context in which a text was written.

In my treatment of Ps 102, I will make room for both retrieval and sus-picion. I will also add another layer, concentrating on the bodily, enfleshed representation of the psalmist as a matter of vital interest, expressed both in voice and in body. Psalms scholars have recently devoted attention to the laments as offering speech for those who suffer. As biblical scholar Melody Knowles recognizes, "voice" is an especially important concept in feminist scholarship, serving as a symbol of effective and powerful selfhood.[8] Voice is also a common theme in studies of trauma and suffering, especially con-cerning trauma's propensity to overwhelm voice and language. Indeed, there is a productive conversation to be had between feminist scholars, scholars of lament, and trauma theorists regarding voice. The laments provide words that give shape and form to overwhelming experiences, helping the disempowered reassert their personhood through language. This aspect of the laments should resonate significantly for feminists.

If the voice of the psalmist is important for feminist readers, the *body* of the psalmist is also critically important. The psalmist's body is her way of entering into conversation with God, her entry point into theological discourse. The laments do not offer a disembodied voice of theological despair. Rather, they offer a fully human, corporeal being, experiencing and feeling the world, her community, and her relationship with God through her body.[9] Though I do not assume that the historical psalmist of Ps 102 was female, or that the psalm was written for use by women specifically, the laments are important for feminists because of what counts as authoritative experience in one's address to God and the community: the embodied experience of the psalmist is an authoritative discourse in these texts. As a category of experience, the language of the body is of vital theological interest for feminist readers, and the laments offer a model of enfleshed selfhood for modern use.

My discussion of Ps 102 will progress through the psalm's three sections, which I am calling "the bodily experience of suffering" (vv. 1-11); "communal trauma and the suffering self" (vv. 12-22); and "the return to the body" (vv. 23-28). My intent is to reembody Psalms interpretation, to "feel with" the psalmist, to recognize the voice *and* body of the psalmist, and to hear the body as an authoritative source of intelligence about both the psalmist's experience and the political experience of Zion. Though the psalmist begins her prayer with description of her own wasted body, her suffering is connected to that of her community. Attentiveness to the body of the psalmist trains our reading practices to see and hear the enfleshed experience of the psalmist in her prayer.

The Bodily Experience of Suffering: Psalm 102:1-11

[1]A prayer of the needy one when he is faint
  and pours his plea before YHWH.
YHWH, hear my prayer,
  let my cry come before you.
[2]Do not hide your face from me
  in my time of distress.
Turn your ear to me.
  When I cry, answer me quickly.

³For my days have vanished like smoke,
     and my bones burn like a furnace.
⁴My body is stricken and withered like grass,
     because I forget to eat my food.
⁵Because of the sound of my groaning,
     my bones show through my skin.
⁶I am like a great owl in the wilderness,
     an owl among the ruins.
⁷I lie awake;
     I am like a lone bird on a roof.
⁸All day my enemies revile me;
     those who deride me use my name as a curse.
⁹For I have eaten ashes like bread,
     and my drink I mix with tears,
¹⁰because of your wrath and your fury;
     for you have lifted me up and cast me away.
¹¹My days are like a lengthening shadow;
     I wither like grass.

The first five verses of this psalm offer a descriptive accounting of bodily experience. The body is the basis of the psalmist's prayer to God, the basis of her understanding of herself and of her self-presentation to God and community. The portrait of the suffering body is extensive and painful. The superscription in verse 1 identifies this prayer as one of a "needy" or "lowly" person—a designation, often employed in laments of the individual, that signifies the humble, needy circumstances in which the psalmist exists.[10] The psalmist is wasted (v. 1); she weeps (literally, "my drink I mix with tears," v. 9), groans (v. 5), and withers (vv. 4, 11). She experiences her body as weakened and diminished. Her body withers like grass; her strength becomes so exhausted that she does not feed herself (v. 4). In verse 9 the psalmist returns to the imagery of eating, explaining that when she does eat, it is as if she eats ashes and not bread. This theme resumes in verse 11 with a more comprehensive reference to her withering existence: "My days are lengthening like a shadow; I wither like grass."

That the psalmist is too weak to eat is a way of explaining her physical symptoms, possibly related to illness or impending death. But it is also language of impaired agency on a more fundamental level. The psalmist's self-description in these verses resonates with observations theologian Serene Jones makes about the diminished agency trauma victims often experience: "Trauma survivors can lose confidence that they are effective actors in the world, because, in the original event, they experience just the opposite: a state of frozen *powerlessness*."[11] Jones's discussion of the experience of trauma victims could easily describe the speaker in Ps 102. The psalmist feels her body to be impaired to the point of ineffectiveness.

The psalmist's sense of powerlessness is readily apparent in images of physical ephemerality. Her physical existence seems fleeting as her life drifts away: "For my days have vanished like smoke" (v. 3). Similarly, in verse 11, the psalmist says that her days "are lengthening like a shadow." The days of her physical existence are inconsequential, intangible like smoke and shadow, almost a trick of the light. On one level, the image of days vanishing intimates the rapid approach of death; the psalmist feels her time on earth is short. The image of days like smoke can also be read another way, however, as an expression of powerlessness. The intangibility of her days, contrasted with the withering body, all contribute to a portrait of impermanence, as if the psalmist wonders if her physical existence is real, concrete, and perceptible to others.

Though images of the self as smoke and shadow do not necessarily connote pain as imagery of weaponry and wounds elsewhere in the laments does, this language of physical ephemerality is not an insignificant expression of fleetingness and dissipation.[12] The second line in verse 3 contributes to and clarifies the physical sensation, the lived experience of feeling as inconsequential as smoke: "My bones burn like a furnace." The psalmist's experience of ephemerality is felt like fire; the smoke that represents her powerlessness is generated by the psalmist's charred bones. The "punch" of this image of fleetingness is in the second line, which does not simply reiterate the first line but intensifies the image, articulating the agony of the psalmist's bodily existence. The fleeting smoke indicates her deeper, perhaps less externally visible, pain. As the psalmist's body burns from the inside out, her existence becomes an excruciating hell.

Imagery of bones depicts not only pain but intense physical vulnerability. Normally, bones provide the human body structure, capacity, and the possibility of agency. In Ps 102 the psalmist feels her structure to be painfully unstable and vulnerable. Not only are the psalmist's bones burning; they protrude: "Because of the sound of my groaning, my bones show through my skin" (v. 5). Here the bones convey painful physical vulnerability. The bones that create the skeletal order of her physical existence are threatened and exposed. This image of bodily exposure symbolizes lack of protection, vulnerability that she also expresses in the social realm.

In the first section of this psalm, images of physical powerlessness mingle with images of abandonment, isolation, and social marginalization. Compromised structure, vulnerability, and lack of agency, all of which the psalmist feels in her body, also extend to marginalization in her social environment (vv. 6-8). When the psalmist is in the company of others, she is mostly the object of disdain and mockery, reviled by her enemies and used as a curse (v. 8). The psalmist's sense of isolation is so intense that the boundaries between death and life begin to blur. The images in verse 6 of a great owl in the wilderness, an owl in the ruins, indicate the psalmist's sense of being on the brink of nothingness, precarious physically and emotionally.[13] The image is repeated and intensified in the next verse, where she resembles a "lone bird on a roof" (v. 7). The birds mentioned in these verses are particularly associated with locations of devastation.[14] Trauma theorist Judith Herman describes the experience of trauma victims that contextualizes this imagery:

> Traumatized people feel utterly abandoned, utterly alone, cast out of the human and divine systems of care and protection that sustain life. Thereafter, a sense of alienation, of disconnection, pervades every relationship, from the most intimate familial bonds to the most abstract affiliations of community and religion. When trust is lost, traumatized people feel that they belong more to the dead than to the living.[15]

The psalmist is distanced from every relationship and source of emotional and physical care, utterly alone. She is a creature of the ruins, a resident of a wasteland as close to death as is possible while still drawing breath.

It is not just the psalmist's enemies who abandon her, however. In verses 9-10, the psalmist clearly sees God as directly involved in her suffering. God casts her away and makes her the object of anger: "For I have eaten ashes like bread, and my drink I mix with tears, because of your wrath and your fury; for you have lifted me up and cast me away" (vv. 9-10).

The question of the psalmist's understanding of God is discussed more fully below, but it should be recognized here that her sense of God's active role in her suffering is clear. Though the act of prayer itself seems to reflect the psalmist's confidence in God's continuing receptivity, the psalmist also asserts that God is an agent in her suffering. The psalmist's divine and human relationships are unstable and in flux, contributing to her profound feeling of social abandonment and physical distress.

While the psalmist experiences extraordinary isolation, she is also confident that this information about her body, her physical existence, is relevant. The authority of the psalmist's prayer, the foundation upon which she comes before God and community, is her bodily experience. She evidently believes that this experience matters to God. Though the psalmist begins her prayer with a thorough depiction of her personal bodily experience, the language of the body expresses not only physical pain but also alienation from the social world in which she is deeply embedded. Her thoroughly embodied sense of self is informed by her surroundings: the relationships, divine and human, that create the potential for her to thrive. The body is never just language of the individual in this psalm but also language of the relational. In the next section of the psalm, the alienation and marginalization evident in the psalmist's physical experience connects to the experience of the politically traumatized Zion.

Communal Trauma and the Suffering Self: Psalm 102:12-22

¹²But you, YHWH, are enthroned forever;
  your fame endures throughout the ages.
¹³You will rise and take pity on Zion,
  for it is time to be compassionate toward her;
  the time has come.
¹⁴Your servants take delight in its stones,
  and pity its dust.
¹⁵The nations will fear the name of YHWH,
  all the kings of the earth, your glory.
¹⁶For YHWH has built Zion;
  he has appeared in all his glory.
¹⁷He has turned to the prayer of the destitute,
  and has not despised their prayer.
¹⁸May this be written down for a coming generation,
  so that people yet to be created may praise YHWH.
¹⁹For he looks down from his holy height.
  YHWH beholds the earth from the heavens,
²⁰to hear the groans of the prisoner,
  to free those condemned to death,
²¹to announce in Zion the name of YHWH,
  his praises in Jerusalem,
²²when the nations gather together,
  the kingdoms to serve YHWH.

Perhaps the aspect of this psalm most often discussed in previous
scholarly treatments is the abrupt shift from elements typical of individual
laments to the psalm's Zion references.[16] Why are there Zion elements in
this psalm? Why the shift from matters that seem relevant to an individual
on her deathbed to matters that relate more to large-scale political events in
Zion? Some scholars interpret this abrupt shift as a sign of redaction, even
recommending removal of these verses, since Zion elements in a lament
psalm are so atypical.[17]

Redaction is certainly one explanation. But the feminist phrase "the
personal is political" provides another lens through which to interpret the
combining of personal lament and Zion themes in Ps 102.[18] "The personal
is political" captures a central theme of modern feminist thought, that the
individual often experiences the injustices and ills of the larger social environment in her personal life and in her body. In like manner, the boundaries
between individual and community break down in this psalm. The social
dis-ease of an alienated community is reflected in the language of the suffering body; the desire for restored community is felt as an illness in the body.
In fact, in verse 17 the psalmist refers to herself as "destitute," recalling the
prior portrayal of physical and social diminishment in verses 1-11. From a
feminist perspective, this psalm bears witness to a kind of integrated indi-
vidual/communal personhood, informed by the authority of embodiment.

Increasingly today, the political is understood not as something external to the body and mind of the individual but as an aspect of lived existence
that takes up residence in the bodies of individuals. In fact, trauma theorists
discuss the effects of overwhelming individual or communal violence, which
sometimes permanently alters cognitive functions.[19] Communal situations
and political structures are not "out there" but take up residence in human
bodies. Psalm 102 reflects what trauma theorist Arlene Audergon says of
the traumatized self: "An orientation is required that is at once personal,
communal and political."[20]

Zion's trauma reflects the psalmist's perception that she is intimately
connected both to her local community and to her nation. The psalmist's
bodily experience becomes a way of speaking about not only her own social
isolation but also Zion's political situation. It is not just the psalmist's vulnerability within her community that causes her physical pain but the condition of the community itself. The language of the body in this psalm is
a rich, multivalent discourse, a language that the psalmist clearly believes

authorizes her experience before God and reflects her embeddedness in the political suffering of her nation.

God's relationship to the psalmist's suffering is voiced in the first section (vv. 1-11), but it dominates the second section (vv. 12-22)—though in an unexpected way. In verse 11, as mentioned above, the psalmist depicts God as an agent in her suffering: speaking to God, she says she eats ashes and drinks tears "because of your wrath and your fury; for you have lifted me up and cast me away." In contrast, in verses 12-22, God is characterized as the powerful redeemer of Zion, one who will act on behalf of the destitute and who will strike fear in the hearts of other nations that have not shown compassion to Zion: "The nations will fear the name of YHWH, all the kings of the earth, your glory. For YHWH has built Zion; he has appeared in all his glory" (vv. 15-16). In verses 12-22, God is powerful, compassionate, and salvific, and the psalmist approaches God with absolute confidence. In fact, she is so confident that God will save Zion and will act on behalf of the nation's suffering that she instructs the listener to write down her assurance, as if for evidence: "May this be written down for a coming generation, so that people yet to be created may praise YHWH" (v. 18). The psalmist's confidence that God will redeem Zion's suffering is palpable in her lofty language about God's mercy and power.

These portrayals of God seem contrary. Is this a God who causes suffering or one who practices compassion and redemption? Yet according to trauma theorists and theologians, we should expect to see confusion in the central theological frameworks of those who experience overwhelming pain and suffering. This psalmist does seem to hold competing views of God. She struggles to make them fit into her experience of suffering. She does not offer a unified theological expression, but one that bears witness to the fragmentary nature of trauma, in which enduring pain defies coherent answers.

Though tension stands between these portrayals of God, they both reflect the psalmist's confidence in God's power, whether it is power to cause suffering or to bring redemption. What is most interesting, in fact, is not that the psalmist's understandings of God conflict with each other but that the psalmist does not frame these understandings in the way we might expect. She does not ask *why* God has caused her and her community to suffer. Nor does she explicitly challenge God's use of power or ask how a good God could allow and even contribute to her suffering. Though the questioning of divine abuse of power appears in other psalms (e.g., Ps 88), this theodicy question does not drive Ps 102. Especially in light of the psalmist's eloquent articulation of her suffering and her belief in God's role in it, the question is, *Why does this prayer not pose the theodicy question?* How can the psalmist affirm God's power to cause and alleviate suffering without questioning God's use of that power in her life? Especially in a situation in which the psalmist feels her agency to be dramatically curtailed both personally and politically, does this failure to hold God accountable represent a theology that actually contributes to her ongoing powerlessness?

Though a prayer that celebrates God's control even of her suffering may seem contradictory and potentially damaging to one who feels herself to be powerless, Serene Jones argues that survivors of trauma often need to believe that their world is intelligible and trustworthy.[21] What seems like a relinquishment of agency may in fact be an attempt to create a sense of order in a world that seems fundamentally broken and untrustworthy. To regain agency, survivors of trauma often need to believe the world to be a space that is understandable, that offers them a way of existing that makes sense again.[22] In this light, the psalmist's assertions of God's authority and power are not necessarily a relinquishment of agency, reinforcing her powerlessness, but a way of imagining herself as capable of being in the world again, of returning from the ruins and wilderness to reconstruct meaning. Indeed, the idea of God's enthronement and power causes the psalmist to feel confident and even hopeful about the future, and even to communicate her hope to future generations (v. 18).

Though the theodicy question has been prevalent in theological treatments of suffering, trauma theory expands the ways theology responds to suffering.[23] Those who treat survivors of trauma have found that the "why" of suffering is often not the most helpful or relevant question. Theologians of trauma are often interested not merely in rational understanding but in strategies for survival, for facing the challenge of remaining, for living in the middle between death and life. In the throes of a traumatic event, the key question is not *why* we *suffer* but *how* we *survive*. How does one stand upright on the shifting ground of trauma? How does one live with its effects? How does one pray when the ground continues to shift? What practices can lead one who suffers into full personhood and full relationship with God, self, and others? These questions drive Ps 102, which offers not a disembodied theology of suffering but a prayer based on bodily experience. The psalmist finds the possibility of thriving and of agency, for herself and for Zion, in a powerful and capacious God.

The psalm could easily have ended with this optimistic call for all nations to serve the God of Zion. Yet, as we will see, the psalmist's description of her bodily experience returns in the final section, connecting it with the first.

The Return to the Body: Psalm 102:23-28

[23]He drained my strength in midcourse;[24]
    he shortened my days.
[24]I say, "My God, do not take me away
    in the midst of my days,
you whose years go on
    for generations upon generations.
[25]Long ago you established the earth;
    the heavens are the work of your hands.
[26]They will perish, but you will remain.
    All of them will wear out like a garment;
you change them like clothing and they pass away.
    [27]But you are the same, and your years never end.
[28]May the children of your servants dwell safely
    and their children endure in your presence."

The psalmist's description of diminished bodily experience is not as developed here as in the first section. But after the highly confident hymnic elements in verses 12-22, it communicates that the psalmist's confidence in God's ultimate intention to save the destitute does not undermine the authority of her ongoing painful physical experience. This return to the traumatized body is theologically significant. Trauma does not end even after moments of supreme confidence in God's ability to heal and restore. Moments of clarity and hope are always interrupted by the past, often in physical ways. As theologian Shelly Rambo says, trauma is not a singular event but one "that continues, that persists in the present. Trauma is what does not go away. It persists in symptoms that live on in the body, in the intrusive fragments of memories that return."[25] One may witness moments of hope, moments of new life, but the memories remain, as does the challenge to live with those experiences. So the psalmist comes back to the body in pain.

This final return to bodily experience leads to proclamation of God's power and ultimate sway over the conditions of the psalmist's suffering. In verse 25 the psalmist refers to God as creator: "Long ago you established the earth; the heavens are the work of your hands." This is a new characterization: whereas in the previous section God was responsible for creating and sustaining Zion, in these final verses God's power reaches from the local to the global. Enemies become like clothing that will eventually wear out (v. 26). But God is not constrained by time, place, and the vicissitudes of human transience: "You are the same, and your years never end" (v. 27). Again, the psalmist does not acknowledge God's global, creative, enduring power in order to ask about theodicy. Rather, acknowledgment of God's vast and enduring power provides reason to hope for the future: "May the children of your servants dwell securely and their offspring endure in your presence" (v. 28).

Though creation language is always on some level a discourse of power, it is also a discourse of physical intimacy. In Ps 139:15, for instance, the psalmist uses creation imagery to indicate the special responsibility God has for the psalmist's life: "My bones were not hidden from you. When I was created in secret, I was intricately woven in the recess of the earth." This psalm's depiction of God as creator not only invokes God's superior power but also claims God's ongoing, continuing role as sustainer of creation, including the psalmist's own body. In talking about God's involvement in the establishment of the earth, and referring to the heavens as the work of God's hands, the psalmist connects God's character as creator with her physical security and the ability of her children to live in safety. In fact, mention of God's hands suggests personal involvement in the world's very construction.

God's intimate relationship with creation is not cause for passive submission to suffering. Instead, the relationship of enduring care connects God to the psalmist in the very structure of the places in which she lives, the earth and Zion. Her acknowledgment of God's power provides the possibility of agency, the expression of hope for the future. That expression of hope does not erase her ongoing experience of physical suffering and trauma, but it does allow her to manage the uneven path between present suffering and the potential future.

Implications and Conclusions

The lament psalms offer language and theological assumptions that place authoritative value on bodily intelligence, especially important in the context of suffering and trauma. That the body in pain matters in the lament psalms should not be missed by modern readers. For those who suffer, the laments provide an important language of embodiment, a vital articulation of enfleshed selfhood. The individual laments offer a necessary theological response to the experience of trauma and suffering. Herein lies the importance of a hermeneutic of creative resiliency, combining a hermeneutic of suspicion with a hermeneutic of retrieval. Of course, the psalmist's bodily experience exists within a complex rhetorical world and should be critiqued as well as appreciated. Yes, the laments reflect patriarchal ideology. But as a mode of address, the embodied selfhood represented in the psalmists' speech emerges as a fleshly authority, a privileged way of knowing the self, the community, and God. Anthony Gilby, a sixteenth-century interpreter of the Psalms, said, "Whereas all other scriptures do teach us what God saith unto us . . . [the psalms] do teach us, what we shall saie unto God."[26] The Psalms do not offer unambiguous language for feminist readers. They may not teach *what* we shall say. Rather, they suggest *how* we shall say it: with confidence that the experience of our bodies matters to our Creator and should be recorded for future generations.

For Further Reading

Brown, William P. *Seeing the Psalms: A Theology of Metaphor.* Louisville, Ky.: Westminster John Knox, 2002.

Cannon, Katie Geneva, Emilie M. Townes, and Angela D. Sims, eds. *Womanist Theological Ethics: A Reader.* Louisville, Ky.: Westminster John Knox, 2011.

Day, Linda, and Carolyn Pressler, eds. *Engaging the Bible in a Gendered World.* Louisville, Ky.: Westminster John Knox, 2006.

Declaisse-Walford, Nancy L. "Psalms." Pages 221–31 in *Women's Bible Commentary: Revised and Updated.* Edited by Carol A. Newsom, Sharon H. Ringe, and Jacqueline E. Lapsley. Louisville, Ky.: Westminster John Knox, 2012.

Herman, Judith. *Trauma and Recovery: The Aftermath of Violence—from Domestic Abuse to Political Terror.* New York: Basic Books, 1977.

Isherwood, Lisa, and Elizabeth Stuart. *Introducing Body Theology.* Sheffield: Sheffield Academic, 1998.

Jones, Serene. *Trauma and Grace: Theology in a Ruptured World.* Louisville, Ky.: Westminster John Knox, 2009.

Knowles, Melody. "Feminist Interpretation of the Psalms." Pages 424–36 in *The Oxford Handbook to the Psalms.* Edited by William P. Brown. Oxford: Oxford University Press, 2014.

Lee, Nancy C. *Lyrics of Lament: From Tragedy to Transformation.* Minneapolis: Fortress, 2010.

Mandolfo, Carleen. "Finding Their Voices: Sanctioned Subversion in Psalms of Lament." *Horizons in Biblical Theology* 24 (2002): 27–52.

Rambo, Shelly. *Trauma and Spirit: A Theology of Remaining.* Louisville, Ky.: Westminster John Knox, 2010.

Tanner, Beth LaNeel. "Hearing the Cries Unspoken: An Intertextual-Feminist Reading of Psalm 109." Pages 283–301 in *Wisdom and Psalms: A Feminist Companion to the Bible.* Edited by Athalya Brenner and Carole Fontaine. Sheffield: Sheffield Academic, 1998.

CHAPTER 13

"MISSING WOMEN" IN JUDGES 19–21
A Feminist Biblical Theology Concerning Violence against Women

Jo Ann Hackett

What are women worth? In what ways does violence in a patriarchal society touch the lives of women? In what kinds of societies is it so important to have a son that the mother's life is threatened by the number of pregnancies or abortions she is expected to undergo until a son is born? And what kind of message does female infanticide and abortion of female fetuses send to all females in the society?

In the modern world, "missing women"[1] refers to the millions of women who would be alive today if they had been allowed to live, instead of being aborted as fetuses or dying as newborns because of female infanticide. The men who might have married these women are known as "surplus men."[2] Most reports of missing women concern the one-child rule in China, but the same situation exists in a number of other countries. The extended story in Judg 19–21 bears a great resemblance to these modern tragedies. Both the modern and the ancient cases involve societies that prefer sons over daughters and men over women. Both stories begin with horrific violence against females (whether women, newborns, or fetuses); both involve groups of men without women to marry; both problems are "solved" by imposing more violence on women; and both are examples of the lack of agency that females have in their respective societies. In more general terms, they describe violence against the most vulnerable in society for the benefit of the strong, with the blessing of those in power.

Missing Women in Judges 19–21

We will first explore the biblical narrative with modern missing women in mind. Judges 21 follows the horrific story of the Levite's secondary wife[3] in Judg 19 and the resulting war between Benjamin and the rest of Israel in Judg 20.[4] In Judg 19 (as in Gen 19), we have stories of failed hospitality offered by one *ger* to other *gerim*—that is, people who are traveling or living outside their home territory and family.[5] In ancient Israelite village culture, there was no police force to uphold the rights of victims and punish criminals, so living within one's home territory was necessary for protection from violence. Protection took the form of blood vengeance: if someone from another family or group abused someone from one's family or group, a "redeemer" from that family punished those responsible. *Gerim*, living as they did outside a group from which their redeemers would come, did not have the luxury of such redemption.

Our story begins with the ordinary and escalates toward exaggeration, forcing readers who are attempting to read it as history to swallow greater and greater improbabilities. We will instead read it not as history but as story. A Levite from Judah is living and working as a *ger* in "the far reaches of Ephraim."[6] He marries a secondary wife from Bethlehem in Judah (Judg 19:1). The two have a falling out,[7] and the secondary wife returns to her father in Bethlehem (v. 2). The Levite follows her and, after finding her at her father's house and spending several days with the overly hospitable father, makes his way north again with his wife and servant. They stop at Gibeah in Benjamin hoping for hospitality, but they get none until an old man, an Ephraimite who is living there as a *ger* himself, offers them a place to stay. He implies that they should not stay out at night in Gibeah (v. 20).

When the old man takes in the Levite and his secondary wife, he is offering them some protection from the people of the town, people who know that the travelers are "from away." Some men of the town, however, do not accept the old *ger*'s authority to offer protection, and they attempt to humiliate him by asking for sex with the Levite. "Just as they were enjoying themselves, men from the town, worthless men, surrounded the house, pounding on the door. They said to the old man who owned the house, 'Send out the man who has come to your house so that we can have sex with him'" (v. 22). The next verse is quite jarring: the old man offers his daughter and the Levite's secondary wife as substitutes but begs the townsmen to leave the man alone. He clearly has no regard for his daughter, over whose sexuality he has power, or his guest's secondary wife, who is not his to offer. Eventually, the Levite throws his secondary wife to the crowd, who rape her all night.[8] The brutality of the men of Gibeah is compounded by the Levite's own brutality: first, in throwing his secondary wife to them to rape all night,[9] and second, in his irritation with and callous treatment of her the next morning:

> The woman came at dawn and fell at the door of the house where her master was until it was light. Her master got up in the morning and opened the doors of the house and went out in order to go along his way, and there was his secondary wife, fallen at the door of the house with her hands on the threshold. He said to her, "Get up so we can get moving!" but she didn't answer. So he put her on the donkey, and the man went on his way home. (vv. 26-28)

His next act, upon returning home, is to cut his wife into twelve pieces, to be sent to the twelve tribes of Israel, in order to compel them to gather and decide what to do with the people of Gibeah. We do not know when the secondary wife died, whether on the threshold or on the way home or, possibly, when the Levite cut her into pieces. The narrator portrays the Levite lying to his fellow Israelites who respond to his call, first reporting that the men had come to kill him, which is not the story as we know it, and then omitting to mention that it was he who gave his secondary wife to the men of Gibeah,[10] eventually causing her death.[11]

Because Benjamin will not turn over the city of Gibeah for punishment, war results between all of Benjamin and the rest of Israel. In the course of winning the war, the Israelites rashly kill everyone in Benjamin, including the women (or so the story tells us; remember that we are reading this story as a narrative and not history). They leave alive six hundred Benjaminite men who have fled from them.

The beginning of Judg 21 tells us, "Now, the men of Israel had sworn at Mitspah [where they had gathered for the war], 'Let no Israelite man give his daughter in marriage to a Benjaminite'" (v. 1). This is the first mention of the oath, which renders the Israelite killing of all the Benjaminite women not only monstrous but impractical. They fear that because of their various actions there will be no one in Israel to marry the remaining six hundred Benjaminite men: "The people went to Bethel and sat there till evening before God,[12] and they raised their voices and cried bitterly. They said, 'Why, YHWH, god of Israel, have you done this thing in Israel, that today one tribe from Israel is lacking?'" (v. 2). The women from Benjamin, of course, are missing because of indifference, rape, and violence, beginning with the Levite's actions toward his secondary wife and the brutality of Gibeah's men. Extreme violence to one woman has led to massive violence against a tribe, including the women, which in turn led to the problem the Israelite men have brought upon themselves.

How do they solve this problem? Modern societies that face an over-abundance of men look for women elsewhere, women who are so little respected that their families will sell them to the "surplus" men from countries that have remarkably unsustainable "sex ratios at birth."[13] The Israelites make similar arrangements. They first determine that because no men from the city of Jabesh-Gilead had joined them in the battle with Benjamin, they have the right to, and must, kill everyone in Jabesh-Gilead:

> They [the Israelites] said, "Is there anyone from among the tribes of Israel who did not go up to YHWH at Mitspah?" And there wasn't a man there from Jabesh-Gilead. . . . The congregation sent twelve thousand of the warriors there and commanded them, "Go and kill the residents of Jabesh-Gilead with the sword, including the women and children, and this is [exactly] what you should do: destroy every man and woman who has had sex, 'but keep alive the marriageable women.'"[14] And they did. They found from among the residents of Jabesh-Gilead four hundred marriageable women who had never had sex, and they brought them to the camp at Shiloh, in the land of Canaan. (vv. 8, 10-12)

They carry out their vow, sparing four hundred virgins who would make the kind of wives that the Benjaminites need: they are Israelite, and they are not being given away by Israelite men. Had any Israelite men done so, they would have been acting in violation of the first vow mentioned, not to marry their daughters to Benjaminites. The men of Jabesh-Gilead cannot break the vow since they are dead. Such is the relentless logic of violence.

The Israelites come up with a similar plan to acquire the remaining two hundred women the Benjaminites need:

> The elders of the congregation said, "What shall we do for wives for the remaining men, since every woman from Benjamin has been destroyed?[15] There must be an inheritance for the survivors of Benjamin; a tribe cannot be blotted out from Israel. But we cannot give them any of our daughters as wives." . . . And [the Israelites] said, "There is a festival to YHWH in Shiloh every year. . . ." And they instructed the Benjaminites, "Go and hide in the vineyards, and when you see that the young women of Shiloh have come out to dance, leave the vineyards and each one of you grab

yourselves your wife from among the young women of Shiloh, and go back to the land of Benjamin." (vv. 16-18a, 19a, 20-21)

The Israelites explain to the Benjaminites that if any fathers or brothers object to this rape, they will be told that they have done a good thing for Israel and have not, in doing so, broken their vow because they did not give their daughters to the Benjaminites. No Israelites have "given" their daughters to Benjaminites, and yet the six hundred extra men have been provided with Israelite wives. These Benjaminites and the women they took are not truly married in the typical Israelite sense: The women's male kin and the male kin of the Benjaminites did not make contracts providing for protection of the women from whatever future problems might occur. The women were simply carried away to be sex partners, in an act amounting to rape.[16] Rape at the beginning and rape at the end—and throughout, a total lack of respect for women's lives, women's protection from violence, women's worth.

From another point of view, Megan Case has argued that, dreadful as the "solution" depicted in this story is, it at least describes premonarchic Israel as a society that could handle its own problems without introducing kingship.[17] If read without the editorial sentences at the end of chapter 21 ("In those days, there was no king in Israel. Everyone did what seemed good to them"), the story of the abduction at Shiloh might have supported an antimonarchic stance. The "clever" solution that so abuses women might have been less significant than the positive outcome of replenishing one of the tribes.[18] The editor of Judges, nevertheless, uses this story to further exemplify the chaotic situation in Israel before a king took over.

Missing Women in Deuteronomic Laws

Judges 19–21 contain particularly horrific stories of women's lives and situations. While there is no reason to believe the stories are historic, they portray a society in which women's lives are most worthwhile when they are saving the lives or fortunes of men. These stories are not so different, however, from two of the laws of war in Deuteronomy, a book whose influence is to be found in many places in the Deuteronomistic History, of which Judges is a part. Both of these laws concern women who are taken by force after a battle has been won against people who live far from Israel. First, Deut 20:10-15a states,

> When you approach a city to wage war against it, call out to it in peace [to offer peaceful terms]. And if they answer you "peace," and open [their gates] to you, everyone who is in it will become forced labor and will work

for you. But if it does not respond peacefully to you, you will wage war with it and besiege it, and YHWH will give it to you. You should kill all the males with the sword, but the women, the children, and the cattle, and everything that is in the city, all its booty, you will take for yourselves. And you will consume the booty of your enemies which YHWH has given to you. Thus you shall do to all the cities that are very far away from you.

The last sentence is key. This process applies to cities that are not neighbors of the Israelites waging the war. When they win the war, everything is theirs to do with as they wish, except all the males who are to be killed. In the next chapter, there is a further rule about women who are taken as prisoners of war:

When you go out to war against your enemies and YHWH your god gives them to you, and you take captives, if you see among the captives a beautiful woman and you desire her and take her for your wife, you will bring her into your house. She will shave her head and cut her nails, and remove the garment she wore in captivity, and live in your house, and cry for her father and her mother for a month. After that, you may have sex with her and be her husband, and she will become your wife. But if you are not pleased with her and you send her away, you may not sell her for money. You must not treat her like a slave, because you have violated her. (Deut 21:10-14)

The ideas involved in these two laws about female prisoners of war resemble the actions in Judges: the men whom the women would otherwise have married are killed (as in Jabesh-Gilead), and the women are taken away from their homes by force (as at Shiloh). There is no male relative to object to their forced marriages or to contract a traditional marriage arrangement in which male relatives of the bride and groom agree upon the terms. While these women are not described as virgins, their situations resemble those of our women in Judg 21: during a war, they are carried away from their homes and into forced marriages. In the two Deuteronomy passages, the men are not acting out of desperate need as the six hundred Benjaminites were, nor are they trying to circumvent a harmful oath; they are simply exercising their "rights" as Israelite men who have been successful in war. In Judg 21, the Benjaminite men have been *unsuccessful* in war, but even that would not have hurt them had it not been for the oath, which was not reported at the time it was supposedly taken.

In both Deuteronomy and Judges, the women lack agency, and their fates lie entirely in the hands of males, who use their bodies to satisfy a variety of needs. In Judges, the division between Benjamin and the rest of Israel is brought about by the Israelite men who fought Benjamin. Women are forced to solve a problem that men have created among themselves, as is so often the case.[19] The two laws from Deuteronomy cited above present not a problem to be solved but an opportunity to be grasped. In Deut 20, the women resemble the four hundred virgins in Jabesh-Gilead, whose fathers and brothers were murdered during the war. A ritual of separation is described in Deut 21, in which the women metaphorically put aside their attachment to their faraway homes and families by shaving their heads, cutting their nails, and changing their clothes. It is the kind of ritual we might imagine the women of Jabesh-Gilead and Shiloh performing to mark their new, forced Benjaminite status.

Missing Women Today

The period of the judges is presented to us in the Hebrew Bible as occurring more than three thousand years ago, but the issue the Israelites faced in Judg 21 is remarkably similar to one faced today by several countries in which sons are preferred over daughters.[20] In many societies today, girls are treated very differently from boys. They are often not as well nourished and can therefore die of otherwise simple diseases. They are not as well educated, nor provided the same health care. If a woman in such a society decides to remain childless, she is often considered strange and threatening.[21] It is this perceived difference in value between men and women that ties their stories to the violence against women in Judg 19–21. More specifically, because they are perceived as being less valuable than boys, many females today are "missing," having died before or at birth. Widespread practices of gender-selected infanticide and abortion have resulted in a dearth of marriageable women, which in turn results in further violence against women, as I will outline below.

Although many people blame today's low female birth rates on the steps countries have taken to lower their populations, such as China's one-child rule, demographer Christophe Guilmoto begs to differ. If those steps were at fault, we would expect the number of boy babies born and the number of girl babies born to diminish equally, but almost nowhere has that been the case. Instead, we find that in many Asian and Caucasus countries today, the ratio of infant boys to infant girls (called the "sex ratio at birth" or SRB) is amazingly high. Guilmoto has written extensively on these soaring SRBs and has observed three conditions in countries experiencing them: (1) rapid development, which means that prenatal screening is easily available; (2) abortion as a common method of birth control; and (3) a drop in fertility that was already happening before sex selection became an issue.[22] Adding traditional son preference to the easy access to technology has created such lopsided gender ratios that several countries are now desperately looking for solutions.

The case of government-instituted birth control that most Western people know about is the one-child rule in China (a rule that has recently been changed).[23] But China's fertility rate was actually falling before the institution of the rule in 1980. More pertinent is that in 1982 ultrasound machines became available in China, first to the urban elites with whom sex selection started.[24] They eventually became available also in rural and poor areas, especially as machines developed that were portable and PC-driven.[25] Ultrasound became a cheap, easy, and readily available technology for determining the sex of a fetus fairly early in pregnancy. There is no stigma against abortion in China,[26] and son preference is still so strong that the combination of these two realities with the availability of ultrasound often results in the abortion of several female fetuses before a male fetus is brought to term. Many Chinese couples still bring girls to full term, especially if the girl is the first baby, so not all the babies that are born are male, but the ratio in various parts of China runs from a normal 106 to 100 to an unsustainable 121 to 100 and even higher.[27] The issue, then, is a perfect storm comprised of a falling fertility rate, so that a family might have only one child, coupled with patriarchy and the newly available technology of sex selection.

The problem of too many men and not enough women is not confined to China. The same falling fertility rate was also evident in Albania, Armenia, Azerbaijan, and Georgia before they began sex selection. In 1995 Armenia's, Georgia's, and Azerbaijan's number of male babies per 100 female babies was around 105; in 2000 Azerbaijan's was 115, Georgia's 118, and Armenia's 120.[28] The reason for the initial falling fertility rate is a familiar one: the fertility rate began to fall once the societies' standard of living increased following the end of the Soviet Union. As is so often the case, when people get to the point of having more material rewards than previous generations have had, they give birth to fewer children with whom to share it. The family is better off materially if they do not need to support so many children. Furthermore, when economic opportunities come to the cities, many people leave the agricultural life for the promise of making an easier living in the city. While agricultural families benefit from more children to help them with the many jobs that need to be done on a farm, those who make their living with individual jobs in cities make no more money and do not have easier lives when they have children. Children, in fact, simply use the family's resources, and so families arrange to give birth to fewer children. The problem for these countries, as for China, comes in when widespread selection for one gender accompanies the falling fertility rate.

In the past, people who gave birth to girls had two choices in their quest for a son: some women birthed girl after girl until they finally had a boy; others practiced female infanticide, resulting sometimes in a great age difference between the first female child and the second male child. In other ways, women's status has risen as technology has advanced and parents have experienced higher standards of living. But in the case of births, technology has played a bittersweet role for women. On the one hand, ultrasound allows them to find out a fetus's sex long before birth, so female infanticide has become almost nonexistent. But on the other hand, finding out the fetus's sex fairly early in the pregnancy allows for easy abortion of females, who in China, for example, would otherwise grow up to need weddings and dowries, who after marriage are generally not able to care for their elderly parents, and who are prohibited from performing the rites of ancestor worship.[29] So if a couple's first pregnancy results in a girl, subsequent pregnancies, checked by ultrasound, are allowed to come to term only if the fetus is male. Families operating in this way have either a single baby who is male or a first baby who is female and a second male child. If they survive, these babies grow into a generation in which only a few more than half of the men have the opportunity to marry. No society operates according to such simple rules, but the trend is real, and, especially in China, the first generation with this lopsided gender ratio is already grown. There, the male birth ratio has risen from 105 in 1982 to around 120 in 1990 to an incredible 150 in 2000.[30]

South Korea is the one country that has walked away from the brink of an SRB of 117 in 1990 to obtain a normal birth ratio today, but their public solution to high SRB is only one of the reasons. In 1990, South Korea's government became worried about the imbalance in their sex ratio and the marriage squeeze that would accompany it. Their concern for what men would experience in the future led to a campaign to convince people to abandon sex selection for males and begin producing girls. They outlawed the use of ultrasound for sex identification and made a few highly publicized arrests. The SRB fell but rose again when the arrests halted. So the government once again made high-profile arrests, and the SRB fell permanently.

This government crackdown, however, has not done as much for the SRB as the Korean people have on their own. They had had enough of the campaigns for the control of population and sex selection and the associated risks and punishments for working outside the system, and they simply stopped having babies almost altogether. They now produce between 1 and 1.25 children per couple, the lowest fertility rate in the world.[31]

There have been surplus men long enough in history and in enough societies that we have seen the results when the ratio of men to women is outlandishly high. Societies with high SRBs are unstable and violent, most likely because testosterone behaves differently in men who have daily access only to other men than it does in those who are married or have children. Men who are married or have children seem to have a lower testosterone level than bachelors, for instance, perhaps for evolutionary reasons. Less aggression, a result of lower testosterone, will more likely keep a male away from dangerous situations and allow him to pass his genes on to the next generation.[32] Such an argument about testosterone has been used to explain much of the wildness of the Wild West in our own history, a territory that was settled almost entirely by men.[33] In our discussion about missing women, then, we must also include the possibility that tens of millions of surplus men could have a destabilizing effect on their societies, a by-product of sex selection that makes finding solutions to the problem of unsustainably high SRBs even more urgent.

In modern societies, several solutions to this problem have been tried. The obvious one is to bring women in, with or without their cooperation, from countries where the standard of living is not as high, so the money earned by selling a young woman is substantial—that is, to find men who are willing to sell female family members who lack protection from the deals being made for their futures and their very lives. Such trafficking is especially active at the borders between countries.[34] Chinese men have enticed or bought women especially from poor parents in Vietnam.[35] Taiwan is another country that is suffering from surplus men and that is trying to solve that problem by resorting to poorer countries and families. Taiwanese surplus men, for instance, go on one-week "marriage tours" to Vietnam.[36] In one incident, three Vietnamese women were advertised for sale on Taiwan's eBay.[37]

It is obvious from a practical standpoint that the solution must eventually be something other than finding women from poorer countries, since those women will become scarce as well. Brides brought from other cultures suffer from, among other things, an inability to understand their new cultures or even to speak the languages their husbands and new families speak. Even within India, for example, cultures and languages in one area can be vastly different from those in another. Polyandry exists in some places, but such cases are rare and usually hidden, since they are frowned upon.[38] An accidental result of surplus men's turning to other cultures for brides is that the children who are produced can be binational, bilingual, and even considered biracial in societies that have been quite closed in the past. The number of "mixed" marriages would seem to encourage liberalization of customs developed when the societies were insular, but the effects of such mixing are not yet known.[39]

It would seem logical, and has seemed logical to many, that a woman's status would rise in a society in which women are scarce. And in one sense it has: men must pay more to marry women than they used to. But this is a bonus for the parents, not the woman. Her status may rise or fall; she may be happy or abused; she may be under the thumb of her husband and/or her mother-in-law for the rest of her life. These facts of life have nothing to do with scarcity. And in fact, some families expect even more from a woman who cost them more.[40] In addition, many girls are kidnapped and offered to the highest bidder or offered back to the family for large sums of money.

A puzzling feature of the missing women issue comes from the demand for prostitutes as an outlet for the surplus men. In China, so many Vietnamese women have been kidnapped and sold into prostitution that native prostitutes have realized the value of their services and have organized to pressure their government for better conditions.[41] This empowerment of women who would ordinarily be considered victims epitomizes the problems feminists have with the missing women issue in Asia and the Caucasus. On the one hand, Western feminists have for decades rallied around a woman's "right to choose" and are loath to interfere in that right or to support a government's interference. On the other hand, this "right to choose" has meant in Asia and elsewhere the abortion of many more female fetuses, not at all the "right to choose" that feminists would like to champion.

The entire situation of missing women in today's societies is one of contradictions and uncomfortable conversations in the West. It was, first of all, the opening of Asian and Caucasian countries to Western economies that allowed people in those countries to aspire to a higher standard of living. That standard of living led to a lower fertility rate, as has usually been the case. It was also a Western push for birth control in countries where the birth rate seemed to be spiraling out of control that convinced women in those countries that having fewer children was advantageous. This push for birth control, added to a higher standard of living, produced lower and lower birth rates, until most of the countries in Asia today do not have the "replacement level" birth rates of 2.1 necessary for preventing a shrinking population. And it was Western technology that facilitated son selection in countries where abortion is commonplace and where son preference remains a powerful force.

Antiabortion groups in the West have not missed the opportunity that the phenomenon of missing women has given them. The fact that many Asian Americans exhibit the same son preference in the United States as in their home countries brings the issue of abortion directly onto U.S. soil.[42] Members of the Christian right have used information about sex-selective abortions in less than 2 percent of the U.S. population to find a position on which they can garner widespread agreement.[43] Feminists are concerned about the effect of this activism on women's ability to choose safe and legal abortion in the United States.

Sex selection in the United States has moved well beyond use of ultrasound and abortion. In the United States, it is now possible to use in vitro fertilization to select against many features in embryos: genetic diseases and propensity toward other defects; breast cancer; colon cancer; Alzheimer's; sex-linked diseases; gender. Preimplantation genetic diagnosis is used by an increasing number of Americans, even those who have no trouble conceiving, precisely because it allows screening for disease and sex selection. The difference in the United States is that sex selection most often means choosing a female baby rather than a male, since girls are perceived as more successful and cooperative in school and as easier to raise.[44]

Conclusion

We have come a long way from the six hundred Benjaminite men who found substitutes for their "missing women" through violence against other Israelites and forced marriage with women who lacked protection. In both the ancient story and in modern high SRB societies alike, chosen "solutions" cause problems for others. The Israelites pass the problem they themselves have created on to the people of Jabesh-Gilead and Shiloh. The people in high SRB societies today can see that the logical result of a low fertility rate combined with son preference is catastrophic, but they often rely on foreign women, trafficking, and even kidnapping to fix their ratio problems.[45]

Both ancient and modern societies desperate for wives and mothers skew the power relationship between men and women, between women and their rulers, and between various groups of men themselves. There is probably no practical and ethical solution to the lack of marriageable women in any society, so the men who desire wives and families, and the men who govern them, will always find loopholes or Band-Aids to cover up the real problem, which is the failure to value females, a failure so comprehensive that even women cooperate in preferring sons to daughters. Women, no matter what their status, are vulnerable to whatever violence those with power over them choose to deliver. From ancient Israel to the modern world, women are missing because of the violence imposed upon them, and they remain undervalued and abused in the solutions devised to seek balanced population ratios. The contribution of the West to this situation has been the technology that so facilitates the violence.

The men of Israel killed all the women of Benjamin with no forethought and only later saw it as a problem. The book of Judges presents this as the nadir of Israel's corporate life: civil war, degradation and violation of women, and the dissolution of their society into chaos. In similar fashion, today's societies that undervalue women have created a problem—so obvious in hindsight—that is now coming home to roost for millions of surplus men. Women's lack of agency and several societies' insistence on maintaining that lack of agency are not sustainable, and loopholes will cease to be available. The future will bring either cooperation or chaos. Whether because of our religious faiths or because of our philosophies, people of good conscience must answer the call to advocate for a changed attitude toward women and girls.

For Further Reading

Attané, Isabelle, and Christophe Z. Guilmoto, eds. *Watering the Neighbour's Garden: The Growing Demographic Female Deficit in Asia.* Paris: Committee for International Cooperation in National Research in Demography, 2007.

Carter, Jimmy. *A Call to Action: Women, Religion, Violence, and Power.* New York: Simon & Schuster, 2014.

Fontaine, Carole. *With Eyes of Flesh: The Bible, Gender, and Human Rights.* Sheffield: Sheffield Phoenix, 2008.

Hackett, Jo Ann. "Violence and Women's Lives in the Book of Judges." *Interpretation* 58 (2004): 356–64.

Hvistendahl, Mara. *Unnatural Selection: Choosing Boys over Girls, and the Consequences of a World Full of Men.* New York: Public Affairs, 2011.

Niditch, Susan. *Judges: A Commentary.* Old Testament Library. Louisville, Ky.: Westminster John Knox, 2008.

CHAPTER 14

ZECHARIAH'S GENDERED VISIONS
A Feminist Biblical Theology of Reconciliation

Ingrid E. Lilly

The twentieth century is infamously hailed as the century of global-scale war. The Holocaust, genocide, strife within nations, and modern warfare pose pressing questions about the nature of conflict and how communities recover and heal. In the crucible of modern conflict, numerous thinkers devoted to peacebuilding, secular and religious alike, turn to concepts of reconciliation.

Many theological insights into reconciliation have resulted from responses to modern conflicts. Hannah Arendt's concepts of revenge, forgiveness, and reconciliation grow out of her work on the Holocaust.[1] Miroslav Volf's concept of exclusion and embrace starts from his analysis of ethnic cleansing in the former Yugoslavia.[2] Leymah Gbowee's peace work overcame civil strife in Liberia.[3] And Desmond Tutu's reflections on forgiveness grew out of his work on the Truth and Reconciliation Commission that redressed crimes under apartheid in South Africa.[4] Among the lessons in these masterful efforts to conceive reconciliation, one shared feature is that context matters.

What does the Hebrew Bible offer these discussions? And how can one exhume a feminist theology of reconciliation from biblical literature? Our foray into a contextual and feminist theology of reconciliation will examine a piece of Israelite literature devoted to postconflict rebuilding, Zechariah. One of only three Hebrew prophetic books entirely set in the postexilic period, Zechariah imagines life for people recovering from war. Zechariah 1–8 comprise visions (chs. 1–6) and oracles (interspersed and chs. 7–8) about Israel's restoration in the land after the Babylonian exile.⁵ Called a "theological prolegomenon to restoration" by David Petersen, Zechariah offers practical visions and theological reflection on building a postconflict polity.⁶

Inasmuch as Zechariah offers visions for rebuilding after war, it does so with reference to its heritage of conflict. For example, Zech 8:10 speaks of the injustices and social ills of the past:

> For before those days there were no wages for people or for animals, nor was there any peace for those who went out or came in because of the foe, and I [YHWH] set all humanity, each one, against his neighbor.⁷

In one of several examples of plain-speak about social conflict, Zechariah names extreme economic poverty and the conditions of foreign siege as factors that led to internal local strife. Neighbors were pitted against neighbors. As we will see, the term "neighbor" (rea) serves as a recurrent index for conflict and reconciliation in Zechariah. Enmity between neighbors implies a conflicted society that can be transformed only when neighbors live together in peace.

In a more overtly theological judgment on this period of conflict, Zech 7:9-10 presents a moral standard for peace, which, up to that point, had failed to be honored:

> Render true judgments. Show kindness and mercy to one another. Do not oppress the widow, the orphan, the alien, or the poor; and do not devise evil in your hearts, each man against his brother.

Where the state of conflict is described as pitting neighbor against neighbor or brother against brother, YHWH's call to reconciliation is premised on justice and truth. This path to reconciliation generates mercy (hesed) and compassion (raham) between relations. Truth, justice, mercy, and compassion—these features of Zechariah's postconflict theology commend the book as an ideal place to engage biblical ideas of peacebuilding and reconciliation.

At the outset, we are well prepared to explore feminist issues when we do theology in context. Feminist theology, when done well, understands how gender is situated in a broader set of intersections: all people possess gender, class, race, and sexual orientation. Feminist theology is conscious of all inequalities premised on arbitrary divisions of peoples and the granting of unmerited social privileges. To explore reconciliation, then, requires context as a means to expose how different groups of people experience and recover from conflict, particularly when inequality mars the process.

It is important to state at the outset that Zechariah's visions for a postwar society are predominantly male. What does it mean for women when reconciliation is enacted and produces peace that is targeted largely at men's experience? A short reflection on gender and reconciliation in South Africa will help us think about this issue. Then, our first project in looking at Zechariah's context will be naming the maleness in Zechariah's visions. Especially important is the vision of the new priest in Zech 3 who plays a role in enacting a society of peace. Our examination of masculinity is not only important for women. It reveals the specific contextual ways that gender operates, and it reminds us that feminist analysis can become more attentive to all gender dynamics that produce gendered marginalization and subordination. Turning to two passages about women and reconciliation in Zech 8 and 5, we will see that Zechariah holds some surprising opportunities to explore the way that social inequality impacts reconciliation.

Contexts for Theology: Zechariah and South Africa

The historical context of Zechariah's theology centers on the dream of local autonomy and represents the strongest vein in Zechariah. After years of war, forced migration, and local strife, Zechariah offers a vision for an autonomous society at peace. The eight visions in chapters 1–6, especially, imagine the features of a native messianic movement. They describe new leadership roles charged with rebuilding the temple and overseeing its community. Hope for a temple galvanizes expectation that YHWH will return to dwell in Jerusalem. These features make for an era of peace in a land that belongs to a people in a way that matters to them.

The visions are religious dreams of empowerment. Judah was a small, far-flung kingdom crushed by imperial expansion. Jerusalem underwent two rounds of military invasion and deportation at the hands of the Babylonian kingdom (597/587 BCE). Its central temple was destroyed, and the city was dismantled along mostly class lines, with numerous elite Judeans forcibly moved. The desire for local autonomy and the chance to rebuild represent the recovery of lost power after a devastating conflict.

One of the most significant known conflicts, with effects long outlasting open warfare, stemmed from forced migration.[8] The waves of Jerusalem deportees were compelled to settle in faraway places. After roughly seventy years of regional aftermath, those migrants began to return under a Persian brand of imperial politics. Their return introduced new problems and opened old wounds.

Much about this socially complex world is unknown or not well understood. A careful analysis of a historical set of conflicts is simply not possible.
However, some broad-brush context can be described. Certainly, it is easy
to imagine a basic material conflict over repossession of land. We also know
that the internationally displaced Judeans were likely sons and daughters
of Judah's skilled and literate class. Their religious and political ideas were
nourished in international contexts of resettlement. They returned to the
land of their ancestors to rebuild the temple and begin establishing a religion in Jerusalem, sanctioned by the new international power. This scenario
presents several potential sites of conflict and tension: "native" versus imperial identity, old versus new economic systems, local versus international
religious ideas. As Zechariah's messianic movement dreams of rebuilding temple and community, any number of historical conflicts could have
required the work of reconciliation for peacebuilding.

In terms of a feminist approach to reconciliation, the most significant
question becomes this: Where are the women? On the face of it, this is a
history of men. With few exceptions, men held the preconflict positions of
leadership; men defended the city against siege; skilled men were targeted
as forced migrants; and men led the empowerment movement to return to
Jerusalem to rebuild the temple. In the biblical literature devoted to these
events, men star; women come along for the ride.

In the precise case of gender, the male-centered history of conflict
and rebuilding in Zechariah resembles the case of reconciliation in South
Africa. South Africa's Truth and Reconciliation Commission (TRC) offers
very helpful insights into the gendered nature of conflict and reconciliation.
A remarkable theology of forgiveness informed the TRC, but its enactment
failed many South African women.[9] A brief description of this problem will
shed light on the gendered nature of conflict and reconciliation.

The TRC was an initiative born in South Africa to address a history of
violence under apartheid during the years 1960–1993. Its successes place
it as a model for numerous modern efforts at reconciliation.[10] However, its
definition of gross violation tended to be those wrongs inflicted on men by
men.[11] In an official report, the TRC admitted that the process had failed
women:

> The definition of gross violations of human rights adopted by the Com-
> mission resulted in blindness to the types of abuse predominantly expe-
> rienced by women. In this respect, the full report of the Commission and

the evidence presented to it make it very clear that while women are not the only sufferers, they bear the brunt of the suffering.[12]

The TRC attempted to rectify the gender blindness of the reconciliation process with special hearings for women, but these were initiated too late, and few women came forward.

The TRC is not alone in (belatedly) recognizing the gendered nature of conflict and reconciliation. The UN Security Council notes that "civilians, particularly women and children, account for the vast majority of those adversely affected by armed conflict."[13] In seven major resolutions, the UN council emphasizes that war impacts women differently. For example, sexual violence against women increases in conflicted and war-torn societies. Rape can be a common weapon of war, a sexual violation across enemy lines. But sexual violence increases within in-groups as well, especially in refugee camps or as a consequence of social breakdown during conflict.[14]

In addition to the gendered ways that people experience conflict and war, gender roles often change during and after violent conflict. The changes to economic systems and social institutions mean that traditional roles go into flux.[15] This brings additional challenges but many opportunities as well.

Biblical literature references some of these gendered experiences of war. For example, Zech 14:2 describes an apocalyptic destruction of Jerusalem during which "the city shall be taken and the houses looted and the women raped." To name rape as a gendered experience of war goes a long way toward a feminist theology of reconciliation. All too often, marginalized experiences are not named and remain invisible. Reconciliation cannot happen without bringing wrongs into public view.

In another passage of Zechariah, we find a clear description of gendered isolation during the process of mourning after war:

> The land shall mourn, each family by itself; the family of the house of David by itself, and their wives by themselves; the family of the house of Nathan by itself, and their wives by themselves; the family of the house of Levi by itself, and their wives by themselves; the family of the Shimeites by itself, and their wives by themselves; and all the families that are left, each by itself, and their wives by themselves.
>
> (Zech 12:12-14)

Particularly striking here is the attention given to the way that wives grieve conflict in isolation from their kinship groups. Whether gendered loss owes to the gendered practices of warfare like rape, as in Zech 14:2, or to different social attachments to material loss, such as damage to or loss of homes, crops, animals, children, sacred spaces, Zech 12:12-14 could not be more clear that Israelite women experience conflict and loss differently than Israelite men do. Although we are not focusing on other intersections of identity here, it is also important to note that recovery isolates different kinship groups, as well. The passage attests to the complex and intersectional nature of conflict, and it alludes to the multiple wrongs that need to be redressed by reconciliation.

Hence, Zechariah holds much promise for thinking about marginalized identities in a feminist theology of reconciliation. However, the TRC case and Israelite history remind us that reconciliation is often about those in institutional or cultural positions of power. Peacebuilding on the societal level does not provide meaningful reconciliation at all intersections of social identity.[16] Nevertheless, a feminist theology of reconciliation must grapple with marginalization in all its forms, especially gendered experiences of conflict.

Zechariah 3: Masculinity and Reconciliation

Zechariah's visions tackle the ways that gender roles adapt and go through changes during and after violent conflict. Rebuilding involved a redefinition of male roles, a point that would be lost in a feminist theology that only focuses on women. Our attention to masculinity can reveal much about the gendered nature of reconciliation in Zechariah.

Zechariah opens with a veritable manifesto about masculinity. In the first line of speech in chapter 1, we read, "YHWH is sore displeased with your fathers" (1:2). Zechariah's opening speech goes on to urge, "Do not be like your fathers" (v. 4); to ask, "Your fathers, where are they?" (v. 5); and to describe how YHWH's commandments "overtook your fathers" (v. 6, author's trans.). In the six verses introducing the book, the Israelite "fathers" are referenced four times in exaggerated repetition.[17]

The opening of the book gives way to a presentation of a better, more ideal, and more successful world than that crafted by the men of the prior age. Their wrongs appear to be failure to live up to the commandments which inspired the prophets of old. Setting Israelite society into a patrilineal logic, as opposed to a governmental one (we might have expected to hear about the failings of past Israelite leaders, officials, judges, priests, etc.) highlights a social fabric rooted in basic patriarchal clan/family identity.

Nevertheless, Zechariah offers governmental solutions to foster a society that enables reconciliation among men. Specifically, Zechariah redefines communal life around new social institutions that represent changes in male leadership roles. These institutional changes are presented in Zechariah 3–4, with chapter 3 offering the strongest statement of reconciliation in Zechariah's eight visions.

Zechariah 3–4 introduce two leaders: Joshua, the high priest, and Zerubbabel, the prince of Davidic lineage. The two of them together are the "sons of the *yitshar*" (4:14)—the anointed ones. Postexilic theology here presents a modified Judean royal messianism organized as a diarchy (government by two). The changed circumstances of the Persian period frustrated historical hopes for a local monarchy. The prophetic compromise was the diarchy, in which king and priest would sit on thrones with "a counsel of peace" working between them (6:13).

Zechariah 3, therefore, is especially interesting for masculinity and reconciliation, for it introduces the innovative masculinity of messianic priesthood. The entire chapter is devoted to a description of Joshua as the high priest. Local temples were key institutions in the Persian-period leadership structures. And for Zechariah, the political moment was propitious; there was an international vacuum that quickly converted into Persian imperial license to rebuild the temple.[18] Hence, the theological and political longing for a native kingdom under a Davidic messiah eventually needed to find expression in the politically possible. In this way, the millennial movement fueling Zechariah's social vision was an adaptive one aimed at the realistic recovery of lost power after foreign invasion.[19] The recovery of local power invested the priesthood with new significance and redefined masculinity for Zechariah's postconflict society.

The vision of priesthood opens by calling Joshua a "brand plucked from the fire" (v. 2). This man stands vulnerable to the gaze of YHWH and his angel. Though unencumbered by the litigious accusations of Satan (vv. 1-2), who would no doubt render harsher judgments, Joshua is described as clothed with filthy garments (v. 3). The clothing explicitly represents his iniquity (*'avon*), and those men attending him remove it, dress him in fresh robes, and crown him with a turban. This new kind of man, dressed in the new garb of priesthood, initiates a new reality, which one should make sure to note is made possible by this male entourage that surrounds him. In a powerful choice of terms, the entourage consists of "neighbors" (*rea*) who are called "men of the sign" (v. 8, author's trans.). The men who act as signs, responsible for Joshua's investment ritual, set the stage for the coming of the messianic "shoot," or the Davidic leader described in chapter 4 and the primary goal of the entire set of visions, YHWH coming to "dwell in your midst" (e.g., Zech 2:11). The theological imperative in Zechariah's postconflict society is for YHWH to return to the temple, a sphere overseen by Joshua.

On the one hand, the emergence of a new masculinity is a collective response to war. Joshua is shaped by his immediate male cohort who literally redress and cleanse him. The priesthood represents the whole community's best chance, as victims of war, to seek empowerment in the Persian period. Hence, postconflict gender transformations emerge in solidarity with collective efforts to recover lost power.[20]

The scene, on the other hand, is a judicial proceeding. Joshua's trial becomes an individual gender transformation. The adversary (hasatan) is denounced by YHWH for preparing a harsh judgment on Joshua. Instead, because YHWH "has chosen Jerusalem" (v. 2), certain amnesties are granted for the sake of setting up a new polity of peace. In other words, instead of raking Joshua over the coals, his Jerusalem cohort transforms him in a ritual that resembles a postconflict tribunal of amnesty.

Zechariah 3 suggests that a gender transformation among the leadership makes possible reconciliation among the more general population. Recall that the strongest statement of conflict in Zechariah used the term "neighbors": "I set all humanity, each one, against his neighbor" (8:10b). At the end of chapter 3 and the vision of Joshua, YHWH says to the community, "[Y]ou all, each man [ish] will invite his neighbor to come under his vine and fig tree" (3:10). Elsewhere, the image of personal vine and fig trees is explicitly associated with social peace (1 Kgs 4:25; 2 Kgs 18:31). Hence, Joshua's priestly role opens up an umbrella of peacebuilding in the community. Verse 10 implies a society of peacebuilding agents. Neighbors interact; theirs is a society of mutual hospitality. In the context of a postconflict society, this looks like much more than just tolerance; it is reconciliation.[21]

Zechariah 8: A Just Society for Reconciliation

Under the umbrella of a postconflict society oriented toward reconciliation and peacebuilding, the privileged gender arrangement can extend its benefits outward. Zechariah 3 connected the gender transformation of Joshua with a society-wide capacity for reconciliation. In the same way, Zech 8 offers a set of discourses that could widen the circle of reconciliation to include Israelite women. Indeed, the oracles in Zech 8 open with a promising scene:

> Old men and old women shall again sit in the streets of Jerusalem, each with staff in hand because of their great age. And the streets of the city shall be full of boys and girls playing in its streets. (vv. 4-5)

Calling Jerusalem a "city of truth" and its people the "seed of peace," YHWH pronounces his intentions to cause "goodness to spring up in Jerusalem" (vv. 3, 12, 15). A veritable peacebuilding program is described at the end when YHWH states,

> These are the things that you shall do: Speak the truth, each man [ish] to his neighbor. Render truth and judgments that make for peace in your gates. Do not scheme in your hearts for evil, each man [ish] against his neighbor, and love no false oath; for these are things I hate. (vv. 16-17, author's trans.)

Peacebuilding is set "in your gates," a reference to public judicial proceedings. The line "render truth and judgments that make for peace" shows the interplay between truth telling and the concept of fair judgments that will make for peace (shalom). The ultimate goal here is not just truth but a process that will build peace, best portrayed by our opening image: a public space for old men and women and young boys and girls to be at ease side by side.

Although the judicial proceeding seems to extend the benefits of reconciliation outward, Zech 8 describes a male judicial sphere. The crucial passage in verses 16-17 commands "each man" ('ish) to enact judgments that make for peace. Many feminist theologians, with some basis in Hebrew grammar, would opt for inclusive language here. Hence, we can hear a charge to each person ('ish) in which women, along with men, are called to do truth and justice work. While this may not be how the original authors and earliest readers understood the charge, we can certainly affirm the benefits when women and marginalized genders take agency in formal reconciliation processes. In any case, Zech 8 portrays peacebuilding as a public space for all genders (at various ages) to experience public ease. Whether women are empowered as agents of judicial processes is less clear. So while Zech 8 may not offer a robustly feminist theology of reconciliation, it does highlight the ongoing importance of reconciliation work. Reconciliation does not happen in one single instant. A society of reconciliation must open up forms of agency to engage the ongoing transformative work of reconciliation.

Zechariah 5: Ungendering Symbols and a Feminist Theology of Reconciliation

In a society where men hold the governmental, religious, and judicial leadership positions, women can still stand to benefit from living in a society of reconciliation. However, Zech 8 is not the most robust place to uncover feminist agency for reconciliation.

If women can play only a potential role in Zech 8's theology of reconciliation, they will find far greater challenges in Zech 5 but also potentially more powerful opportunities. On the face of it, the seventh of Zechariah's visions (5:5-11) presents an extremely vexing problem: a gendered representation of social ill. When social ill is mapped onto a subordinate or marginalized gender, the process of rebuilding alienates that identity from the experience of reconciliation.

In the vision, a woman is thrust down into a small basket, a heavy lid locks her inside, and she is sent away from the community, branded as wickedness.[22] In the symbolism of the vision, her treatment and departure represent an ethical purification of the postconflict society. Here more than anywhere else in Zechariah's visions, we encounter the challenge that religions pose in the project of peacebuilding. For here we must come to terms with Zechariah as an explicitly religious and theological peacebuilding program and not just a social vision. Marvin Sweeney names the misogyny often brought to Zech 5, in which a theological correlation is forged between woman and sin. In light of the New Testament blame levied on Eve, the vision is read in step with a Christian tendency to gender sin.[23]

However, as many interpreters argue, religion is at work here in a much different and more specific way. Attention to the context where the primary concern is preparing the temple for YHWH's return, this passage is specific to an ancient theology of temple purification. If we read the vision in this lens, the woman symbolizes a goddess, likely the Mesopotamian Queen of Heaven, frequently condemned during the rise of monotheistic Yahwism.[24] The goddess is expunged from YHWH's temple and brought to a temple in Babylon. Verse 11 drives home this reading. The prophet asks, "Where is she going?" with reference to those bringing her away:

> To the land of Shinar, to build a house for it; and when this is prepared, they will set the basket down there on its base.

Hebrew "house" (*bayit*) frequently refers to a temple. Ancient Near Eastern context strengthens this point. As Carol Meyers notes, there is a double entendre between the basket ('*ephah*) with the cult room of a Mesopotamian temple (*E-pa*) and wickedness (*harish'ah*) with the goddess name Asherah. Further, the basic measurements of the basket and lead weight cannot hold a human-sized woman. Meyers considers the woman a cult statue.[25]

Interpreting the woman in a basket as a cult statue for a goddess has a few good payoffs for a feminist reading. Most prominently, it salvages the vision from that strain of Christian theology in which "woman" is the cause of and symbol for sin. Human women are not wickedness in the basket. On the contrary, women and men stand on equal footing in relation to iniquity and reconciliation. Reading the woman as a cult statue also activates a justice concern present in the passage. In verse 6 "basket" ('*ephah*) is a unit of measure, and in verse 7 "leaden cover" (*kikar 'opheret*) is a term for a round piece of lead used as a weight. There is a possible allusion here to economic justice, as weights and measures could be manipulated for selfish gain. As a probable source of conflict, economic abuse may have been justified on religious grounds. Representing both the wicked economic practices and the religion that justified them, the wickedness in the measuring basket must be expunged from the temple.

It may be hard for feminists to let go of their dismay that economic wickedness is symbolized by a woman. But symbols can hold multiple meanings. In an important sense, with Carolyn Walker Bynum, we need to affirm that "gender-related symbols are sometimes 'about' values other than gender."[26] Rejecting the idol in the '*ephod* as a religious system of economic injustice, Zechariah empowers religious people to reform, to examine their religious heritage, and to root out its collusion with economic wickedness. An intersectional feminist theology affirms the vision's concern for people who fall prey to economic predation; reconciliation must confront systemic wrongdoing that causes conflict between economic classes.

Zechariah 5: Gendered Scapegoating and a Feminist Theology of Reconciliation

And yet, as Bynum goes on to point out, "all symbols arise out of the experience of 'gendered' users." We must ask, "For whom does it mean?"[27] A feminist theology of reconciliation cannot ignore the way that gendered symbols give rise to thought.[28] We already saw that some Christian theology takes liberties with Zechariah's woman in a basket, reinforcing the Christian view of women as the origins of evil.

Indeed, the literal level of the vision remains troubling. There are few other references to women in Zechariah's visions and none as explicit. The word used is "woman" (*'ishah*), not idol or cult statue.[29] Athalya Brenner names Zech 5:5-11 among her list of "offensive" prophetic passages.[30] The symbol of the banished woman reflects "chauvinism and xenophobia," especially, as Brenner notes, "from the perspective of human-interactions."

With Brenner, we can ask Bynum's question: Who were the "gendered users" of Zechariah's symbolic discourse? Historically, such a symbol did give rise to thought. The men of postexilic Jerusalem eventually concocted a program that sent foreign women away from Jerusalem. The book of Ezra describes how the postexilic community enacted a program of mass divorce, banishing foreign women for being inadequate to carry the holy seed. That they were a gateway to foreign religious practices probably strengthened the social imperative to expunge them. They were scapegoated as socially dangerous, banished from postexilic society as it rebuilt its identity and institutions.

What is the role of scapegoating in a theology of reconciliation? A feminist should be on guard when societies find religious cause to label social groups as pariahs. David Janzen is basically correct to call the expulsion of foreign women in Ezra a "witch-hunt."[31] René Girard's theory of violence, which develops the mechanism of social scapegoating, will run in this direction as well.[32] As a marginalized gender, the woman in the basket is a convenient scapegoat, blamed for domestic problems. The woman is sent away in an act of collective expulsion whereby a community achieves unity by directing enmity against a common enemy. While the people who send her away feel they are solving the problem of their domestic conflicts, the woman in the basket is actually a victim of her own conflict society. What does reconciliation even mean for a scapegoated victim of a conflict society?

I must here express my amazement that we need not abandon Zech 5 to explore this question further. Symbolism already lends itself to more than one interpretation, and linguistic opportunities in Zech 5:5-11 make possible a reversal of fate for the woman in the basket. Verses 9-11 are key, beginning in verse 9:

> Then I looked up and saw two women coming forward. The wind was in their wings; they had wings like the wings of a stork, and they lifted up the basket between earth and sky.

Two women conduct her expulsion. These women can fly; their wings resemble those of the stork. Lifting the basket, they usher the woman away "between earth and heaven." The two flying women not only whisk her away, but they are tasked with building a house for her (v. 11). There, she will be set "on her place."

Preparing the ground for a different interpretation, we can first note that this is not expected treatment for foreign cult objects. When King Josiah reformed Israelite religion and censured Canaanite worship, he burned down the temples and killed all the priests (2 Kgs 22–23). Deuteronomy sanctions the violent eradication of cult objects, as stated in the injunction "[t]he images of their gods you must burn with fire" (Deut 7:25).

In contrast, Zechariah's vision is strikingly serene. The woman's voyage is handled by women. She is lifted up on the air by birds' wings and installed in a house built specifically for her. Moreover, the phrase "wings of a stork" poetically evokes the language of God's *hesed* A stork is already a benign and even pastoral species. But in Hebrew, the term stork (*hasidah*) shares its root with *hesed*, which means "loving-kindness." God's *hesed* represents a devoted love not unlike the instincts of a bird to its young. In fact, *hesed* is elsewhere likened to refuge-giving wings (Ps 36:7). Even as the woman's confinement in the basket is described in violent terms, a rather startling benevolence attends the excommunication of the woman marked as iniquity.

We do not know what becomes of the woman once the basket touches down in Shinar and is set "on its place." What enduring scar trails on after her violent confinement? Her excommunication and ethical censure excludes her from any native pathways to reconciliation with her old community. Indeed, scapegoats do not fare well in judicial proceedings.

And yet, following her to her place in Shinar could provide one of the most important insights into a feminist postconflict reconciliation. The role of *hesed* in her life and the designated space to which she is brought bespeak a future of possibility. From this position of agency, grounded in a new world, the censured woman can outlive the mark her old society placed upon her. Shall the woman in a basket become a leader? What would her return to Jerusalem look like? Is she morally obligated to reconcile with her old community, or shall she rebuild a life in Shinar facing a new set of reconciliations?

The United Nations has recognized the significance of women in postconflict reconciliation. The Security Council, referenced above, strongly resolves that women must lead in all stages of conflict resolution:

> Reaffirming that women's and girls' empowerment and gender equality
> are critical to efforts to maintain international peace and security, and

emphasizing that persisting barriers to full implementation of resolution 1325 (2000) will only be dismantled through dedicated commitment to women's empowerment, participation, and human rights, and through concerted leadership, consistent information and action, and support, to build women's engagement in all levels of decision-making.[33]

The vision of the woman in the basket reminds me of aspects in the life of Leymah Gbowee, who emerged a national leader for peace work in the wake of a failed reconciliation process in Liberia. According to her autobiographical reflections in *Mighty Be Our Powers*, Gbowee bore numerous negative female stereotypes during the Liberian conflict. As a marginalized woman, she struggled to find confidence in her leadership positions.[34] As a single mother, she struggled with religious judgments on her character.[35] Of her abusive marriage, she describes how "the words came at [her]": "*Lazy bitch, Liar, Whore.*" Gbowee italicizes the words to signal the way they hung in the air she breathed.[36] Her abusive husband hurled accusations of juju magic at her, claiming she had "bewitched him into taking responsibility for children that weren't even really his."[37] Flipping the significance of the label, Gbowee adopted the plastic self-description "witch" to describe the sacred power of female solidarity in peacebuilding.[38]

In so many ways, Gbowee allowed differently gendered spaces (usually meetings of women) to transform the negative social labels that trapped her in depression, inactivity, and self-loathing. As if describing life in the basket, Gbowee reflects,

> Depression is a strange thing. You feel so helpless, so drained, that no matter how bad the place you find yourself, you sink into it, thinking, it's too hard to move. I'll just stay here.[39]

But Gbowee did not stay there. She doggedly devoted herself to peacebuilding among women, extending the courage she gained outward toward multiple sectors of society. She confronted the male spheres of conflict in Liberia, calling them out as patriarchal war. Leymah Gbowee went on to win a Nobel Peace Prize, and Liberia emerged from its civil war, electing its first woman president.

On the personal level, Gbowee overcame the ways in which she was socially scapegoated as a marginalized victim of conflict. Her work in transforming gender expectations and commitment to peacebuilding stemmed in part from her ability to read against the grain. At one point in her autobiography, she describes the confidence she drew from the powerful and transformative role of prostitutes in biblical literature. In an interview with

Bill Moyers, Gbowee charts her development as a leader with reference to a Hebrew prophet—citing how God used prostitutes, unexpected and even unwilling people who have little more than conviction.[40] Her courage to resignify the labels "prostitute" and "witch" reflects the transformative gender work she undertook in her self-definition. As Bynum might say, she made the gendered symbol of a prostitute carry a different value. The different value, a political and social agency, empowered her to become a leader in reconciliation and peacebuilding.

Conclusion

A feminist contextual theology of reconciliation finds many good footholds in Zechariah. Our analysis of chapters 3, 5, and 8 prompts reflection on how power works, how gender changes during and after conflict, the nature of truth telling versus scapegoating, the importance of judgments that make for peace, and what it means to empower agents of reconciliation.

Zechariah 3 explores gender transformations within patriarchal leadership. We saw how a modified priesthood both empowered Judah after its devastation from war and enacted a ritual process of reconciliation for the society. The vision of Joshua begins as a judicial proceeding and becomes a ritual of amnesty. His gender transformation sets off a chain of events that, for Zech 3, prepares for YHWH's return and widespread reconciliation among neighbors. Historically, all of this peacebuilding happened in male spheres, as the phrase "men of the sign" underscores. The vision of Joshua prompts reflection on how postconflict empowerment and social stability can be a public good that extends certain benefits outward.

Zechariah 8 enhances and deepens the concept of a society of reconciliation. Where Zech 3:10 describes neighbors who were formerly in conflict engaging in mutual hospitality, Zech 8:16-17 outlines an ongoing process for dealing with conflict. A society of reconciliation requires judgments that make for peace. Certainly important for a feminist theology of reconciliation is a gender-inclusive vision for peace, as we saw in 8:4-5. Old men and women holding canes can sit side by side in public spaces without fear of violence or gross conflict.

And yet, according to 8:16, truth telling and judgments for making peace fall in the sphere of men ('ish). The time when this matters most is in a scenario like that of Zech 5, the scapegoating of the woman in the basket. Her victimization is the result of gendered judgments about how to expunge wickedness. Although her society is patriarchal institutionally and discursively, and she becomes a victim of a violent act of scapegoating, the vision forges a postconflict path with promising features. She is brought a safe distance from the community that violated and negatively marked her.

The two women that interest me the most in this postconflict society of reconciliation are (1) the old woman with the cane who gets up from her public bench and seeks justice in the gates of her city and (2) the scape-goated woman who is flown away to a new place by stork-winged women. How will they engage the ongoing work of reconciliation?

For Further Reading

Arendt, Hannah. *Eichmann in Jerusalem: A Report on the Banality of Evil.* Revised and Enlarged Edition. New York: Viking, 1965.

———. *The Human Condition.* Chicago: University of Chicago Press, 1958.

Gbowee, Leymah. *Mighty Be Our Powers: How Sisterhood, Prayer, and Sex Changed a Nation at War.* With Carol Mithers. New York: Beast Books, 2011.

MacGinty, Roger, ed. *Routledge Handbook of Peacebuilding.* New York: Routledge, 2013.

PBS. "Women, War, and Peace." Five-part documentary. New York: WNET, 2014. http://www.pbs.org/wnet/women-war-and-peace/.

Tutu, Desmond. *No Future without Forgiveness.* New York: Doubleday, 1999.

Volf, Miroslav. *Exclusion and Embrace: A Theological Exploration of Identity, Otherness, and Reconciliation.* Nashville: Abingdon, 1996.

CHAPTER 15

PATH AND POSSESSION IN PROVERBS 1–9
A Feminist Biblical Theology of Flourishing

*Christine Roy Yoder**

What is the good life? How does one achieve it? How does a person navigate life well? What habits, activities, traits, and relationships promote human well-being? Within the Hebrew Bible, the book of Proverbs wrestles overtly with these age-old questions, pondering what aspects of life are vital to individual and communal welfare. Proverbs is a collection of collections, a composite of two-line proverbs and longer instructions that the sages or scribes of ancient Israel gathered over time. Generation after generation affirmed its teachings to be reliable expressions of the community's knowledge and values gained through experience about how to get along well in the world.

Proverbs 1–9 introduces and motivates the book's vision of the good life. Presented as instructions by a father to his sons[1] in an affluent urban household, the opening chapters establish what Carol Newsom calls "the eudaimonic ideal," or understanding of what constitutes human flourishing, that frames and informs Proverbs as a whole.[2] That ideal, the father repeatedly contends, is wisdom, which a person gains through the cultivation of certain virtues (see 1:1-7). Wisdom is "your life" (4:13; cf. 8:35). Wisdom protects as a shield (e.g., 2:7) and stands guard against a myriad of dangers (e.g., 2:11-12).

* I am pleased to dedicate this essay to Carol A. Newsom, with gratitude for her inspiring work, invaluable wisdom, and gracious collegiality and friendship.

Wisdom is a most desirable woman who bestows on her lover the benefits of esteem in the community, wealth, health, and honor by God (e.g., 3:13-18; 4:4-9; 8:1-21). Wisdom is the mythic "tree of life," a source of nourishment and healing (3:18; cf. Gen 2:9; Rev 22:2). Moreover, wisdom is at the side of God during creation: she is delight, playing between God, humanity, and the world (8:22-31). When people embrace wisdom, therefore, they find joy and align themselves with the structures and generative forces of creation. Wisdom is happiness. Wisdom is the good life.

No one disputes that this depiction of the good life reflects a decidedly male and upper-class point of view.[3] Readers are addressed as "my son" (e.g., 1:8; 2:1, author's trans.). Women are portrayed as either wholly good or wholly bad, while men are their beneficiaries or hapless victims. The father also assumes that his sons have freedom and capacity to act in the world, along with access to resources and opportunities. It is thus not surprising that women often find Prov 1–9 complicated and disorienting, its claims about the good life at once intriguing and alienating. Alert to these aspects of the father's worldview, I am interested in whether and how his conception of the good life might nonetheless be an important resource for women. Despite its intractable male bias, that is, are there ways in which this instruction might resonate with women's experiences and empower their agency?

I find promise in how the parent talks about life itself. Whereas wisdom is the singular goal of human existence, the father's use of two distinct metaphors for life signals that there are different ways to reach it. He presents what is called a dual metaphor: life is a journey, and life is a possession.[4] The first metaphor draws from the domain of space (location); the second, from the domain of acquisitions (object). The combined result is a location/object pair: two metaphors for the same concept that reinforce and challenge each other. That the father does this is significant. More than simply skillful rhetorical flourish, metaphors structure human understanding and inform critical reflection. They are modes of reasoning, lenses through which we perceive and make sense of the world, ourselves, and our relationships. Accordingly, by entwining multiple ways of thinking about life and the attainment of wisdom, the parent fosters agency. By providing diverse perspectives by which to interpret life, he cultivates the capacities of discernment, agility, and imagination, making it more likely that the next generation will adjust adroitly and quickly to life's circumstances and thereby flourish. The following explores each metaphor more closely. I then conclude with some implications, particularly for women, of their interweaving.

Life as a Journey: The Good Life as the Path
to Wisdom

The first and most prevalent metaphor for life in Prov 1–9 is that of a journey—a trek that takes time, covers a lot of ground, and moves in a particular direction.[5] The metaphor is familiar to most readers still today. Consider such expressions as "she had a head start in life," "his life is moving in the right direction," "you are hurrying through life," or "I'm not going anywhere."[6] In this metaphorical mapping, the quality of a person's life is measured principally in spatial terms: the wise and just orient themselves and move properly in the world; the foolish and wicked are disoriented and eventually dispelled from it. Life is conceptualized in terms of a person's motion in space.

Personal attributes or states of being are destinations in the landscape. Wisdom personified as a woman stands at the center of things. Not only does she delight daily in the inhabited and cultivated places of God's world (8:31), but she moves about in the heart of a city, a celebrated stronghold of human culture. She calls out "in the street, in the squares . . . at the busiest corner . . . at the entrance of the city gates" (1:20-21; cf. 8:1-3)—right in the middle of everyday commerce and civic and social happenings, right in the places most symbolic of power and authority. She is the quintessential insider. Indeed, those who seek wisdom go "up" to find her, in the direction usually assigned to authority and status, goodness and virtue (e.g., the moral "high ground"; cf. 25:6-7).[7] Wisdom is "on the heights" (8:2), and she speaks "from the highest places in town" (9:3).

In contrast, foolishness personified as a woman is "outside" the community. The parent introduces her as a "stranger" (*zarah*) and a "foreigner" (*nokriyyah* [2:16]), terms that situate her beyond boundaries, as "off limits," whether social, legal, ethnic, or sexual.[8] Although she frequents many of the same places as wisdom ("now in the street, now in the squares" [7:12]), she moves along the edges and corners of those spaces to "stalk" (6:26) and "lie in wait" for her victims (7:12). Her front stoop is at a high place in the city, but its location proves similarly deceiving. Those who cross her threshold discover too late that, like her feet (which can be a euphemism for her genitalia [5:5, 27]), her house (or womb)[9] "sinks down" to death, in the direction often associated with depravity (2:18). Her guests are in the depths of Sheol or the underworld; by implication, they must ascend an insurmountable distance to return to the land of the living—hence the parent's warning "[those who go to her] do not regain the paths of life" (2:19).

Situated in this geography that is symbolically framed by women—wisdom as center, inside, and up; folly as outside and down—a person is a traveler. Recurrent in Prov 1–9 are terms for a "path" (i.e., *derekh*, *'orah*, *ma'gal*, and *netivah*), and nearly all of the characters are said to have one, from God (8:22), to wisdom (8:20), to folly (2:18; 5:5), to a solitary ant (6:6). There are starting points (e.g., 1:7; 8:22). A person enters a path (4:14) and may depart from it (e.g., 2:12). Parents guide their children on certain paths (4:11). And every path is under the watchful eyes of God (5:21). With thick lines, the parent draws two primary roads across the map: the way of wisdom and justice ("the way of life" [6:23]) and the way of folly and wickedness (the way of death [e.g., 2:18; 5:5]). People travel on one or the other, so these ways are public and well trod, not the individual "off road," blaze-your-own-trail paths of rugged individualism. The way of life is pleasant, peaceful, and increasingly bright "like the light of dawn" (4:18; cf. 2:9; 3:17; 8:20). The way of death is engulfed in deep darkness (4:19) and winds downward crookedly (e.g., 2:15). It is riddled with obstacles and traps (e.g., 1:17-19; 4:19).

Every decision and behavior is a movement of the body, a step further down the path. Life is moving, or not, on one's way. The instructions teem with verbs of physical motion (e.g., walk, run, stumble, enter, avoid, go, turn away, and pass by, all in 4:12-19 alone). Prepositions and relative directions situate the reader in the topography (e.g., in, out, on, near to, right, left). The verb "to walk or go" (*hlkh*) occurs as a metaphor over fifteen times, as in "walk blamelessly" (2:7), "[those who] walk in the paths of darkness" (2:13), and "walk on the way of the good" (2:20). Invitations to consider various ways of being in the world also begin with the same verb, giving the sense of physical tug and pull in different directions. A street gang calls out, "Walk [*hlkh*] with us!" (1:11). The parent urges, "Go [*hlkh*] to the ant!" (6:6) to learn about self-motivated industriousness. The "strange" woman beckons, "Come [*hlkh*], let us take our fill of love-making" (7:18), while wisdom offers a quite different feast: "Come [*hlkh*], eat of my bread!" (9:5).

The good life is the path to wisdom. A person must commit and set out before knowing what wisdom is exactly and then orient and move the body and parts of it to stay on the path. The wise are "upright" (*yesharim* [2:7, 21; 3:32; cf. 8:8-9]) and walk "straight" ahead (*yshr* [9:15]). They "steer" their hearts to understanding (2:2) and keep their feet from "turning aside" to foolishness and evil (7:25; cf. 3:7; 4:27). They put distance between themselves and anyone or anything that might deter them from their course, a practice that is underlined by a series of commands: "Do not enter the path of evildoers. Do not stride on the way of the wicked. Avoid it. Do not move over to it. Turn aside from it and move on" (4:14-15). The wise diligently stay far away from folly and do not go near the door to her house (5:8). At the same time, the wise draw near to everyone and everything that encourages them ahead in wisdom and well-being (e.g., "keep to the paths of the just" [2:20]; "do not turn aside from parental instruction" [4:5; cf. 5:7]). The parent acknowledges that this physical comportment and navigation through life is not easy. It requires constant watchfulness and self-discipline (4:25-27):

> Keep your eyes looking forward,
>   let your gaze be straight ahead.
> Keep straight the path of your feet,
>   and all of your ways will be steady.
> Do not swerve to the right or to the left;
>   turn your foot from evil.

The metaphorical demeanor and movements of fools and the wicked are predictably the opposite. Adjectives of physical contortion, especially "twisted" and "crooked," frequently characterize their decisions and actions (e.g., 2:12; 6:14; cf. 8:13). They "abandon" the path of life in favor of dark and meandering roads (2:13, 15). They "stray" (5:23) and "stumble" and do not know what trips them up (4:19). They "miss" wisdom, as in missing a target (8:36). Personified folly exemplifies their ignorant bumbling: she "does not keep to the path of life; her ways wander and she does not know it" (5:6). Her lack of direction, compounded with her lack of understanding, signals the lack of a worthy purpose. Moreover, unlike the wise, who usually move thoughtfully and deliberately, fools and the wicked hurry off in the wrong direction. The street gang, for example, "runs to evil" and hurries to shed blood (1:16; cf. 6:18). A youth without sense rushes after folly "like a bird rushing into a snare" (7:23). In the end, what destroys the naïve is all this "turning about" (*meshuvat*, from *shuv*, "to turn, return")—that is, their "waywardness" (1:32, so NRSV).

That personified wisdom and folly stand at crossroads and corners (1:21; 7:8, 12; 8:2), places of decision making, highlights the role of personal responsibility to stay on the path to wisdom. One must choose again and again to press on. At the same time, the parent identifies forces that enable or impede movement. In doing so, he invokes the community's "iconic narrative" or expression of the foundational structures of reality and the nature and tendencies of the world—namely, how the world "works."[10] Because God made the world with wisdom (3:19-20; 8:22-31), wisdom is woven into the fabric of creation, giving it shape, meaningful order, and a coherence that God continues to uphold. So the parent names God and wisdom explicitly as forces or agents who facilitate a person's movement along the path of life. God "makes one's path straight" (3:6) and "keeps one's foot from being caught" (3:26). Wisdom is a "shield" to those who walk with integrity (2:7). Wisdom "guards" and "keeps watch" over their paths (2:8; cf. 2:11) and is a lamp and light to see by (6:23). Parental instruction "leads" and keeps company with the wise on their way, "watching over" them when they sleep and talking with them when they wake (6:22). Wisdom "saves" one from the path of evil (2:12). In short, the world is not neutral. Because God created and sustains it, God sees to it that those who choose the path to wisdom encounter few if any obstacles.

Conversely, the parent names forces and impediments that trip up those who choose the path of folly and wickedness. The terrain is crooked and shadowy (7:21). The wicked lurk about, driven by a relentless and restless need to "make someone stumble" (4:16). Snares and traps pepper the landscape. Ironically, the wicked get caught in traps of their own making (1:18; 5:22); fools bind themselves, "like a bird in the hand of the fowler," by their poor judgment (6:1-5); and poverty attacks the lazy like a highway robber and armed warrior (6:11). Folly herself stalks the unsuspecting (6:26). The parent invokes the mythic notion of a woman as a trap with the claims that her eyelashes "capture" them (6:25) and that her speech "pushes" them to follow her "like an ox to the slaughter . . . a stag toward the trap . . . a bird into a snare" (7:21-23). Folly "lays low" her victims (7:26). In a world formed by God's wisdom, the trail of foolishness is deadly.

At times it is not clear what encourages or impedes a person's progress. Instead, there is the so-called divine passive, an implicit reference to divine wisdom at work in the deepest structures of the world. For example, disaster comes "like a whirlwind" to those who refuse discipline (1:26-27; cf. 3:25). The parent does not say that wisdom sends the storm or that God does. The tempest simply happens because that is the way the world "works": the world eventually expels wickedness.[11] Likewise, calamity "descends suddenly" on villains and scoundrels (6:15). Proverbs 2 concludes confidently that "the upright will abide in the land and the innocent will remain in it, but the wicked will be cut off from the land, and the treacherous will be rooted out of it" (2:21-22). Said differently, the wise have a place in the world; they are located here; but, in the end, the wicked have no place. To have no place, no space at all in the landscape, is the worst possible fate in a metaphor that measures the quality of a person's life in spatial terms.

Contrary to all expectations, in this metaphor a person never arrives at the good life and stays there. There is no climactic exclamation of "I've arrived," no moment of enduring perfection, no ultimate achievement of wisdom and clarity. Paradoxically, those who seek wisdom continue the search even after finding it (e.g., 1:5-6). They gather happily to wait patiently and expectantly, as lovers do, outside of wisdom's house ("watching daily at my gates, waiting beside my doors" [8:34]). And they hear wisdom's invitation to "turn aside" and enjoy the feast of her household as perpetual and immediate (9:1-6). That this first metaphor for life yields no final, permanent destination means that the spotlight stays bright on the journey itself. The journey to wisdom is not a means to an end, a path that moves one eventually to some perfect and abstract realization of wisdom and thus to well-being. Rather, as the parent tells it, the journey to wisdom *is* the good life.

Life as a Possession: The Good Life as Gift

The second metaphor for life in Prov 1–9 is that of a possession. Whereas the journey metaphor privileges motion, its dual does not require movement at all. One gives and takes, attains or discards, well-being. People strive to possess a good life, to gather it to them. Consider such contemporary expressions as "I seized the opportunity," "he has a rich life," "happiness slipped through my fingers," and "the good life is finally in her grasp."

Personal attributes and states of being in this metaphor are physical objects. The parent describes wisdom, for example, as fine jewelry, worn as a beautiful garland on the head, pendants around the neck, or rings on the fingers (1:9; 3:22; cf. 6:21; 7:3); its value exceeds that of exquisite jewels, fine gold, and choice silver (3:15; 8:19). Similarly, the wise metaphorically wear loyalty and instruction around their throats (3:3; 6:21). One may hold "good" in the hands but must never refuse to return it to "its owner" (3:27-28). Foolishness is water that has been stolen—sweet at first taste but, in the end, bitter and poisonous (9:14; cf. 5:4).

The good life results from attaining desirable objects and avoiding or discarding undesirable ones. The most desirable object, without question, is wisdom (2:15). Like treasure hunters or miners, those who want to survive, and even thrive, search tirelessly for it (2:1-5; cf. Job 28:3-4, 9-11). The parent presses early and often that one should "take" instruction (*lqḥ* [1:3; 2:1;

4:10; 8:10])[12] and "store it up" (*tspn* [2:1]). With regard to wisdom personified, the language is often simultaneously economic and marital, as with the instruction to "acquire" wisdom (*qnh* [e.g., 1:5]). The verb *qanah* commonly means to acquire or buy with cash or the exchange of goods (e.g., Prov 17:16; 23:23); it is also used for marriage, as when Boaz "acquires" Ruth as his wife (Ruth 4:5, 10). The entwining of the economic and marital reflects a social-historical context in which a marriage was typically a business transaction negotiated between two families, and a wife was counted among a husband's possessions. Note the seamless back and forth in this instruction and how it conveys a transactional notion of a person's relationship to wisdom:

> Acquire [*qeneh*] wisdom; acquire [*qeneh*] understanding....
> Do not forsake her, and she will keep you;
>   love her, and she will guard you.
> The beginning of wisdom is this: Acquire [*qeneh*] wisdom!
>   Above all of your possessions [*qinyanekah*], acquire [*qeneh*] insight.
>   (4:5-7)

Elsewhere, the parent intensifies the pressure to possess wisdom with such verbs as "keep hold" (*hzq* [3:18; 4:13]), "hold fast" (*tmkh* [3:18; 4:4]), "keep" (*shmr* [5:2]), and "do not let go" (*rph* [4:13]). The result is an unremitting appeal to attain wisdom first, before any other possession—to grasp and hold onto wisdom in a world of many competing and enticing desirable objects (e.g., the street gang's quick loot [1:11-14]).

Despite considerable effort, however, one cannot attain wisdom alone. Everyone must search for wisdom as for treasure and a most desirable companion (2:4). Everyone must "set down" their naïveté (9:6) and heed reproof and instruction. But in the end, God "gives" wisdom (*ntn* [2:6-8]) and "stores up" wisdom for the just (*tspn* [2:7]). Wisdom—the good life—is a gift. Moreover, this wisdom proves to be, to borrow the familiar marketing slogan, the "gift that keeps on giving." Wisdom enables a person to thrive in the world. Wisdom "gives" happiness (3:13, 18; 8:32, 34);[13] she is joy (8:30b), rejoicing before God and in the world. Those who acquire her enjoy health and long life (3:16, 18; 8:14; cf. 3:8). They "inherit" honor and prosperity (*nhl* [3:14, 16; 4:9; 8:15-16, 18-19, 21]). Wisdom even adorns the wise with fair garlands and crowns for their heads, signs of favor, nobility, and marriage (4:9; cf. 1:9). The wise prosper in the world, indeed they flourish, because they seek wisdom, *not* her many benefits.

Fools and the wicked miss that very important distinction. They reject wisdom, the most desirable possession, even when it is handed to them: they "give up" instruction (*ntsh* [1:8]) and "refuse" wisdom's reproof (*'bh* [1:25, 30]). Fools prefer to live by their wits instead (the "wisdom of [their] own eyes" [e.g., 3:7]). As a result, they grab wrongheaded objects, including quick money (1:13-14) and disposable, illicit relationships (6:27). In the end, the parent argues, in a world formed by God's wisdom, fools find themselves empty-handed (5:8-14). Gone is their wealth, the loss of which is particularly grave because it goes to "others," "strangers"—people not of one's family (5:9-10). Lost is any hard-earned honor. And imperiled is their health, their flesh and body consumed (5:11). Whereas wisdom gives life, greed and foolishness take it away (*lqh* [1:19]).

Conclusion: Attaining the Good Life

So how does one attain the good life? How does a person flourish? Proverbs 1–9 presents two alternatives side by side: stay on the path to wisdom and acquire wisdom as your most desirable possession. Both options reveal important aspects of the parent's worldview. He assumes a world of discernible order, a world formed and maintained by divine wisdom, and therefore a landscape of stark, if not always clear,[14] choices between wisdom and foolishness, righteousness and wickedness. Perhaps this sense of an intelligible order reflects the relatively stable social-historical context of the Persian period in which Prov 1–9 came together. Perhaps it simply implies such a world.[15] Whichever the case, the parent assumes the capacity to navigate freely in that structured world and to make decisions that shape one's circumstances. The dual metaphors convey confidence that a person is able, with discipline and guidance, to attain a good life. Certainly, not all readers will share these assumptions.

Even so, the parent's dual metaphors for life can empower agency—not only of the "sons" he addresses directly, but of women who now listen alongside. The two metaphors reinforce each other in significant ways. Both initially locate wisdom outside of oneself as a place or an object. Inherent is the conviction that people need knowledge from beyond themselves for wholeness. To survive and thrive, therefore, we turn outward to the world and learn variously from traditions, other people and cultures,[16] everyday happenings, and creation itself ("go to the ant!" [6:6-8; cf. Prov 30]). On the one hand, this dynamic takes seriously the extent to which we are formed by the people and world around us; culture exerts considerable force on human lives in ways that may be oppressive or liberating. Women have long known they dare not downplay that reality. One consequence of doing so is what

Serene Jones calls the "highly agentic woman" who "appears daily on television commercials and in so-called professional women's magazines; she is the emancipated woman who, by strength of will, fights off sexist forces of cultural expectation and makes it in a 'man's world' of corporate success and power."[17] Ironically, an overestimation of women's agency can place a heavy and unwieldy burden on the very people it seeks to liberate.

On the other hand, women dare not underestimate their capacities. Both metaphors for life in Prov 1–9 presume that people have the ability and responsibility to participate intentionally in their own formation and that of their community. Commitment to wisdom is necessary. Verbs of attentiveness and action, discernment and decision making, abound: walk, turn aside, steer, take, acquire, hold fast, and set down. Accountability is assumed. Consequences are named. And the never ultimately realized ends of the metaphors remind readers that the attainment of well-being is a disciplined, ongoing, negotiated process. Far from a template of *the* good life—or some static, universal concept of human flourishing—Prov 1–9 insist on wisdom that is woven into creation, born of everyday experience, informed by tradition, and worked out with others amid the messy and often difficult particularities of life. Both metaphors envision a person to be the subject of her own life, an embodied agent in God's world.

The two metaphors are also mutually corrective. The life as a journey metaphor presses readers to take a long view at the good life, to look to the horizon of a brighter future, to look to the destination of wisdom, and to take the next step. Wisdom is a lifelong trek, a place to which one moves, a space in which one enters, a common and bounded region in which people can thrive, a house in which one finds shelter, other seekers of well-being, and a prepared meal on the table (9:1-6). The good life is staying on the path to wisdom and progressing deliberately onward, planning ahead, anticipating, avoiding, or navigating around pitfalls and dead ends, and knowing where one is and where one is going next. It requires trusting those who came before, companioning those alongside, and making the path even more apparent and safe for those who follow. A failed life in Prov 1–9 is missing the path in the first place, wandering away from it, being directionless, tripping up others on their way, or insisting on a different path in the direction of injustice and harm—as the parent's many descriptions of the fools and wicked indicate.

In contrast, the life as possession metaphor urges an immediate view. At issue is claiming wisdom—the most desirable object—in the moment, doing what is necessary to acquire, hold on, and share or display well-being in everyday circumstances. This is the metaphor that asks what one should gather to oneself and what one must set aside or refuse for the sake of flourishing now. That relationships, including that of a parent and child, are construed by this metaphor primarily in transactional terms (e.g., "I give you good precepts" [4:2]) commends paying attention to what one gives and takes away in every encounter. The good life is thus an urgent, present undertaking. A failed life is to refuse even to look for wisdom and to turn away insight and instruction when others offer it.

That both metaphors invite different modes of reasoning about life teaches one last important facet of wisdom: wise people often affirm truths that are in tension with one another and draw on them as is fitting in the immediate circumstances. No single claim, no one perspective on a matter, no one logic always works. This is particularly true when the matter is complex, as in the case of defining and attaining the good life. As Edward Slingerland notes with regard to complicated topics, people "often shift from situation to situation—or, sometimes even within the same utterance—between different and mutually incompatible conceptual models."[18] The parent does this frequently, as the following demonstrate:

> Such are the ways of all who are greedy for gain,
>   it takes away the life of its possessors. (1:19)

> Keep sound wisdom and shrewdness;
>   they will give vitality to your throat,
>   and adornment for your neck.
> Then you will walk on your way securely,
>   and your foot will not stumble. (3:21b-23)

> I have taught you in the way of wisdom
>   I have led you in the paths of uprightness.
> . . . .
> Hold fast to discipline, do not let go;
>   guard it, for it is your life. (4:11, 13)

In the end, Prov 1–9 does not insist on a single, consistent, "right" metaphor for life as inherent to establishing the eudaimonic ideal. Rather, the parent's use of dual metaphors equips women and men with alternative conceptions with which to reason, make decisions, and navigate skillfully through life's challenges and joys—more possibilities, that is, to embrace wisdom and flourish.

For Further Reading

Newsom, Carol A. "Woman and the Discourse of Patriarchal Wisdom: A Study of Proverbs 1–9." Pages 142–60 in *Gender and Difference in Ancient Israel*. Edited by P. Day. Minneapolis: Augsburg Fortress, 1989.

Strawn, Brent A., ed. *The Bible and the Pursuit of Happiness: What the Old and New Testaments Teach Us about the Good Life*. New York: Oxford University Press, 2012.

Whybray, R. Norman. *The Good Life in the Old Testament*. New York: T&T Clark, 2002.

CHAPTER 16

COUNTERIMAGINATION IN ISAIAH 65 AND DANIEL 12
A Feminist Biblical Theology of Hope

Amy C. Merrill Willis

What is hope? This is a basic question to be sure, but one that is surprisingly elusive. The poet Emily Dickinson famously called hope "the thing with feathers."[1] In her poetic imagination, hope provides spiritual and individual comfort: it can keep one warm in chill air and accompany one in difficult places. Hope is the bird that delights us with limitless sweetness and demands not a crumb even in its own extremity. Unlike humans with their heavy bodies that can never overcome gravity's pull or time's sway, hope is not earthbound, but light, and makes its perch in the soul. For Dickinson, hope has an undemanding utility. It gives so much yet requires so little.

As a theological term, however, hope is a weightier matter. Even in casual use, the word "hope" is tied to our experience of time, especially our expectations of the future. Beyond the casual use, hope is freighted with even greater significance. In the biblical imagination, the thing that is hoped for is more than individual comfort and solace—it is nothing less than the salvation and redemption of God's people. But what is the substance of that salvific hope, and how is hope nurtured? As it is evoked in the prophets and re-visioned through feminist theology, hope is vital to human flourishing, but it is not something that just comes to humans like Dickinson's bird. Rather, hope entails a vigorous act of counterimagination about the future that makes moral and emotional demands on us in the present.

229

Between Optimism and Escapism

The Hebrew word *tiqvah*, which is often translated as "hope" in various English versions of the Bible, actually refers to confidence or trust in God. This correlation is obvious in Ps 71:5: "For you are my hope [*tiqvati*], my Lord God; my confidence [*mivtahi*] since the time of my youth."[2] Certainly, trust and confidence in God constitute an attitude important to the life of faith, but the Hebrew term *tiqvah* does not quite name the substance of biblical expectations about the future. Hope refers to an idea that differs from confidence; nor should hope be confused, as it often is, with optimism. A robust understanding of hope is different from both of these.

Since the concept refers to both an action and an attitude or emotion, theologians such as Fraser Watts and Miroslav Volf have found valuable insight in the discipline of psychology. Drawing on psychological theory, they both argue that hope is more than trusting in God and entails something riskier than optimism. Watts writes, "The clearest difference between optimism and hope lies in the confidence with which a future event is predicted."[3] Strictly speaking, optimism is based on certainty, given all the facts in evidence. One can have optimistic expectations about the future when one has evidence that such a future is highly probable. Volf calls this "extrapolative cause and effect thinking."[4] That is, based on past evidence, optimism leads one to draw rational conclusions about good outcomes that will result from present circumstances. While hope also involves positive expectations, hopefulness is not based on confidence in good outcomes. Rather, hope is an attitude that can exist only when the prognosis looks bleak. Authentic hope lives in the midst of trouble. It exists where there is no certainty about a good outcome, where positive expectations are not warranted by the present evidence. Volf puts the contrast this way: "Optimism is based on the possibilities of things as they have come to be. . . . Hope can spring up even in the valley of the shadow of death; indeed, it is there that it becomes truly manifest."[5] Indeed, in the experience of women and men caught up in tragedy, suffering, and grief, hope is what is necessary to make it through the valley.

Even though it is a risky undertaking, genuine hopefulness moves one toward well-being, community, and affirmation of life. The act of hoping does not mean wishing for everything that one wants or nurturing fantastical expectations. Genuine hopefulness is responsive to reality, seeking the good for self and others even while acknowledging difficult and painful circumstances. In this regard, Watts distinguishes between genuine and pathological forms of hope.[6] Pathological hope, instead of contributing to one's well-being and the good of others, devolves into wishful thinking, denial, isolation, and escapism.

Laura Lippman illustrates such toxic hope in her novel *What the Dead Know*. The novel portrays young parents in the years after their teenage daughters disappear from a Baltimore mall. When police investigations fail to turn up information about their children's fate, the couple must manage their grief on their own. Over time they each adopt a different attitude. Dave clings to hope, to the idea that the girls will be found. But Miriam comes to realize that the girls are probably dead. The recognition, though painful, frees her from the need for a happy ending. She can grieve their deaths and create a new, though diminished, life. Dave, who cannot relinquish his hope, finds that it is "an impossible emotion to live with . . . a demanding and abusive companion."[7] Far from viewing hope as a comforting feathered creature, Dave names it the hope-griffin, an animal whose claws knead into him and eventually tear him apart. Dave is unwilling to embrace the possibility of their deaths and, consequently, his life comes to an emotional halt. His hope, which is really denial, drives him to despair.

Feminist theologian Ivone Gebara calls attention to a sustaining hope that is rooted in reality.[8] Gebara highlights the story of Isabel Allende caring for her comatose daughter, as recounted in Allende's memoir *Paula*.[9] Initially, Allende's hope is for Paula's recovery, and that hope is urgent and stubborn despite her own terror and feelings of powerlessness. She decides to write about the ordeal to give form and meaning in the midst of her terror. She hopes that this act will in some way "bring [Paula] back to life." She writes for Paula so that after she awakens she will not feel lost. But as Paula's coma lengthens, Allende recognizes the diminishing probability of recovery. Allende's hope, and her purpose for writing, shifts. She no longer writes for Paula, for she realizes that Paula will never read those pages, but she continues to write for herself because it is her source of salvation. When the inevitable tragedy arrives, Allende recognizes it as a sacred and mysterious moment filled with the love of family members who have gathered around her dying daughter. Though the moment brings her pain and loss, it does not bring despair.

Envisioning Hope in the Hebrew Bible

I noted above that the Hebrew Bible's word for hope, *tiqvah*, does not describe the substance of hope, the things for which one should hope. There is a notable exception to this, however, found in Jer 29:11, a verse frequently quoted out of context for devotional and sentimental purposes. Hard upon the news of disaster, the oracle provides a skeletal framework of hope:

> For I know the plans that I have made for you, says the LORD,
>   plans for shalom and not for evil
>   to give you a future with hope.

The oracle intimates several important aspects of hoping, the most prominent of which is its temporal quality. Hope, as already noted, has to do with a future condition, with what may come to be. Divine activity makes this future hope nascent in the present. In God's very act of knowing, planning, and declaring, the future begins to take root and spring up now. God's plan insists that—contrary to the evidence of the present (and in this case the prophet is speaking of the national catastrophe and personal suffering inflicted on Judeans by the Babylonian Empire)—the future make room for shalom, a state of well-being that includes physical, social, and spiritual wholeness within God's community.

Because the anticipated future does not match the present, hope depends on the imagination. Since hope is not based on cause-and-effect reasoning or certainty of a good outcome, it must be nourished by the ability to conjure a reality that is different from the present. This work not only asserts that such a future is possible; it envisions that future in a concrete way. At the beginning of this essay, I used the word "counterimagination" to indicate this activity: the imagination must counter not only the present reality of brokenness and loss but also other imagined scenarios. The imagination can go in all directions, including skepticism and darkness. Having an active imagination is no guarantee that one can envision a hopeful future. The hopeful imagination is one that recognizes and confronts dark possibilities but counters the lure of resignation and fatalism. Authentic hope chooses to imagine that shalom is still possible.

In the Hebrew Bible, such acts of imagination most often appear in prophetic oracles of salvation and deliverance. While there are a number of texts that imagine an alternative future, I propose to focus on two that are especially distinctive, Isa 65:17-25 and Dan 12:1-3. These texts offer two very different visions of deliverance, both of which commentators call eschatological. Eschatology, or the theology of "last things," is fundamentally concerned with some kind of significant future expectation. The term often refers to depictions of the end of the world.[10] Yet the language of "the end" that sometimes appears in these biblical passages is ambiguous; it can refer to all kinds of endings—the end of a particular political order, the end of a political and religious crisis, or the end of one historical period of time but the inauguration of another. That is, eschatological moments are not just endings but often new beginnings. Sometimes these moments are major turning points *within* history rather than the end of history and of the cosmos itself.

Commentators typically identify Isa 65 as an example of prophetic eschatology and Dan 12 as apocalyptic eschatology. The precise difference between prophetic and apocalyptic eschatology has sparked an inconclusive debate, but two obvious differences are dating and situation. Isaiah 65 reflects the difficulties and concerns of the Judean community after the return from the Babylonian exile, in the years following 538 BCE. It draws on the Isaianic tradition preserved in Isa 1–55 to address those difficulties. Daniel 12 responds to the particular crisis of 167–164 BCE when a foreign king, Antiochus IV Epiphanes, outlawed the practice of Judaism in Jerusalem and defiled the temple. Daniel's visions in chapters 7–12 make constant references back to the Isaianic tradition as well, drawing on language from every part of the book of Isaiah. Despite this shared source, each text envisions the future and the prospects of salvation quite differently.

Hope in Isaiah 65

There are few passages in the Hebrew Bible that imagine well-being with greater clarity than Isa 65:17-25. It begins with YHWH's declaration of an impending act of cosmic renewal: "See! I am creating a new heaven and a new earth" (v. 17). The grammar suggests immediacy in God's intention; the new creation is both anticipated and already undertaken. To use a phrase familiar to Christians, God's new creation is "already and not yet."

Eschatological visions of the future often recapitulate the primeval conditions of creation.[11] This is the case in Isa 65, where re-creation reverses the garden of Eden's tragedies. Whereas Gen 3:14-19 describes human banishment, cursedness (vv. 14, 17), difficult childbirth (v. 16), and hard manual labor to eke out a minimal existence (vv. 17-19), Isa 65:23 announces a future in which the people

> will not labor in vain,
>> or bear children for calamity,
> for they will be offspring blessed by YHWH.

Reversing the order of punishments found in Gen 3, the oracle describes a time of blessedness in the form of productivity and abundance that has eluded humanity since its banishment from the Garden. Indeed, the people will live out abundant days, virtually untouched by death. Verse 22b announces, "Like the days of the tree will be the days of my people," indicating lifespans of a century or more. The verse also evokes the tree of life itself (Gen 2:9)! During those long lives, "they will plant vineyards and will eat their fruit" (Isa 65:21). They will enjoy respite from laboring in unproductive fields, respite that the inhabitants of Eden never enjoyed. Moreover, the difficulties of childbearing will be undone. Women will no longer endure the prospect of birthing and nurturing children only to see them die as infants or meet an untimely death in youth. Indeed, the vision rejoices in the prospect of children who live well past a hundred years without fear of early demise.

The passage begins with the announcement of a new heaven and a new earth and invokes the creation imagery of Eden, but the place of YHWH's creative activity is Jerusalem.[12] Jerusalem is a complex symbol; it evokes both the historical city and the Jerusalem of mythic imagination—the site of God's cosmic mountain that connects heaven and earth. But it cannot be reduced to either of those things. In using the language of the new Jerusalem, the passage maintains a constant tension between the cosmic and the particular. The new creation is universal, encompassing all things. At the same time, it is also a particular locality whose history and features are well known to the reader.

In the new Jerusalem, God's creative work has more to do with reordering society than just bringing things into being.[13] To speak of God's creating something can mean that God is making something that did not previously exist, but this meaning does not fully encompass God's creative activity. Indeed, at various points in the Hebrew Bible, one sees God ordering the environment and human life as a necessary part of God's creative work. The Hebrew verb "to create" (br', Isa 65:17) encompasses the acts of producing and ordering. In this passage, the emphasis is on ordering; the new creation is really a renovated social order.

Domestic life is at the heart of the renewed Jerusalem; hence, the passage focuses specifically on children, homes, vineyards, and even farm animals.[14] Of special concern are the health and stability of the family, Israelite society's fundamental unit. Quite remarkably, the oracle announces that infant mortality, a chronic problem in ancient Israel where mortality rates were approximately 50 percent,[15] will be eradicated (v. 20). Having survived infancy, children can look forward to a life free of trauma, war, and slavery, all of which were potential calamities children faced in Israel (v. 23b). The family will not be divided or diminished (v. 23d). Parents will be able to keep their children close, provide for them, and see them grow up without fear of catastrophe, and will know that they will be able to contribute to the upbuilding of the home.

The future that the oracle imagines is remarkably mundane. Although it does imagine extraordinary lifespans, it does not set its sights on streets paved with gold or pearly gates. Indeed, true hope does not require a grandiose imagination. In verses 21-23, the oracle focuses on remarkably basic life-sustaining activities—building homes and planting vineyards (vv. 21-22), laboring in the fields and raising children (v. 23).[16] Unlike their ancestors in Jerusalem at the time of the Babylonian exile, when they were evicted from land and homes (v. 22), or in the frustrating early days after returning from Babylon, the people will soon experience the satisfaction of seeing their work come to fruition (v. 21). They will be able to shelter their families and provide them with food and drink.

This vision of well-being, however, is not simply focused on the human inhabitants of the land. The prophet is also concerned with nonhuman creation. In the passage, the quality of human life is integrally connected to, dependent upon, and measured by the fecundity of the natural world. The prophet asserts that humans will live as long as the trees and will thrive on the abundance of grapes and the fertility of the soil. The manifest harmony between humans and the environment extends to the animal world as well. In a reworking of Isa 11:6-9, Isa 65:25 pictures wolf and lamb, lion and ox, predator and prey, wild and domestic animals dwelling peaceably together. What is the secret of their newfound harmony? Is it their new vegetarian status, highlighted in verse 25? Or is it a transformation of their inner nature as well—a change of diet along with changed internal appetites and desires? Whatever is the case, the passage envisions a reversion to the vegetarian condition of animals and humans as described in Gen 1 and 2.[17] Strikingly, the serpent, long the symbol of fear and enmity in the Hebrew Bible, has not been banished from this rejuvenated social order. It still has a place in the new creation, though it does not enjoy reversion to its original state. It remains a dust-eater, as in the curse language of Gen 3:14. Perhaps this is because the serpent is less threatening to the human occupants of the new Jerusalem this way.

Having unraveled the destructive experiences of family and community life, the oracle then announces the repaired relationship between God and humanity (v. 24). Isaiah 56–66 as a whole witnesses to the community's broken relationship with God. In the first part of Isa 65, the prophet puts the blame on those who refused to hear God's voice and refused to answer God's calls (65:1-12). Despite this, Isa 65:24 insists that failure of communication will be rectified through God's action. That is, God assumes the responsibility for the failure and for its repair. God will reverse positions and move from being the one who calls to a responsive, dialogical partner. Even before the community prays, even as they are in the act of speaking, God will respond. God will be constantly attentive and present, eschewing the absenteeism and silence that the people had accused the deity of in the past.

Hope in Daniel 12

While Isa 65 ponders a future primarily focused on the mundane world and the simple abundance of a restored domestic life, Dan 12:1-3 describes a future hope that is decidedly more cosmic in scope and political in orientation. This passage is part of an apocalyptic oracle of deliverance, announced by the angel Gabriel to the wise man Daniel. As an apocalyptic text, it discloses heavenly secrets that reveal the true nature of earthly events in the present even as it projects a future resolution of those events. In this oracle, Gabriel describes a cosmic deliverance of the faithful Jews, undertaken by the archangel Michael, the commander of God's angelic army:

> At that time, Michael, the great prince
>   who protects your people, will arise.
> It will be a time of distress such has never been
>   since the beginning of the gentile nations up to that point.
> At that time, your people will be rescued,
>   all those whose names have been written in the book. (Dan 12:1)

Michael's entrance into the tribulations of the faithful Jewish community represents an otherworldly intervention into history. Michael is God's agent, breaking into human events from beyond history. As the oracle envisions it, God's action comes during unprecedented political and religious crisis, signaled by the repeated use of the phrase "at that time." "That time" is the point at which the atrocities perpetrated by the Syrian king Antiochus IV have reached a tipping point.[18] Antiochus's military and political force can no longer be contained by human forces, necessitating divine intervention on behalf of a beleaguered, suffering community. The deliverance imagined is military and eschatological. Michael acts as a warrior doing battle against Antiochus's troops. Michael's military victory will not only rescue the people; it will mark the turning point at which all human empires pass away and God's judgment and eternal rule will break into human time. No longer will God's people be subject to foreign empires and exploitative kings.

Daniel 12 does not fully imagine the eschatological future in the way that Isa 65 does. Instead of describing a renovated political or social order, the apocalyptic oracle announces the resurrection of the dead:

> Many of those who dwell in the dust of the earth will arise;
>> some to everlasting life, and some to reproach and everlasting shame.
> But the wise ones will shine like the brightness of the sky;
>> and those who lead many to righteousness will be like the stars
>> forever. (Dan 12:2-3)

While it has influenced the Christian notion of a general resurrection of all the dead in Christ, the resurrection in this passage encompasses only some of the dead—both the righteous and the unrighteous. This latter group most certainly includes the king himself, while the former includes those faithful Jews who led some kind of unarmed resistance to the foreign king and have been martyred. The king and his unrighteous cohort are resurrected to punishment and dishonor, but the righteous are elevated to a new state of being in which they will shine like the stars in the sky (v. 3). Their resurrected state has a transcendent, cosmic quality to it—the righteous will either be granted immortality as astral bodies or be elevated to an angelic state like that of Gabriel and Michael, who are often described as stars.

Although the passage speaks to a particular historical situation, its desires speak to widespread concerns about death and injustice. For many, the experiences of suffering and tragic death challenge the human sense-making ability. Tragedy and death easily corrode one's sense of a meaningful universe. But Dan 12 counters the corrosive effects of tragedy by offering a vision transcending death.[19] Resurrection asserts that death is not itself a judgment on those who have died. Though unjustified death is tragic, resurrection vindicates the lives and work of the dead. Moreover, resurrection asserts that the foreign king's violent overturn of the universe will be set to right. In Dan 12, God restores justice and righteous rule through the resurrection events.

The Bible's Legacy—It's about Time

Isaiah 65 and Dan 12 are only two of many visions of a transformed future found in the Bible. My readings used literary, historical, and theological

methods to show how these texts envision a future that many readers have
found inspiring. Indeed, these passages have funded an eschatological
thinking that has held powerful sway in the West. Even so, the legacy of
these texts, both culturally and theologically, is an ambivalent one.

In American society in particular, the popular imagination is of two
minds about eschatological expectations. On the one hand, American
culture has a long history of fascination with utopian ideals, of looking
forward to an idealized future free from the sin and suffering of the present. America's puritan ancestors, writers like Cotton Mather and Jonathan
Edwards, anticipated a time when God's work of transforming the world
and creating a time of perfect peace would take place on American soil. The
widespread popularity of Edwards Hicks's nineteenth-century paintings,
a series called *The Peaceable Kingdom*, also attests to this utopian fascination. These paintings have become virtual icons of American folk art.
Based on Isa 11, and thus resonant with Isa 65, Hicks's depiction of an
idyllic time when the lion would lie down with the lamb fuse the future
Eden with echoes of the American countryside.[20] Western civilization as a
whole has tended to be future oriented, to seek out its destiny and worth in
the promises of a better future. Westerners yearn to live happily ever after
in a perfect future world.

Nevertheless, Western culture is not entirely convinced that the future
will bring good things. Popular movies and novels about the collapse of
human society abound. These stories link visions of the future to catastrophic doom, not to an ideal future where war, poverty, and illness have
been eliminated.[21] The turn of the millennium at the end of 1999 serves as
a good example. While many celebrated the end of one era and the inauguration of the new by building monuments such as the millennium dome in
London, others warned of a Y2K technological glitch that could cripple all
the planet's computer networks and bring whole countries to a halt. Such
anxieties reflect neither trust nor hope but skepticism, perhaps understandable after a century filled with wars, genocides, terrorism, and the advent of
nuclear weapons.[22]

This profound confusion about the future—which encompasses fascination and fear, hope and dread—is part of the Bible's legacy in the modern world. Flora Keshgegian argues that Western conceptions of time and
history have been shaped by biblical visions in various ways.[23] She notes
that the biblical accounts of creation, sin, redemption, and re-creation have
shaped Western culture to view time and history as a narrative moving in

linear fashion from a beginning point toward an end point. This end point, however, is more than a stopping place; in Christian and Jewish thinking, this end point is typically perceived as a telos, or history's goal, consummation, and fulfillment. Christian and Jewish interpreters have tended to link the redemption of history's traumas with the telos, thinking that history will reach its culmination when God's peaceable kingdom is established and wounds and warfare are overcome. Biblical texts such as Isa 65 and Dan 12 have helped to shape a widespread view of history as a story that is inevitably moving toward a happy ending.

This idea of a happy ending is not inherently bad. Indeed, Keshgegian notes that biblical visions, especially apocalyptic visions like Dan 12, allow those caught in tragic circumstances to see meaning in the human experience of time.[24] Nevertheless, the teleological interpretation has been damaging to human well-being. It has been linked to a progressive view of time, the idea that the future will continue on a path toward advancement and improvement in every part of life. This view of time, however, fails to make sense of a world that is not getting better for many. The gap between promise and reality has generated confusion and skepticism rather than hope.

Although the Hebrew Bible affirms that history is the arena of God's work, the teleological view of history has, somewhat ironically, depleted our commitment to the present world.[25] When we emphasize the future as the point at which history is redeemed, time becomes something that we are simply passing through, something to withstand and endure. Such a view suggests that human experiences in the past and present are always points at which history *fails* to find meaning; these experiences are not valuable in themselves, since only the future can bring redemption. This thinking discourages believers from dwelling in the present and encourages them to look away to the next age's distant horizon.

The search for a utopian future can have disastrous effects that these biblical visions never intended to foster. Ivone Gebara, working and living among women in dire conditions in Latin America, expresses her deep skepticism toward promises of otherworldly salvation. When co-opted by religious and political leaders interested in maintaining the status quo, such promises can anesthetize people to present injustices: "Talk that refers to a happy outcome at the end of time is able not only to allay the fear of life and death but also to be taken over by the powerful. . . . The powerful always speak of justice in the afterlife; they present happiness as the goal of the journey, as the *beyond* of history."[26] Thus, utopian expectations can devolve into pathological forms of hope, undermining attempts to work for justice. When the promise of redemption is always delayed, Gebara writes, "tomorrow becomes an endless frustration."[27] Under these circumstances, hope becomes little more than escapism, a fruitless activity no longer grounded in reality.

The Time and Place for Salvation

Instead of grounding hope in the search for a happy ending, Gebara and Keshgegian ask how salvation and redemption can involve the present and the near future. This means rethinking traditional concepts of salvation. Redemption involves deliverance from evil, sin, and suffering. It promises reparation of what is broken and makes shalom possible. But what kind of salvation should one imagine? Gebara eschews visions of salvation as once-and-for-all events abstracted from the present world. Such visions locate God's redemptive work at one decisive moment in the future that encompasses all peoples. But this prospect is almost completely disconnected from most women's experiences. Biblical visions of eschatological redemption are almost never used to address the evils and the joys, the fears and the hopes, that so many women experience in the present. Apocalyptic visions like that of Dan 12 concentrate on the political sphere and on powerful male agents and their concerns. Most of the world's women, however, are not among the powerful, nor do they have the luxury to devote their time to the political sphere. For many women and men, daily life is devoted to providing for children and caring for the sick, the dying, and the dead. Often these things are done amidst dehumanizing poverty, powerlessness, and violence, where salvation means finding basic necessities.

Gebara re-visions salvation in more immediate, provisional, and mundane terms than traditional Christian theology does. God's work is to be seen in life-affirming acts of community. Redemption is found in "tiny events" of present living and sharing. It is "an everyday salvation, a salvation of the here and now, a salvation for this life and this moment. It is a far cry from the grand projects of world economy, official statistics, a religious apocalypse, a far cry from the salvation of heaven."[28] These small moments are not grand, nor are they once-and-for-all; they come and go even as suffering and evil still abound. Nevertheless, moments of grace that women experience every day are fundamentally salvific and should not be overlooked. They include "shared bread, wounds healed, gestures of tenderness, the straightened posture of a stooped woman, hunger satisfied for the moment, the birth of a child, a good harvest. All these can be held up as symbols of life and therefore of salvation."[29]

This emphasis on "the now" of salvation does not preclude consideration of the future. Indeed, narrow concern for the present without regard for the future can easily slip into irresponsible hedonism. But Gebara sees the salvific present as part of the creative tension between "the already and the not-yet" at work in Isa 65 and other biblical texts. Her purpose is not to resolve that tension by eliminating the future dimension of hope but to push back against attempts to eliminate the present character of salvation. The salvific present is a foretaste of what could be, a gesture toward what one hopes for. Moreover, the salvific present is not just about the individual. Gebara argues that the intimate and provisional experiences of grace must also be connected to concern for the community and its need for systemic justice. The struggle for justice remains necessary.

Gebara's thinking is rooted in the feminist concepts of relatedness and interdependence. Like many feminist theologians, she valorizes women's experiences of caring for others and relying on their care. Every human is caught up in an inextricable web of relations. Moreover, this web of relatedness includes nonhuman creation.[30] Christian interpreters have too long seen the earth as expendable. The arena for God's redemptive activity must be extended to include all living beings and the natural environment itself.[31]

Can These Texts Be Saved? Hope in Isaiah 65 and Daniel 12 Revisited

Viewed in the light of feminist suspicions about "the end," these oracles raise new questions for thoughtful readers. How can they nurture authentic hope instead of pathological escapism? How can they speak to women's everyday experiences and empower them? Of course, biblical passages always require interpreters. How might these texts, read through a feminist lens, speak hope?

There are many points of intersection between this feminist construction of hope and Isa 65, which is, first and foremost, a vision of redemptive space rather than redemptive time. The passage explicitly places redemption in Jerusalem. Moreover, it places redemption in the sphere of domestic life, agricultural life, and animal life, not that of Jerusalem's religious and political institutions. The temple, the battles to restore the high priesthood, and the imperial politics of Persian rule—all the places of social power and conflict—are rendered invisible by the vision. The passage gives a view from the ground: vineyard, house, and farmyard come into focus. The passage makes visible the traditional work of women in caring for children and families. These are invoked not as a mark of female subordination and the failure of history but as the sign of shalom! Indeed, Gebara's symbols of life and redemption—"shared bread, hunger satisfied, the birth of a child, a good harvest"—resonate closely with the renewed world in Isaiah. And while the prophet does not exactly envision an ecofeminist ethic in this depiction of nonhuman creation, the oracle still attests to a fundamental integration between human and nonhuman life that can support such an ethic.

The vision abounds with images of divine nearness, of an immanent God, embedded in relationships. God's redemptive actions are interwoven with human work: God will draw close to the people in prayerful exchange, and their delight will reflect God's own delight and joy (65:18-19). Keshgegian affirms that "God is on the side of life, forever. . . . Contrary to the evidence and signs, God is present, making life happen."[32] In Isa 65, God's redemptive presence is shown primarily through evidence of life—in the fecundity of the natural world and the length of human years.

Just as divine activity is immanent in the human community, so the time of that activity is also near. Although Isa 65 can be used to support utopian expectations of an idealized future, the oracle's use of time offers another interpretive option. Earlier, I noted the tension of the "already and the not yet" in the passage. Clearly, the passage speaks about the future, but it is a future that is breaking into the present. In verses 17-18, God's creating activity is a dynamic and ongoing process that is visible now. The prophet's purpose in depicting this future is surely not to defer these salvific moments but to validate those present activities of care and nurture that are central to God's salvific concerns.

While Isa 65 harmonizes well with the feminist vision of redemption, Dan 12 voices expectations of time, place, and redemptive agency that do not follow the feminist cadences of hope quite so closely. Nevertheless, feminist readers ignore apocalyptic texts at their peril. It is only by reclaiming and revaluing apocalyptic texts that readers ensure that these texts nurture authentic hope instead of passivity and fatalism.

While Dan 12 decidedly focuses on the future, apocalyptic time never moves in one clear, unbroken direction toward that future.[33] Throughout Dan 7–12, the writers play with the arrow of time. They look back, casting the past in the form of a future prediction, but they also look ahead to anticipate what is to come. Sometimes time is ruptured altogether. The difference between this kind of time and teleological time is significant. Teleological time promises a happy ending in such a way as to dismiss present suffering, much like the well-intentioned person counseling a grieving friend by saying, "Don't worry! It will turn out fine in the end." But Daniel's apocalyptic time contemplates the future to gain knowledge about the present. That knowledge is itself empowering.

The oracle of deliverance in Dan 12, together with the visions leading up to it, functions to bring meaning and coherence to the chaotic present. Antiochus's pronouncement outlawing Judaism in 167 BCE was unprecedented. Moreover, many events before and after this, including the armed conflict between some Jewish groups and the king's forces, divided the Jews of Jerusalem and caused terror. Earlier Israelite ways of thinking argued that such tragedies were God's work in history. But Daniel's vision of judgment on the unrighteous dead emphasizes that God's power cannot so easily be identified with human events and power-hungry kings. Daniel's visions validate the efforts of the community who was resisting, apparently through nonviolent means, Antiochus's program of terror and domination.

By giving the present experience of persecution a narrative form with a defined ending, the vision allows the community to see its situation as temporary. Such a view of the present does challenge the feminist construction of hope, since it urges the community to see the destructive present as finite and transient. But this challenge serves as a reminder that embeddedness in the world and in time is itself an ambivalent reality. That is, if feminist theology reminds us that dwelling in the world, and not just passing through it, is important to nurturing genuine hope, then the apocalyptic view reminds us that the experience of being embedded in the present is sometimes an oppressive one that can create despair.

Emphasis on divine transcendence in Dan 12 represents a similar clash with feminist visions of hope. For those who wrote the vision, God is not embedded in the community's life but exists outside of it. God's redemptive activity breaks in from outside the world and beyond history. Such an emphasis on God's transcendent power shifts the calculus of human agency somewhat, but it by no means eliminates it. The apocalyptic vision emphasizes that the human ability to shape history is limited, both for the foreign king who imagines himself as all powerful and for the dominated community living at the king's mercy. Here, significant exercise of agency involves understanding God's sovereign plan and aligning oneself to it. Indeed, *knowing* is in itself a symbolic action that attempts to change the world on the symbolic and imaginative level, even if it cannot make concrete changes. This work of knowing is expressed through the writing of the visions themselves.[34] In this way, it is not unlike Isabel Allende's attempt to nurture her hope and "bring Paula back to life" by writing her memoir. For Allende, no less than the scribal community that wrote Daniel, writing gives form and meaning to experiences of terror, and it thereby delivers from terror's paralyzing effects.

The disagreements between Daniel's oracle and the feminist construction of hope do not diminish either perspective's ultimate affirmation of life. Indeed, Daniel's affirmation of resurrection may also be seen as an affirmation of the embodied life. Daniel 12 asserts that God is on the side of life and that God values the practices of righteousness and justice that are lived out in the body. The ongoing challenge is to see how that embodied life, which in Daniel is so very far removed from our own, can nevertheless include the world and work of mortals who live ordinary lives, care for family members, go to work, seek God, and yearn for justice.

Conclusion

It is a great privilege to offer this essay in honor of Carol A. Newsom. I came to Emory University in 1995 as a young graduate student to study apocalyptic texts with her. Since that time, Carol has nurtured and challenged my love for these difficult texts. She has also understood that this is more than an academic pursuit for me; it is a genuine calling. That I have been able to pursue this calling as a scholar and a teacher is due in no small way to her efforts. I am profoundly indebted to her for all kinds of things: her patience as I plodded through a lengthy dissertation process; the many letters of recommendation she wrote for me; and the kindness she showed at the birth of my children, knowing that they too were part of my calling and hope.

The work of hope is a communal effort; one cannot hope in solitude without guaranteeing failure. There have been times during my academic journey when I have been unable to imagine a future for myself. In so many of those moments, Carol helped me reimagine. Her particular brand of hope comes by way of metaphor and story: When I was certain that my story would have a catastrophic ending, Carol would gently and humorously redirect the narrative. When I spoke of the racehorse that broke its leg before crossing the finish line, she spoke instead of making a silk purse out of a sow's ear. When I spoke of things lost and ruined, she spoke of gems found in small packages. When I lamented the impending death of my career, she told a simple story of resurrection, embodied in the life of a thriving colleague. Such acts of hope manifest Carol's nimble intellect, to be sure, but also her wisdom and compassion.

Hope imagines a future of well-being and then works to bring it into existence through small and large practices of wisdom, compassion, and justice. It is a risky and courageous thing to do, to help one another by shouldering this work. But the dialogue between these biblical texts offers rich resources for going about this necessary task.

For Further Reading

Keshgegian, Flora. *Time for Hope: Practices for Living in Today's World.* New York: Continuum, 2006.

Newsom, Carol A., Sharon Ringe, and Jacqueline Lapsley, eds. *The Women's Bible Commentary.* 3rd ed. Louisville, Ky.: Westminster John Knox, 2012.

Polkinghorne, John, and Michael Welker, eds. *The End of the World and the Ends of God: Science and Theology on Eschatology.* Harrisburg, Pa.: Trinity, 2000.

BIOGRAPHY OF CAROL A. NEWSOM

Carol A. Newsom was born July 4, 1950, in Birmingham, Alabama, to parents Donald L. and Imogene P. Newsom. She graduated summa cum laude from Birmingham–Southern College in 1971 and received her M.T.S. (1975) from Harvard Divinity School and her Ph.D. with distinction (1982) from Harvard University. She has been teaching in the Old Testament department at Emory University since 1980, where she is now Charles Howard Candler Professor of Old Testament and directs the Graduate Division of Religion.

She is the author of nine books, including commentaries on Job and Daniel and several works on Qumran literature. In addition, she coedited with Sharon Ringe (and later with Jacqueline Lapsley) three editions of the *Women's Bible Commentary*. She has published countless essays, juried articles, encyclopedia and reference entries, and book reviews. She serves on the editorial boards of several prominent journals, study Bibles, and series, including *Journal of Biblical Literature*, *New Oxford Annotated Bible*, and Old Testament Library, and in 2011 she served as president of the Society of Biblical Literature. A much sought-after lecturer, she has appeared as close to home as Columbia Seminary and as far away as the University of Otago in Dunedin, New Zealand. Most importantly, she has directed or codirected twenty-five Ph.D. dissertations, fifteen of which have been subsequently published. When offered a dinner to celebrate her inauguration as SBL's president, in

San Francisco in 2011, and asked whom she wanted to invite, Carol said there was no one she wanted to celebrate with more than the many Emory graduates she has taught over the years, whom she considers her "children."

Her fruitful scholarly life has been affirmed by numerous awards, from Phi Beta Kappa during college to the Candler School of Theology "Wings of Eagles" Teaching Award, the SBL Outstanding Service in Mentoring Award, and Emory University's Emory Williams Distinguished Teaching Award, as well as numerous study grants and fellowships. She has received honorary doctoral degrees from Birmingham–Southern College (2006), the University of Copenhagen (2009), and Virginia Theological Seminary (2013).

Carol Newsom lives in Decatur, Georgia, with her spouse of forty-two years—Dr. Rex D. Matthews, who serves as Associate Professor in the Practice of Historical Theology at Candler School of Theology—and with a pair of Chesapeake Bay retrievers, Django and Suki. Besides being a consummate host and adventurous chef, Carol enjoys growing vegetables at a community garden and in her front yard and keeping tabs on the wildflowers blooming in the mountains of north Georgia.

SELECTED BIBLIOGRAPHY OF
CAROL A. NEWSOM'S WRITINGS

Books Written

Songs of the Sabbath Sacrifice: A Critical Edition. Harvard Semitic Studies 27. Atlanta: Scholars Press, 1985.

Job. New Interpreters Bible. Nashville: Abingdon, 1996.

Qumran Cave 4: VI; Poetical and Liturgical Texts, Part 1. With E. Eshel et al. Discoveries in the Judean Desert 11. Oxford: Clarendon, 1998.

Angelic Liturgy: Songs of the Sabbath Sacrifice. With J. Charlesworth. The Princeton Theological Seminary Dead Sea Scrolls Project. Louisville, Ky.: Westminster John Knox, 1999.

The Book of Job: A Contest of Moral Imaginations. New York: Oxford University Press, 2003. Paperback ed., 2009.

The Self as Symbolic Space: Constructing Identity and Community at Qumran. Boston: Brill, 2004. Paperback ed., Atlanta: Society of Biblical Literature, 2007.

1QHodayot^a with Incorporation of 1QHodayot^b and 4QHodayot^{a-f}. Hartmut Stegemann with Eileen Schuller. Translation of texts by Carol Newsom. Oxford: Clarendon, 2009.

The Hodayot (Thanksgiving Psalms): A Study Edition of 1QH^a. With Eileen M. Schuller. Atlanta: Society of Biblical Literature, 2012.

Daniel: A Commentary. Old Testament Library. Louisville, Ky.: Westminster John Knox, 2014.

Books Edited

Harper's Bible Commentary. With J. Mays (gen. ed.) et al. San Francisco: Harper & Row, 1988. Rev. ed., 2000.

The Women's Bible Commentary. With Sharon H. Ringe. Louisville, Ky.: Westminster John Knox, 1992. Translated into Dutch as *Met eigen ogen.* Meinema: Zoetermeer, 1995. Translated into Italian as *La Bibbia delle donne.* Torino: Claudiana, 1996. Translated into Japanese. Tokyo, 1998.

Women's Bible Commentary: Expanded Edition with Apocrypha. With Sharon H. Ringe. Louisville, Ky.: Westminster John Knox, 1998. Translated into Korean, 2013.

Oxford Annotated Bible. With M. Coogan (gen. ed.) et al. New York: Oxford University Press, 2001. Rev. ed., 2010.

Women's Bible Commentary: Twentieth Anniversary Edition, Revised and Updated. With Sharon H. Ringe and Jacqueline M. Lapsley. Louisville, Ky.: Westminster John Knox, 2012.

Articles, Book Chapters, and Shorter Critical Text Editions and Translations

"The Development of 1 Enoch 6–19: Cosmology and Judgment." *Catholic Biblical Quarterly* 42 (1980): 310–29.

"A Maker of Metaphors: Ezekiel's Oracles against Tyre." *Interpretation* 38 (1984): 151–64. Reprinted as pages 188–99 in *Interpreting the Prophets.* Edited by J. Mays and P. Achtemeier. Philadelphia: Fortress, 1987. Reprinted as pages 191–204 in *This Place Is Too Small for Us: The Israelite Prophets in Recent Scholarship.* Edited by R. Gordon. Winona Lake, Ind.: Eisenbrauns, 1995.

"The Masada Fragment of the Qumran Sabbath Shirot." With Yigael Yadin. *Israel Exploration Journal* 34 (1984): 77–78.

"The Past as Revelation: History in Apocalyptic Literature." *Quarterly Review* 4 (1984): 40–53.

"Merkabah Exegesis in the Qumran Sabbath Shirot." *Journal of Jewish Studies* 38 (1987): 11–30.

"Retelling the Story of the Exodus." *Quarterly Review* 7 (1987): 71–100.

"4Q370: An Admonition Based on the Flood." *Études Qumrâniennes: Mémorial Jean Carmiqnac*. Edited by F. García Martínez and E. Puech. *Revue de Qumrân* 13 (1988): 23–43.

"The Psalms of Joshua from Qumran Cave 4: A Preliminary Edition." *Journal of Jewish Studies* 39 (1988): 56–73.

"Woman in the Discourse of Patriarchal Wisdom: A Study of Proverbs 1–9." Pages 142–60 in *Gender and Difference in Ancient Israel*. Edited by P. Day. Philadelphia: Augsburg Fortress, 1989. Reprinted as pages 116–31 in *Reading Bibles, Writing Bodies: Identity and The Book*. Edited by T. Beal and D. Gunn. New York: Routledge, 1997.

"Apocalyptic and the Discourse of a Sectarian Community." *Journal of Near Eastern Studies* 49 (1990): 135–44.

" 'He Has Established for Himself Priests': Human and Angelic Priesthood in the Qumran Sabbath Shirot." Pages 101–20 in *Archaeology and History in the Dead Sea Scrolls*. Edited by L. Schiffman. Sheffield: Sheffield Academic, 1990.

"Kenneth Burke Meets the Teacher of Righteousness: Rhetorical Strategies in the Hodayot and the Serek ha-Yahad." Pages 121–31 in *Of Scribes and Scrolls: Studies on the Hebrew Bible, Intertestamental Judaism, and Christian Origins*. Strugnell Festschrift. Edited by H. Attridge, J. Collins, and T. Tobin, S.J. Lanham, Md.: University Press of America, 1990.

"The Sage in the Literature of Qumran: The Functions of the *Maskil*." Pages 373–82 in *The Sage in Ancient Israel*. Edited by J. Gammie and L. Perdue. Winona Lake, Ind.: Eisenbrauns, 1990.

" 'Sectually Explicit' Literature from Qumran." Pages 167–87 in *The Bible and Its Interpreters*. Edited by W. Propp and B. Halpern. Winona Lake, Ind.: Eisenbrauns, 1990.

"4Q374: A Discourse on the Exodus/Conquest Traditions." Pages 40–52 in *The Dead Sea Scrolls: Forty Years of Research*. Edited by D. Dimant and U. Rappaport. Leiden: Brill, 1992.

"The Case of the Blinking I: Discourse of the Self at Qumran." Pages 13–23 in *Semeia 57: Discursive Formations, Ascetic Piety and the Interpretation of Early Christian Literature*. Pt. 1. Edited by V. Wimbush. Atlanta: Society of Biblical Literature, 1992.

"Job." Pages 130–36 in *The Women's Bible Commentary*. Edited by C. Newsom and S. Ringe. Louisville, Ky.: Westminster, 1992.

"Considering Job." *Currents in Research: Biblical Studies* 1 (1993): 97–131.

"Cultural Politics in the Reading of Job." *Biblical Interpretation* 2 (1993): 119–34.

"Knowing as Doing: The Social Symbolics of Knowledge at Qumran." Pages 139–53 in *Semeia 59: Ideological Criticism of Biblical Texts*. Edited by D. Jobling and T. Pippin. Atlanta: Society of Biblical Literature, 1993.

"Response to Norman Gottwald's 'Social Class and Ideology in Isaiah 40–55: An Eagletonian Reading.'" Pages 73–78 in *Semeia 59: Ideological Criticism of Biblical Texts*. Edited by D. Jobling and T. Pippin. Atlanta: Society of Biblical Literature, 1993.

"The Moral Sense of Nature: Ethics in the Light of God's Speech to Job." *Princeton Seminary Bulletin* 15 (1994): 9–27.

"370. 4Q Admonition on the Flood." Pages 85–97 and pl. xii in *Qumran Cave 4: XIV, Parabiblical Texts, Part 2*. Edited by J. VanderKam. Discoveries in the Judean Desert 19. Oxford: Clarendon, 1995.

"374. 4Q Discourse on the Exodus/Conquest Tradition." Pages 99–110 in *Qumran Cave 4: XIV, Parabiblical Texts, Part 2*. Edited by J. VanderKam. Discoveries in the Judean Desert 19. Oxford: Clarendon, 1995.

"Job and Ecclesiastes." Pages 177–94 in *Old Testament Interpretation: Past, Present, and Future (Essays in Honor of Gene M. Tucker)*. Edited by J. Mays, K. Richards, and D. Petersen. Nashville: Abingdon, 1995.

"378–379. 4Q Apocryphon of Joshua." Pages 241–88 and pls. xvii–xx in *Qumran Cave 4: XVII, Parabiblical Texts, Part 3*. Edited by J. VanderKam. Discoveries in the Judean Desert 22. Oxford: Clarendon, 1996.

"4Q378 and 4Q379: An Apocryphon of Joshua." Pages 35–85 in *Qumranstudien*. Edited by H.-J. Fabry, A. Lange, and H. Lichtenberger. Göttingen: Vandenhoeck & Ruprecht, 1996.

"Bakhtin, the Bible, and Dialogic Truth." *Journal of Religion* 76 (1996): 290–306.

"Songs of the Sabbath Sacrifice." Pages 28–32 in *Prayer from Alexander to Constantine: A Critical Anthology*. Edited by M. Kiley et al. New York: Routledge, 1997.

"Daniel." Pages 201–6 in *Women's Bible Commentary: Expanded Edition with Apocrypha*. Edited by C. A. Newsom and S. H. Ringe. Louisville, Ky.: Westminster John Knox, 1998.

"Psalm 151." Pages 335–36 in *Women's Bible Commentary: Expanded Edition with Apocrypha*. Edited by C. A. Newsom and S. H. Ringe. Louisville, Ky.: Westminster John Knox, 1998.

"Job and His Friends: A Conflict of Moral Imaginations." *Interpretation* 53 (1999): 239–53.

"Common Ground: An Ecological Reading of Genesis 2–3." Pages 60–72 in *The Earth Story in Genesis*. Edited by N. Habel and S. Wurst. The Earth Bible 2. Sheffield: Sheffield Academic, 2000.

"Apocalyptic Subjects: The Social Construction of the Self at Qumran." *Journal for the Study of the Pseudepigrapha* 12 (2001): 3–25.

"Probing Scripture." *Christian Century*, January 3–10, 2001, 21–28.

"The Book of Job as Polyphonic Text." *Journal for the Study of the Old Testament* 97 (2002): 87–108.

"The Consolations of God: Assessing Job's Friends across a Cultural Abyss." Pages 347–58 in *Reading from Right to Left*. Edited by C. Exum and H. Williamson. Sheffield: Sheffield Academic, 2003.

"Elihu's Sapiential Hymn (Job 36:24–37:13): Genre, Rhetoric and Moral Imagination." Pages 347–58 in *Relating to the Text: Interdisciplinary and Form-Critical Insights on the Bible*. Edited by C. Mandolfo and T. Sandoval. London: T&T Clark, 2003.

"Genesis 2–3 and 1 Enoch 6–16: Two Myths of Origin and Their Ethical Implications." Pages 7–23 in *Shaking Heaven and Earth*. Edited by C. R. Yoder, K. M. O'Connor, E. E. Johnson, and S. P. Saunders. Louisville, Ky.: Westminster John Knox, 2005.

"Spying Out the Land: A Report from Genology." Pages 437–50 in *Seeking Out the Wisdom of the Ancients: Essays Offered to Michael V. Fox on the Occasion of His Sixty-Fifth Birthday*. Edited by R. Troxel, K. Friebel, and D. Magery. Winona Lake, Ind.: Eisenbrauns, 2005. Reprinted as pages 19–30 in *Bakhtin and Genre Theory in Biblical Studies*. Edited by R. Boer. Semeia Studies 63. Atlanta: Society of Biblical Literature, 2008.

"Rhyme and Reason: The Historical Résumé in Israelite and Early Jewish Thought." Pages 215–33 in *Congress Volume Leiden 2004*. Edited by A. Lemaire. Supplements to Vetus Testamentum 109. Leiden: Brill, 2006.

"Dramaturgy and the Book of Job." Pages 375–93 in *Das Buch Hiob und seine Interpretationen*. Edited by T. Krüger et al. Zürich: Theologischer Verlag, 2007.

"Re-considering Job." *Currents in Biblical Research* 5 (2007): 155–82.

"Response to *How Are the Mighty Fallen? A Dialogical Study of King Saul in 1 Samuel*." *Horizons in Biblical Theology* 29 (2007): 29–39.

"Constructing 'We, You, and the Others' through Non-polemical Discourse." Pages 13–21 in *Defining Identity: We, You, and the Others in the*

Dead Sea Scrolls. Edited by F. García Martínez and M. Popović. STDJ 70. Leiden: Brill, 2008.

"Daniel." Pages 257–60 in *Theological Bible Commentary*. Edited by G. R. O'Day and D. L. Petersen. Nashville: Abington, 2009.

"Reflections on Ideological Criticism and Postcritical Perspectives." Pages 541–60 in *Method Matters: Essays on the Interpretation of the Hebrew Bible in Honor of David L. Petersen*. Edited by J. M. LeMon and K. H. Richards. Atlanta: Society of Biblical Literature, 2009.

"Pairing Research Questions and Theories of Genre: A Case Study of the Hodayot." *Dead Sea Discoveries* 17 (2010): 270–88.

"Rhetorical Criticism and the Dead Sea Scrolls." Pages 198–214 in *Rediscovering the Dead Sea Scrolls: An Assessment of Old and New Approaches and Methods*. Edited by M. Grossman. Grand Rapids: Eerdmans, 2010.

"Rhetorical Criticism and the Reading of the Qumran Scrolls." Pages 683–708 in *Oxford Handbook of the Dead Sea Scrolls*. Edited by J. Collins and T. Lim. New York: Oxford University Press, 2010.

"Why Nabonidus: Excavating Traditions from Qumran, the Hebrew Bible, and Neo-Babylonian Sources." Pages 57–79 in *The Dead Sea Scrolls: Transmission of Traditions and Production of Texts*. Edited by S. Metso, H. Najman, and E. Schuller. STDJ 92. Leiden: Brill, 2010.

"Daniel." Pages 159–72 in *The Oxford Encyclopedia of the Books of the Bible*. Vol. 1. Edited by M. D. Coogan et al. New York: Oxford University Press, 2011.

"Flesh, Spirit, and the Indigenous Psychology of the *Hodayot*." Pages 339–54 in *Prayer and Poetry in the Dead Sea Scrolls and Related Literature*. Edited by J. Penner, K. M. Penner, and C. Wassen. STDJ 98. Leiden: Brill, 2011.

"God's Other: The Intractable Problem of the Gentile King in Judean and Early Jewish Literature." Pages 31–48 in *The "Other" in Second Temple Judaism: Essays in Honor of John J. Collins*. Edited by D. C. Harlow, M. Goff, K. M. Hogan, and J. S. Kaminsky. Grand Rapids: Eerdmans, 2011.

"Models of the Moral Self: Hebrew Bible and Second Temple Judaism." *Journal of Biblical Literature* 131 (2012): 5–25.

"Positive Psychology and Ancient Israelite Wisdom." Pages 117–35 in *The Bible and the Pursuit of Happiness*. Edited by B. Strawn. New York: Oxford University Press, 2012.

"Religious Experience in the Dead Sea Scrolls: Two Case Studies." Pages 205–22 in *Experientia II*. Edited by R. Werline and C. Shantz. SBL Symposium Series. Atlanta: Society of Biblical Literature, 2012.

"The Book of Job and Terrence Malick's *Tree of Life*." Pages 228–42 in *A Wild Ox Knows: Biblical Essays in Honor of Norman C. Habel*. Edited by A. Cadwallader. Sheffield: Sheffield Phoenix, 2013.

"Now You See Him, Now You Don't: Nabonidus in Jewish Memory." Pages 270–81 in *Remembering Biblical Figures in the Late Persian and Early Hellenistic Periods*. Edited by E. Ben Zvi and D. Edelman. New York: Oxford University Press, 2013.

"Evil in the Hebrew Bible: The Case of the Wisdom Literature." Forthcoming in *Evil*. Edited by A. Chignell. Oxford Philosophical Concepts Series. New York: Oxford University Press, 2014.

"The Reuse of Ugaritic Mythology in Daniel 7: An Optical Illusion?" Pages 85–100 in *Opportunity for No Little Instruction: Studies in Honor of Richard J. Clifford, S.J. and Daniel J. Harrington, S.J.* Edited by C. Frechette, C. Matthews, and T. Stegeman. New York: Paulist, 2014.

"The Rhetoric of Jewish Apocalyptic Literature." Pages 218–34 in *The Oxford Handbook of Apocalyptic Literature*. Edited by J. J. Collins. New York: Oxford University Press, 2014.

"Selective Recall and Ghost Memories: Two Aspects of Cultural Memory in the Hebrew Bible." Pages 41–56 in *Memory and Identity in Ancient Judaism and Early Christianity: A Conversation with Barry Schwartz*. Edited by Thomas Thatcher. Semeia Studies. Atlanta: Society of Biblical Literature, 2014.

SELECTED ENCYCLOPEDIA AND REFERENCE ARTICLES

Harper's Bible Dictionary. Edited by P. Achtemeier. New York: Harper & Row, 1985. "Habakkuk," 364; "Scroll," 915.

Dictionary of Pastoral Care. Edited by R. Hunter. Nashville: Abingdon, 1990. "Wisdom Tradition, Biblical," 1326.

Anchor Bible Dictionary. Edited by N. Freedman. New York: Doubleday, 1992. "Angels," 1:248–53; "Gabriel (Angel)," 2:863; "Joshua, Psalms of," 3:1015; "Raguel (Angel)," 5:610; "Songs of the Sabbath Sacrifice," 6:155–56; "Uriel (Angel)," 6:769.

The Oxford Study Bible. Edited by M. Jack Suggs, K. D. Sakenfeld, and J. R. Mueller. New York: Oxford University Press, 1992. "The Dead Sea Scrolls and Other Jewish Literature," 101–11.

The HarperCollins Study Bible. Edited by W. Meeks et al. San Francisco: HarperCollins, 1993. "Baruch, Introduction and Annotations," 1617–26.

Dictionary of Biblical Interpretation. Edited by John H. Hayes. Nashville: Abingdon, 1999. With S. E. Schreiner, "Job, Book of," 587–99.

Encyclopedia of the Dead Sea Scrolls. Edited by J. VanderKam et al. New York: Oxford University Press, 2000. "Job, Book of," 412–13; "Mysticism," 591–94; "Songs of the Sabbath Sacrifice," 887–89; "Throne," 946–47.

Dictionary of New Testament Background. Edited by C. A. Evans and S. E. Porter. Downers Grove, Ill.: InterVarsity Press, 2002. "4Q374–377 Apocryphon of Moses"; "4Q378–379 Apocryphon of Joshua"; "4Q400–407 Songs of the Sabbath Sacrifice."

The Eerdmans Dictionary of Early Judaism. Edited by J. J. Collins and D. C. Harlow. Grand Rapids: Eerdmans, 2010. "Job, Book of"; "Songs of the Sabbath Sacrifice"; "Theodicy."

Oxford Bibliographies Online. 2011. "The Book of Daniel"; "The Book of Job"; "Dead Sea Scrolls."

The Oxford Encyclopedia of the Books of the Bible. 2 vols. Edited by M. D. Coogan et al. Oxford: Oxford University Press, 2011. "Daniel," 1:159–72.

NOTES

Abbreviations in the text and notes follow the standard abbreviations of the Society of Biblical Literature.

CHAPTER 1: INTRODUCTION

1   Kathy Davis, "Embodying Theory: Beyond Modernist and Postmodernist Readings of the Body," in *Embodied Practices: Feminist Perspectives on the Body* (ed. Kathy Davis; London: Sage, 1997), 5.

2   See especially, in this volume, Katie Heffelfinger's discussion of these themes as they arise in Psalms and Isaiah. Many thanks to her for contributing to this discussion.

3   Phyllis Trible, "Five Loaves and Two Fishes: Feminist Hermeneutics and Biblical Theology," *Theological Studies* 50 (1989): 289.

4   Leo Perdue, *Reconstructing Old Testament Theology: After the Collapse of History* (Minneapolis: Fortress, 2005), 160–61; James Mead, *Biblical Theology: Issues, Methods, and Themes* (Louisville, Ky.: Presbyterian Publishing, 2007), 108–12.

5   Among some recent explicitly feminist and theological efforts is Juliana Claassens, *Mourner, Mother, and Midwife: Reimagining God's Delivering Presence in the Old Testament* (Louisville, Ky.: Westminster John Knox, 2012).

6   Carol A. Newsom, "Bakhtin, the Bible, and Dialogic Truth," *Journal of Religion* 76 (1996): 290–306.

7   These include not only Carol A. Newsom's commentary on Job (in *The New Interpreter's Bible* [ed. Leander Keck et al., vol. 4; Nashville: Abingdon, 1996], 317–638) but also, and more explicitly, *The Book of Job: A Contest of Moral Imaginations* (New York: Oxford

University Press, 2003) and several articles developing the themes of her book: "The Book of Job as Polyphonic Text," *Journal for the Study of the Old Testament* 97 (2002): 87–108; "Cultural Politics in the Reading of Job," *Biblical Interpretation* 2 (1993): 119–34; "Considering Job," *Currents in Research: Biblical Studies* 1 (1993): 97–131; "The Moral Sense of Nature: Ethics in the Light of God's Speech to Job," *Princeton Seminary Bulletin* 15 (1994): 9–27; "Job and His Friends: A Conflict of Moral Imaginations," *Interpretation* 53 (1999): 239–53; and "Re-considering Job," *Currents in Biblical Research* 5 (2007): 155–82.

8   Mikhail Bakhtin, "Discourse in the Novel," in *The Dialogic Imagination* (ed. M. Holquist; trans. C. Emerson and M. Holquist; Austin: University of Texas Press, 1981), 259–422; *Problems of Dostoevsky's Poetics* (ed. and trans. C. Emerson; Minneapolis: University of Minnesota Press, 1984).

9   Newsom, "Bakhtin, the Bible, and Dialogic Truth," 293–94.

10 Newsom, "Bakhtin, the Bible, and Dialogic Truth," 305.

11 Newsom, "Bakhtin, the Bible, and Dialogic Truth," 305.

12 Walter Brueggemann, *Old Testament Theology: An Introduction* (Nashville: Abingdon, 2010), 5.

CHAPTER 2: TULL

1   Marc Bekoff, "Considering Animals—Not 'Higher' Primates: Consciousness and Self in Animals; Some Reflections," *Zygon* 38 (2003): 229–45. See also Nicola Hoggard Creegan, "Being an Animal and Being Made in the Image of God," *Colloquium* 39 (2007): 185–203.

2   As Hoggard Creegan says, "Theologians must pay attention to our animal inheritance, not as a fleeting fact to be reconciled in a moment, but as a way of looking at the world which requires long pondering in conversation with the biblical text" ("Being an Animal," 203).

3   W. Sibley Towner, "Clones of God: Genesis 1:26-28 and the Image of God in the Hebrew Bible," *Interpretation* 59 (2005): 341–56; Theodore Hiebert, *The Yahwist's Landscape: Nature and Religion in Early Israel* (New York: Oxford University Press, 1996), 156.

4   See Andreas Schüle, "Made in the 'Image of God': The Concept of Divine Images in Gen 1–3," *Zeitschrift für die alttestamentliche Wissenschaft* 117 (2005): 1–20; Annette Schellenberg, "Humankind as the 'Image of God': On the Priestly Predication (Gen 1:26-27; 5:1; 9:6) and Its Relationship to the Ancient Near Eastern Understanding of Images," *Theologische Zeitschrift* 65 (2009): 97–115.

5   Elaine Pagels (*Adam, Eve, and the Serpent* [New York: Random House, 1989], esp. 39, 55–56, 100–101), for example, describes how the early church's understanding of *imago Dei* affirmed the worth, dignity, and nobility of the whole human race equally, constituting good news for enslaved people in the Roman Empire and comforting those persecuted by the Roman government.

6   Phyllis Trible (*God and the Rhetoric of Sexuality* [Overtures to Biblical Theology; Philadelphia: Fortress, 1978], 20) says: "As the most basic way to know humankind in its fullness, 'male and female' is the vehicle of a metaphor whose tenor is 'the image of God.'... 'Male and female' is the finger pointing to the 'image of God.'"

7 Javier R. Alanis, "The *Imago Dei* as Embodied in Nepantla: A Latino Perspective," *Currents in Theology and Mission* 32.6 (2005): 445–55; Vítor Westhelle, "Creation Motifs in the Search for a Vital Space: A Latin American Perspective," in *Lift Every Voice: Constructing Christian Theologies from the Underside* (ed. Susan Brooks Thistle-thwaite and Mary Potter Engel; San Francisco: Harper, 1990), 146–58 (158); and Ada Maria Isasi-Diaz, *En La Lucha / In the Struggle: Elaborating a Mujerista Theology* (Minneapolis: Fortress, 1993).

8 Lynn Townsend White Jr., "The Historical Roots of Our Ecological Crisis," 4, http://www.uvm.edu/~gflomenh/ENV-NGO-PA395/articles/Lynn-White.pdf; originally published in *Science* 155 (1967): 1203–7.

9 White, "Historical Roots," 4.

10 See discussion of these shifting viewpoints in Hoggard Creegan, "Being an Animal," 186–92. For examples of recent attempts to reassert human uniqueness, see especially J. Wentzel van Huyssteen, *Alone in the World? Human Uniqueness in Science and Theology* (Grand Rapids: Eerdmans, 2006); and Ian Tattersall, *Becoming Human: Evolution and Human Uniqueness* (Orlando: Harcourt, 1998).

11 See esp. Langdon Gilkey, "Nature as the Image of God: Signs of the Sacred," *Theology Today* 51 (1994): 127–41. Leslie A. Muray ("Human Uniqueness vs. Human Distinctiveness: The *Imago Dei* in the Kinship of All Creatures," *American Journal of Theology & Philosophy* 28 [2007]: 299–310) similarly recommends extending the *imago Dei* to nonhumans.

12 Sallie McFague, "An Earthly Theological Agenda," in *Ecofeminism and the Sacred* (ed. Carol J. Adams; New York: Continuum, 1993), 84–98 (92).

13 Anne M. Clifford, "Feminist Perspectives on Science: Implications for an Ecological Theology of Creation," *Journal of Feminist Studies in Religion* 8 (1992): 65–90 (84). Rosemary Radford Ruether says, "We need to discover our actual reality as latecomers to the planet. . . . Nature does not need us to rule over it, but runs itself very well, even better, without humans" ("Symbolic and Social Connections of the Oppression of Women and the Domination of Nature," in *Ecofeminism and the Sacred* [ed. Carol J. Adams; New York: Continuum, 1993], 13–23).

14 Although White laid blame on the Bible itself, Clifford ("Feminist Perspectives," 71–73), citing Carol Merchant (*The Death of Nature: Women and the Scientific Revolution* [New York: Harper & Row, 1980], 164–90), traces Bacon's use of Gen 2–3 to promote nature's subjugation. See also Catarina J. M. Halkes (*New Creation: Christian Feminism and the Renewal of the Earth* [Louisville, Ky.: Westminster John Knox, 1992]), who more extensively traces the connection of dominion with the *imago Dei* back to early Christianity.

15 Hoggard Creegan, "Being an Animal," 197.

16 Peter Enns, *The Evolution of Adam: What the Bible Does and Doesn't Say about Human Origins* (Grand Rapids: Brazos, 2012), xv.

17 Enns, *Evolution of Adam*, xv; see also p. 139.

18 Brigitte Kahl calls Gen 1:26-28's history of interpretation "an instructive lesson in one-sided and selective Bible-reading" ("Human Culture and the Integrity of Creation: Biblical Reflections on Genesis 1–11," *Ecumenical Review* 39 [1987]: 128–37 [130]).

19 Acceptance of evolution's full implications seems to await a more favorable view of other life. As David Clough ("All God's Creatures: Reading Genesis on Human and Non-human Animals," in *Reading Genesis after Darwin* [ed. Stephen Barton and David Wilkinson; Oxford: Oxford University Press, 2009]) puts it, readers of Gen 1 are post-Copernican in cosmology but still resolutely pre-Darwinian in their views of themselves as creatures.

20 William P. Brown, *The Seven Pillars of Creation: The Bible, Science, and the Ecology of Wonder* (New York: Oxford University Press, 2010), 63.

21 The NRSV and NIV follow the ancient Syriac translation and the opinions of a large number of scholars in restoring the three-letter word meaning "wild animals (of the earth)" to v. 26 (as in v. 25), rather than reading "all (the earth)," which abruptly interrupts the list of species.

22 Hiebert, *Yahwist's Landscape*, 157; Ellen Davis, *Scripture, Culture, and Agriculture: An Agrarian Reading of the Bible* (Cambridge: Cambridge University Press, 2009), 29.

23 Hiebert, *Yahwist's Landscape*, 66.

24 The other instances of this verb in relation to agriculture (Gen 4:2, 12; Deut 15:19; 28:39; 2 Sam 9:10; Zech 13:5; Isa 19:9; 30:24) do nothing to suggest a relationship of rule or even ownership in relation to the ground—the work described is humble, albeit necessary.

25 Hiebert, *Yahwist's Landscape*, 63.

26 Carol A. Newsom ("Genesis 2–3 and 1 Enoch 6–16: Two Myths of Origin and Their Ethical Implications," in *Shaking Heaven and Earth* [ed. C. R. Yoder et al.; Louisville, Ky.: Westminster John Knox, 2005], 11) maintains, in fact, that Gen 2 ends without constructing a clear boundary between the incipient humans and the other animals. That boundary emerges only later, when the humans, unlike the other animals, view themselves as naked and in need of covering.

27 Hiebert, *Yahwist's Landscape*, 60.

28 Bekoff, "Considering Animals," 239, emphasis in original.

29 Joshua M. Moritz ("Human Uniqueness, the Other Hominids, and 'Anthropocentrism of the Gaps' in the Religion and Science Dialogue," *Zygon* 49 [2012]: 65–96 [92]) suggests, in view of the significant tension between biblical interpretation and theological doctrines, that "the doctrine of the *imago Dei* has been irretrievably lost and that theologians might want to cut their losses and give up the search."

30 Ivone Gebara, *Longing for Running Water: Ecofeminism and Liberation; Biblical Reflections on Ministry* (Minneapolis: Augsburg Fortress, 1999), 122.

31 Gebara, *Longing for Running Water*, 54.

32 Thomas Berry, *The Dream of the Earth* (San Francisco: Sierra Club, 1988), 46.

33 Edward O. Wilson, *The Creation: An Appeal to Save Life on Earth* (New York: W. W. Norton, 2006), 91.

34 Wilson, *Creation*, 91.

35 John Cobb, "Protestant Theology and Deep Ecology," in *Deep Ecology and World Religions* (ed. David Landis Barhill and Roger S. Gottlieb; Albany: State University of New York Press, 2001), 213–28 (220).

36 Sallie McFague, "The World as God's Body," *Christian Century*, July 20–27, 1998, 671–73, http://www.religion-online.org/showarticle.asp?title=56. See also her *The Body of God: An Ecological Theology* (Minneapolis: Fortress, 1993).

37 McFague, "World as God's Body."

38 Martin Buber, *I and Thou* (trans. Ronald Gregor Smith; London: Continuum, 2004), 14–15; original publication: *Ich und Du* (Berlin: Shocken, 1923).

39 Buber, *I and Thou*, 75, emphasis in original.

40 Vicki Hearne, *Animal Happiness* (San Francisco: HarperCollins, 1994), 173.

41 Stephen Webb, *On God and Dogs: A Christian Theology of Compassion for Animals* (New York: Oxford University Press, 1998), 4.

42 Webb, *On God and Dogs*, 4.

43 Webb, *On God and Dogs*, 103–4.

44 Peter Smith, "Religious Orders Sisters of Loretto and Abbey of Gethsemani Deny Access to Land for Gas Pipeline," *Courier Journal*, August 17, 2013, http://www.courier-journal.com/article/20130801/NEWS01/308020044/ Religious-orders-Sisters-Loretto-Abbey-Gethsemani-deny-access-land-gas-pipeline.

45 ARC, "Touching Hearts and Minds: Faith Environmental Action," ARC News and Resources, http://www.arcworld.org/news.asp?pageID=506.

CHAPTER 3: LEE

1 Edward F. Campbell, *Ruth: A New Translation with Introduction, Notes and Commentary* (New York: Doubleday, 1975), 28–29.

2 On Ruth as an Abrahamic figure, see Phyllis Trible's classic exposition, "A Human Comedy: The Book of Ruth," in *God and the Rhetoric of Sexuality* (Philadelphia: Fortress, 1978), 31–59.

3 Campbell, *Ruth*, 83. See also Jacqueline E. Lapsley, *Whispering the Word: Hearing Women's Stories in the Old Testament* (Louisville, Ky.: Westminster John Knox, 2005), 89–108.

4 Biblical laws extending special protection to widows and orphans reflect their extreme vulnerability (see, e.g., Exod 22:21-23; Deut 27:19; cf. Isa 1:17).

5 Ruth contains a number of subtle allusions to the ancestral narratives: a famine-driven migration into a foreign land that threatens the safety of Israel's matriarchs ("there was a famine in the land" only at Gen 12:10; 26:1; and Ruth 1:1); Naomi's use of the divine epithet "Shaddai" in Ruth 1:20-21 (traditionally rendered as "Almighty"), which is associated with the promise of fecundity in Gen 28:3; 35:11; 49:25; the intertextual echoes of Tamar's story (Gen 38) in Ruth 3. The references, however, become explicit in Ruth 4:11-12, which I will discuss more fully below.

6 Of course, infertility is not an exclusively female issue, but biblical patriarchy typically saw it in that light.

7 Jacob Neusner, *Ruth Rabbah: An Analytical Translation* (Atlanta: Scholars Press, 1989), 189. *Ruth Rabbah* is a compilation of Jewish homiletic expositions of Ruth, dating to the late fifth and early sixth centuries.

8 Patrick D. Miller writes, "Theologians have long maintained that theology is at least in part an outgrowth of prayer . . . that it is not simply a matter of believing and then praying to God in the light of what one believes. That very belief is shaped by the practice of prayer" (*They Cried to the Lord: The Form and Theology of Biblical Prayer* [Minneapolis: Fortress, 1994], 1). See also Patricia K. Tull (*Esther and Ruth* [Interpretation Bible Studies; Louisville, Ky.: Westminster John Knox, 2003], 56–57), who notes the

importance of attending to Naomi's and Ruth's discourse about God, in addition to that of the narrator. Tull observes three different theological perspectives at play in the first chapter of Ruth.

9   The child's value is also directly connected to his mother, whom the women declare to be "more . . . than seven sons!" (4:15b).

10   The rabbis too saw something of this dynamic. Commenting on the fortuitous appearance of the closer kinsman-redeemer in 4:1, they imagine the following divine logic: "Boaz did his part, and Ruth did her part, Naomi did her part; so said the Holy One . . . 'I too shall do mine'" (*Ruth Rabbah* to Ruth 4:1, in Neusner, *Ruth Rabbah*, 173).

11   I offer this somewhat awkward translation to make explicit the use of the Hebrew verb "to give." The verb has various nuances in the Hebrew Bible, including "to make/ constitute" (hence the more common rendering "May the LORD make the woman . . . like Rachel and Leah").

12   Mieke Bal, *Lethal Love: Feminist Literary Readings of Biblical Love Stories* (Bloomington: Indiana University Press, 1987), 84–87. Adele Berlin likewise describes the function of the text as a "literary intensifier" (*Poetics and Interpretation of Biblical Narrative* [Winona Lake, Ind.: Eisenbrauns, 1994], 173).

13   Adele Berlin argues that continuity of people and land is the Hebrew Bible's overarching theme, which reaches a critical moment here in Ruth ("Ruth and the Continuity of Israel," in *Reading Ruth: Contemporary Women Reclaim a Sacred Story* [ed. Judith A. Kates and Gail Twersky Reimer; New York: Ballantine, 1994], 255–60).

14   Since an imperative following a jussive or cohortative usually expresses purpose or result, the two imperatives are best understood as the consequence of the opening clause.

15   C. J. Labushchagne was the first to make this argument, basing his case on Job 21:7-8; Joel 2:22; Prov 31:3 ("The Crux in Ruth 4:11," *ZAW* 79 [1967]: 36–67). But the meaning of *hayil* in those texts is disputed.

16   Ironically, the narrative that has belabored the importance of preserving "the dead man's name on his inheritance" (4:5, 10) actually memorializes Boaz's name and that of his progeny.

17   There are additional intertextual echoes between these texts and Ruth. The house that YHWH establishes for David is characterized by secure rootedness, signified by the notion of "rest" (cf. Ruth 1:9; 3:1). References to the "great name" (2 Sam 7:9; Ruth 4:11, 14) and to Ephrathah (1 Sam 17:12; Ruth 4:11; cf. 1:2) also reinforce the Davidic connection.

18   Tamar resorts to trickery and prostitution (Gen 38). But the scandalous elements of these stories may function as a critique of the patriarchal culture that places women in such desperate straits.

19   Francine Klagsbrun, "Ruth and Naomi, Rachel and Leah: Sisters under the Skin," in *Reading Ruth* (ed. Kates and Reimer), 264.

20   Ilana Pardes, *Countertraditions in the Bible: A Feminist Approach* (Cambridge, Mass.: Harvard University Press, 1992), 98–117.

21   The expression "that I may have children through her" (NRSV), in Hebrew, literally reads, "that I may be built up through her."

22 Much more common is the notion of the "father's house." The strong impulse to define reality in patriarchal terms can be seen in some ancient manuscripts that revert to "father's house" even in Ruth 1:8.

23 Carol Meyers, "Returning Home: Ruth 1:8 and the Gendering of the Book of Ruth," in *Feminist Companion to Ruth* (ed. Athalya Brenner; Sheffield: JSOT Press, 1993), 85–115.

24 Various scholars have noted that the construction of the tabernacle in Exodus and the Solomonic temple in 1 Kings are modeled after God's "building" of creation. See Raymond C. Van Leeuwen, "Building God's House: An Exploration in Wisdom," in *The Way of Wisdom: Essays in Honor of Bruce K. Waltke* (ed. J. I. Packer and Sven K. Soderlund; Grand Rapids: Zondervan, 2000), 204–11.

25 In the Hebrew text, the words for "wisdom" and "woman" are plural, which may be rendered "the wisest of women" (JPS) or "the manifold wisdom of women" (author's trans.; cf. Prov 1:20; 24:7; Sir 4:11; Ps 49:3). This text closely echoes Prov 9:1, where Woman Wisdom builds her house. The significance of her seven-pillared house is deliberately ambiguous, making it amenable to various interpretations—cosmological, cultic, and domestic. Wisdom's domicile thus encompasses multiple spheres of meaning and represents the center of a good and well-ordered society. On the significance of Wisdom personified as a woman, see Claudia Camp, *Wisdom and the Feminine in the Book of Proverbs* (Sheffield: Almond Press and JSOT Press, 1985).

26 For an extended analysis of this figure, see Christine Yoder, *Wisdom as a Woman of Substance: A Socioeconomic Reading of Proverbs 1–9 and 31:10-31* (Beihefte zur Zeitschrift für die alttestamentliche Wissenschaft 304; Berlin: De Gruyter, 2001).

27 See Eunny Lee, "Ruth the Moabite: Identity, Kinship, and Otherness," in *Engaging the Bible in a Gendered World: An Introduction to Feminist Biblical Interpretation in Honor of Katharine Doob Sakenfeld* (ed. Linda Day and Carolyn Pressler; Louisville, Ky.: Westminster John Knox, 2006), 89–101.

28 *Malbim on the Book of Ruth: The Commentary of Rabbi Meir Leibush Malbim* (trans. Rabbi Shmuel Kurtz; Jerusalem: Feldheim, 1999), 133.

29 For a comparison of Ruth and Tamar, see Ellen van Wolde, "Texts in Dialogue with Texts: Intertextuality in the Ruth and Tamar Narratives," *Biblical Interpretation* 5 (1997): 1–28.

30 For a lengthier discussion of this material, see Judith A. Kates, "Transfigured Night: Midrashic Readings of the Book of Ruth," in *Scrolls of Love: Ruth and the Song of Songs* (ed. Peter S. Hawkins and Lesleigh Cushing Stahlberg; New York: Fordham University Press, 2006), 57.

31 Julia Kristeva, *Strangers to Ourselves* (trans. L. S. Roudiez; New York: Columbia University Press, 1991 [1988]), 75–76, emphasis in original.

32 Neusner, *Ruth Rabbah*, 109.

33 A. LaCocque, "Subverting the Biblical World: Sociology and Politics in the Book of Ruth," in *Scrolls of Love* (ed. Hawkins and Stahlberg), 25, emphasis in original.

34 For a postcolonial critique of the notion of home in the book of Ruth, see also Kwok Pui-lan, *Postcolonial Imagination and Feminist Theology* (Louisville, Ky.: Westminster John Knox, 2005), esp. 100–121.

35 "Open houses" reflect the expansiveness of God's own house, which also invites the participation of foreign builders (1 Kgs 5:6-11; 7:13; cf. Isa 44:28; 2 Chr 36:23; Ezra 1:2-4) and grants them vital access to its sacred precincts (1 Kgs 8:41-43).

36 See Kathryn Turner, *God and Creation in Christian Theology: Tyranny or Empowerment?* (Oxford: Basil Blackwell, 1988).

37 Walter Brueggemann gives a sociocultural account for these trends in biblical scholarship in "The Loss and Recovery of Creation in Old Testament Theology," *Theology Today* 53 (1996): 177–90. He rightly notes that while creation theology "cannot be subsumed under or equated with feminist consciousness, it also cannot be separated from it" (188).

38 Phyllis Trible makes creation the starting point of her proposal concerning the possible contours and content of a feminist biblical theology ("Treasures Old and New: Biblical Theology and the Challenge of Feminism," in *The Open Text: New Directions for Biblical Studies?* [ed. Francis Watson; London: SCM Press, 1993], 32–56).

39 Terence Fretheim speaks of originating creation, continuing creation, and completing creation not only in the physical universe but also in the social, cultural, and national orders of life. See *God and World in the Old Testament: A Relational Theology of Creation* (Nashville: Abingdon, 2005), esp. 1–28, 91–97.

40 Fretheim likewise characterizes the God of the Old Testament as a "power-sharing God," entering into mutual relationships with creatures, so that "God is not the only one who has something important to do and the power with which to do it" (*God and World*, 21).

CHAPTER 4: MANDOLFO

1 My use of the masculine singular pronoun in reference to the divine is to be understood not in any ontological sense but rather as a reflection of the biblical text, in which the divine is widely understood as male.

2 Melissa Raphael, *The Female Face of God in Auschwitz: A Jewish Feminist Theology of the Holocaust* (New York: Routledge, 2003), 35–37.

3 Raphael, *Female Face*, 29–34

4 Raphael, *Female Face*, 28.

5 "Levinas's first magnum opus," *Totality and Infinity* (1961), influenced in part by the dialogical philosophies of Franz Rosenzweig and Martin Buber, sought to accomplish this departure through an analysis of the "'face-to-face' relation with the Other" (Emmanuel Levinas webpage, http://www.levinas.sdsu.edu/, accessed May 2013).

6 For Melissa Raphael, "there is no divine presence without human presence—the *hinneni* or 'here I am'" ("The Female Face of God in Auschwitz," in *Wrestling with God: Jewish Theological Responses during and after the Holocaust*, ed. S. Katz, S. Biderman, and G. Greenberg; Oxford: Oxford University Press, 2007, 648–62 [658]).

7 Raphael, "Female Face of God," in *Wrestling with God* (ed. Katz, Biderman, and Greenberg), 653.

8 Regina Schwartz, *The Curse of Cain: The Violent Legacy of Monotheism* (Chicago: University of Chicago Press, 1998).

9 Raphael, "Female Face of God," in *Wrestling with God* (ed. Katz, Biderman, and Greenberg), 661, emphasis in original.

10 Even texts such as Isaiah 40–55 (Second Isaiah) that many valorize as redemptive are only such insofar as they are following on the heels of and compensating for the vicious assault suffered by Israel at the hands of God earlier in Isaiah (and many of the other eighth-century through sixth-century prophets). See Carleen Mandolfo, *Daughter Zion Talks Back to the Prophets* (Atlanta: Society of Biblical Literature, 2007), ch. 5.

11 This data is drawn from Samuel Balentine's painstaking analysis of this phrase, in *The Hidden God: The Hiding of the Face of God in the Old Testament* (Oxford: Oxford University Press, 1983), 45.

12 Emmanuel Levinas, "Useless Suffering," in *Wrestling with God* (ed. Katz, Biderman, and Greenberg), 450–54 (453, emphasis added).

13 Robert D. Biggs et al., eds., *The Assyrian Dictionary of the Oriental Institute of the University of Chicago* (Chicago: Oriental Institute, 2005), 122.

14 "Akk. [*sedu*] has a double meaning; it is primarily used to indicate a protective spirit, but it is also used for a malevolent demon, particularly in the [plural]" (L. Koehler and W. Baumgartner, *Hebrew and Aramaic Lexicon of the Old Testament* [Leiden: Brill Academic, 2002]).

15 Judith Butler, *Precarious Life: The Powers of Mourning and Violence* (New York: Verso Books, 2004), 145, emphasis added.

16 Isa 8:17; 50:6; 53:3; 54:8; 59:2; 64:7.

17 Isa 8:17; 54:8; 59:2; 64:7.

18 It should be noted that Deuteronomy probably in fact postdates the prophetic texts under consideration.

19 In the Psalms, only the "wicked" think that the hiding of God's face is a good thing: "They [i.e., the wicked] think in their heart, 'God has forgotten, he has hidden his face, he will never see'" (Ps 10:11).

20 The last clause of this verse is difficult to translate, but my translation captures the essence of the Hebrew.

21 Note the contrast of this verse with the more traditional wisdom understanding of God's watchfulness in Prov 15:3: "The eyes of the LORD are in every place, keeping watch on the evil and the good." Here, divine watching is necessary for the just maintenance of human concerns.

22 Except, notoriously, Richard Rubenstein, who declared the death of the God of the covenant, in *After Auschwitz: Radical Theology and Contemporary Judaism* (Indianapolis: Bobbs-Merrill, 1966).

23 Rubenstein, *After Auschwitz.*

CHAPTER 5: HEFFELFINGER

1 Glenn Morrison, "'God Writes Straight with Crooked Lines': Eros, Agape and the Witness of Glory. An Encounter between the Philosophy of Emmanuel Lévinas and Feminist Liberation Theology," *Colloquium* 33, no. 1 (2001): 23.

2 Gerald G. O'Collins, "Salvation," in *Anchor Bible Dictionary* (6 vols.; ed. David Noel Freedman; London: Doubleday, 1992), 5:908; J. Richard Middleton and Michael J. Gorman, "Salvation," in *New Interpreter's Dictionary of the Bible* (5 vols.; ed. Katharine Doob Sakenfeld; Nashville: Abingdon, 2009), 5:52.

3 See, e.g., Middleton and Gorman, "Salvation," in *New Interpreter's Dictionary* (ed. Sakenfeld), 5:48, 53; and the discussion of cosmic features in Isa 51–52 below.

4 Unless otherwise noted, translations throughout the essay are my own.

5 Rebecca S. Chopp, *Saving Work: Feminist Practices of Theological Education* (Louisville, Ky.: Westminster John Knox, 1995), 55.

6 See, e.g., the description of "post-biblical feminists" offered by Elisabeth Schüssler Fiorenza, *Sharing Her Word: Feminist Biblical Interpretation in Context* (Edinburgh: T&T Clark, 1998), 44–45.

7 See Kathleen M. O'Connor, "The Feminist Movement Meets the Old Testament: One Woman's Perspective," in *Engaging the Bible in a Gendered World: An Introduction to Feminist Biblical Interpretation in Honor of Katharine Doob Sakenfeld* (ed. Linda Day and Carolyn Pressler; London: Westminster John Knox, 2006), 23.

8 Elsa Tamez, "Women's Rereading of the Bible," in *Voices from the Margin: Interpreting the Bible in the Third World* (ed. R. S. Sugirtharajah; London: SPCK, 1995), 52.

9 Chopp, *Saving Work*, 35; Valerie Saiving, "The Human Situation: A Feminine View," in *Womanspirit Rising: A Feminist Reader in Religion* (ed. Carol P. Christ and Judith Plaskow; San Francisco: Harper & Row, 1979), 25–42; Linda Hogan, *From Women's Experience to Feminist Theology* (Sheffield: Sheffield Academic, 1995), 176.

10 Chopp, *Saving Work*, 35.

11 Gerardine Meaney, *Gender, Ireland, and Cultural Change: Race, Sex, and Nation* (London: Routledge, 2010), xvii.

12 Kathy Davis, "Embodying Theory: Beyond Modernist and Postmodernist Readings of the Body," in *Embodied Practices: Feminist Perspectives on the Body* (ed. Kathy Davis; London: Sage, 1997), 10.

13 See, e.g., Christl M. Maier, *Daughter Zion, Mother Zion: Gender, Space and the Sacred in Ancient Israel* (Minneapolis: Fortress, 2008), 210.

14 Martha C. Nussbaum, *Upheavals of Thought: The Intelligence of Emotions* (Cambridge: Cambridge University Press, 2001), 25, 1.

15 Nussbaum, *Upheavals of Thought*, 43.

16 Nussbaum, *Upheavals of Thought*, 1.

17 Corrine Carvalho, "The Beauty of the Bloody God: The Divine Warrior in Prophetic Literature," in *Aesthetics of Violence in the Prophets* (ed. Chris Franke and Julia M. O'Brien; London: T&T Clark, 2010), 146.

18 For "rebuking consolation," see Richard J. Clifford, *Fair Spoken and Persuading: An Interpretation of Second Isaiah* (New York: Paulist, 1984), 170.

19 Since the pronouns refer to the "forearm," English translations typically use "it," as is correct in English usage.

20 Meaney, *Gender, Ireland, and Cultural Change*, xvii.

21 Uta Schmidt, "Zion and the Servant of God Structuring and Gendering Isaiah 49–55" (presented to the Formation of Isaiah Section, SBL Annual Meeting, San Francisco, November 20, 2011), 5; Maier, *Daughter Zion, Mother Zion*, 212.

22 See further the argument of Jeremy M. Hutton, "Isaiah 51:9-11 and the Rhetorical Appropriation and Subversion of Hostile Theologies," *Journal of Biblical Literature* 126 (2007): 271–303.

23 See Joan Judge, "Blended Wish Images: Chinese and Western Exemplary Women at the Turn of the Twentieth Century," in *Beyond Tradition and Modernity: Gender,*

Genre and Cosmopolitanism in Late Qing China (ed. Grace S. Fong et al.; Leiden: Brill, 2004), 128; and Suzanne Kennedy Flynn, "Countess Courageous," *World of Hibernia* 4, no. 3 (1998): 8.

24 Hutton, "Isaiah 51:9-11," 295.

25 Carvalho, "Beauty of the Bloody God," in *Aesthetics of Violence* (ed. Franke and O'Brien), 150.

26 Meaney, *Gender, Ireland, and Cultural Change*, 3; see also Cathy Leeny, *Irish Women Playwrights 1900–1939: Gender and Violence on Stage* (Irish Studies 9; Oxford: Peter Lang, 2010), 7.

27 See further Meaney, *Gender, Ireland, and Cultural Change*, esp. xv, 5.

28 Carol A. Newsom, "Response to Norman K. Gottwald, 'Social Class and Ideology in Isaiah 40–55,'" *Semeia* 59 (1992): 77.

29 James L. Mays, *Psalms* (Interpretation: A Bible Commentary for Teaching and Preaching; Louisville, Ky.: Westminster John Knox, 1994), 215.

30 Mays, *Psalms*, 216.

31 William P. Brown, *Seeing the Psalms: A Theology of Metaphor* (London: Westminster John Knox, 2002), 27.

32 Nussbaum, *Upheavals of Thought*, 43.

33 Tamez, "Women's Rereading," in *Voices from the Margin* (ed. Sugirtharajah), 52.

CHAPTER 6: LAPSLEY

1 "To go through the Book of Psalms is to be led increasingly toward the praise of God as the final word. While doxology *may* be the beginning word, it *is* clearly the *final* word" (Patrick D. Miller Jr., *Interpreting the Psalms* [Philadelphia: Fortress, 1986], 67), emphasis in original.

2 Unless otherwise noted, all translations are my own. This particular verse reflects the NRSV.

3 Patrick Miller, "The Poetry of Creation: Psalm 104," in *God Who Creates: Essays in Honor of W. Sibley Towner* (ed. William P. Brown and S. Dean McBride Jr.; Grand Rapids: Eerdmans, 2000), 97.

4 Elaine James, "Landscapes of Desire: The Song of Songs, the Body, and the Earth" (Ph.D. diss., Princeton Theological Seminary, 2013), 36.

5 William P. Brown, *Psalms* (Interpreting Biblical Texts Series; Nashville: Abingdon, 2010), 151.

6 Frank-Lothar Hossfeld and Erich Zenger, *Psalms 3: A Commentary on Psalms 101–150* (ed. K. Baltzer; trans. L. M. Maloney; Minneapolis: Fortress, 2011), 617, emphasis in original.

7 "Perhaps a poor, lowly Christian had his eyes fixed on a pagan, rich and powerful perhaps, had his eyes fixed on the flower of the field, and was perhaps halfway to choosing him for a patron rather than his God" (Augustine, Sermon 33A.3, cited in *Psalms 51–150* [ed. Quentin F. Wesselschmidt and Thomas C. Oden; Ancient Christian Commentary on Scripture: Old Testament; Downers Grove, Ill.: InterVarsity, 2007], 8:416).

8 Mitchell J. Dahood, *Psalms 101–150* (AB 17:2; Garden City, N.Y.: Doubleday, 1970), 341. A merism consists of two contrasting words that signify an entirety (e.g., "God made *the heavens and the earth*"—i.e., everything).

9   See, e.g., Isa 40:23-24.

10 For a full discussion of the theology conveyed by the Hebrew word *'ashere* underlying these English expressions, see Ellen Charry, *God and the Art of Happiness: An Offering of Pastoral Doctrinal Theology* (Grand Rapids: Eerdmans, 2010).

11 J. Clinton McCann, Jr., "Psalms," in the *New Interpreters Bible Commentary*, vol. 4 (ed. Leander E. Keck; Nashville: Abingdon, 1996), 1264; cf. James Luther Mays, *Psalms* (Interpretation; Louisville, Ky.: Westminster John Knox, 1994), 439. According to McCann, "Wickedness is essentially autonomy, which is strongly disavowed by both Psalms 1 and 146" ("Preaching on Psalms," 39).

12 The psalm possesses what some commentators call an "anthological style." See John S. Kselman, "Psalm 146 in Its Context," *Catholic Biblical Quarterly* 50 (1988): 589. This same feature, along with some Aramaisms, suggest a postexilic date for the psalm.

13 Jer 7:6 ("if you do not oppress the alien, the orphan, and the widow; if you do not shed the blood of the innocent in this place; if other gods you do not follow, to your own hurt"; cf. Jer 21:12) provides some of the specific content of the summary statement "executes justice for the oppressed."

14 Kselman, "Psalm 146 in Its Context," 593–94.

15 McCann, "Psalms," 1264.

16 In his manuscript, King placed the words in quotation marks, having found the ideas and vocabulary in an 1853 collection of sermons by Theodore Parker (*Ten Sermons of Religion* [Boston: Crosby, Nichols, 1853], 84–85).

17 Carol A. Newsom, *The Book of Job: A Contest of Moral Imaginations* (Oxford: Oxford University Press, 2003), 121.

18 Hossfeld and Zenger, *Psalms 3*, 611.

19 Hossfeld and Zenger, *Psalms 3*, 611.

20 Rosemary Radford Ruether, "Ecofeminist Thea/ologies and Ethics," in *Religion and the Environment*, vol. IV: *Connections: Science, Ethics, Eco-feminism, Consumerism, Sustainability, and Spirituality* (Critical Concepts in Religious Studies; ed. Roger S. Gottlieb; New York: Routledge, 2010), 143.

21 Patricia K. Tull, *Inhabiting Eden: Christians, the Bible, and the Ecological Crisis* (Louisville, Ky.: Westminster John Knox, 2013), 61.

22 Chris J. Cuomo, *Feminism and Ecological Communities: An Ethic of Flourishing* (London: Routledge, 1998), 73.

23 Cuomo, *Feminism and Ecological Communities*, 65.

24 Ivone Gebara, *Out of the Depths: Women's Experience of Evil and Salvation* (trans. Ann Patrick Ware; Minneapolis: Fortress, 2002), 58.

25 Ruether, "Ecofeminist Thea/ologies and Ethics," in *Religion and the Environment* (ed. Gottlieb), 145, emphasis added. Ruether discusses the theologies of Gebara and other ecofeminists from Africa, India, and North America.

26 Aldo Leopold, *A Sand County Almanac* (New York: Ballantine Books, 1966), 21.

CHAPTER 7: STEWART

1   Michael J. Sandel, *Justice: What's the Right Thing to Do?* (New York: Farrar, Straus & Giroux, 2009), 216.

2   The force of the conjunction *ki* in v. 12 ("*for* he delivers the needy") is debated, with some commentators suggesting that it provides the rationale for YHWH's favor upon the king (i.e., may this happen *because* he delivered the needy) and others interpreting v. 12 as a condition (i.e., may this happen *if/when* he delivers the needy). See for instance Walter Houston, "The King's Preferential Option for the Poor: Rhetoric, Ideology, and Ethics in Psalm 72," *Biblical Interpretation* 7 (1999): 350; Mitchell Dahood, *Psalms II: 51–100* (AB 17; Garden City, N.Y.: Doubleday, 1968), 182; Frank-Lothar Hossfeld and Erich Zenger, *Psalms 2: A Commentary on Psalms 51–100* (ed. Klaus Baltzer; trans. Linda M. Maloney; Hermeneia; Minneapolis: Fortress, 2005), 202.

3   See Phyllis A. Bird, "Poor Man or Poor Woman? Gendering the Poor in Prophetic Texts," in *Missing Persons and Mistaken Identities: Women and Gender in Ancient Israel* (Minneapolis: Fortress, 1997), 67–78.

4   Abraham J. Heschel, *The Prophets: Volume 1* (New York: Harper & Row, 1962), 216.

5   For a feminist reading of this metaphor, see, e.g., Renita J. Weems, "Gomer: Victim of Violence or Victim of Metaphor?" *Semeia* 47 (1989): 87–104.

6   For a discussion of the patriarchal worldview implicit in Proverbs, see Carol A. Newsom, "Woman and the Discourse of Patriarchal Wisdom: A Study of Proverbs 1–9," in *Gender and Difference in Ancient Israel* (ed. P. Day; Minneapolis: Augsburg Fortress, 1989), 142–60.

7   Carol A. Newsom, *The Book of Job: A Contest of Moral Imaginations* (New York: Oxford University Press, 2003), 87.

8   Newsom, *Book of Job*, 154.

9   The Hebrew term *'āmon* is difficult to translate (cf. NRSV, "master worker"); for a discussion of the various options, see Michael V. Fox, "*'Amon* Again," *Journal of Biblical Literature* 115, no. 4 (1996): 699–702. I follow Fox, who reads the form as an infinitive absolute of the verb *'mn* ("to raise," "to be raised"), here functioning as an adverb to complement the main verb.

10 William P. Brown notes, "Delightful play thus binds Wisdom to both the divine and human spheres, not in a relationship of servile dependence—Wisdom is not Yahweh's codependent—but in the freedom of interdependence" (*The Ethos of the Cosmos: The Genesis of Moral Imagination in the Bible* [Grand Rapids: Eerdmans, 1999], 278).

11 Brown, *Ethos of the Cosmos*, 278.

12 See William P. Brown, "To Discipline without Destruction: The Multifaceted Profile of the Child in Proverbs," in *The Child in the Bible* (ed. Marcia J. Bunge et al.; Grand Rapids: Eerdmans, 2008), 78.

13 Anne Marie Goetz, "Gender Justice, Citizenship and Entitlements: Core Concepts, Central Debates and New Directions for Research," in *Gender Justice, Citizenship, and Development* (ed. Maitrayee Mukhopadhyay and Navsharan Singh; Ottawa: International Development Research Centre, 2007), 18.

14 See the most recent report of the United Nations Development Programme, which draws its conclusions based on analysis of life expectancy, wealth, education, and participation in the political process: *Human Development Report 2013: The Rise of the South; Human Progress in a Diverse World* (New York: United Nations Development Programme, 2013), 31–33.

15 Martha C. Nussbaum, *Women and Human Development: The Capabilities Approach* (New York: Cambridge University Press, 2000), 41.

16   E.g., see Raghav Gaiha, "Does the Right to Food Matter?" *Economic and Political Weekly* 38, no. 40 (2003): 4269–76. This article analyzes the right-to-food campaign in India.

17   Beverly Wildung Harrison, *Justice in the Making: Feminist Social Ethics* (ed. Elizabeth M. Bounds et al.; Louisville, Ky.: Westminster John Knox, 2004), 16.

18   Houston, *Justice*, 104–5.

19   Ada María Isasi-Díaz, "Justice and Social Change," in *Dictionary of Feminist Theologies* (ed. Letty M. Russell and J. Shannon Clarkson; Louisville, Ky.: Westminster John Knox, 1996), 161.

20   Isasi-Díaz, "Justice and Social Change," in *Dictionary of Feminist Theologies* (ed. Russell and Clarkson), 161.

21   Naila Kabeer, "Empowerment, Citizenship and Gender Justice: A Contribution to Locally Grounded Theories of Change in Women's Lives," *Ethics and Social Welfare* 6, no. 3 (2012): 216–32.

22   Lila Abu-Lughod, "Do Muslim Women Really Need Saving? Anthropological Reflections on Cultural Relativism and Its Others," *American Anthropologist* 104, no. 3 (2002): 788.

23   Kabeer, "Empowerment, Citizenship and Gender Justice," 231.

24   Heschel, *Prophets*, 215.

CHAPTER 8: HOWARD

1   This question and its answer are from "Catechism for Young Children," written by Joseph Engels. It is based on the Westminster Shorter Catechism and has been promulgated and edited by Reformed churches since the nineteenth century. The answer itself draws on 2 Pet 1:21: "For the prophecy came not in old time by the will of man: but holy men of God spake as they were moved by the Holy Ghost" (KJV).

2   See Helena Zlotnick, "From Jezebel to Esther: Fashioning Images of Queenship in the Hebrew Bible," *Biblica* 82 (2001): 477–95.

3   For more detailed treatments of the role of writing in these texts, see Susan Niditch, *Oral World and Written Word: Ancient Israelite Literature* (Library of Ancient Israel; Louisville, Ky.: Westminster John Knox, 1996), 82–83; and William M. Schniedewind, *How the Bible Became a Book: The Textualization of Ancient Israel* (Cambridge: Cambridge University Press, 2004), 27–29.

4   On literacy as a privilege of the elite, see Christopher A. Rollston, *Writing and Literacy in the World of Ancient Israel: Epigraphic Evidence from the Iron Age* (Archaeology and Biblical Studies 11; Atlanta: SBL, 2010).

5   Mieke Bal, "Lots of Writing," *Semeia* 54 (1991): 77–102.

6   Sandra Beth Berg, *The Book of Esther: Motifs, Themes and Structure* (Society of Biblical Literature Dissertation Series 44; Missoula, Mont.: Scholars Press, 1979), 59–72.

7   Berg, *Book of Esther*, 61.

8   Berg, *Book of Esther*, 70.

9   Esther's receipt and subsequent embrace of her royal status provide her official, titular authority. Yet she also exercises an otherwise unexplained charm over the eunuch Hegai (2:9): an ephemeral, ineffable authority. Since the qualification for replacing Vashti as queen of Persia is to please the king overnight, Esther's initial charms over

the king are more easily explained as sexual. At 5:2, the ephemeral authority seems to reemerge, but not without sexual innuendo, as Esther touches the king's "golden scepter that was in his hand." See also Timothy K. Beal, *The Book of Hiding: Gender, Ethnicity, Annihilation, and Esther* (Biblical Limits; London: Routledge, 1997), 76.

10 The Hebrew text adds one more phrase to this verse: "and speak according to the tongue of his people." The phrase does not appear in the Septuagint, and the NRSV relegates the phrase to a note, rather than including it in the body of the translation. Syntactically the phrase is attached to the content of the declaration, as if every man is also being told to speak in his own language. However, given the concern the book shows for communicating to the whole of the empire in ways all its subjects can understand, the phrase makes more sense either as dittography or as a gloss on the earlier phrases concerning the letters. The idea of "speaking" would introduce an oral component to the communication involved with the letters, but textuality remains the overwhelming emphasis.

11 Just two of many examples include the giving of the law at Sinai, when the law is famously written on two stone tablets, and at Exod 17:14, when God tells Moses regarding Amalek, "Write this as a reminder in a book."

12 On the issue of the infinite interpretability of texts, I am deeply informed by John D. Caputo, *More Radical Hermeneutics: On Not Knowing Who We Are* (Studies in Continental Thought; Bloomington: Indiana University Press, 2000). Caputo affirms that not only written texts but also speech—anything committed to language—is indeterminate, infinitely subject to interpretation.

13 Some translations, including the JPS Tanakh and the New King James Version, render this phrase as a declaration instead of a question. Regardless, Jezebel is incredulous about Ahab's refusal to use his royal authority to its fullest extent.

14 Deuteronomy's law of the king (Deut 17:14-20) also presumes the tendency of kings to take indiscriminately, as it specifically forbids the king to acquire many horses or wives.

15 One could also say that Ahab fails to act like a man, given the ways kingship and masculinity are intertwined throughout the Deuteronomistic History. See Cameron B. R. Howard, "1 and 2 Kings," in *Women's Bible Commentary* (3rd ed.; ed. Carol A. Newsom et al.; Louisville, Ky.: Westminster John Knox, 2012), 164–83.

16 Caputo, *More Radical Hermeneutics*, 206.

17 Phyllis Trible, "Exegesis for Storytellers and Other Strangers," *Journal of Biblical Literature* 114, no. 1 (1995): 3–19.

18 Trible, "Exegesis for Storytellers," 5.

19 Trible, "Exegesis for Storytellers," 5–6.

20 Trible, "Exegesis for Storytellers," 7.

21 Trible, "Exegesis for Storytellers," 12. The translation of Proverbs is Trible's.

22 For an overview of Jezebel in the history of interpretation, including exceptions to the demonizing of Jezebel, see Josey Bridges Snyder, "Jezebel and Her Interpreters," in *Women's Bible Commentary* (3rd ed.; ed. Newsom et al.), 180–83.

23 I am deeply grateful to Lauren Baird for this and many other insights that she offered in personal correspondence upon reading an earlier draft of this essay.

24 Bal, "Lots of Writing," 95.

25 Beal, *Book of Hiding*, 121.

CHAPTER 9: BOORER

1   It is generally held that Num 20:1-12 is a Priestly text and Num 12 is non-Priestly. My approach will differ from that of many feminist analyses of texts involving Miriam that focus on the present text only—e.g., Phyllis Trible, "Subversive Justice: Tracing the Miriamic Traditions," in *Justice and the Holy: Essays in Honor of Walter Harrelson* (ed. Douglas Knight and Peter Paris; Atlanta: Scholars Press, 1989), 99–109; Claudia Camp, *Wise, Strange and Holy: The Strange Woman and the Making of the Bible* (Journal for the Study of the Old Testament: Supplement Series 320; Sheffield: Sheffield Academic, 2000), 191–278.

2   By being mentioned first in v. 1, and with a fem. sing. verb, Miriam is accentuated.

3   This is the only place where Moses is said to have a Cushite wife. There is much debate concerning whether she is to be identified with Zipporah or, as is more probable, she is to be seen as a second wife of Ethiopian/Egyptian origin. For our purposes what is important is that she is foreign, not an Israelite.

4   This time using the verb *'mr*, not *dbr b-*.

5   The phrase *'mn b-* is ambiguous and can mean either that Moses is entrusted (as leader) with YHWH's house—that is, the Israelites—or that Moses is the most trusted of all YHWH's household, Israel. It will primarily be taken in the first sense in this discussion.

6   NRSV translation notwithstanding, there is no actual mention of whiteness in the Hebrew here. Whether or not whiteness is implied is debated. Some scholars see a reference to whiteness and interpret this as playing on the black skin of the Cushite, with the implication that Miriam's punishment is linked with the crime. See Trible, "Subversive Justice," in *Justice and the Holy* (ed. Knight and Paris), 105; Rodney Sadler, *Can a Cushite Change His Skin? An Examination of Race, Ethnicity, and Othering in the Hebrew Bible* (New York: T&T Clark, 2005), 37–40; Mukti Barton, "The Skin of Miriam Became as White as Snow: The Bible, Western Feminism, and Colour Politics," *Feminist Theology* (2001): 68–80 (73–74). Others maintain that there is no white/black contrast here, that "like snow" refers not to whiteness but to the flakiness of the skin disease. See Wilda Gafney, *Daughters of Miriam: Women Prophets in Ancient Israel* (Minneapolis: Fortress, 2008), 84.

7   See Phyllis S. Kramer, "Miriam," in *Exodus and Deuteronomy* (ed. Athalaya Brenner and Carole Fontaine; 2nd Series; Sheffield: Sheffield Academic, 2000), 104–33 (122–24).

8   See S. David Sperling, "Miriam, Aaron and Moses: Sibling Rivalry," *Hebrew Union College Annual* 70–71 (1999–2000): 39–55 (47).

9   See Imtraud Fischer, "The Authority of Miriam: A Feminist Reading of Numbers 12 Prompted by Jewish Interpretation," in *Exodus and Deuteronomy* (ed. Brenner and Fontaine), 159–73 (160).

10 An asterisk indicates that only part of the verse (or verses) is being referred to. In this case it refers to v. 8a*ab*.

11 See Suzanne Boorer, "The Place of Numbers 13–14* and Numbers 20:2-12* in the Priestly Narrative (Pg)," *JBL* (2012): 45–63 (50–52). For simplicity's sake, this coherent story as outlined here will be referred to as "Num 12:1-12," on the understanding

that it is only the portions indicated above and not vv. 1-12 in their present form that are meant.

12 The notice of Miriam's death and burial may have been added to the Priestly itinerary in v. 1 at a later time—that is, later than the coherent story that follows in Num 20:2-12 as outlined here.

13 As I have noted elsewhere ("Place of Numbers 13–14"), in the Priestly narrative, which extends throughout Genesis and Exodus and into these Numbers passages, the tent of meeting is situated inside the camp, in the midst of the Israelites.

14 See Boorer, "Place of Numbers 13–14," 61–62.

15 Those who see non-Priestly Num 12 as earlier than the Priestly text of Num 20:1-12 tend to see the features of this text, both its tensions and its signs of unity, as owing to the combination of two earlier traditions on a preliterary level (e.g., Martin Noth, *Numbers: A Commentary* [London: SCM Press, 1968], 92–93, 96). Those who see Num 12 as later than Num 20:1-12 explain the same features of the text as resulting from an author's drawing on, and combining, motifs from diverse pentateuchal texts (e.g., Thomas Römer, "Israel's Sojourn in the Wilderness and the Construction of the Book of Numbers," in *Reflection and Refraction: Studies in Biblical Historiography in Honour of A. Graeme Auld* [ed. Robert Rezetko et al.; Leiden: Brill, 2007], 436, 439–40, 442).

16 See also Exod 33:18-23 in relation to Moses beholding the form of YHWH in Num 12:8.

17 See Camp, *Wise, Strange and Holy*, 275: "'Mouth to mouth' suggests the impossibility that Moses could get the message wrong or change its transmission."

18 See the Hebrew wordplay between "spit" (*yrq*, v. 14) and "only" (*raq*, v. 2). See Thomas Dozeman, "Numbers," in *The Interpreter's Bible* (ed. Leander Keck; 12 vols.; Nashville: Abingdon, 1998), 2:110.

19 Prohibition of exogamous marriages seems to have been a major issue, at least primarily, in the postexilic period. See Sadler, *Can a Cushite Change*, 36.

20 Miriam is also described in Exod 15:20 as Aaron's sister. But the tradition of a sibling relationship among all three of them is thought to be late. See Rita J. Burns, *Has the Lord Indeed Spoken Only through Moses? A Study of the Biblical Portrait of Miriam* (Atlanta: Scholars Press, 1987), 81, 84, 90.

21 Alternatively, it could be interpreted as both the prophetic function, symbolized by both Miriam and Aaron, and the priestly function, symbolized by Aaron, being subordinated to Moses, the incomparable mediator: Römer, "Israel's Sojourn in the Wilderness," in *Reflection and Refraction* (ed. Rezetko et al.), 439–40.

22 Katharine Sakenfeld, "Numbers," in *Women's Bible Commentary* (ed. Carol A. Newsom, Sharon Ringe, and Jacqueline Lapsley; Louisville, Ky.: Westminster John Knox, 2012), 84. See also Fischer, "Authority of Miriam," in *Exodus and Deuteronomy* (ed. Brenner and Fontaine), 169.

23 Camp, *Wise, Strange and Holy*, 253.

24 Camp (*Wise, Strange and Holy*, 191, 194, 197–98, 226, 229–31, 278) explains why Miriam had to become an outsider, whereas Aaron remains an insider, by combining the motif of Miriam as Aaron's sibling with the Priestly genealogies that identify who are priests—that is, by birthright. As sister of Aaron, Miriam is part of the Priestly

genealogy, but she is excluded from priesthood because of her gender. Her leprosy, a form of impurity, simply dramatizes her exclusion further.

25 Camp, *Wise, Strange and Holy*, 251

26 Camp, *Wise, Strange and Holy*, 252.

27 Moreover, Aaron's descendants succeed him in this office (Num 20:22-29). See Camp (*Wise, Strange and Holy*, 262–76), who argues convincingly that Moses stands for the authoritative written word, which is appropriated in future generations by the priesthood, the descendants of Aaron who is portrayed as Moses' divinely authorized mouth piece.

28 Camp, *Wise, Strange and Holy*, 249.

29 That is, post-Priestly and therefore to be interpreted in light of both earlier and later texts.

30 See Mmapula Kebaneilwe, "This Courageous Woman: A Socio-rhetorical Womanist Reading of Proverbs 31:10-31" (Ph.D. diss., Murdoch University, 2013).

CHAPTER 10: GALAMBUSH

1 See, e.g., Gosta W. Ahlstrom, *Who Were the Israelites?* (Winona Lake, Ind.: Eisenbrauns, 1986). Ironically, the poem in Deut 32:8-9 seems to reflect this view, though here El Elyon, the high god, assigns the land of Israel along with its people to YHWH.

2 This essay focuses on the role YHWH plays as a character in the text and as the patron deity of Israel. Historically, a male god YHWH will be referred to as "he" particularly because YHWH's masculinity may have been understood as bound up with the ways in which he asserts dominance in the text. The use of the masculine pronoun thus designates YHWH as worshiped in ancient Israel and does not attribute gender to God as such.

3 Thomas W. Mann, *Divine Presence and Guidance in Israelite Traditions: The Typology of Exaltation* (Eugene, Ore.: Wipf & Stock, 2010).

4 Ahlstrom, *Who Were the Israelites*, 59; Jon Levenson, *Sinai and Zion: An Entry into the Hebrew Bible* (Minneapolis: Winston, 1972).

5 Horeb/Sinai is first mentioned as YHWH's home in Exod 3:1, but then throughout the Torah. Cf. Judg 5:5; Ps 68:8, 17; Neh 9:13.

6 This portrayal of YHWH as an outsider is probably accurate.

7 See, e.g., Deut 20:10-19. Note that in vv. 10-15 the Israelites are to treat towns outside the promised land according to standards that were well established in ancient Near Eastern warfare—enslaving the residents of towns that surrendered. It is only within the land (vv. 16-19) that the population is to be slaughtered without exception.

8 The Mesha inscription is probably the best-known example.

9 In this context it is baffling that Israel's name is based on the name of El, one of the high gods of Canaan, rather than on the newcomer, YHWH.

10 On the complexity of the commandments, see Y. Hoffman, "The Deuteronomistic Concept of the Herem," *Zeitschrift für die alttestamentliche Wissenschaft* 111 (1999): 196–210.

11 For an accessible discussion, see Israel Finkelstein and Neil Asher Silberman, *The Bible Unearthed: Archaeology's New Vision of Ancient Israel and the Origin of Its Sacred Texts* (New York: Free Press, 2001). For a closer examination of the data, see Lester

Grabbe, *Ancient Israel: What Do We Know and How Do We Know It?* (London: T&T Clark, 2008). Unfortunately, scholarly assurances that the conquest narratives represent only a "utopian" or "ideal" scenario leave the problem of genocide as an "ideal" unaddressed. See, among others, Moshe Weinfeld, *The Promise of the Land: The Inheritance of the Land of Canaan by the Israelites* (Berkeley: University of California Press, 1993); and Hoffman, "Deuteronomistic Concept."

12 See, e.g., the summaries in Grabbe, *Ancient Israel*, 65–76; and Finkelstein and Silberman, *Bible Unearthed*, 97–118.

13 See Dafna Langgut et al., "Dead Sea Pollen Record and History of Human Activity in the Judean Highlands (Israel) from the Intermediate Bronze into the Iron Age (~2500–500 BCE)," *Palyngology* 38, no. 2 (2014), doi:10.1080/01916122.2014.906001.

14 Although the date by which Israel became a nation-state in its own right is debated, by the ninth century BCE several known inscriptions refer to Israel (the Northern Kingdom of the Bible), among them the Monolith Inscription, which mentions Ahab as a ruler of regional status.

15 Contrary to biblical claims that the Northern Kingdom were inveterate Baal-worshipers, the Mesha inscription attests to YHWH as (northern) Israel's god in the mid-ninth century.

16 See, e.g., John Day, *Yahweh and the Gods and Goddesses of Canaan* (Bloomsbury: T&T Clark, 2002).

17 Morton Smith, *Palestinian Parties and Politics That Shaped the Old Testament* (New York: Columbia University Press, 1971). The belief that YHWH commanded monolatry (the exclusive worship of only one god regardless of whether others also existed) appears as early as prophetic texts such as Hosea, which may date to the eighth century BCE. The Bible as we have it, however, received heavy editing and at least some composition in the fifth through second centuries BCE.

18 Ehud Ben Zvi points out that the Babylonians were likely to have left some of the Judean elite in place for the sake of social stability ("Inclusion in and Exclusion from Israel as Conveyed by the Use of the Term 'Israel' in Post-Monarchic Biblical Texts," in *The Pitcher Is Broken: Memorial Essays for Gosta W. Ahlstrom* [ed. S. Holloway and L. Handy; Sheffield: JSOT Press, 1995], 95–149). Assuming this was the case, the returnees would have been challenged by a separate, nonreturnee elite, who did not share the returnees' belief that the "good figs" had been sent into exile, with the "bad figs" left behind in the land (see Jer 24:1-5). See also John Kessler, "Images of Exile: Representations of the 'Exile' and 'Empty Land' in the Sixth to Fourth Century BCE Yehudite Literature," in *The Concept of Exile in Ancient Israel and Its Historical Contexts* (ed. Ehud Ben Zvi and Christoph Levin; Berlin: De Gruyter, 2010), 309–51.

19 A wonderful example of this dynamic can be found in Ps 82, in which God becomes enraged at the divine council and declares that they will no longer be divine but will now "die like mortals" (v. 7). The psalm's author clearly expects the reader to take the council's existence for granted. God's decision that the lower gods will now become mortal paves the way for the psalm's monotheistic conclusion: "Rise up, O God, judge the [entire] earth!" (v. 8).

20 Ironically, in chap. 9, Ezra charges the earlier returnees with having married women from among "the Canaanites, the Hittites, the Perizzites, [and] the Jebusites," all peoples whom the conquest narrative claims had been wiped out centuries earlier by

Joshua. On the question of who counts as Israel in postexilic texts, see Ben Zvi, "Inclusion," in *Pitcher Is Broken* (ed. Holloway and Handy); Daniel Smith-Christopher, "Between Ezra and Isaiah: Exclusion, Transformation, and Inclusion of the 'Foreigner' in Post-exilic Biblical Theology," in *Ethnicity and the Bible* (ed. M. Brett; New York: Brill, 1996), 117–42; and Bob Becking, "On the Identity of the 'Foreign' Women in Ezra 9–10," in *Exile and Restoration Revisited: Essays on the Babylonian and Persian Periods in Memory of Peter R. Ackroyd* (ed. G. Knoppers and L. Grabbe; London: T&T Clark, 2009), 31–49.

21 See discussion in Daniel Smith-Christopher, *The Religion of the Landless: The Social Context of the Babylonian Exile* (Bloomington, Ind.: Meyer-Stone, 1989).

22 Ben Zvi ("Inclusion," in *Pitcher Is Broken* [ed. Holloway and Handy]) argues that the narrative of return provides a tool for reconciliation between returnee and those in the land. The whole nation's ancestors sinned; consequently, the leaders, representing the people as a whole, were taken into exile. Now that the punishment has been completed, the groups can move forward together. This model is attractive, though it presumes that at least a majority of those in the land are open to the "YHWH alone" policy of the biblical authors.

23 Raymond Westbrook, *A History of Ancient Near Eastern Law* (Leiden: Brill, 2003), 1:37–38, 377, 580.

24 Christiana Van Houten, *The Alien in Israelite Law: A Study of the Changing Legal Status of Strangers in Ancient Israel* (Sheffield: JSOT Press, 1991); Rolf Rendtorff, "The Ger in the Priestly Laws of the Pentateuch," in *Ethnicity and the Bible* (ed. Brett), 77–87; and Jacob Milgrom, *Leviticus 17–22: A New Introduction and Commentary* (Anchor Bible 3a; New York: Doubleday, 2000), 1704–7.

25 It is unclear whether Abraham ceases to be a *ger* with the purchase of the burial cave.

26 The Bible speaks only of male *gerim*. Although some women were surely considered *gerim*, this essay follows the biblical texts in referring to the *ger* as male.

27 This fact calls into question the translation of *ger* and *'ezrah* as "sojourner" and "native" or "native born," respectively. Presumably, any Israelite is a "native" (that is, a native to the group, Israel) regardless of where he or she was born, while the *ger* remains a *ger* even if her or his ancestors were residents of the land. Jacob Milgrom is surely correct that Num 15:14 legislates for the *ger* throughout Israel's generations in the land rather than the *ger*'s (*Numbers* [Philadelphia: Jewish Publication Society, 1989], 120). Narratives such as that describing Israel's four hundred years as *gerim* in Egypt assume the possibility of permanent status as a *ger*.

28 See discussion in Rendtorff, "Ger in the Priestly Laws," in *Ethnicity and the Bible* (ed. Brett).

29 It would be inaccurate to think of the *ger* as "non-Jewish" in the contemporary, religious sense, as the *ger* is circumcised and keeps the laws of the Torah. In this regard the *ger* is more fully a member of the community than the so-called God-fearers of Acts 13, as the *ger* is circumcised and allowed to offer sacrifices in the temple.

30 Westbrook, *History of Ancient Near Eastern Law*, 37–38, 377, 580.

31 See Bruce Wells, "What Is Biblical Law? A Look at Pentateuchal Rules and Near Eastern Practice," *Catholic Biblical Quarterly* 70 (2008): 223–43.

32 Ben Zvi, "Inclusion," in *Pitcher Is Broken* (ed. Holloway and Handy), 100.

33 In this vein, the tradition in which "Canaanites" are left in the land "as a snare" to test Israel may represent a strategy of acknowledging the continued land rights of "heterodox" Judeans.

34 See, e.g., Robert Allen Warrior, "A Native American Perspective: Canaanites, Cowboys, and Indians," in *Voices from the Margin: Interpreting the Bible in the Third World* (ed. R. S. Sugirtharajah; Maryknoll, N.Y.: Orbis Books, 1991), 289, 291–92.

35 Shira Milgrom, *"Ki Teitzei*: We Are What We Remember," in *Ten Minutes of Torah: Reform Voices of Torah*, at www.reformjudaism.org/learning/torah-study/ki-teitzei/ ki-teitzei-we-are-what-we-remember?m_source=WU&utm_medium=email&utm _content=20140905&utm_campaign=WeeklyParsha.

CHAPTER 11: MELCHER

1 Lisa Sowle Cahill, "Christian Character, Biblical Community, and Human Values," in *Character and Scripture: Moral Formation, Community, and Biblical Interpretation* (ed. W. P. Brown; Grand Rapids: Eerdmans, 2002), 3–17.

2 Cahill, "Christian Character," in *Character and Scripture* (ed. Brown), 4–5.

3 M. Daniel Carroll R., "He Has Told You What Is Good: Moral Formation in Micah," in *Character Ethics and the Old Testament: Moral Dimensions of Scripture* (ed. M. Daniel Carroll R. and Jacqueline E. Lapsley; Louisville, Ky.: Westminster John Knox, 2007), 104.

4 Carroll R., "He Has Told You," in *Character Ethics* (ed. Carroll R. and Lapsley), 104.

5 *Aristotle's Nicomachean Ethics* (trans. Robert C. Bartlett and Susan D. Collins; Chicago: University of Chicago Press, 2011), 42, 1109b–1130.

6 *Stanford Encyclopedia of Philosophy*, s.v. "Moral Responsibility," by Andrew Eshleman, last revised March 26, 2014, http://plato.stanford.edu/entries/moral-responsibility/.

7 *Nichomachean Ethics* 1110a–111b4. Cf. *Stanford Encyclopedia of Philosophy*, s.v. "Moral Responsibility."

8 John Martin Fischer, "Recent Work on Moral Responsibility," *Ethics* 110 (1999): 93–139.

9 Fischer, "Recent Work," 99.

10 Carol A. Newsom, "Models of the Moral Self: Hebrew Bible and Second Temple Judaism," *Journal of Biblical Literature* 131 (2012): 5–25.

11 Newsom, "Models of the Moral Self," 12.

12 Newsom, "Models of the Moral Self," 13.

13 Newsom, "Models of the Moral Self," 12.

14 Carol Gilligan, "Remapping the Moral Domain: New Images of Self in Relationship," in *Mapping the Moral Domain: A Contribution of Women's Thinking to Psychological Theory and Education* (ed. C. Gilligan et al.; Cambridge, Mass.: Harvard University Press, 1988), 3–19.

15 Gilligan, "Remapping the Moral Domain," 8.

16 Gilligan, "Remapping the Moral Domain," 4.

17 Gilligan, "Remapping the Moral Domain," 8.

18 Musa W. Dube, *Postcolonial Feminist Interpretation of the Bible* (St. Louis: Chalice, 2000); and Kah-Jin Jeffrey Kuan and Mai-Anh Le Tran, "Reading Race Reading Rahab: A 'Broad' Asian American Reading of a 'Broad' Other," in *Postcolonial*

Interventions (ed. T. B. Liew; The Bible in the Modern World 23; Sheffield: Sheffield Phoenix, 2009), 27–44.

19 Dube, *Postcolonial Feminist Interpretation*, 49.

20 See the preceding chapter, in which Julie Galambush explores the implications of the land as divine gift and the accompanying justification of extermination of the people who occupied it.

21 Robert G. Boling notes, "The roots for 'spy, explore' (*rgl*, 'to go about on foot, to hoof it'; *ḥpr*, 'to explore'), are used three times at the outset (vv. 1, 2, 3), so that there will be no misunderstanding the nature of their mission west of the Jordan" (*Joshua: A New Translation with Notes and Commentary* [Anchor Bible 6; Garden City, N.Y.: Doubleday, 1982], 143).

22 Mary Joan Winn Leith suggests that there may be a hidden ethnic slur in the treatment of Rahab ("The Archaeology of Rahab," *Biblical Archaeology Review* 33 [2007]: 22, 78).

23 Rahab's status of exemplar continues in two passages in the Christian Scriptures. Heb 11:31 states, "By faith, Rahab the prostitute did not perish with those who were disobedient, because she had received the spies in peace." James 2:25 also uses Rahab as an exemplar: "Likewise, was not Rahab the prostitute also justified by works when she welcomed the messengers and sent them out by another road?"

24 Koehler, L., W. Baumgartner, and J. J. Stamm, *The Hebrew and Aramaic Lexicon of the Old Testament*, (trans. and ed. under the supervision of M. E. J. Richardson. 4 vols. Leiden, 1994–1999), 2:340.

25 "They were, after all, just a couple of patrons from whom it was not customary to require credentials" (Boling, *Joshua*, 146).

26 Michael D. Coogan, *A Brief Introduction to the Old Testament: The Hebrew Bible in Its Context* (2nd ed.; New York: Oxford University Press, 2012), 169.

27 Peter F. Lockwood, "Rahab: Multi-faceted Heroine of the Book of Joshua," *Lutheran Theological Journal* 44 (2010): 39–50 (42).

28 Gilligan, "Remapping the Moral Domain," 8.

29 Though many interpreters have seen a subtle reference to God in Mordecai's words, some scholars emphasize the ambiguity reflected in Mordecai's speech as well as in the book of Esther taken as a whole. Timothy K. Beal, for instance, says, "Here again, one could read this as an affirmation of divine providence or of chance and accident. Perhaps, Esther has risen for a reason, that is, to fulfill God's plan for deliverance. Or perhaps the Jews are simply lucky to have her there" ("Esther," in *Ruth and Esther* [Berit Olam; Collegeville, Minn.: Liturgical, 1999], 66). Adele Berlin comments about Esth 4, "God is most present and most absent in this chapter. Religious practice and the mention of God's name come closest to the surface here, and are most obviously suppressed. It is hard to read about fasting, mourning, and crying out without seeing God as the addressee to whom all these actions are directed. It is hard to plead for salvation from anyone but God" (*Esther* [JPS Bible Commentary; Philadelphia: Jewish Publication Society, 2001], 44).

30 Gilligan, "Remapping the Moral Domain," 8.

31 Gilligan, "Remapping the Moral Domain," 8–9.

CHAPTER 12: COTTRILL

1 "PTSD: Not a New Ailment on 'Wartorn' Battlefield," *NPR*, November 8, 2010, https://www.npr.org/templates/story/story.php?storyId=131096344.

2 Shelly Rambo, *Trauma and Spirit: A Theology of Remaining* (Louisville, Ky.: Westminster John Knox, 2010), 7.

3 See also Pss 3, 6, 38, 69.

4 All translations are my own. Verse numbering follows the NRSV, which differs from the Hebrew numbering.

5 See Linda Day and Carolyn Pressler's use of these terms in the introduction to *Engaging the Bible in a Gendered World* (ed. Linda Day and Carolyn Pressler; Louisville, Ky.: Westminster John Knox, 2006), xvii.

6 See the analyses of Beth LaNeel Tanner, "Hearing the Cries Unspoken: An Intertextual-Feminist Reading of Psalm 109," in *Wisdom and Psalms: A Feminist Companion to the Bible* (ed. Athalya Brenner and Carole Fontaine; Sheffield: Sheffield Academic, 1998), 283–301; and David Clines, "The Book of Psalms, Where Men Are Men: On the Gender of Hebrew Piety" (paper presented at the annual meeting of the SBL, Philadelphia, November 2005). In her feminist treatment of Ps 45, Nancy Bowen ("A Fairy Tale Wedding? A Feminist Intertextual Reading of Psalm 45," in *A God So Near: Essays on Old Testament Theology in Honor of Patrick D. Miller* [ed. Nancy R. Bowen and Brent A. Strawn; Winona Lake, Ind.: Eisenbrauns, 2003], 70–71) makes a particularly striking claim: "My work with this psalm leads me to suggest that it may be appropriate to omit Psalm 45 from our acts of corporate worship."

7 See esp. Nancy L. Declaisse-Walford, "Psalms," in *Women's Bible Commentary: Revised and Updated* (ed. Carol A. Newsom et al.; Louisville, Ky.: Westminster John Knox, 2012), 221–31; Lisa W. Davison, "'My Soul Is Like the Weaned Child That Is with Me': The Psalms and the Feminine Voice," *HBT* 23 (2001): 155–67; Patrick D. Miller, "Things Too Wonderful: Prayers of Women in the Old Testament," in *Biblische Theologie und gesellschaftlicher Wandel: Für Norbert Lohfink SJ* (ed. Georg Braulik et al.; Freiburg: Herder, 1993), 237–51; Carleen Mandolfo, "Finding Their Voices: Sanctioned Subversion in Psalms of Lament," *HBT* 24 (2002): 27–52; and Nancy C. Lee, *Lyrics of Lament: From Tragedy to Transformation* (Minneapolis: Fortress, 2010).

8 Melody Knowles, "Feminist Interpretation of the Psalms," in *The Oxford Handbook to the Psalms* (ed. William P. Brown; Oxford: Oxford University Press, 2014), 424.

9 As with most biblical texts, ancient composers and compilers assumed male readers. But women have no doubt prayed the psalms since their composition. Here, therefore, I employ female pronouns to facilitate experiencing this psalm more directly as female readers.

10 Only Pss 88 (v. 15) and 102 are iterations in the voice of the *ani* ("needy, wretched, or afflicted one"), though the psalmist describes himself as afflicted elsewhere: 22:25; 25:16; 34:6; 69:30; 70:6; 86:1; 109:22.

11 Serene Jones, *Trauma and Grace: Theology in a Ruptured World* (Louisville, Ky.: Westminster John Knox, 2009), 17, emphasis in original.

12 See, e.g., the use of threatening weapon imagery in other lament psalms: 7:13, 14; 11:2; 37:14-15.

13 These verses contain two Hebrew words, *kos* and *qa'at*, that are differentiated in English translation in various ways. William P. Brown renders the Hebrew as "scops owl" and "tawny owl," respectively. *Seeing the Psalms: A Theology of Metaphor* (Louisville, Ky.: Westminster John Knox, 2002), 146.

14 See Brown, *Seeing the Psalms*, 146.

15 Judith Herman, *Trauma and Recovery: The Aftermath of Violence—from Domestic Abuse to Political Terror* (New York: Basic Books, 1977), 52.

16 See Robert C. Culley, "Psalm 102: A Complaint with a Difference," *Semeia* 62 (1993): 19–35.

17 See Andrew Witt, "Hearing Psalm 102 within the Context of the Hebrew Psalter," *Vetus Testamentum* 62 (2012): 585.

18 The phrase is often credited to Carol Hanisch, who published a speech entitled "The Personal Is Political," in *Notes from the Second Year: Women's Liberation* (ed. Shulie Firestone and Anne Koedt; New York: Radical Feminism, 1970), 76–78.

19 See Rambo, *Trauma and Spirit*, 21.

20 Arlene Audergon, "Collective Trauma: The Nightmare of History," *Psychotherapy and Politics International* 2, no. 1 (2004): 16.

21 Jones, *Trauma and Grace*, 57.

22 In a related way, this need for God to be in control may be helpful in understanding some of the prophets' rhetoric in the Hebrew Bible, especially the argument that enemy attacks upon Israel and Judah are the direct result of God's displeasure. On one level, such language seems to blame the victim. But through the lens of trauma theory, such rhetoric may be understood as providing a wounded nation a sense of order and agency in a situation of utter chaos. Providing an intelligible reason for the trauma and a sense of possibility for the future, even if it meant assigning blame, may have been the prophets' way of helping others endure a world of suffering.

23 Rambo, *Trauma and Spirit*, 5.

24 The subject of this verse is unclear, though it can be inferred that the psalmist speaks of God.

25 Rambo, *Trauma and Spirit*, 2.

26 Anthony Gilby, trans., *The Psalms of David* (London: Henry Denham, 1581), sig. A3v; cited in *Rivkah Zim, English Metrical Psalms: Poetry as Praise and Prayer, 1535–1601* (Cambridge: Cambridge University Press, 1987), 28.

CHAPTER 13: HACKETT

1 Amartya Sen, "More than 100 Million Women Are Missing," *New York Review of Books*, December 20, 1990. Mara Hvistendahl estimated in 2011 that the number of missing women has risen to 160 million (*Unnatural Selection: Choosing Boys over Girls, and the Consequences of a World Full of Men* [New York: Public Affairs, 2011], 6).

2 Hvistendahl, *Unnatural Selection*, 14.

3 Hebrew *pilegesh* is traditionally translated "concubine," a word that is anachronistic and often negative. The *pilegesh* in ancient Israel was a married woman, but probably one whose family was too poor to hope for bridewealth or to offer a dowry, and so the marriage stood in less esteem than that undertaken through a contract worked out between the males of both families. Today, many scholars translate the

word as "secondary wife," as I will, even though it is a mouthful. See Michael Patrick O'Connor, "The Women in the Book of Judges," *Hebrew Annual Review* 10 (1986): 277–94.

4 The first essay I know of that dealt with this passage from a feminist point of view was Trible's "An Unnamed Woman: The Extravagance of Violence," in *Texts of Terror* (Philadelphia: Fortress, 1984), 64–91.

5 For a thorough discussion of the issues at stake, see Victor Matthews, "Hospitality and Hostility in Judges 4," *Biblical Theology Bulletin* 21 (1991): 13–21.

6 All translations from Hebrew in this essay are my own.

7 The versions differ on the reasons for the falling out: the Hebrew Masoretic Text says that she prostituted herself, while the Greek Septuagint, translated from a different ancient Hebrew text, says that she became angry with him.

8 This story is often thought to be about homosexuality, but although the men at first asked to perform homosexual acts with the old man's guest, the Levite's secondary wife was clearly a good enough substitute for them. Demanding to perform homosexual rape is not the same thing as being homosexual. See Susan Niditch, "The 'Sodomite' Theme in Judges 19–21: Family, Community, and Social Disintegration," *Catholic Biblical Quarterly* 44 (1982): 365–78; see further Alice A. Keefe's insightful article, "Rapes of Women/Wars of Men," *Semeia* 61 (1993): 79–97.

9 One wonders whether he would have dared to do this to a more prominent wife, risking her family's redeemer holding him responsible.

10 Gale Yee, "Ideological Criticism: Judges 17–21 and the Dismembered Body," in *Judges and Method: New Approaches in Biblical Studies* (ed. Gale Yee; Minneapolis: Fortress, 1995), 146–70 (166).

11 On Judg 19 as an anti-Benjamin and thus anti-Saul story, see David Jobling, "Structuralist Criticism: The Text's World of Meaning," in *Judges and Method* (ed. Yee), 91–118 (100–101). The story suggests that King Saul himself, since he is a Benjaminite, must have been a product of the forced Benjaminite marriages. See Edmund Leach, "Anthropological Approaches to the Study of the Bible in the Twentieth Century," in *Structuralist Interpretation of Biblical Myth* (by Edmund Leach and D. Alan Aycock; Cambridge: Cambridge University Press, 1983), 26–28.

12 The ark of the covenant was at Bethel at that time (Judg 20:27), and since the ark can represent the presence of YHWH himself (see Num 10:35-36), to sit "before God" is to sit in the presence of the ark.

13 The sex ratio at birth (SRB) is the number of baby boys born divided by the number of baby girls born. We will discuss this issue later in the essay.

14 The final phrase, "but keep alive the marriageable women," is supplied by the Greek text.

15 The verb in Hebrew is just as I have translated it: a passive verb that does not in any way express the Israelites' responsibility for the dead Benjaminite women.

16 In fact, "to carry away" is a rare and archaic meaning for the English verb "to rape," according to the *Oxford English Dictionary*, a meaning that has become "archaic" in my own lifetime.

17 In personal communication.

18 See also Susan Niditch, *Judges: A Commentary* (Old Testament Library; Louisville, Ky.: Westminster John Knox, 2008), 210–11.

19 See, e.g., Sherry Ortner's classic essay "Is Female to Male as Nature Is to Culture?" in *Woman, Culture, and Society* (ed. M. Z. Rosaldo and L. Lamphere; Stanford: Stanford University Press, 1974).

20 Nicholas D. Kristof and Sheryl WuDunn identify gender inequality as the chief feature that predicts whether societies will have untenable sex ratios (*Half the Sky: Turning Oppression into Opportunity for Women Worldwide* [New York: Vintage, 2009], xiv–xvii).

21 Hvistendahl, *Unnatural Selection*, 173–74.

22 Hvistendahl, *Unnatural Selection*, 10.

23 Whereas previously each parent had to be an only child in order to qualify to have a second child, now only one parent needs to be an only child in order for the couple to be eligible. Michelle FlorCruz, "China's Reformed One-Child Policy Hurts Female Job Applicants Planning on Second Child," *International Business Times*, March 5, 2014; Tania Branigan, "China May Opt for 'Two Children' Policy in Future, Says Senior Official," *Guardian*, March 4, 2014, http://www.theguardian.com/world/2014/mar/04/china-may-opt-two-children-policy. It should also be noted that the rule was not enforced in all places and at all times, and it was always the case in many places that if the first child a couple had was a girl, they could apply to have a second in order to be sure of a son; the application was generally honored (Hvistendahl, *Unnatural Selection*, 21n).

24 Though ultrasound was first used in India for sex selection, the process spread like wildfire to other countries in Asia, to the astonishment of scholars studying sex ratios (Hvistendahl, *Unnatural Selection*, 49).

25 Hvistendahl, *Unnatural Selection*, 50–51. Hvistendahl has harsh words for GE, the company that first introduced the PC-operated ultrasound.

26 Hvistendahl, *Unnatural Selection*, 10. Hvistendahl also mentions the high abortion rates in Vietnam, South Korea, and the Caucasus.

27 Hvistendahl, *Unnatural Selection*, 5; Li Shuzhuo et al., "Imbalanced Sex Ratio at Birth and Female Child Survival in China: Issues and Prospects," in *Watering the Neighbour's Garden: The Growing Demographic Female Deficit in Asia* (ed. Isabelle Attané and Christophe Z. Guilmoto; Paris: Committee for International Cooperation in National Research in Demography, 2007), 25–44.

28 France Meslé et al., "A Sharp Increase in Sex Ratio at Birth in the Caucasus: Why? How?" in *Watering* (ed. Attané and Guilmoto), 73.

29 Li et al., "Imbalanced Sex Ratio," in *Watering* (ed. Attané and Guilmoto), 38. They point out that the governments of Taiwan and China have begun to support people in their old age, so they will not need a son to do it, and to update the laws about marriage, inheritance, and education, so that women will be able to take the place that traditionally only a son could.

30 Li et al., "Imbalanced Sex Ratio," in *Watering* (ed. Attané and Guilmoto), 27–28.

31 Hvistendahl, *Unnatural Selection*, 235–38. For a similar view on Japan, see John W. Traphagan, "Japan: Death by Demographics?" *National Interest*, January 20, 2014, http://nationalinterest.org/commentary/japans-looming-demographic-disaster-9736.

32 Hvistendahl, *Unnatural Selection*, 200. Hvistendahl cites several studies that show that married men commit fewer and less serious crimes than unmarried men, for

instance, but admits that the causal relationship between testosterone and societal behavior is not truly understood.

33   Hvistendahl, *Unnatural Selection*, 204–8.

34   Le Bach Duong et al., "Transnational Migration, Marriage and Trafficking at the China-Vietnam Border," in *Watering* (ed. Attané and Guilmoto), 393–425.

35   Hvistendahl, *Unnatural Selection*, 167.

36   Hvistendahl, *Unnatural Selection*, 15.

37   Hvistendahl, *Unnatural Selection*, 172.

38   Hvistendahl, *Unnatural Selection*, 189–90.

39   Hvistendahl, *Unnatural Selection*, 172. One wonders whether a similar situation might have greeted those women from Jabesh-Gilead and Shiloh when they arrived in Benjamin.

40   Hvistendahl, *Unnatural Selection*, 171–73.

41   Hvistendahl, *Unnatural Selection*, 186.

42   Hvistendahl, *Unnatural Selection*, 239–43.

43   Hvistendahl, *Unnatural Selection*, 43, 240–41.

44   Hvistendahl, *Unnatural Selection*, 249–58. Preimplantation genetic diagnosis has become so sophisticated that a technique that was once used for livestock breeding is now being tested for human sperm: they are spun in a centrifuge until the heavier X-carrying sperm separate from the lighter Y-carrying sperm, permitting accurate sex selection before the sperm are even joined with eggs.

45   Megan Case, personal communication.

CHAPTER 14: LILLY

1   Hannah Arendt, *The Human Condition* (Chicago: University of Chicago Press, 1958); Arendt, *Eichmann in Jerusalem: A Report on the Banality of Evil* (rev. and enl. ed.; New York: Viking, 1965); Arendt, *On Violence* (New York: Harcourt Brace Jovanovich, 1970).

2   Miroslav Volf, *Exclusion and Embrace: A Theological Exploration of Identity, Otherness, and Reconciliation* (Nashville: Abingdon, 1996).

3   Leymah Gbowee, *Mighty Be Our Powers: How Sisterhood, Prayer, and Sex Changed a Nation at War* (with Carol Mithers; New York: Beast Books, 2011).

4   Desmond Tutu, *No Future without Forgiveness* (New York: Doubleday, 1999).

5   Widely considered a book with two exclusive sections, chs. 1–8 and 9–12, the book's composition history and composite genres recommend focusing on Zech 1–8, also known as First Zechariah (hereafter just Zechariah unless otherwise noted).

6   David L. Petersen, *Haggai and Zechariah 1–8: A Commentary* (Philadelphia: Westminster, 1984), 119.

7   My translation follows the NRSV except when necessary for my discussion.

8   See John Ahn, *Exile as Forced Migration: A Sociological, Literary, and Theological Approach on the Displacement and Resettlement of the Southern Kingdom of Judah* (Beihefte zur Zeitschrift für die alttestamentliche Wissenschaft 417; New York: De Gruyter, 2011).

9   See Tutu, *No Future without Forgiveness*.

10 See Robert I. Rotberg, "Truth Commissions and the Provision of Truth, Justice, and Reconciliation," in *Truth v. Justice: The Morality of Truth Commissions* (ed. R. Rotberg and Dennis Thompson; Princeton, N.J.: Princeton University Press, 2000), 3–21. Rotberg nevertheless fails to use the terms "women," "woman," "girl," or "gender" in his advocacy for the moral project of the South African TRC.

11 Truth and Reconciliation Commission, *TRC Final Report—Volume 1* (1998), 29, www.justice.gov.za/trc/report/index.htm.

12 Truth and Reconciliation Commission, *TRC Final Report—Volume 4* (1998), 318, §144, www.justice.gov.za/trc/report/index.htm.

13 See the UN Security Council Resolutions, available at http://www.unwomen.org/en/about-us/guiding-documents (accessed October 27, 2013).

14 See the five-part documentary "Women, War, and Peace," *PBS* (New York: WNET, 2014), http://www.pbs.org/wnet/women-war-and-peace/.

15 Maria O'Reilly, "Gender and Peacebuilding," in *Routledge Handbook of Peacebuilding* (ed. Roger MacGinty; New York: Routledge, 2013), 57–68 (esp. 61–62).

16 See Madeline Fullard and Nicky Rousseau, "Truth-Telling, Identities, and Power in South Africa and Guatemala," in *Identities in Transition* (New York: International Center for Transitional Justice, 2009), 1–4, http://ictj.org/publication/truth-telling-identities-and-power-south-africa-and-guatemala (accessed April 21, 2014).

17 Historical criticism on Zechariah concludes, with significant reason, that Zech 1:1-6 was added as an introduction, bringing Zechariah into conversation with Deuteronomistic theology. Joseph Blenkinsopp, *A History of Prophecy in Israel* (rev. and enl. ed.; Louisville, Ky.: Westminster, 1996), 204.

18 Rebuilding the temple was the central focus of the three postexilic prophetic books: Haggai, Zechariah, and Malachi.

19 See W. Michael Ashcraft, "Progressive Millennialism," in *The Oxford Handbook of Millennialism* (ed. Catherine Wessinger; Oxford: Oxford University Press, 2011), 44–65.

20 This comes across in the case studies of Melissa M. Wilcox, "Gender Roles, Sexuality, and Children in Millennial Movements," in *Oxford Handbook of Millennialism* (ed. Wessinger), 171–90.

21 See Walter Brueggemann, "'Vine and Fig Tree': A Case Study in Imagination and Criticism," *CBQ* 43 (1981): 188–204.

22 "Wickedness" or "iniquity" are readings found in the Greek and Syriac versions as well as one Hebrew witness. Other Hebrew manuscripts read, "their eyes." This essay will assume the reading "iniquity," especially as it is the chosen interpretation in the NRSV, the King James, and most English translations of the Bible.

23 Marvin A. Sweeney, *The Twelve Prophets*, vol. 2: *Micah, Nahum, Habakkuk, Zephaniah, Haggai, Zechariah, Malachi* (Berit Olam; Collegeville, Minn.: Liturgical Press, 2000), 620.

24 See Jer 7:18 and 44:17.

25 Carol L. Meyers and Eric M. Meyers, *Haggai, Zechariah 1–8* (AB 25B; New York: Doubleday, 1987), 296–303.

26 Carolyn Walker Bynum, "Introduction," in *Gender and Religion: On the Complexity of Symbols* (ed. Carolyn Walker Bynum et al.; Boston: Beacon, 1986), 2–3.

27 Bynum, "Introduction," in *Gender and Religion* (ed. Bynum et al.), 3.

28 Paul Ricœur, *The Symbolism of Evil* (trans. Emerson Buchanan; Boston: Beacon, 1969), 347–57.

29 Other visions capitalize on both the literal and the figurative levels. So in Zech 5:1-4, the scroll figuratively acts as a curse, but it also says something about the authority of textualization, writing, and the rise of Scripture in the Persian period.

30 Athalya Brenner, "Introduction," in *Feminist Companion to the Bible: The Latter Prophets* (ed. Athalya Brenner; Sheffield: Sheffield Academic, 1995), 21–39 (esp. 26).

31 David Janzen, *Witch Hunts, Purity, and Social Boundaries: The Expulsion of the Foreign Women in Ezra 9–10* (Sheffield: Sheffield Academic, 2002), esp. 19–21.

32 René Girard, *Violence and the Sacred* (trans. Patrick Gregory; Baltimore: Johns Hopkins University Press, 1997).

33 United Nations Security Council (SC), Resolution 2122, 1, October 18, 2013. See also SC, Resolution 1325, 1, October 30, 2000 (resolution beginning, "Reaffirming the important role of women . . ."); SC, Resolution 2106, §§7 and 11, June 24, 2013; SC, Resolution 1960, 2–3, December 16, 2010 (resolution beginning, "Recognizing the efforts . . ."). All above documents available at http://www.unwomen.org/en/about-us/guiding-documents.

34 For instance, Gbowee faced social judgments in her first appointment to a leadership position in WIPNET (Women in Peacebuilding). Gbowee, *Mighty Be Our Powers*, 115–16.

35 Gbowee, *Mighty Be Our Powers*, 122.

36 Gbowee, *Mighty Be Our Powers*, 65–66.

37 Gbowee, *Mighty Be Our Powers*, 62.

38 Gbowee, *Mighty Be Our Powers*, 113.

39 Gbowee, *Mighty Be Our Powers*, 67. Throughout her reflections, Gbowee reiterates the concepts developed in an important all-female activity she used to empower victims called "Shedding of the Weight." Gbowee's own experience with the unburdening ritual felt like "a wound in [her] had healed," and she went on to say that "women can't become peacemakers without releasing the pain that keeps them from feeling their own strength" (113).

40 Bill Moyers, "The Journal: Women Fight for Peace," *PBS* video, 53:09, June 18, 2009, http://video.pbs.org/video/1157137218.

CHAPTER 15: YODER

1 This was a common setting for instruction in the ancient Near East. See, e.g., the Sumerian *Instructions of Shuruppak* and the epilogue of the Egyptian *Instruction of Anii*. Ecclesiastes also addresses "my son" (12:12). In Proverbs, the father-to-son setting continues through chapters 1–9 and occurs occasionally later in the book (19:27; 23:15, 19, 26; 24:13, 21; 27:11).

2 Carol A. Newsom, "Positive Psychology and Ancient Israelite Wisdom," in *The Bible and the Pursuit of Happiness: What the Old and New Testaments Teach Us about the Good Life* (ed. B. A. Strawn; New York: Oxford University Press, 2012), 121.

3 Previous studies explore this in detail, including Carol A. Newsom's now classic "Woman and the Discourse of Patriarchal Wisdom: A Study of Proverbs 1–9," in

Gender and Difference in Ancient Israel (ed. P. Day; Minneapolis: Augsburg Fortress, 1989), 142–60.

4   See George Lakoff, "The Contemporary Theory of Metaphor," in *Metaphor and Thought* (2nd ed.; ed. A. Ortony; Cambridge: Cambridge University Press, 1993), esp. 218–29; George Lakoff and Mark Johnson, *Philosophy in the Flesh: The Embodied Mind and Its Challenge to Western Thought* (New York: Basic Books, 1999), esp. 61–70, 178–211.

5   Lakoff and Johnson, *Philosophy in the Flesh*, 194.

6   Lakoff, "Contemporary Theory of Metaphor," in *Metaphor and Thought* (ed. Ortony), 223.

7   George Lakoff and Mark Johnson, *Metaphors We Live By* (2nd ed.; Chicago: University of Chicago Press, 2003), 14–21.

8   The term *zarah* elsewhere in the Hebrew Bible designates an "outsider," someone not of one's family (e.g., Deut 25:5), tribe (e.g., Num 1:51; 18:4, 7), or community (i.e., "foreigners" [e.g., Hos 7:8-9; Isa 1:7]). Such a "stranger" is often considered illegitimate (e.g., Hos 5:7), forbidden (e.g., Jer 2:25), and/or an enemy (e.g., Isa 29:5; Jer 30:8). The second term, *nokhriyyah*—contrary to many modern translations ("adulterous," so NRSV)—typically denotes a "foreigner," usually a non-Israelite (e.g., Deut 17:15; Judg 19:12; 1 Kgs 8:41), but sometimes any person who is outside a person's family (e.g., Gen 31:15). The parent thus identifies the woman as "other" without indicating explicitly what makes her so.

9   The term "house" (*bayit*) may serve as a metaphor for a woman's body and/or her womb. For a helpful study of this in biblical and rabbinic literature, see Gail Labovitz, *Marriage and Metaphor: Constructions of Gender in Rabbinic Literature* (Lanham, Md.: Lexington Books, 2009).

10   Carol A. Newsom, *The Book of Job: A Contest of Moral Imaginations* (New York: Oxford University Press, 2003), 122–23.

11   Martin Luther King Jr. once echoed this worldview: "Let us remember that there is a creative force in this universe working to pull down the gigantic mountains of evil, a power that is able to make a way out of no way and transform dark yesterdays into bright tomorrows. Let us realize that the arc of the moral universe is long, but it bends toward justice" ("Where Do We Go from Here?" accessed September 25, 2013, https://kinginstitute.stanford.edu/king-papers/documents/where -do-we-go-here-delivered-11th-annual-sclc-convention).

12   The noun "instruction" (*leqah* [1:5; 4:2; 9:9]) derives from the same root as the verb often translated "take," signaling further the notion of teaching as an exchange or trade.

13   The term "happy" or "fortunate" forms an *inclusio* around the tribute to wisdom in 3:13-18.

14   Notably, personified wisdom and folly resemble each other. Both women seek the youth's attention, persuade with their speech, move about in the city, have houses, and offer wealth and luxuries. Moreover, both women issue verbatim invitations from the highest places in town ("you who are naïve, turn in here" [9:4, 16]). Discerning the difference between them, therefore, requires attentiveness, experience, and skill—which the parent aims to teach.

15   Newsom, "Positive Psychology," in *Bible and the Pursuit* (ed. Strawn), 134.

16 Proverbs includes two collections that are attributed to foreigners (Agur in Prov 30 and King Lemuel's mother in Prov 31:1-9), one that is an artful adaptation of the Egyptian *Instructions of Amenemope* (22:17–24:22), and many proverbs with close parallels in other ancient Near Eastern wisdom traditions.

17 Serene Jones, *Feminist Theory and Christian Theology: Cartographies of Grace* (Guides to Theological Inquiry; Minneapolis: Fortress, 2000), 38.

18 Edward Slingerland, "Conceptual Metaphor Theory as Methodology for Comparative Religion," *Journal of the American Academy of Religion* 72 (2004): 8.

CHAPTER 16: MERRILL WILLIS

1 "Hope is the thing with feathers," reprinted by the Poetry Foundation from *The Complete Poems of Emily Dickinson* (ed. Thomas H. Johnson; Cambridge, Mass.: Belknap, 1945, 1983).

2 Unless otherwise noted, translations in this essay are my own.

3 Fraser Watts, "Subjective and Objective Hope: Propositional and Attitudinal Aspects of Eschatology," in *The End of the World and the Ends of God: Science and Theology on Eschatology* (ed. J. Polkinghorne and M. Welker; Harrisburg, Pa.: Trinity, 2000), 57.

4 Miroslav Volf, "Not Optimistic," *Christian Century*, December 28, 2004, 31.

5 Volf, "Not Optimistic," 31.

6 Watts, "Subjective and Objective Hope," in *End of the World* (ed. Polkinghorne and Welker), 60.

7 Laura Lippman, *What the Dead Know* (New York: HarperCollins, 2007), 199.

8 Ivone Gebara, *Out of the Depths: Women's Experience of Evil and Salvation* (trans. Ann Patrick Ware; Minneapolis: Fortress, 2002), 26–30.

9 Isabel Allende, *Paula* (New York: HarperCollins, 1994). Quoted in Gebara, *Out of the Depths*, 26–30.

10 The best and most concise discussion of this difficult term remains that of John Collins, "Apocalyptic Eschatology as the Transcendence of Death," *Catholic Biblical Quarterly* 36 (1974): 21–43.

11 Richard L. Schultz, "Intertextuality, Canon, and 'Undecidability': Understanding Isaiah 65's New Heavens and New Earth (Is 65:17-25)," *Bulletin for Biblical Research* 20, no. 1 (2010): 33.

12 The name "Jerusalem" includes a form of the Hebrew root from which the term "shalom" comes. While the original meaning of the name is not certain, in Christian and Jewish circles there is a tradition of calling Jerusalem "the city of Peace" or "the city of Shalom." Walter Brueggemann makes use of this tradition in his commentary *Isaiah 40–66* (Louisville, Ky.: Westminster John Knox, 1998), 248. See further Bruce Schein, "Jerusalem," in *Harper's Bible Dictionary* (ed. Paul J. Achtemeier; San Francisco: Harper & Row, 1985), 463–73.

13 God's ordering activity is also on display throughout Gen 1 and Job 38.

14 Brueggemann, *Isaiah 40–66*, 248.

15 Carol L. Meyers, "Everyday Life: Women in the Hebrew Bible," in *The Women's Bible Commentary, Expanded Edition* (ed. C. A. Newsom and S. Ringe; Louisville, Ky.: Westminster John Knox, 1998), 255.

16 Margaret Dee Bratcher, "Salvation Achieved: Isaiah 61:1-7; 62:1-7; 65:17–66:2," *Review and Expositor* 88 (1991): 177–88.

17 Gen 1:29-30 speaks explicitly of God's intention that humans and animals be vegetarians. It is not until Gen 9:3, after the flood, that the deity permits humans to eat meat.

18 The king is not identified by name in Daniel 7–12; however, the consensus within critical scholarship is that these chapters were written between 167 and 164 BCE and reflect the kingship of Antiochus IV. His infamous reputation is remembered both within and outside of the Hebrew Bible.

19 Collins, "Apocalyptic Eschatology," 30–37.

20 Schultz, "Intertextuality," 35–36.

21 Several insightful books have chronicled end-time belief, apocalypticism, and utopianism in Western history. See especially Frederic J. Baumgartner, *Longing for the End: A History of Millennialism in Western Civilization* (New York: Palgrave, 1999); and Daniel Wojcik, *The End of the World as We Know It: Faith, Fatalism, and Apocalypse in America* (New York: New York University Press, 1997).

22 For further reading on this point, see Richard Bauckham, "Conclusion: Emerging Issues in Eschatology in the Twenty-First Century," in *The Oxford Handbook of Eschatology* (ed. Jerry L. Walls; New York: Oxford, 2008), 671–89.

23 Flora Keshgegian, *Time for Hope: Practices for Living in Today's World* (New York: Continuum, 2006), 17–45.

24 Keshgegian, *Time for Hope*, 115–20.

25 Keshgegian, *Time for Hope*, 74–79.

26 Gebara, *Out of the Depths*, 122, emphasis in original.

27 Gebara, *Out of the Depths*, 127.

28 Gebara, *Out of the Depths*, 22–23.

29 Gebara, *Out of the Depths*, 115.

30 Gebara, *Out of the Depths*, 122–33.

31 Keshgegian, *Time for Hope*, 134–38.

32 Keshgegian, *Time for Hope*, 179.

33 There continues to be disagreement about the character of time in Daniel and in the book of Revelation, which has borrowed heavily from Daniel. Some scholars maintain that apocalyptic literature depends on cyclical views of time; some maintain that it is characterized above all by a linear and teleological character; and some maintain, as I do, that apocalyptic literature admits elements of both.

34 Amy C. Merrill Willis, *Dissonance and the Drama of Divine Sovereignty in the Book of Daniel* (New York: Continuum, 2010), 26–35.

LIST OF CONTRIBUTORS

SUZANNE BOORER is Senior Lecturer in Old Testament/Hebrew Bible at Murdoch University, Perth, Western Australia.

AMY C. COTTRILL is the Denson N. Franklin Associate Professor of Religion at Birmingham–Southern College, Birmingham, Alabama.

JULIE GALAMBUSH is Associate Professor of Religious Studies at the College of William and Mary, Williamsburg, Virginia.

JO ANN HACKETT is Professor of Middle Eastern Studies and Religious Studies at the University of Texas at Austin.

KATIE M. HEFFELFINGER is Lecturer in Biblical Studies and Hermeneutics at the Church of Ireland Theological Institute, Dublin, Ireland.

CAMERON B. R. HOWARD is Assistant Professor of Old Testament at Luther Seminary, Saint Paul, Minnesota.

JACQUELINE E. LAPSLEY is Associate Professor of Old Testament at Princeton Theological Seminary, Princeton, New Jersey.

EUNNY P. LEE is an independent scholar currently working in northern New Jersey.

INGRID E. LILLY is a visiting scholar at the Pacific School of Religion, Berkeley, California.

CARLEEN MANDOLFO is Associate Professor of Hebrew Bible at Colby College, Waterville, Maine.

SARAH J. MELCHER is Chair of the Theology Department at Xavier University, Cincinnati, Ohio.

AMY C. MERRILL WILLIS is Associate Professor of Religious Studies at Lynchburg College, Lynchburg, Virginia.

ANNE W. STEWART is Director of External Relations at Princeton Theological Seminary, Princeton, New Jersey.

PATRICIA K. TULL is A.B. Rhodes Professor Emerita of Old Testament at Louisville. Presbyterian Seminary, Louisville, Kentucky; and Affiliate Developer for Hoosier Interfaith Power and Light, Indianapolis, Indiana.

CHRISTINE ROY YODER is Professor of Old Testament at Columbia Theological Seminary, Decatur, Georgia.

SCRIPTURE INDEX

8:9	102	22:17–24:22	287n16
8:10-11	103	23:15	285n1
8:10	223–24	23:19	285n1
8:13	221	23:23	224
8:14, 15-16	102, 224	23:26	285n1
8:17, 18-21	102	24:7	263n25
8:18-19	224	24:13	285n1
8:19	223	24:21	285n1
8:20-21	103	24:23-25	99
8:20	220	24:26	102
8:21	224	25:6-7	219
8:22-31	10, 103, 218, 222	27:11	285n1
8:22	220	29:4, 26	99
8:27-31	103	30	225, 287n16
8:30	224	31	120
8:31	219	31:1-9	287n16
8:32	224	31:3	262n15
8:34	223–24	31:10-31	138
8:35	104, 217	31:10	39
8:36	221	31:15	38
9:1-6	223, 226	31:16	120
9:1	263n25	31:17	39
9:3	219	31:20	39
9:4	286n14	31:21	38
9:5	220	31:24, 25	39
9:6	224	31:27	38
9:9	286n12	31:31	39
9:14	223	Ecclesiastes	
9:15	220	3:11	23
9:16	286n14	12:12	285n1
11:1	98	Song of Songs	
12:4	39	3:4	38
14:1	38	8:2	38
15:3	265n21	Isaiah	
16:10	99	1–55	233
16:11	98	1:7	286n8
16:13	99	1:17	95, 261n4
17:16	224	5:48, 53	266n3
17:23	99	8:1	110
19:27	285n1	8:17	50, 265n16, 265n17
19:28	99	11	238
20:8, 26	99	11:6-9	235
21:15	99	19:9	260n24

SUBJECT/AUTHOR INDEX